THE BHAGAVAD-GITA FOR THE MODERN READER

What is the *Bhagavad-Gita*? Is it just a religious text? When was it composed? How relevant is it to the modern world?

This book answers these foundational questions and more. It critically examines the *Bhagavad-Gita* in terms of its liberal, humanist and inclusive appeal, bringing out its significance for both present times and novel applications. The author elaborates the philosophy underlying the text as well as its ethical and spiritual implications. He also responds to criticisms that have been levelled against the text by Ambedkar, D. D. Kosambi and, more recently, Amartya Sen. The volume proposes new ways of utilising the text in diverse fields, such as business and management and scientific research.

Eclectic and accessible, this work will be of interest to scholars of philosophy, religion, history, business and management studies, as well as the general reader.

M. V. Nadkarni is presently Honorary Visiting Professor at the Institute for Social and Economic Change (ISEC), Bengaluru, and a Member of the Governing Body at the Centre for Multi-disciplinary Development Research (CMDR), Dharwad, Karnataka, India. An economist by professional training, with specialisation in agricultural and ecological/environmental economics, he is actively interested in development economics, political economy, history, sociology, philosophy, ethics, religion and Gandhian Studies. He was the Indian Council of Social Science Research (ICSSR) National Fellow for two years (2002–04) and Vice Chancellor of Gulbarga University, Karnataka, India from 1999 to 2002.

THE BHAGAVAD-GITA FOR THE MODERN READER

History, interpretations and philosophy

M. V. Nadkarni

Routledge
Taylor & Francis Group
LONDON AND NEW YORK

First published 2017
by Routledge
2 Park Square, Milton Park, Abingdon, Oxon OX14 4RN

and by Routledge
711 Third Avenue, New York, NY 10017

Routledge is an imprint of the Taylor & Francis Group, an informa business

British Library Cataloguing in Publication Data
A catalogue record for this book is available from the British Library

Library of Congress Cataloging in Publication Data
A catalog record has been requested for this book.

ISBN: 978-1-138-20231-3 (hbk)
ISBN: 978-1-315-43900-6 (ebk)

Typeset in Sabon
by Apex CoVantage, LLC

यस्य मूलं त्वया प्रोक्तं ममेति ह्यर्पये कथम् /
कोऽहमर्पणकर्ता स्यां यस्यास्तित्वं त्वया कृतम् //१//

त्वं स्वीकुरुष्वाखिलकार्यकर्तः कृतन्तु किञ्चित् तव प्रीतिजातम् /
गीतार्थसारस्तु जनेषु गम्यः त्वदीयकार्येऽस्मि निमित्तमात्रम् //२//

भणिता भगवद्‌गीता बह्वीभिः भाष्यभङ्गिभिः /
तासां तलिनतात्पर्यं ग्रन्थेऽस्मिन् विनिवेदितम् //३//

विभ्रमे भर्त्सिता गीता वितर्केण विमर्शकैः /
सतर्कं खण्डनं तेषां विनयेनैव भाषितम् //४//

कालक्रमेण गीतायाः प्रयोगा आगता नवाः /
कथनं चापि तेषां हि विस्तरेण समर्पितम् //५//

वाचकेषु व्यवस्थायिन् विश्वेशऽऽ विश्ववत्सल /
वन्दित्वाऽनेन ग्रन्थेन विनम्रं त्वां यजाम्यहम् //६//

Transliteration

Yasya mulam tvaya proktam mameti hyarpaye katham /
Koaham arpana-karta syam yasyastitvam tvaya kritam //1//

Tvam sweekurushwakhilakaryakartah kritam tu kimchit tava pritijatam /
Gitarthasarastu janeshu gamyah tvadiya karyesmi nimittamatram //2//

Bhanita Bhagavadgita bahvibhih bhashya-bhangibhih /
Tasam talina-tatparyam granthesmin viniveditam //3//

Vibhrame bhartsita Gita vitarkena vimarshakaih /
Satarkam khandanam tesham vinayenaiva bhashitam //4//

Kalakramena Gitaya prayoga agata navah /
Tesham kathanam chaapi savistarena samarpitam //5//

Vachakeshu vyavasthayin Vishwesha-a Vishwa-vatsala /
Vanditvaanena granthena vinamram tvam yajamyaham //6//

Translation

How can I dedicate this as mine whose source is (as) told by You?
Who am I to dedicate whose existence is created by You? //1//

Even then, Oh Doer of Everything, accept
what little is done born from your love!
The essence of the Gita needs to be disseminated among people;
I am just an instrument (*nimitta*) in Your own work. //2//

The Bhagavad-Gita is spoken of by numerous waves of (*bhangibhih*) commentaries;
their underlying (*talina*) purport (*tatparyam*) is narrated in this book. //3//

The Gita has been criticised in confusion by critics with false arguments;
their refutation is presented (here) logically and politely only. //4//

In the course of time, new applications (*prayogah*) of the Gita have come into vogue;
their narration is also offered in good detail. //5//

Through this book, I salute (and) propitiate (*yajami*) You in all modesty, the Lord of the universe,
(who is) affectionate to all, and nicely abiding among the readers. //6//

[The original Sanskrit verses and their translation are both by the author]

CONTENTS

PREFACE

I have been exposed to the *Shrimad-Bhagavad-Gita* (the Gita in short) since childhood. However, it was only after my retirement from salaried service in 2002 that I could give a serious attention to it, and I started a systematic study of its many translations along with commentaries and interpretations. The sheer simplicity and at the same time complexity and profundity of the Gita fascinated me. The deep desire that was dormant during all these decades to know what all the tremendous literature on the Gita added up to, and how the Gita helps humankind, came to the surface as a compelling force. This book is as much a product of my struggle to understand the Gita in all its aspects as it is an outcome of equally strong urge to share this knowledge with all those who may not have the time or patience to read the vast literature on the Gita on their own. The adage that one gains by sharing applies conspicuously to knowledge.

There are, however, thousands of books already on the Gita including some 2,000 translations in English, not counting many in Indian languages. Why this book again? Is there anything special about it? There is, I plead. First of all, it has a historical perspective, exploring not only its origin, but also its long career in terms of translations, global spread, and influence particularly in India both before and after independence. The book starts with an introduction which explains what made the Gita a sacred book over two-and-half millennia, its place in the Mahabharata and the question of the date of its composition and also of authorship (see Chapter 1). The next four chapters (2–5) trace four main phases in the subsequent career of the Gita. The classical interpreters in the first phase like Shankara focused on the metaphysical and *sadhana* aspects of the Gita, mainly in the Vedic tradition. During the next phase, paradoxically under the colonial rule, the Gita was launched on a global travel and accepted as a text of universal interest to all mankind, not just to the Vedic tradition within India. I have explained why. In the later phase of the colonial rule, the Gita assumed a special relevance for the nationalist struggle and social reform in India and was recognised as a progressive and activist text. In the contemporary phase, the ethical content of the Gita and its relevance for guiding even day-to-day mundane life were recognised without detriment to its being a source of spiritual inspiration and teaching. Once again with redoubled strength, its universal relevance was emphasised in the contemporary phase. The story of how the Gita began to reach wider audience through translations in Indian regional languages has also formed a part of this narrative. Interestingly, the Gita also has had its own career! It is marked by two features: first, it has been continuously applied to address the issues of each phase; second, its audience is deepening in the sense of reaching down to even common people beyond scholars and also widening across countries and religions. It was exciting to narrate the story of this career.

The second distinctive feature of the book is that while most of the books on the Gita go verse by verse and chapter by chapter, I thought it is useful to view it as a whole. It is by so studying that one can comprehend its philosophy in all its aspects – moral, metaphysical and paths to spiritual striving or *s̲adhan̲a* that it has shown. Before arriving at this understanding, I had to take due note of most of the main interpretations of the Gita. There is a long history of these interpretations since Shankara in the eighth century to the present, which is reviewed in this book (see Chapters 2–5). The approach to presenting these interpretations here is not one of mechanically summarising them, but of bringing out their contributions to the understanding of the Gita. The reader can know about the main interpreters of the Gita, over thirty of them, along their background and thoughts, within a single book. In the process, there is also an attempt to see how far these interpretations are helpful to solve the problems of the present.

Third, I have my standpoint through which I have viewed the Gita in writing this book. It is not in terms of the traditional classification of Vedanta philosophy into Advaita, Vishi̲s̲h̲ta-advaita, and Dvaita, though certainly I have taken due note of them and commented on them by arguing that they need not be taken as mutually irreconcilable, but as different aspects of a complex but comprehensive Ultimate Truth. All the three philosophies have significantly enriched Indian philosophy. My standpoint is in terms of the modern values we cherish – equality, human dignity, justice, respect for differences in faiths and the need to build a peaceful and prosperous world in which there is fair play, without poverty and deprivation. Is the Gita relevant here? This is the main standpoint from which I have tried to understand the Gita. The greater relevance of the Gita consists not so much in showing us a path to renounce this world, as in making our travel in this world itself from birth to death, *sharira-yatra*, as the Gita calls it, meaningful, fruitful and enjoyable. The Mahabharata calls it as *loka-yatra*, or people's travel in the world (Amur 2013). Many of the ancient as well as modern interpreters valued the Gita for the guidance it provides in sailing through the conflict-ridden turbulent ocean of *samsara* (day-to-day life in this practical world), not by escaping from it but by facing it. Ethical teachings of the Gita along with its guidance to shape our mind and attitudes helpful in this task are therefore particularly emphasised in this book. What is great about the Gita is that its God is not jealous of other gods; it does not preach intolerance to differences in faiths. On the other hand, it preaches that God is the same whatever be the name and form through you worship Him, and the worship reaches Him. Its approach to differences in faiths is to reconcile them. It is, therefore, a universal and inclusive sacred text. Gandhi was particularly fascinated by this feature of the Gita, as he was also by its emphasis on truth and non-violence, and ethics in general, which he treated as the main message of the Gita. That is what makes our travel in this world worthwhile and happy. While the Gita was a source of inspiration for freedom fighters as well as social reformers during nationalist struggle before independence in India (see Chapter 4), it also has astoundingly novel applications in the present times. Three such areas are identified in the book, where the teachings of the Gita can be very helpful: (a) business enterprise, leadership, and management; (b) theory and methodology of seeking truth in scientific research; and (c) making our personal lives and relationships happy and fruitful (Chapter 8).

The Gita, however, does not expect us to get bogged down into the mundane matters, but to have a higher purpose. Whether or not one believes in gaining *moksha* in the sense of liberation from the cycle of births and deaths, the Gita shows the path to freedom from bondage of the confines of narrowness and weaknesses like hatred and jealousy, and to realise the divinity within us all. The path shown by it for success in sailing through *samsara* serves also in *sadhana* or spiritual striving. The Gita has no doubt rich ethical content, but is not confined to it. The Gita has a philosophy of happiness, which all humankind is entitled to, and also guidance to give about attaining this happiness. This philosophy has been explained both in general and then specifically in its three major aspects: (a) ethics, (b) theology and metaphysics and (c) proposed paths of *sadhana* (in Chapter 6). To understand the Gita, we need to comprehend all these aspects. It is stressed here that selfless service for the good of all (*sarva-bhuta-hita*) or promoting the welfare of people (*loka-sangraha*) is an intrinsic part of *sadhana* preached by the Gita. Its karma-yoga has hardly any significance if it does not include such service.

Fourth, the book devotes an entire chapter (the seventh) to respond to the criticisms made against the Gita, including those by Dr B. R. Ambedkar, Kosambi, and Amartya Sen. Since most of the criticisms are not just due to differences in perspectives but also mainly due to improper understanding of the Gita, the chapter clarifies the issues with cool logic, trying to remove the misunderstandings. Neither do I mind rationalism and agnosticism, nor do I subscribe to any fanatical or intolerant interpretation of Hinduism, but I also think that to attack the Gita is hardly a brilliant and effective strategy to defeat fanaticism. Having been trained as a professional social scientist (economist) has helped me to be analytical, rational and objective, shunning fanaticism and blind belief. My admiration for the Gita is based mainly on its humanist and ethical appeal.

As Swami Bhoomananda Tirtha says, it would be doing injustice to the Gita if it is seen only as a sacred text meant for the recluse and the retired, instead of grasping its larger significance (Bhoomananda 2014, Vol. I: 15). My book presents the Gita in its wider perspective. The Gita should not be seen as a sacred book of Hindus only. I do not, however, subscribe to demands like declaring it as a 'national book' or prescribing it as a compulsory teaching in schools to the exclusion of sacred texts of other religions. Besides, the Gita is not the only sacred text even within Hinduism.

My book is addressed to a general contemporary reader who has interest in religion and Indian philosophy, and not only to scholars in this field, though they too would find it interesting. Hence my style of writing is simple even when dealing with complex and profound issues. Wherever technical terms are used, they are adequately explained in the text itself. A Glossary is also added to the book.

I have generally followed the Key to Transliteration given in the following text, but I have also used the simple well-known forms after using the Key once or twice. For example, after using the correct word, *Shrimad-Bhagavad-Gita* once or twice, the simple term 'Gita' is used without transliteration marks; similarly, after using 'Krishna', the word has been used subsequently without transliteration marks.

I had the benefit of consulting several scholar friends, whose suggestions have been very helpful. Among them are Professors Mallepuram G. Venkatesh (former vice chancellor, Karnatak Sanskrit University, who assured me that my response to the criticisms of the Gita is cautious and polite enough), Shrinivasa Varakhedi, P. R. Panchamukhi and K. S. Kannan. Since I am not a pundit in Sanskrit, I got my dedication verses checked by Professors Varakhedi, Panchamukhi and Mallepuram, who kindly helped me in correcting my mistakes. If mistakes remain, they are mine. Professor G. S. Amur took the trouble to go through an initial draft of the book and gave valuable advice. My brother, Dr Kishore Nadkarni, served as a sounding board, whose comments on initial chapters put me on guard. I am also grateful to Professor R. S. Deshpande, my daughter Saraswati, sons Anirudh and Makarand for encouragement and support. My daughter-in-law Amita helped by neatly arranging all the chapters in different files as required by the publisher. Subhashree Banerjee taught me how to type in Sanskrit on the computer with Google typing aid. From Vishnu Kedar, I learnt linking up footnotes with the main text. I cannot fail to thank Mr B. B. Chand and Dr Pradeep Hegde of ISEC Library for their kind help by getting books and other references on time. My being an honorary visiting professor at ISEC has been a source of strength and stimulus in all my works after retirement.

I am grateful to the three anonymous reviewers of the publisher for their valuable suggestions and appreciation of the book. I may not have followed all their suggestions, though I have a great respect for them. The responsibility for views expressed and for any errors in the book is, therefore, mine. I am greatly indebted to Dr Shashank Sinha, the publishing director of Routledge India, for all the encouragement and support, and the personal interest he took in getting this published soon. I am also grateful to his colleagues for processing the book in good time.

Though my wife, Ganga, is physically not with me since 2003, she has continued to be a constant source of strength. She would have loved to read this book. I miss her deeply. I also miss my sister-in-law, Girija (Ammu) Pandit, who was a keen student of the Gita and would have received this book with her usual enthusiasm and spread a word about it among her numerous friends and relatives. I greatly miss my senior friend and colleague, Professor V. M. Rao. There was hardly a book or an article with which I did not bother him for critical comments, and he always obliged. He wrote the Foreword for my previous book on ethics. This book also would have benefited from his sage advice.

KEY TO TRANSLITERATION

(In the alphabetical order of Sanskrit)

Vowels

a – o as in son	a – a as in master
i – i as in if	i – ee as in feel
u – u as in full	u – oo as in boot
ri – ri as in Krishna	au – ow as in now

Consonants

kh – ckh as in blockhead	gh – gh as in log-hut
ch – ch as in chain	chh – chh as in catch-him
jh – dge as in hedgehog	
t – t as in ten	th – th as in anthill
d – d as in den	dh – dh as in godhood
n – n as in under	
t – t as in Gita	th – th as in thin
d – th as in then	dh – th as in this
n – as in not, singer, bench	
ph – ph as in loophole, or as f in fit	bh – bh as in abhor
y – y as in yard	v, w – as in avert, awake
sh – sh as in cherish, *shankara*	sh – sh as in show, *shashtha* (sixth)
s – s as in Sun	
h – h as in hot	l – second l as in Malayalam

Note: Illustrations of pronunciation are mostly from Harshananda (2008, Vol. I: x), but the key followed here is different, consisting simply of underlining, not using symbols which need special software. This key was successfully used in Nadkarni (2013).

1

SIGNIFICANCE OF THE GITA, ITS DATE AND AUTHORSHIP

As a sacred text

The *Shrimad-Bhagavad-Gita*, or the *Gita* in its well-known short form, is the most popular sacred text of the Hindus. The prefix, *Shrimat(d)*, is normally used for some of the later sacred texts in Hinduism, signifying utmost respect given to them, *Shrimad-Ramayanam, Shrimad-Bhagavatam* being a few other examples. What constitutes a sacred book? First and foremost, a sacred book is an authoritative source of guidance and inspiration both in leading day-to-day life consistent with ethical values *and* in pursuing peace of mind and spiritual realisation. In describing itself both as *brahma-vidya* and *yoga-shastra* (in the colophons), the Gita tells what constitutes a sacred book. *Brahma-vidya* means the knowledge of the Ultimate Truth or reality; in imparting such a knowledge, it presents a discussion of metaphysics and theology. But this knowledge is not a question of mere book learning. One's life should reflect the basic urge for spiritual realisation. That is, to acquire *brahma-vidya*, or spiritual knowledge, one should also behave in a certain way consistent with or aimed at this goal. That is where striving for it becomes relevant. *Yoga-shastra* is the science of spiritual striving (yoga) or *sadhana* (striving). Yoga here does not just mean adopting certain postures of the body, but has the much wider connotation of leading a life of spiritual orientation and rigorous discipline – morally and mentally. A sacred book serves thus as a guide to both *brahma-vidya* and *yoga-shastra*.

Second, a sacred book resonates across space and time, not being specific or limited to a particular given context alone, but having a universal significance or relevance. Though the immediate context of the Gita is to remove Arjuna's despondency, the purpose of Krishna or the Gita is not just to give a pep talk to him. When Arjuna asks

Krishna what is best (*shreya*) for him, Krishna's reply is about not only what is best for Arjuna particularly but also what is best generally or universally for all (Dayananda 1989: 20). Arjuna is a symbol of a human being in struggle. Krishna's Gita is meant for all. This is very clear from verses 68 to 70 in the last chapter of the Gita, viz. Chapter 18, where Krishna makes his intention for its wider dissemination quite evident, though of course among those who are faithful and devoted. Krishna says that one who teaches or expounds on the Gita with devotion among his devotees is dearest to him and will ultimately become one with him. Verse 71 of the same chapter promises that even if one merely listens to this teaching, he or she will have auspicious destiny. The text is clearly not limited to Arjuna, who is only a pretext for the profound teaching.

Third, a sacred book is also one which is faithfully accepted by a large number of people at least of a group or creed. Though many leaders of Hinduism including Gandhi and Sri Aurobindo emphasise that sacred books are not substitutes for reasoning, reasoning alone may not suffice when humans try to probe what is beyond merely mundane and go in the pursuit of spiritual solace and contentment. Even in helping to lead a life of virtue, a sacred book should harmonise reason and faith; reasoning in it should be convincing while faith inspires and prods. Both Gandhi and Aurobindo emphasise further that a scripture should enable one to elevate himself or herself above ordinary existence and *experience* the truth that the scripture expounds. Recitation and verbal understanding of the text, though necessary, are not enough.

Hinduism does not have one single exclusive sacred text, and the greatest, most ancient and original sacred texts of Hinduism are the *Vedas*. They are followed by the *Upanishads*, most of which are appended at the end of the Vedas themselves. The scriptures of Hinduism are more like a common pool multilingual library, where you pick and choose a certain book which you find particularly useful and inspiring, without insisting that all other books be destroyed or condemned, nor requiring that all the books must be read equally thoroughly to qualify for access to the library. What is more, it is not a sacrilege to add to this library. It does not diminish the significance of the books accessed earlier in any way. First came the Vedas and Upanishads, and then the classic epics – the Ramayana and the Mahabharata, the *Vedantasutras* (also known as the *Brahmasutras*), the *Yogasutras, Narada-Bhaktisutras*, the *Shastras* and *Smritis*, the *Puranas* including the eminent *Bhagavata Purana*, and the *Kural* in

Tamil by Thiruvalluvar. All these emerged in the ancient, or the classical, period well before the end of the first millennium CE. This was not the end. Except for the *Kural*, all the literature mentioned earlier is in Sanskrit. There was no bar in having more scriptures, now in the vernacular. In the medieval era were added the *Jnaneshwari* (an explanation of the Gita in Marathi in verses by Jnaneshwar), the *Vachanas* (sayings) of Shivasharan̲as in Kannada, *Ra̱macharitama̱nasa* of Goswa̱mi Tulasidas in Hindi, and the lyrical poetry of the numerous bhakti sants in regional languages. One's lifetime is not enough to go through and understand all this literature. I may say in a lighter vein that Hindus invented rebirth so that they can take up reading in the next life what they craved to finish but could not in the present life!

Not many Hindus, however, opt for a rebirth, if they can help it. Devout Hindus prefer to have self-realisation or enlightenment in this very birth! Spiritual enlightenment is open to everyone in Hinduism, irrespective of gender, class and caste. Hindus needed a scripture which would guide them to engage with the life they face in an ethically correct way, taking the pleasures and frustrations in their stride with equanimity and, at the same time, realise the Divine. Of course, they had a wide choice of the texts. But the four Vedas and over a dozen Upanishads constituted a very vast literature, offering a formidable challenge for ordinary humans to learn them in the first instance, let alone following them after attaining some understanding of them. The Bhagavad-Gita provided a solution. As Yogananda and other celebrities have declared, the Gita provided the essence of all the 'ponderous' four Vedas, the 108 Upanishads, and the six systems of Hindu philosophy, constituting – 'a universal message for the solace and emancipation of all mankind' (Yogananda 2002, Vol. 1: 169), in lucid and relatively easy-to-understand Sanskrit, and in a compact form of only 700 verses in eighteen chapters. One could easily read a single chapter a day or even a few verses a day and feel blessed. Quite a few Hindus have learnt the whole of the Gita by heart. The *Gita̱-Dhya̱nam* (Meditating on the Gita), which is ritually recited before the Gita, picturesquely states that all the Upanishads are like cows, and Shri̱ Krishna – the son of a cowherd – milked them for the benefit of people having a pure mind, with Arjuna being the calf, and the nectar of the Gita is the milk (verse 4). This verse explains why the Gita came to be accepted as the most popular sacred book of Hindus. It acknowledges that the Gita is intended to be the essence of the Upanishads conveyed for the benefit of people, Arjuna providing an excuse, and the Mahabharata war a dramatic context to take off. What is more, the milkman is no less than God Himself, though in human incarnation as Krishna! The God of the Gita is not just the abstract Brahman, but more a personal God who loves and likes to be loved. This is in great contrast with the abstract and impersonal God of the Upanishads. To make it endearing, the Gita is in the form a dialogue between Krishna and Arjuna, with the latter asking searching questions again and again, and the former responding patiently in detail with deep affection. Krishna tells Arjuna emphatically: 'Definitely dear you are to me' (*Ishtoasi mey dridham*, XVIII.64, i.e. Chapter 18 and verse 64); and again, 'I promise, beloved you are to me!' (*Pratijaney priyoasi mey*, XVIII.65). It is as if Lord Krishna invites the devout listeners and readers of the Gita to place themselves in the position of Arjuna and enjoy the Lord's unbounded love and protection. Arjuna is only an exemplar of a devotee, who is also a friend treated with love. The Gita does not see a devotee as a servant or slave, nor it needs a devotee consider himself or herself that way. A devotee can question God and engage in a dialogue with him as an intimate friend. Krishna assures that a devotee or a seeker can obtain peace with the knowledge that He, the Divine, is a friend (*suhrida*) of all beings (V.29). He affirms in verse after verse (XII.14–20) that he loves his devotees. The Gita emphasises not only devotee's love of God, but also God's abundant love for devotees. When a devotee loves God heartily with abandon, that is enough to earn Divine love. Krishna also makes it clear that whatever little a devotee offers to him as a token of genuine love, he accepts it without reservation – be it a leaf, a flower, a fruit or even a little water! (IX.23–24). It made religion easy and accessible to all. No other sacred text before it had achieved this revolution in religion. Bal Gangadhar Tilak points out, in his preface to his famous work, *Gita-Rahasya*, a traditional compliment to the Gita, which says: 'It is quite enough if one thoroughly studies the Gita. What is the use of dabbling in other *Shastras*?' (1936: li).[1] It is no surprise, therefore, that the popularity of the Gita as a sacred text grew spontaneously *without anyone imposing it*. For quite a few people, the Gita as a book became an icon by itself, to be revered and worshipped, without having to understand its contents. However, many of these people end up trying to study and absorb the contents as well and benefit by its guidance.

The Gita's popularity also owes to its dramatic context of conflict. The dialogue took place right in the battlefield, with Lord Krishna urging a confused Arjuna to fight. The Gita is certainly not a text on the ethics of war. It does not discuss whether wars are justified or when they are. But if one is confronted with a war which is inevitable, it teaches how to face it with equipoise. Even this is not its only purpose. As Gandhi explained, the war which Arjuna faces is only a metaphor for situations of conflict between forces of good and evil inherent in the human condition. The Gita teaches that we have to face the conflicts and cannot run away from them in a cowardly manner (Gandhi 1980: 12–14). Not only is the war in the Gita an allegory, but even the fact of Lord Krishna being the charioteer (*sarathi*) of Arjuna is also of great allegorical significance. Before the war, Duryodhana and Arjuna were given a choice by Krishna between the whole of Krishna's army on the one side and the unarmed non-fighting Krishna on the other. Arjuna chose Krishna, while Duryodhana chose his army. What is more, Arjuna wanted Krishna as his charioteer. In the struggle for life, one need not be alone. One has to invoke Krishna or the Divine Spirit as *sarathi* to be with us to guide, inspire and empower. The significance of the Gita's inspiring and empowering teaching becomes apparent when we note why many people commit suicides when they give up facing problems. The Gita can give courage and cure demoralisation. One needs to face the struggle of life with wisdom and equanimity. The Gita teaches that it is also the duty of each individual to help all persons and the society in general to cope with this struggle. This is conveyed in the Gita's teaching on *loka-hita* and *loka-sangraha*, which will be discussed subsequently in more detail.

When a flood of religious literature followed the Vedas and the Upanishads, the *Shastras* which appeared subsequently made a distinction between two types of literature – the *Shruti* and *Smriti*. The former included the foundational texts like the Vedas and Upanishads, consisting of prayers, ethical axioms and principles, and philosophical probes. The latter are secondary texts, covering the great epics, *Shastras* including *Smritis*, and the *Puranas*. They derive their authority from the former by explaining and illustrating what is contained in the former and indicating guidelines for conducting day-to-day lives. Sometimes there was a risk that the *Smriti* texts could deviate from the former, developing their own theories and rules which are not in conformity with the *Shruti* texts. In such cases, the *Shastras* themselves ruled that what is stated in the *Shruti* prevails over whatever is said in the *Smritis*. It is clear that only the *Shruti* texts are regarded as authoritative and sacred, and the *Smriti* texts as secondary or supplementary. Where would the Gita fit in?

The Gita is a part of the Mahabharata, appearing in the *Bhishma Parvan* (as Chapters 23–40 according to the 'Critical Edition' of Bhandarkar Oriental Research Institute (BORI), Pune, and Chapters 25–42 according to the more popular Gita Press Gorakhpur edition). The *Bhishma Parvan* is the sixth out of eighteen *Parvans* of the great epic, which itself has 117 chapters (122 chapters according to the Gorakhpur edition), which include the Gita's eighteen chapters. But the Mahabharata is regarded as a *Smriti* text, secondary and not foundational. Therefore, the tradition does not accord the status of *Shruti* to the Gita on par with the Vedas and Upanishads (Radhakrishnan 1923, Vol. 1: 519). How then could the Gita be considered as a sacred text, if being regarded as a foundational authority is a hallmark of a sacred text? First of all, the Mahabharata is not just another *Smriti* text, but even regarded as the fifth Veda (*Panchama Veda*) by some. But the importance of the Gita transcends beyond being a part of the Mahabharata and can be regarded as a stand-alone text too. The Gita is taken as not only conveying the essence of the Vedas and Upanishads, but also giving its followers much more even within its small size. It is both a *brahma-vidya* (the science of Brahman, the ultimate reality) and also a *yoga-shastra* (the science and practical art of realising that reality), as stated in the colophons. For this reason, the Gita itself is regarded as an Upanishad in the colophons, which appear at the end of every chapter of the Gita. Colophons mention the name of each chapter respectively, and the title of each chapter ends with the suffix *yoga*, indicating that each is a discipline itself. Incidentally, the colophons are not given in some of the modern printed texts of the Gita, but they were given invariably in popular texts meant for daily recitation. The colophon at the end of the first chapter of the Gita, for instance, reads as follows:

> *Om Tad-sat iti Shrimad-Bhagavad-Gitasu Upanishadsu Brahma-vidyayam Yogashastre Shri Krishna-Arjuna-samvade Arjuna-vishada-yogo nama Prathamodhyayah.*

It literally means: *Om tad-sat*! (Invocation of the Brahman, the Truth). Here ends the first chapter named 'the Yoga of Arjuna's Agony', in the dialogue between Shri Krishna and Arjuna in the Divine Songs (which are) Upanishads, *brahma-vidya* as well as *yoga-shastra*.

It may look puzzling that colophon uses the word *samvade* (dialogue) in singular, but the words *Gitasu* (songs, referring to the Gita) and *Upanishadsu* (Upanishads) in plural. Apparently, it may be because each chapter could be considered as a song, a discipline and an Upanishad in its own right, with the whole constituting a unity in terms of the referred dialogue. To me, however, the use of the plural has tremendous additional significance as borne out from the history of the Gita given later in this and succeeding chapters. The Gita is amenable to a variety of interpretations, and in this sense, we have Shankaracharya's Gita, Ramanujacharya's Gita, Madhvacharya's Gita, *Jnaneshwari*, Edwin Arnold's Gita, Gandhi's Gita, Annie Besant's Gita, B. G. Tilak's Gita, Aurobindo's Gita and so on. And yet, we have one dialogue, one integrated Gita. It is one as well as many!

There is no doubt that the Gita has borrowed from a few Upanishads, sometimes whole or parts of verses.[2] Working with detachment is emphasised both in the Gita and in the Upanishads (see, e.g. the Isha Up.). Yet, the Gita is neither a mere compilation of quotations from the Upanishads, nor a mere summary of them, but has a contribution of its own to make. For instance, there is hardly any discussion of bhakti in the Upanishads, but it finds a significant place in the Gita. The concept of the descent (*avatar*) of God to solve the problems of the world came into the Gita first; it was not there in the Upanishads. The concept of God in the Gita is personal unlike in the Upanishads, where the Brahman is the impersonal force permeating the whole universe. Nevertheless, the Gita takes a holistic and fresh look at the Vedas and Upanishads and presents a synthesis along with its own contribution in a succinct, yet readable style. The *Brahmasutras* also contain the philosophical essence of the Upanishads, but their format in the form of dense axioms was beyond the reach of even the commonly learned persons. The Gita was on the contrary formatted to be a popular sacred text.

The very first verse of *Gita-Dhyanam* (Meditation on the Gita) makes it clear that the Gita was taught by God Himself (Narayana), addressed to Arjuna, and composed as a book by the ancient sage Vyasa as a part of the Mahabharata (*Parthaya pratibodhitam Bhagavata Narayanena swayam/Vyasena grathbhitam purana-munina madhye Mahabharatam//*). The divine origin of the Gita, in which devout Hindus believe, is thus considered to be a major reason, though not the only one, for regarding it as a sacred scripture. But the Mahabharata has many philosophical dialogues attributed to various persons, including dialogues between Lord Krishna and his devotees (such as the *Anu-Gita*, the *Uttara-Gita* and the *Uddhava-Gita*, the first two being dialogues between Krishna and Arjuna like the Bhagavad-Gita). However, none has attained the popularity and status of the Bhagavad-Gita. So it is not just the divine origin attributed to the Gita which made it a popular sacred text, but also the nature of its format and the outstanding significance of its contents.

Gandhi played down the criterion of divine origin for a text to be regarded as sacred. Even if texts regarded as sacred had divine origin, they have come down to us through human intervention, and therefore no sacred text of any religion is infallible, he argued. Instead of divine origin, he would apply three tests: first, the text should stand to reasoning; second, its values should be ethical, consistent with the basic principles of truth and ahimsa; and third, it should have teachings which are practical to follow. He observed, 'Every formula of every religion has in this age of reason, to submit to the acid text of reason and universal justice if it is to ask for universal assent. Error can claim no exemption even if it can be supported by the scriptures of the world' (*Young India* 26 February 1929: 74). He did not exaggerate the importance of reason and recognised the due role of faith in religion, but any belief or practice or any religious text which went against the three tests, particularly ethics, would not be acceptable to him. He declared, 'Nothing that is inconsistent with the universally accepted principles of morality has for me the authority of the *Shastras*' (CWMG Vol. 52: 9; Jordens 1991: 92). For the same reason, he would not accept any text as *Shastra* or sacred book which endorsed untouchability and oppression. Gandhi was equally emphatic on practicality. He said: 'It is a misuse of our intellectual energy and a waste of time to go on reading what we cannot put into practice' (CWMG Vol. 32: 228; Jordens 1991: 91–92). It is significant that Gandhi not only just accepted but also regarded the Gita as a basic spiritual and moral guide in his day-to-day life. Obviously, the Gita passed all his stringent tests.

An important requirement for a religious text to be regarded as sacred is, more than its simplicity, its being profound. As Dalal remarks, 'a sacred text has a receding horizon' (2009: 26). The more one learns, the more one feels like knowing and goes deeper. A sacred text requires both contemplation and practice. It needs to be absorbed in a way that our life, even day-to-day living, becomes more meaningful and fulfilling under its guidance. It is not enough to merely recite a text. A sacred text helps not only in choosing life's goals, but also in selecting the means of achieving them. A text cannot inspire contemplation and practice without being profound. The Gita is profound in this sense and came to be regarded as a foundational text.

Even more than the Vedas, the foundation of philosophical Hinduism is traditionally regarded as consisting of the Upanishads, the *Brahmasutras* and the *Bhagavad-Gita*. All these are profound. Together, they are known as the *Prasthanatriya* – the three foundational works.

Different schools of philosophical thought in Hinduism or *Vedanta* sprang out from these works, and no offshoots of Hinduism could ignore them even if they did not accept the Vedas. But in sheer popularity, the Gita prevailed over the other two. The Upanishads are too many for a common Hindu to study, and philosophical and moral thought is spread over all of them. The *Brahmasutras* are at the other extreme, in compact prose as Sutras, but too terse and dense to be popular. The Gita provided a golden mean. It is in the form of a long poem, lucid and lyrical, amenable for chanting. The whole Gita could be learnt by heart if one wished, and the meaning of its verses could be easily understood, in translation and with commentaries if necessary. It could be recited daily, in parts or as a whole depending on one's time and aptitude, which is believed to confer great spiritual merit and solace. Regular recitation of a text is an important sign of its acceptance as sacred. The benefits obtained by recitation of the Gita are eulogised in *Shri Gita-Mahatmyam* ('Greatness of the Gita'), which normally appears at the end of printed texts of the Gita, said to be from the *Varaha-Purana*. It appears that recitation of the Gita as a sacred text had already come into vogue by the time this *Purana* was composed. The *Varaha-Purana* only formalised what was in practice and made the faith of people firmer in the Gita. The Gita is being studied and recited by millions regularly for at least two millennia. And that is how the three great acharyas (Shankara, Ramanuja and Madhva) and others too took it up for editing and commenting upon it.

There were also more profound reasons for accepting the Gita as a sacred text. The Gita from the beginning was never exclusive. It opened the door to the masses of people for spiritual solace and God realisation. It offered a simple religion which any one could follow, rich or poor, man or woman, young or old, irrespective of caste. It transcended the Vedas and even the Upanishads without undermining them. While the Vedas offered a religion of rituals and sacrifices, suitable more to the rich, the Gita offered convenient choices as per the aptitude of persons concerned between contemplation on the Divine, selfless work or service of others, and devotion to the Divine, or, if you like, a suitable combination of all these tailored to the spiritual seekers' personal inclination. What is more, the Gita was practical enough to realise that all cannot be full-time spiritual seekers, and most people would like to combine worldly pursuits with spiritual ambition. So the Gita offered a religion for people who are basically engaged in the world and not addressed to the ascetics who have renounced the world. The Gita gave a personal God to people at large, to whom they could pray and offer their love and devotion and also be loved and protected by Him. The religion it offered was meant for the worldly people. It taught them how to avoid tensions of ordinary life with equanimity and efficiency in work. It offered guidance in leading cheerfully one's worldly activities, but with a sense of purpose and moral backing. While the religion offered by the Upanishads also transcended the Vedas and did not require rituals, it tended to emphasise contemplation on the nature of the self and the Divine most of the time. Their contemplative methods did not very much appeal to the mass of people engaged in worldly affairs but who nevertheless had some spiritual aspirations. The Gita, on the other hand, avoided both the material elitism of the Vedas and the spiritual elitism of the Upanishads, and offered a more realistic and relatively easy-to-follow religion within the reach of the common people. Its religion is simple, so simple in fact that there is no idol worship or temple worship in the Gita. Yet its religion is sophisticated enough to insist on honesty, truthfulness and selflessness and shows the ways of spiritual evolution to the level of perfection.

Moreover, the Gita is non-sectarian in approach and preaches a universal religion. In the *Gita-Dhyanam*, Krishna of the Gita is saluted as *Jagadguru* – world teacher – and not as a teacher of Vaishnavites, or for that matter, Hindus alone. And that is how it came to be accepted by the Vaishnavas, Smartas, Shaivites and Shaktas equally, and it would be no surprise if it appeals also to non-Hindus who are open minded. The universality and tolerant understanding of different religious ways of people are reflected in what Krishna assures: 'In whatever way people try to reach me, I accept and reward them; O Partha (Arjuna), people can follow the path to me from all sides' (IV.11). This assurance is repeated again: 'Whatever form devotees choose to worship with dedication and faith (*shraddha*), I make that *shraddha* steady' (VII.21). The greatness of these statements consists in accepting different conceptions of the Divine and paths to it. The Gita says nowhere that Krishna alone is the true God and other gods are false. It simply says that whichever god or whatever form of God you worship, it goes to the One and same God (IX.23). Though the roots of this belief lie in the Vedas and Upanishads themselves, the credit for popularising it and making it a basic tenet of Hinduism goes to the Gita. The bhakti saints of the medieval era only further emphasised and popularised it.

Consistent with this tolerance and respect for differences, the Gita does not intend to impose its views as God-given. Though considered as a sacred text, it is aware that conflicting views in such texts can be bewildering (*shruti-vipratipanna*, II.53). There could be flaws and inconsistencies even in texts claiming divine origin, since as Gandhi said, these texts have been handed down to us through human media. We cannot give up human reasoning, which after all is itself God-given. After teaching his message, Krishna tells Arjuna at the end to reflect critically on what all was told to him and then do only what he is willing to accept (*Vimarshyetad asheshena yathhetchhasi tatha kuru*, XVIII.63). The Gita also provides guidance in thinking correctly and seeking true knowledge in the same chapter. As Gandhi clarified, human reasoning can be depended upon only if it is unselfish and unprejudiced. Gita's God in any case is not an imposing tyrant, but an understanding, friendly, compassionate and liberal teacher, and gives enough freedom to human beings in choosing their path correctly and wisely in the light of His guidance. Ultimately, a spiritual seeker transcends injunctions of the texts and attains realisation through his or her own efforts (*jijnasurapi yogasya shabda-brahmaativartate*, VI.44). The Gita says that for a realised person who knows Brahman, the Ultimate, sacred texts are of the same use as a small water-body when there is flooding everywhere (II.46). The Gita thus teaches a healthy, undogmatic attitude to sacred texts, though it is itself considered as a sacred text.

Thus, the Gita, though initially regarded as a part of the *Smriti* literature along with the Mahabharata, soon transcended this status and became a sacred book in its own right surpassing the Vedas. This became particularly conspicuous after Shankaracharya took it up for commentary as one of the *Prasthanathriyee*, signalling that what mattered more for religion is its philosophy and ethics rather than its rituals. The astounding rise in its appeal during the modern period since the second half of the eighteenth century owes to this fact more than anything else. The Gita still has the potential to finish its unfinished task of releasing Hinduism from the compulsive clutches of ritualism and blind belief, and emphasising its ethical and philosophical basis. It can be useful in reforming popular Hinduism and taking it to a higher level.

As a part of the Mahabharata

The Gita, as a dialogue between Krishna and Arjuna, has been a part of the great epic, Mahabharata, almost ever since the Mahabharata was created. The occasion for the Gita is the great battle between Kauravas and Pandavas, both contenders to the kingdom which was earlier ruled by Pandu, the father of Pandavas, and later after the demise of Pandu, by Dhritarashtra, the blind brother of Pandu and the father of Kauravas. Pandavas did not, in any case, claim the whole of the kingdom, but only a reasonable part of it which they had ruled before but were cheated out of it and exiled after a game of chess with high stakes. Pandavas returned after fourteen years of exile and laid their claim. When their claim was repeatedly rejected by Duryodhana, the eldest of the Kaurava brothers, Krishna – keen on avoiding a war between the cousins – finally went as an emissary of the Pandavas to plead with the Kauravas, for at least five villages for the five brothers, as they did not want to live in the kingdom whose effective ruler was Duryodhana. Krishna was a close friend of Pandavas, particularly to Arjuna, and had chosen to be on their side. Krishna was humiliated in the Kaurava court and was even tried to be arrested, though he had come only as an emissary. He could not however be arrested, but the war became inevitable between the cousins, as it was now a matter of honour. There was a long history of humiliations, cheating and sufferings imposed on the Pandavas earlier, including an attempt to disrobe Draupadi, the common wife of the five Pandavas, in the open court of Kauravas.

The war, though basically between the cousins, involved most of the kings and armies of northern India joining either side. The Kaurava army was much bigger with eleven *akshohinis* in size, as against the Pandava army of seven *akshohinis*.[3] The armies came to the plains of Kurukshetra in the present-day Haryana to fight it out. On the first day of the war when the armies on both sides stood face to face ready for battle in the battlefield of Kurukshetra, Arjuna was suddenly in no mood for the war. He developed an agony, became acutely conscious of a moral dilemma and a compassion for his cousins, particularly his teacher, elders and other relatives whom he had venerated all his life. His grandfather Bhishma, teacher Drona and numerous other relatives were now on the side of Kauravas. Though sympathetic to the cause of Pandavas, they chose to be on the side of Kauravas because they were employed by them. The first chapter of the Gita and a small initial part of the second are devoted to describing the moral dilemma and agony of Arjuna mostly in his own words. For instance, Arjuna tells Krishna, his charioteer and mentor: 'I do not see any good in killing my own people; I want neither victory nor the pleasures of a kingdom' (I.31). 'Kauravas may be overpowered by greed, but I am not, and can see the evil consequences of a destructive war' (I.38–45). And he lays down his bow and sits down in the chariot, full of tears.

Arjuna was no common warrior; he was well known for his prowess and had defeated the Kaurava army earlier on behalf of king Virata while in exile. His agony was not out of cowardice; he was confident of victory. After several attempts at reconciliation and peace, Pandavas including Arjuna had finally decided on war, which the Kauravas were itching for. Krishna did not lose his cool at this unexpected development of Arjuna's loss of will. He smiled at him and explained that his behaviour would be treated as cowardice by the enemies, and he cannot just run away at this juncture. As a soldier (Kshatriya) on a battlefield, it was his duty to fight; not only his but also the honour of all those fighting on Pandavas' side was involved. A dishonour to Kshatriya is worse than death. Gandhi adds as a comment here that Krishna was right, because if Arjuna had given up the fight, the whole Pandava army would have been demoralised, and the Kaurava army would have pursued and slaughtered them all. Violence could not have been avoided which Arjuna wanted to avoid (Gandhi 1980: 20). Moreover, Arjuna was merely sentimental, and his agony arose out of his attachment to his teacher and relatives whom he did not want to kill, as Gandhi pointed out. Arjuna's compassion and nonviolence were not general or universal covering all, but focused on what he called his own people (*swajana*) (Gandhi 1980: 13). Even Gandhi, a votary of nonviolence, did not see any merit in Arjuna's opting for nonviolence at that juncture.

Arjuna was not easily convinced by Krishna's admonition and call to abandon what could apparently be treated as unmanliness. Krishna, therefore, launches a long philosophical and moral discourse to ultimately convince him that the sin of killing would not attach to him by following his teaching. And that is how the Bhagavad-Gita originated. We will look into the ethics and philosophy of the Gita in subsequent chapters, but presently, we face a question often raised by a few scholars on this episode.

The question raised is whether the Gita is an original part of the Mahabharata or an interpolation. For, how could Krishna launch a long discourse which would have taken several hours, if not days, right in the middle of the battlefield when the fighting was about to begin? Moreover, all the philosophical issues raised in the discourse were not directly necessary to give a morale-boosting pep talk to Arjuna. For instance, how could the teaching on meditation and bhakti as ways of God realisation have been relevant in that urgent context of war? The inference is that the Gita was simply added to the Mahabharata by its talented poet-author who was eager to immortalise his analysis and interpretation of the Upanishads, and give a philosophical basis for the *sanatana dharma* (Hinduism), which common people could understand more easily than the Vedas and Upanishads. It is argued that it was not very unusual for poets in ancient India to supress own identity and attribute authorship to Vyasa, and the Gita may have been an instance of this. The concerned poet may have imaginatively used the dramatic context of the Mahabharata war to launch his own poem. Supporting this hypothesis of the Gita as an interpolation, Meghnad Desai says that even if the Gita were taken out of the Mahabharata, and the preceding and succeeding chapters are joined, it would still make a continuous and coherent flow, and would not make a break in the narrative (Desai 2014: 53).

Kashi Nath Upadhyaya takes up this hypothesis for a detailed critical examination and concludes that the Gita is indeed 'a genuine constituent part of the Mahabharata', and it had been so from the very beginning (Upadhyaya 1971: 4–9). He argues that the Mahabharata is not a historical treatise presenting only an accurate and exact account of events that took place. The author was a talented poet, versed in philosophy, and made use of all occasions to expound his views and analysis of philosophical and ethical issues. There are several other instances of such long discourses in the epic poem, though the Gita is among the more detailed. There are several references to the Gita in other parts of the epic. Upadhyaya refers to the views of eminent scholars like K. T. Telang and B. G. Tilak, who compared the words, combinations of words (*sandhis*) and grammar used in the Gita with those in the Mahabharata and concluded that they were similar. The type of grammar used in both is of pre-Panini period, involving usages which could be considered as mistakes by Panini (Upadhyaya 1971: 7). The revelation of the cosmic form of Krishna in the eleventh chapter of the Gita is not unique to it and occurs elsewhere too at least on four more occasions in the epic (Upadhyaya 1971: 9).

Swami Vivekananda also took up this issue and was convinced that the Gita was an integral and inseparable part of the Mahabharata. He observed at the Paris Congress of the History of Religions in 1900: 'The style of language of the Gita is the same as that of the Mahabharata. Most of the adjectives used in the Gita to explain matters spiritual are used in the *Vana* and other Parvans of the Mahabharata. . . . Such coincidence is impossible without the most general and free use of those words at one and the same time. Again, the line of thought in the Gita is the same as in the Mahabharata' (CWSV 1998, Vol. IV: 428). Sri Aurobindo, who had made a thorough study of the Mahabharata and even tried to separate Vyasa's original from the later accretions, treated the Gita as a central part of the epic, 'the epitome of Vyasa's main emphasis upon the active religious life', 'the undoubted work of the poet' (Minor 1991-a: 63).

There is a great consistency between the philosophical and ethical stands taken in both the Gita and the Mahabharata. The Mahabharata is of great interest to us even today because of the ethical dilemmas raised through various characters and events, and the Gita begins with one such ethical dilemma. Thus, it is entirely coherent with the overall nature of the larger epic and fits very well in it as its integral part. If the Kurukshetra War constitutes the core of the Mahabharata in terms of events, with the Gita dialogue placed at the very beginning of it, the Gita can be regarded as the soul of the epic in terms of dharma, or ethics and philosophy. Desai's remark that even if the Gita were taken out, the flow of the epic would not be affected appears therefore to be irrelevant and trivial, when we take into account the significance of the Gita in the Mahabharata, in terms of both events and philosophy.

Moreover, there have been at least two main recensions of the Mahabharata, the Southern and the Northern, and several editions and versions in each recension, and of course hundreds of palm-leaf manuscripts in different parts of the country. The Bhagavad-Gita is included in the bulk of them, except maybe where the manuscripts themselves were not found in their entirety. This indicates that the Gita was accepted as a part of the Mahabharata in popular tradition since a long time. Four considerations are relevant in finally settling the question of whether the Gita in its present version had since the beginning been a part of the Mahabharata. First is that the Gita has been composed in a way that it appears as an integral part of the epic. If you take away the dramatic context of the Mahabharata war, what is left for the motivation of the Gita? It would rob the Gita of its main teaching to humanity to face conflicts and tensions in life with equanimity and courage, and not run away from them. Second, the Gita has appeared as a part of the epic in almost all its versions since nearly two millennia. Third, its status as a part of the epic has also since times immemorial been embedded firmly in the minds of people for good reasons, whatever a few scholars may say to the contrary. Finally, irrespective of whether a part of the Mahabharata or not, the Gita admittedly has an authority and importance on its own, and has been recited, studied, and venerated as an independent text, though without erasing the context of the Mahabharata war.

Date and authorship

As is well known, the Gita is in the form of a dialogue believed to have taken place between Lord Krishna and Arjuna in the battlefield of Kurukshetra when the battle was about to start. In fact, the whole Gita is presented as a narration by Sanjaya to king Dhritarashtra, Kauravas' father, including the dialogue between Krishna and Arjuna. Blessed by Sage Vyasa, Sanjaya is enabled to observe everything going on in the battle even while sitting in the palace with the king and narrate it to him. Based on astrological data from the Mahabharata, the traditional sources have estimated that the great battle took place in the year 3139 BCE[4] (Before Common/Christian Era), and the Gita Jayanti is observed on Shukla Ekadashi (eleventh day of the bright half) of the month of Margashirsha (according to the Hindu lunar calendar, which comes usually in December), as the day when the dialogue took place. Most of the historians and modern scholars on the Gita, Hindus included, would not, however, accept this year as historically correct, at least not as the date of the composition of the Gita. We will see later what is a more acceptable date according to modern scholars, though a consensus on this is not possible. Moreover, there could well be a gap between the date when the dialogue took place and the date when the present version of the Gita was finally settled and established. Lord Krishna did not write it down himself even as per tradition.

Though Lord Krishna is acknowledged as the original source and author of the Gita, the credit for compiling it in the form of a text (*grantha*) and including it in the Mahabharata is given by tradition to sage Vyasa. He was the genetic grandfather of both Pandavas and Kauravas,[5] and is believed to have been living through and observing all the events of the Mahabharata. The authorship of the Mahabharata as a whole has been attributed by tradition to Vyasa, whose full name was Krishna Dvaipayana – Krishna indicating that he was dark in complexion and Dvaipayana because he was born in an island (*dvipa*) in the river Yamuna (Jamuna). He is also known as Veda-Vyasa. His mother was a fisherwoman named Matsyagandha (woman with fishy smell) and father a Brahmin sage, Parashara. Vyasa could have been a title given to a learned man who is an expert in putting texts together and editing them, as Karve has observed (1991: 7). Vyasa has been credited to have put together in an orderly form all the Vedas composed nearly a millennium earlier and also with having authored – apart from the Mahabharata – many *Puranas* composed centuries later. Apparently, it could not have been the same Vyasa who did it all. According to the tradition, however, Vyasa is a *chiranjeevi*, an immortal.

Karve observes further that there were two types of literature in ancient India. The first and more ancient type consists of the Vedas, which were in the form of mantras, and they were handed down from generation to generation by well-trained priests with scrupulous attention given to safeguard the accuracy of every syllable and word and its pronunciation in every generation. A similar care was taken about the Upanishads too. The Vedas and the Upanishads were considered as sacred, and no liberty could be taken with their texts. The second type consisted of versified narratives sung and passed on from generation to generation by talented bards, who often were themselves composers too (1991: 2–3).The Mahabharata could have been put together by a learned person, titled as Vyasa, and handed down together with additions made by the bards. The bards were known as *Sutas,* who were well sought after by kings and common people alike eager to listen to their stories in the form of songs. The so-called interpolations thus became natural in such Suta literature, to which the two major epics – the Ramayana and the Mahabharata – and the *Purana*s belonged.

According to many scholars, the first version of the Mahabharata was much smaller, consisting of only 8,400 verses, called *Jaya* (victory). It was confined mainly to narrating the victory of Pandavas over the Kauravas. In the course of time, it grew to a larger version consisting of some 24,000 verses, *Bharata*, so called as it narrated the history of events in the dynasty of the ancient emperor Bharata, who is said to have ruled over all of India (and that is how India was named as Bharat) and whose descendants were the Pandavas and the Kauravas. In the third stage of the expansion of the epic, it grew to its present size of 100,000 verses and became the Mahabharata. It is difficult to tell with certainty, when the *Jaya* became the *Bharata*, and when the *Bharata* became the Mahabharata. The Mahabharata war, as a historical event, is believed by historians to have taken place around 1000 BCE (Karve 1991: 1), and the narrative in its first stage may have begun its course soon after. R. S. Sharma, an authority on ancient India, supports this hypothesis when he says that the composition of the epic (in its first stage) started roughly from the tenth century BCE (2011: 2–3). Based on a review of different Sanskritists' views by Pusalker, one may say that the second stage of the epic was reached around 450–400 BCE (1955: xxvi–xxxi). Pusalker observes that the Mahabharata was almost finalised in its present form by the year 200 CE (or AD). He adds that no single definite date can be assigned to this epic and that it existed largely in its present form by the second century BCE (1955: xxvi–xxxii). It is in the third stage that most of the side stories and long discourses intended to explore the intricacies of dharma and *adharma*, and ethical dilemmas were included. The Bhagavad-Gita in its present form was ready probably before the end of the second stage of the Mahabharata and inspired the inclusion of other side stories and long discourses in the great epic in its third stage.

The evolution of the Mahabharata took place in the spirit of an evolving encyclopaedia, which undergoes periodical revisions and additions, often with new authors entering the picture. In fact, the epic *is* of the nature of an encyclopaedia. In the first volume itself, it claims: *Yadihasti tadanyatra yannehasti na tat kvachit* ('What is here is found elsewhere. What is not here is nowhere.') (Mahabharata Critical Edition 1.56.33; Tr. by Gurcharan Das 2009: xli). Such being the case, treating the later insertions as 'interpolations' amounts to being improper and unfair, particularly if the term 'interpolation' is used pejoratively. Those who put the insertions were talented and learned poets who acted on good faith. The so-called interpolations took place not recently, but more than two millennia back. There was a stage when they stopped. They were not whimsical and arbitrary, but were often creative and imaginative (as the following anecdote would show) and played a positive role in the evolution of the Mahabharata, enriching it with insights, stories, and instructive discourses. Badrinath has subtitled his book on the Mahabharata as 'An Inquiry in the Human Condition' (2007). The epic would not have attained this status of a perceptive inquiry had it not been for the many 'interpolations' which reflected the ancient wisdom of centuries.

There is an anecdote in the Mahabharata itself about how the epic was first put to writing, though it is considered as an insertion into a later version of the epic. C. Rajagopalachari in his summary of the Mahabharata in English, which has proved to be the most popular book on the epic, has of course taken care to include this anecdote in the beginning itself besides 107 stories through which he covered the entire epic (Rajagopalachari 2006: 1). Having conceived the epic, sage Vyasa was in search of a stenographer who could take down the whole epic in written form. Brahma, the first of the Trinity of Hindu gods – the creator – advised Vyasa to meditate upon god Ganapati and pray to him to take up the challenging role. Vyasa did so. Ganapati appeared before him, agreed to his request, but smiled mischievously and laid down a condition: his pen should not stop, and Vyasa should dictate without pause! Vyasa agreed and, guarding himself, put a counter-stipulation: Ganapati should first understand the meaning of what is dictated before writing it down! Ganapati agreed. Vyasa began to sing the story of the Mahabharata, and Ganapati smoothly put it all down in writing. But when the shrewd poet needed a pause occasionally, he dictated a puzzling verse (*kuta-shloka*) to keep Ganapati pondering over its meaning, until Vyasa would start dictating again. Apart from its entertainment value, the anecdote perhaps was inserted to explain the presence of several puzzling verses occurring in the course of the epic.

Since the epic was handed down to succeeding generations orally by bards in different parts of the country, there were differences from region to region in the manuscripts which were based on oral accounts. There is even a Javanese adaptation ascribed to 1000 CE, but all the *Parvans* (volumes) of this adaptation have not yet been traced (Lal 2013: 6).Though the majority of manuscripts found were in Devanagari script in which normally Sanskrit literature is written, there have also been manuscripts in other regional scripts like Bengali, Kannada, Maithili, Malayalam, Nepali, Sharada, and Telugu. During the reign of the Mughal emperor Akbar, a free rendering of the epic was done into Persian (Lal 2013: 6). Since there were quite a few differences from manuscript to manuscript of different regions, sometimes some containing extra chapters and verses, a need was felt for taking a critical look into all the available manuscripts and arriving at what was termed as a 'Critical Edition'. This task was undertaken by the BORI, Pune, in 1919, and completed around the middle of the century. V. S. Sukthankar edited the first volume, *Adiparvan*, examined some 235 manuscripts and set out the principles and criteria of preparing the Critical Edition of the epic in his voluminous 'Prologomena'. The edition did not ignore what the editors considered as interpolations or insertions, but important differences from the selected version were recorded in the footnotes for readers' own judgement. Bringing out the Critical Edition has been a major milestone in the history of the Mahabharata.

Interestingly, divergences in the text of the Gita are far less than in case of the Mahabharata as a whole. Based on modern research into the Gita, S. C. Roy concluded: 'The text of the Gita has remained substantially unaltered in spite of numberless interpolations that have taken place in other portions of the Great Epic' (quoted by Pusalker 1955: 163). Pusalker (Pusalker 1955: 144) remarks: 'It is indeed curious how the Bhagavadgita presents such a relatively fixed consistent text for the last 1200 years.' But the estimate of 1,200 years could well be a gross underestimate if we go by other scholars' view, according to whom the Gita may have attained the present final shape before 400 BCE. On the basis of astronomical analysis, M. R. Yardi concludes that the (present) Gita was composed in 450 BCE (1991: 12). Probably, Pusalker took eighth century CE as a benchmark, because Shankar<u>a</u>ch<u>a</u>rya wrote his commentary on the Gita in its present form then. But there were commentaries on the Gita even before, which Shankara and R<u>a</u>m<u>a</u>nuja have referred to, such as the one by Boudh<u>a</u>yana. Telang observes that though Boudhayana's date is not settled, he is known to have lived prior to *Apasthambha Smriti*, the date of which was settled by Buhler as prior to the third century BCE (Telang 1970: 21, 32), which concurs with the date given by Upadhyaya (1971: 17). Boudhayana's commentary could have come only after the Gita in its present form was established. Shankara does not refer to changes in the text of the Gita before him. The present popular version has been stable since then, except for minor variations, with 700+1 verses. The +1 verse appears in some editions at the beginning of Chapter 13 as a question put by Arjuna, omitted in other editions. Thus, the present version of the Gita, commented upon by Shankara, has been with us for no less than 2,500 years. A Kashmiri recension emerged in around 800 CE with 745 verses, but the additional verses do not make any material difference to the content of the Gita (Pusalker 1955: 144). It is the traditional version used by Shankara (with 700 verses) which is extant in the mainstream.

Closely linked with the issue of the date or year as per calendar, there is also the issue of where the Gita fits in the chronological sequencing of major texts, which indirectly helps in settling the date. This question has been discussed at some length by Telang (1970: 7–24), which may be briefly paraphrased here. Telang suggests that the Gita clearly came before the six orthodox schools of Hindu philosophy were systematised into texts (such as Patanjali's *Yogas<u>u</u>tras*), and in this respect, the Gita can be grouped with the Upanishads. There is no attempt at systematisation either in the Upanishads or in the Gita, though they reflect deep philosophical insights. They provided the ingredients for the subsequent systematisation. Telang even observes that there has been no attempt at the standardisation of the meaning of some words in the Gita, like 'Yoga', 'Brahman' or 'Buddhi', which acquired scientific precision only subsequently. He thinks that the Gita precedes even the *Brahmas<u>u</u>tras*, known more popularly as the *Ved<u>a</u>ntas<u>u</u>tras* earlier. A mention of 'Brahmas<u>u</u>tra' in the Gita (XIII.4) does not really refer to the text as such, according to Telang. As the verse itself says in the preceding line, it may refer simply to statements pointing to Brahman found in the Vedas and Upanishads. On the contrary, Telang contends, the *Brahmasu̱tras* themselves refer to the Gita as a *Smriti* (in Sutras I.2.6 and I.3.23). Telang also observes that the Gita mentions (in IX.17) only the three Vedas, *Rig, Yajur*, and *Sa̱ma*, there being no reference to the *Atharva-veda*. This may suggest that the Gita came even prior to the *Atharva-veda*. According to Telang, the Gita comes prior also to Panini, the ancient grammarian, whose date is fixed as not later than the fourth century BCE (Telang 1970: 33). The grammar of the Gita and of the Mahabharata as a whole is considered as pre-Paninian. The *Apasthambha* and *Manu Smritis* came long after the Gita. This is because (as Telang argues), the Gita came at a time when the birth-based caste system was only in a formative stage and the *varṉas* were on the basis of work and aptitude (*guna-karma*) rather than birth. Both *Apasthambha* and *Manu Smritis*, on the other hand, came at a subsequent stage when the birth-based caste system had consolidated itself. Between the two, the former came earlier. On the authority of Buhler, Telang points out that while the *Manu Smriti* can be assigned to the second or third century BCE, the *Apasthambha Smriti* can be to a period of time prior to the third century BCE. If the Gita was composed earlier than the *Brahmasu̱tras* and the *Atharva-veda*, which came much before the two Smritis, its place in all these chronological sequencing points to its date as being not later than the fifth century BCE.

The chronological position of the Gita vis-à-vis early Buddhism also corroborates this conclusion. Telang takes a clear stand on this and argues that the Gita was composed before the rise of early Buddhism (Telang 1970: 24–27). His contention is not based on the negative point of the absence of any reference to the Buddha or Buddhism in the Gita, but on more positive grounds. Telang points out two major differences between the Gita and the Buddha. The Buddha totally rejects the authority of the Vedas and the varṉa order. On the other hand, the Gita does not absolutely reject either the Vedas or the varṉa system. It only protests against ritualism in the Vedas and deplores the emphasis on merely reciting them and just book learning. It points to more profound ways of making our lives meaningful and fulfilled. As regards varṉa system, the Gita places it on 'less untenable basis' (Telang 1970: 25) of work and aptitude, rather than birth. Telang does not interpret it as a defensive stand of the Gita trying to save Hinduism by abandoning its weak points in the light of Buddhist attack, which would have meant that the Gita is subsequent to early Buddhism.

On the other hand, he interprets the rise of Buddhism as a result of dissatisfaction with the success of the reform movement within the sanatana dharma initiated clearly much earlier to Buddhism by the Upanishads – a reform movement which the Gita also joined subsequently. Telang groups both the Upanishads and the Gita together as fellow participants in reversing the decline brought about by Vedic ritualism. He compares the Upanishad–Gita reform movement with the modern reform movement started by Raja Rammohan Roy, and the rise of Buddhism with Keshub Chandra's more radical movement subsequently. Since Telang wrote in the nineteenth century, he could not have foreseen the even more radical Ambedkar movement and the re-emergence of Buddhism after a long gap, again as a protest against the evils in Hinduism. Had he written now, Telang would have considered it as a repetition of history. The main point of Telang, however, is that it is more probable that the Gita came prior to early Buddhism or even the Buddha. There is some controversy about the exact date of the Buddha. But the chief landmark in Buddhist chronology is his *Parinibbana* or death, and there is a fair degree of agreement that it took place between 487 and 477 BCE (Upadhyaya 1971: 32). It is well recorded that the Buddha lived up to eighty years. If the Gita's period is taken to be as at about the same time as the Buddha's lifetime, it will mean sixth century BCE, which would make it close to what was concluded earlier as not later than the fifth century BCE. It is difficult to be more accurate than this about the date of the Gita.

Dr Babasaheb Ambedkar, however, considers the Gita to be post-Buddhist, on the basis of certain points which he thinks the Gita has borrowed from Buddhism. There is a conspicuous reference to *Brahma-nirvana* in the Gita (II.72). He observes that no Upanishad used the word, and that the Gita must have borrowed the word 'Nirvana' from *Mahaparinibbana Sutta*, prefixing 'Brahma' to make it appear as original. He also points out some common concepts or ideas between the Gita and the Buddhist texts, including virtues described as desired like detachment, compassion, purity and desirelessness (Ambedkar 2004: 203–4). There is certainly a significant common ground between the Gita and Buddhism. But both were influenced by Upanishads and the vibrant intellectual environment of the time, which explains the common ground. It is possible, however, that the Gita – at least its final version – may have been composed during the Buddha's time or early Buddhism, in which the words like *Brahma-nirvana* may have been included. In any case, the Gita has its own distinctive features which are not in Buddhism, particularly its theism and the different paths of *sadhana*.

There is a further complication if we agree about the Gita having undergone a few stages of evolution before it attained its present form, indicating multiple authorship. The thesis of multiple authorship has not gone uncontested, but a few scholars agree about it. Yardi mentions those who subscribe to the thesis of multiple authorship of the Gita, both Indian and Western (Yardi 1991: 4). He refers to the *Chhandogya Upanishad* mentioning Devaki-putra (son of Devaki) Krishna, a pupil of Ghora Angirasa; Krishna is said to have studied the Upanishads in depth under the latter. Yardi believes that it is the same Krishna who expounded the Gita to Arjuna, as he was also believed to be Devaki-putra. This teaching as compiled by Vyasa was preserved and handed down to succeeding generations. Shaunaka came into possession of it and incorporated it into the Mahabharata. According to Yardi, Sauti added six chapters to the Gita subsequently, which dealt mainly with the *Sa̲nkhya* philosophy (Yardi 1991: 13, 18). Whether the Gita had one or more authors, it is agreed by many that they were all before Panini, who systematised Sanskrit grammar, because the grammar of the Gita (and the Mahabharata) is pre-Paninian. As noted earlier, Panini came before the fourth century BCE, which means that even the last addition to the Gita must have come before that.

The hypothesis of multiple authorship of the Gita was first raised by European scholars, particularly by Rudolf Otto, whose work on it was first published in German in 1933, and an English translation of which by J. E. Turner was published in 1939, under the title, *The Original Gita: The Song of the Supreme Exalted One*. Interestingly, Gajanan S. Khair also supported the hypothesis much later in India through a similarly titled book, *Quest for the Original Gita* (1969, 1997). Khair thinks there were three authors of the Gita, the first well before the Buddha, the second a little before the Buddha or during his lifetime, and the third in the early phase of Buddhism partly as a response to it, around the third century BCE. While all the three authors made significant and welcome contributions according to Khair, it is only the original Gita identified as such which is authentic and important for Otto.[6] According Khair, the first and the second authors addressed themselves mainly to upper classes and the religious and spiritual elite. The third author, however, kept the common people in mind (Khair 1997: 50–51). Khair even attempts an identification of the exact contribution made by each author and thinks that, in terms of the size, the contribution of the third author was the largest of the three. He makes no attempt, however, to name the three authors, except saying that they were very learned sages who added their contribution in good faith and with good intention. The first author distilled the philosophy of the Upanishads, taking their idea of Brahman, broadened the concept of yajna, making elaborate rituals and animal sacrifices unnecessary for spiritual progress. He also advanced the idea of karma-yoga, the path of selfless service without detachment (Khair 1997: 68, 71–72). The second author was influenced by the *Sankhya* philosophy, and not only added to the Gita a discussion of *trigunas* (*satva, rajas*, and *tamas*) but also went beyond the *Sankhya* philosophy by proposing the concept of *Purushottama* or Paramapurusha, the Highest Soul or the Supreme Soul above all and everything. The original *Sankhya* system did not have this concept and was confined to the twin concept of *prakriti*, the active principle behind the material universe or nature, and numerous Purushas, the individual, conscious, and watching souls. While the original *Sankhya* is agnostic, the Gita is very much theistic (Khair 1997: 68, 72–73). Khair's third author took the idea of Purushottama further, making Him a personal God, amenable to bhakti or devotion and love. The third author felt that the common people needed a personal God to whom they could offer their prayers and devotion, and felt it could work to the advantage of *sanatana dharma*, as against the agnostic faiths like Buddhism, Jainism and Lokayata. He also made the concept of karma-yoga easier to follow by declaring that one has to just surrender the fruits of action to God. He made God accessible to everyone – men, women, high castes and low castes – for everyone is equal in the eyes of God, and caste or gender did not matter (Khair 1997: 75, 128,142). Khair thus explains how the Gita evolved over a period, responding to the needs of time. However, the evolution of the Gita came to a stop after the third author in around the third century BCE, and the interpreters took over thereafter, who brought in the needed flexibility to respond to circumstances prevailing at different times.

The basis for the hypothesis of multiple authorship rests on a perception that there is no unity of a single theme in the Gita, that there is no logical and smooth flow of argument and that there are some inconsistencies. The hypothesis is tried to be proved only through a textual analysis or internal evidence, and speculatively so, and there is not even a shred of external evidence cited anywhere to indicate support to multiple authorship. On the contrary, all available external evidence confirms the traditional view that the Gita first came out of the lips of Lord Krishna and compiled later in verse form by Vyasa as a part of the Mahabharata. As to the absence of a single theme, lack of a smooth logical flow and presence of inconsistencies, which scripture in the world is free from these problems – including the scriptures of Semitic religions? In the case of the Gita, it is known and explicitly acknowledged that it was a free and informal dialogue between two friends, and neither a lecture in a formal academic seminar nor an article in an academic journal! Moreover, it is the basic essence and purpose of the Gita to offer a creative synthesis of different schools of thought and different paths of spiritual pursuit. The apparent inconsistencies have to be interpreted in the light of their respective contexts in any scripture after all! No scripture should be interpreted literally with each sentence taken as applicable to all times, contexts and circumstances, as it would amount to fundamentalism or fanaticism.

Whether we accept the hypothesis of multiple authorship or not, it is not necessary to regard the Gita as a patchwork of interpolations. The additions through which the Gita is presumed by some to have evolved are not whimsical, but thoughtfully done by knowledgeable and perceptive sages, responding to the needs of the time. The Gita does have enough continuity and consistency to be treated as a single integrated work, in spite of apparent inconsistencies which can arise even in the works known to be by one author. The Gita any way has been a delightful challenge to a variety of interpreters each of whom could find a central message, even if they differed from each other in identifying what that message was. Merely because their perceptions and interpretations differed does not mean lack of unity in the original text, just as the different perceptions of the nine blind men in the famous parable could not have denied the oneness of the elephant they perceived. It is these differences which make the Gita so very interesting and even challenging. Besides this, we cannot forget that in its present form, the Gita has been with us for no less than 2,500 years and has acquired enough heritage value and authority. Even if it evolved over time before that and multiple authorship is granted, Lord Krishna remains as its basic source. We can still regard the Gita as one integrated work, and the different paths of spiritual seeking represented in it only reflect the diversity and richness of choices open to its followers who like to benefit from it. If I go to a restaurant for lunch, I would expect some choices open to me according to my taste, and not one dish for all and for all time. If the restaurant offers a rich variety of fare, it is its strength, not weakness. The Gita reflects not inconsistency, but a variety to choose from, according to one's aptitude. One may feel attracted by the notion of the Supreme as *nirguṉa* (without attributes), while another may prefer an intervening personal *saguṉa* God (with attributes) who loves and looks after his devotees.

The former may prefer to follow *jnana-marga* (the path of knowledge or contemplative inquiry), while latter may like to be a *bhakta*, a devotee. Others may not very much bother about the nature of the Supreme, but would concentrate on their just duty of serving others selflessly as a path of liberation. They would choose *karma-marga*. Yet others may like to follow a combination of all the three paths. The Gita is an inspiring guide for all of them.

It is because of its proven ability to provide answers to questions raised by a variety of people, in a variety of contexts, and for well over two millennia by now, and in future too, the Gita can be considered as timeless like the Vedas. It is an eternal intellectual and spiritual resource of humanity to draw upon, which is not exhausted but further enriched by using it.

Notes

1 The original Sanskrit saying quoted in Tilak's Preface is: *Gita sugita kartavya kim anyaiah Shastra-vistarashah?* The translation is as given by Sukthankar (Tilak 1936: li).

2 Radhakrishnan (1996: 525, n3) gives some examples of common verses: BG II.29 and Katha Up. 2.7; BG II.20, VIII.11 and Katha Up. 2.19, 2.15; BG III.42 and Katha Up. 3.10; BG VI.11 and Shvet. Up. 2.10; BG VI.13 and Shvet. Up. 2.8.

3 An *Akshohini* consists of 21,870 chariots (*rathas*), 21,870 elephants, 65,610 cavalry and 109,350 infantry (*Adiparva* 2.15–23). See en.wikipedia.org/wiki/Akshauhini; and Pai (2015: 18). There were eleven of them on the Kaurava side and seven on the Pandava side, making a total of more than four million fighting, both sides together, depending on how many worked on each elephant and chariot. Pai notes incidentally that the digits of these divisions add up to eighteen, coinciding with the eighteen chapters of the Gita and eighteen Parvans of the Mahabharata. It is also mentioned on page 18 of her book!

4 This is as per www.thevedicfoundation.org/bharatiya-history/mahabharat.htm, downloaded on 25 January 2015.

5 Based on the account in the Mahabharata itself, Richard Davis narrates how: 'When the ruling king of the Bharata dynasty, Vichitravirya, dies without fathering a male heir, Vyasa (who is half-brother to the deceased) is called to court in order to impregnate his two widows. Their sons are Pandu and Dhritarashtra, fathers of the Pandavas and Kauravas respectively' (Davis 2015: 36).

6 According to Otto, the original Gita comprised of: I; II.1–13, 20, 22, 29–37; X.1–8; XI.1–6, 8–12, 14, 17, 19–36, 41–51; and XVIII.58–61, 66, 72–73 (Otto 1939: 15; as quoted in Robinson 2013: 46).

2

CLASSICAL COMMENTATORS OF THE GITA

The Gita in the rest of the Mahabharata, and the *Puranas*

The significance and greatness of the Gita was recognised without much lapse of time. The Mahabharata itself says later in the same *Bhishma Parvan* in which the Gita occurs – *Gita sugita kartavya kim anyah Shastra-vistarashah*, that is, 'whoever studies the Gita thoroughly need not bother himself about the prolixity of other Shastric writings' (Yardi 1991: v). The Mahabharata makes use of another occasion in the *Ashwamedhika-parvan* to paraphrase the Gita as narrated to Arjuna by Krishna in what came to be known as *Anu-Gita* (Sharma 1985: 1–11). The war had ended by then and the Pandavas had won, and the context of removing Arjuna's grief and goading him to fight was no longer there. It is in such a changed context that Arjuna requests Krishna to recapitulate what was taught in the Bhagavad-Gita. It is as if Arjuna wanted to know the more enduring teaching of the Gita, with the earlier context removed. Sharma thinks that the *Anu-Gita* is 'the first comment, if not commentary, on the Bhagavad-Gita within the Hindu tradition' (Sharma 1985: 2). The *Anu-Gita* emphasises that the knowledge of Brahman is possible only through sense-control, and the yoga of action has to be based on and guided by *jnana* or knowledge. Sharma observes that the *Anu-Gita* is free from any glorification of Krishna and ends on a *jnana*-oriented note, in contrast to the *bhakti*-oriented concluding note of the *Bhagavad-Gita* (Sharma 1985: 6). However, the *Anu-Gita* has been considered as somewhat less comprehensive and inspiring as compared with the original Gita and did not become popular. Perhaps it was so due to the less dramatic context of the *Anu-Gita*. There are several further references to the Gita in the Mahabharata, which have been cited by Tilak in the Appendix to his *Gita Rahasya*.

Around the time the composition of the Mahabharata including the final form of the Gita was completed, a Vasudeva cult had started becoming popular. Its emphasis was on bhakti as the easiest and the most dependable path of God realisation. As a part of following this path, a practice of daily recitation of the Gita was adopted. It was this practice which must have prevented any further interpolation of the text and stabilised it. A few *Puranas*, which emerged then, refer to the Gita with reverence, including the *Padma-Purana* and the *Skanda Purana*. The *Varaha-Purana* prescribes recitation of its *Gita-Mahatmyam* along with that of the Gita.[1] Tilak mentions two other *Gita-Mahatmyams* in *Padma-Purana* and *Vayu-Purana* respectively. The former is more detailed, with eighteen chapters each corresponding respectively to each of the eighteen chapters of the Gita. Tilak also points out to several Gitas in various *Puranas* inspired by the original Gita, which, however, do not have the same freshness as the original according to him. There is even a *Ganesha-Gita* of *Ganesha-Purana*, which he says is a faithful copy of the *Bhagavad-Gita* except for slight verbal differences (Tilak 1936: 4–8). *Yoga-vasishta* gives a summary of the *Bhagavad-Gita* in its last chapter. There is the *Uddhava-Gita* in the *Bhagavata Purana*, the *Shiva-Gita* in the *Padma Purana*, and the *Devi-Gita* in the *Devi Bhagavata Purana*. These subsequent Gitas, however, hardly reduced the significance attached to the *Bhagavad-Gita*. Endorsement of the *Bhagavad-Gita* by the *Puranas* spread the belief that its mere recitation or of parts of it or even of a few verses in it every day conferred great merit (*punya*). Soon the influence of the Gita spread beyond the followers of the Vasudeva cult and captured the mind of others too.

S. Radhakrishnan observes that the Gita influenced Mahayana Buddhism, and at least two chief works of it, *Mahayana-shraddhotpatti* (The Awakening of Faith in the *Mahayana*), and *Saddharma-pundarika* (The Lotus of the True Law), are deeply indebted to the teaching of the Gita. He adds that through Buddhism, the Gita's influence extended in early times to China and Japan also (Radhakrishnan 1993: 11, n1).

Apart from finding an endorsement in a few Puranas, the Gita attracted a few commentators as well even before Adi Shankaracharya. Baudhayana was a major one among them, who has been referred to in the last chapter of Shankara's commentary. Unfortunately, Baudhayana's commentary (*bhashya*) is not available now. An important feature of the bhashyakaras (commentators) is that they take the text handed down to them as given, treat it with reverence and only try to explain its intricacies and elaborate the meaning though in the light of their own perspective. They avoid being critical of the text, though not of other commentators. If any vagueness or inconsistencies are found in the text, they try to understand and reconcile them, instead of launching an attack on the text on that pretext. In this respect, they are very different from some of the modern scholars of the Gita who treated texts like lab specimens, meant for dissection and critical analysis only. Nevertheless, the earlier commentators cannot be regarded as uncritical, and they played an important role by interpreting a fixed text in the light of changing times, discovering new meanings and new messages. This has been very much the case with the Gita throughout its history.

Though the Gita had slowly started making an impact, in those initial days, the Gita's followers and admirers were not yet in the mainstream of India's religious milieu. In spite of the Upanishads and their emphasis on jn<u>a</u>na or knowledge and ethics, a tradition of complex rituals originating from the *Karma-k<u>a</u>n<u>d</u>a* portion of the Vedas had staged a comeback. The Gita had given a new meaning to the concept of *yajna* as well as karma, but with most people, karma meant rituals. On the other hand, the heterodox faiths like Buddhism and Jainism caught the imagination of those people who found the path of rituals much less appealing.

Shankara

A need arose thus for an eminent and eloquent person who could retrieve the san<u>a</u>tana dharma from the morass of ritualism on the one hand and the challenge of the heterodox faiths on the other. This need was addressed by <u>A</u>di Shankar<u>a</u>ch<u>a</u>rya (Shankara for brevity). He did not have to bother much about opposing Buddhism and Jainism, but focused more on defeating the ritualists through debates, travelling all over the country on foot from Kerala to Kashmir and the Himalayas in the bargain. Once the ritualists were defeated, it could take the wind out of the sails of Buddhism and Jainism.

There is a controversy about the exact years when Shankara lived, but much less dispute about his having had a short life of only thirty-two years. Perhaps there is none else in history who accomplished so much within such a short span of life. Govind Chandra Pande, after examining the views and evidence of most scholars and making his own analysis in an exclusive chapter devoted to arriving at the date of Shankara, concludes that the date of Shankara ranges between 650 and 775 CE (Pande 1994: 41–54, esp.52). Several scholars believe his date to be from 788 to 820 CE (Harshananda 2008, Vol. 3: 192). It is commonly accepted that he lived in the eighth century CE. His parents' home was in Kaladi (also called as Kalati), near modern Alwaye, and he was born in Veliyanad (near Erunakulam in his mother's place), in a pious family. He died at Kedarnath in the Himalayas (Pande 1994: 77–78). Not only in birth and death, but also in work, he spanned the whole of India.

Shankara was a precocious child who could learn quickly and retained in memory what he heard once. By his third year itself, he is said to have memorised a good deal of poetry. His father, Shivaguru, initiated him into Vedic studies at the age of five, but died soon after. Sanskritic education was widespread in Kerala then, available mostly in the premises of major temples. The child Shankara had no difficulty in mastering the Vedas, Upanishads, Shastras and Puranas early in life. At the age of eight, he had an urge to become a *sannyasi* (monk, renunciate), but could not do so without permission from his mother, Aryamba, whom he loved much, and she was reluctant to accede to his wish. An incident helped him in realising his wish. Once when he visited his home back from the place of his study, he was bathing in the river nearby, when a crocodile caught him. Shankara called out to his mother who was nearby and said he might be saved if she released him for renunciation. His mother agreed, and the crocodile also released him miraculously. After leaving his mother to the care of her relations, Shankara left as a peripatetic mendicant in search of a Guru. But before leaving, he promised to his mother that he would be with her at the hour of her death and perform her last rites in spite of being a sannyasi (Pande 1994: 78–81). He kept his promise.

The eight-year-old Shankara travelled north and in his ninth year met his guru, Govindapada, on the banks of river Narmada. Shankara remained with his guru until he was twelve and learnt the intricacies of Vedanta. The guru then advised him to go to Kashi (Varanasi) and write a commentary on the *Brahmasutras*, which he did. Biographers of Shankara agree that he finished writing his famous commentaries on the *Brahmasutras*, ten Upanishads and the Gita, as well as most of his numerous literary works by the time he finished sixteen years (Pande 1994: 83,87,88).

Shankara spent the next sixteen years of his life travelling almost all over the country, defeating opponents in debates, winning disciples, establishing *mathas* (monasteries) in all four directions of India and propagating his doctrine of non-dualism or Advaita. To Shankara goes the credit of organising sanatana dharma on the sound and sustained basis of *mathas* probably for the first time in the history of Hinduism. The acharyas and spiritual leaders who came after him simply followed his example. The *mathas* contributed a good deal in consolidating Hinduism toughening it against the onslaughts of other religions, by continuing the tradition of Vedic studies, providing religious instruction to people, training priests and also promoting social service particularly in times of emergencies.

We cannot afford to miss an incident in his life said to have occurred at Kashi, which became famous. When Shankara was proceeding to the river along with his disciples, he saw a Chandala (outcaste) on the way and asked him to move away. To Shankara's surprise, the Chandala pointed out the inconsistency between his doctrine of spiritual unity and the caste notion of untouchability. Shankara realised his mistake and prostrated at the feet of the so-called outcaste. Shankara has immortalised this incident in five verses, together titled as *Manishapanchakam*, recording Shankara's response to the man whom he now accepted as a guru. Pande observes that this incident could hardly have been a fabrication of later times and believes it to be genuine (Pande 1994: 87). The incident is significant as it demonstrated the social significance of Shankara's philosophy in a very practical way, though unfortunately it hardly succeeded in ending untouchability in India.

With Shankara, Pande observes, the age of *Smritis* and *Puranas* ended, and the age of commentaries or *bhashyas* commenced (Pande 1994: 57).[2] There is a common notion that it was Shankara who almost discovered the Gita hidden in a corner of the Mahabharata and made it famous through his commentary. Such a notion is a bit exaggerated view of his role. Shankara himself, in his introduction to his *Gita Bhashya*, says that there have been commentaries before him, but they could not achieve much because they did not take a total view of the Gita and resolve seemingly contradictory verses and doubts. He explains that that is why he wrote his commentary (cf. para 3 of *Upodghata* or introduction in Warrier's translation with the Sanskrit original, 1983: 3). There is no doubt, however, that though Shankara may not have discovered a lost Gita as such, his *bhashya* gave unprecedented prominence to it. In any case, the commentaries made before Shankara have been lost since long and are not available today.

Shankara interpreted the Gita in terms of his own perspective, as did the acharyas after him from their own respective viewpoints. These perspectives or viewpoints neither were preconceived notions nor were derived from the study of the Gita alone, but also from their study of other texts, particularly the *Brahmasutras* and the Upanishads. What these acharyas did was to take a total view in developing their doctrines, derived from their comprehensive study and contemplation on them, and reapply them to individual scriptures in interpretation. As Arvind Sharma shows almost throughout his book (1985), this attempt landed them in difficulties with particular verses which did not quite fit their doctrines, resulting in over-interpretation or under-representation at times. Sharma observes here: 'Any attempt to straightjacket the Gita leads to odd excesses' (1985: xxv). Whenever someone tries to get a *single* meaning out of a sacred text, it can become one more among many. This is especially so in the discussions on the nature of the Supreme, the relation of the Supreme with individuals and the path to the realisation of the Supreme or Liberation. There just cannot be one exclusive view about it. This does not mean that the interpretations of the eminent acharyas are flawed; after all, this is a problem with any interpreter having one particular perspective. But is it possible to analyse or interpret anything without a perspective?

As is well known, Shankara's overall perspective was Advaita (non-dualism or monism), which he summarised in half a verse: *Brahma satyam jagan mithya jivo Brahmeti na parah* (Brahman is the truth, the world unreal; the soul is Brahman, not anything else). The Gita's explicit support to Shankara's main contention about the soul or the real self (*jiva* or *atma*) being Brahman is to be found in quite a few of its verses (see the first half of the following: II.17, VI.29, VI.31, VIII.3, X.20, XIII.27, XV.15, XVIII.61, and full IV.24, XIII.32). Can this belief lead to arrogance in an individual ('I am God!')? No, because the soul of *everyone* is divine, and not of one person alone. It can lead, however, to enormous self-confidence, motivating each to realise one's immense potentialities. A basic teaching of Advaita is that the ego, identified with body–mind–senses complex, is not the real self or the soul. Arrogance is associated with ego, which actually comes in the way spiritual pursuit. Ego perishes with the body, while the *Atman* is eternal. *Atman* is the Divine presence in all beings, not only human beings, but all beings. In this sense, all life is sacred as it is the explicit expression of the Divine.

The other part of Shankara's summary statement about the world being unreal (*jaganmithya*) has often been wrongly interpreted to mean that Shankara denied the reality of the world. If the world is unreal or false, then what is the meaning and purpose of any work in the world? Would there be any basis for ethics? Shankara had to address these implications; so he explained that what he really meant was that the world is not real in the same sense in which Brahman is real and that the world is only relatively real. While the reality of Brahman is absolute, autonomous, eternal and primary, the reality of the world is dependent, derived, transient and secondary. Based on the Upanishads, he explained that there are two levels of truth – *paramarthika satya* (spiritual or transcendental truth) and *vyavaharika satya* (truth at all practical or mundane levels). The fact that Shankara did not regard the latter as illusory is clear from another word he gave to the occurrence of an illusion, *pratibhasika*, which is not a reality in any sense (Radhakrishnan 1999, Vol. 2: 520). The immense significance of *vyavaharika* in mundane matters is not denied. The *paramarthika satya* may not be realised through sense perception, but the *vyavaharika* can be. Both are real at their own levels. According to quantum physics, the basic reality consists of particles. The table which I use for writing is very real and has immense meaning and significance to me in practical matters. For a scientist, however, its basic reality is in terms of quanta of particles. If I am a spiritual seeker eager to realise the basic reality behind all that exists, it is the *paramarthika satya* which I have to know. But at the same time, I have to live and work in this world, where I have to operate according to the rules of *vyavaharika satya*. Even if the world is a drama, we have to play our roles as actors, that is, as morally responsible human beings. There is an anecdote in the life of Shankara, which brings out this teaching. During one of his travels in the country along with his disciples, they were passing through a forest and saw an elephant coming. They immediately took to their heels. Once they reached a safe place, a disciple asked him in a lighter vein why he ran, wasn't the elephant *mithya* (unreal)? Shankara promptly replied, '*mama palayanam api mithya*!' (My running away also was *mithya*).

Right in his introduction to his *Gita Bhashya* (in *Upodghata*, para 4), Shankara observes that 'the purpose of the science of the Gita is to set forth the *summom bonum* [*nihshreyas*], which consists in the total cessation of the transmigratory life and its causes' (Warrier 1983: 4). Transcending the *Samsara's* cycle of births and deaths has been accepted as the highest goal by almost all the Hindu philosophers and saints, including the three acharyas. But there may be a little difference of opinion about the means of achieving it. According to Shankara, it is achieved only by *atma-jnana-nishtha* (staying with the self-knowledge) preceded by *sarva-karma-sannyasa* (renunciation of all works). *Atma-jnana* means becoming aware of the unity or identity of the self with the Brahman, and realising that the self is different from the ego. Shankara believed that such state cannot be reached through being engaged in action or works. But the Gita itself tells clearly in Chapter 3 (verse 5) how none can rest even for a moment without some action, how work is absolutely necessary for the functioning of the world itself (III.14) and how God Himself always continues in action though He has nothing to gain from it (III.22). Shankara, however, rules out combining knowledge with works as a solution whatever the reasoning (*Tasmat kayapi yuktya na samucchayah jnana-karmanoh* – para III.2 in his *Gita Bhashya*, Warrier 1983: 102). He even declares that karma-yoga is meant only for the ignorant (*Ajnanam eva hi karma-yogah, na jnaninam* – para 5.1 in his *Gita Bhashya*, Warrier 1983: 106). In the context of the Gita, one can make sense of Shankara in three ways: *one*, we have to take him to mean only rituals when he refers to *karma*, while the Gita uses the term in a wider sense. *Second*, even if Shankara takes karma in the wider sense of the Gita, karma or works are relevant only as far as the phenomenal world or *samsara* is concerned. If our goal is transcending it and realising the real self or the Brahman, then karmas are not relevant, as per his philosophy. It is only *jnana* which is. *Third*, as the Gita itself explains, renunciation consists not in ceasing to work, but only in giving up the personal desire for fruits of karma and surrendering the outcome of works into the hands of God.

According to Advaita philosophy, the Brahman is masked or veiled by the world. The latter is a projection on the Brahman, like a scene or picture projected on a cinema screen. We see only the picture and enjoy it, and not the screen. The process by which Brahman is veiled or projected upon is called by Shankara as *maya*. Though the term is usually translated as illusion, it is not its precise connotation. *Maya* is the act of veiling or projection. *Maya* is taken as a power of the Divine by almost all the interpreters of the Gita, since the Gita also says so. The traditional explanation for the purpose of *Maya* is the proneness of the Divine for sport (*lila*). But this goes against the notion of *nirguna* (without attributes) Brahman in Advaita and also against the notion that Brahman is *purna* (complete, perfect, not lacking in anything) who needs no sport to entertain himself. Brahman is therefore said to be inscrutable. Mere human beings are unable to probe into the purpose of the Divine in wielding the power of maya, as they are themselves a part of maya. But when Brahman is worshipped as *saguna Ishwara*, the Lord with attributes of compassion for all beings, the creation is an expression of this attribute.

The world being *mithya* is only one of the ingredients of Advaita philosophy. Its most important ingredient which gave the philosophy its name is that *jiva* or Atman or the soul is the same as Brahman, but distinct from the ego identified with the body–mind complex; that is, Atman and Brahman are not two. The Divine is present in every being as its soul. One way in which Shankara arrived at this conclusion is by reflecting on the fact that the basic nature of both the Brahman and Atman is the same, and that basic nature is one of *sat* (pure existence, truth), *chit* (consciousness) and *ananda* (blissful joy). Both are eternal, though the ego is not. Ego perishes with body. The identity of the *jiva*–Atman and Brahman is realised through deep contemplation, by focusing on pure consciousness or awareness. Another way in which one can arrive at the identity of the *jiva* with the Brahman is by recalling that the Brahman is omnipresent, and therefore It/He is in you and me, and in every being. Omnipresence can also be taken as implying that there is nothing else present, nothing else exists except the Brahman. Thus, the *jiva* cannot be different from the Brahman. Any perception of other things being present is due to *maya*.

Mani Bhaumik, a reputed physicist and co-inventor of laser technology, believes that modern science has brought us closer to appreciate the ancient teaching of Advaita Vedanta – *Aham Brahmasmi* (I am Brahman). He says that each of us completes creation and that 'God is incomplete *without us*' (emphasis in original) (Bhaumik 2005: 30). It means that God lives in us, and his spirit pervades everywhere (Bhaumik 2005: 31). Bringing out the remarkable correlation between modern science and ancient Vedanta, he observes that 'everything is at the deepest level, everywhere. That all is one' (Bhaumik 2005: 32). Bhaumik points out that according to Walter Moore, biographer of quantum visionary Erwin Schrödinger, he was intuitively influenced by Vedanta in formulating quantum mechanics, and perhaps the Vedantic concept of oneness led him to a decade-long search for the unified field theory. 'From the Upanishads, Schrödinger finds it to be so simple and clear: *Tat twam asi*, This is you' (Bhaumik 2005: 177). Bhaumik does not refer to Shankara as such, but it is clear that his reference is to the Advaita Vedanta from the Upanishads. He says: 'Why do the Vedic rishis quietly assert, from the deep well of contemplation, "I am Brahman"? Could it be that the timeless mystical experience of oneness with the *source*, an experience that transcends all faiths and cultures, is actually the closest we humans can ever come to perceiving the universe as it truly is?' (Bhaumik 2005: 216).

Once the identity of *jiva* and Brahman is realised, that is liberation, according to Shankara. It can happen even while living; one does not have to wait for death. This realisation is not possible unless one has a pure mind and moral integrity. It can be aided by prayers to the Divine through *stotras* (praise of God) even in *saguna* form. In the *vyavaharika* world, we can have a personal God in any form including the female, whom we can call Ishwara, or Narayana or Devi or by any name. Shankara himself composed numerous *stotras* in mellifluous verses addressed to various deities with forms including the female, though he believed in the Ultimate being nirguna Brahman. In this type of *Sadhana*, complex Vedic rituals hardly had any role. And that is the reason he gave emphasis to *jnana* or spiritual knowledge as the ultimate means of liberation, and not karma. When he denied a role for karma in liberation, he must have meant only the complex rituals, but not day-to-day activities of living or activities oriented to the welfare of the world (*loka-hita* or *loka-sangraha*) emphasised in the Gita. He accepted both *karma-yoga* and *bhakti-yoga* recommended by the Gita, but he held that both facilitate the achievement of jnana through which alone ultimate liberation is possible (Rangaswami 2012: 317, 331, 334, 352). Swami Anandashram (1902–66), known for the depth of his scholarship in Advaita Vedanta and spiritual accomplishment in the same tradition, clearly stated: 'There is no conflict between bhakti and Advaita; not merely that, some *sadhakas* can even experience Advaita through bhakti' (2014: 7) (Tr. by the author from the Konkani original).

It did not take long for Advaita to attract sharp criticism. Its *maya-vada* (theory of *maya*) was too complicated for popular mind. Even for intellectuals, any suggestion that the world is unreal was difficult to accept as it negated the need for any responsibility and work in the world. The distinction made between *paramarthika satya* and *vyavaharika satya* on the one hand and between the impersonal Brahman and the personal Ishwara on the other could be mistaken as denying the Unity of Truth and God respectively. It was feared that such a theory could distort the essence of the Gita. Moreover, though Shankara appeared to be a reformist, his followers did not quite follow the implication of Advaita for caste discrimination, and the significance of the incident between the untouchable and Shankara resulting in the composition of *Manisha-panchakam* was lost on the followers. The incident was tried to be explained by saying that it was not an untouchable really but Ishwara himself in disguise, and discrimination against lower castes by upper castes continued in practice.

Bhaskara

The first important commentator of the Gita to oppose Shankara was Bhaskara, who lived around 900 CE, a century after Shankara. This Bhaskara, who wrote bhashyas both on the Gita and *Brahma-sutras*, is different from astronomer Bhaskara who lived in the sixth/seventh century CE and also from the mathematician Bhaskara who lived in the twelfth century CE (Harshananda 2008, Vol. 1: 287). Bhaskara is credited for his contribution known as the *Bhedabheda* (difference cum non-difference) or *Dvaitadvaita* (dualism cum non-dualism) doctrine. This was taken up for further elaboration later by Nimbarka of the twelfth century CE, but Bhaskara originated it. In a way, the *Bhedabheda* theory explains rather than opposes Advaita. According to *Bhedabheda*, the 'difference (*bheda*) has in it the characteristic of identity (*abheda*) – the waves are different from the sea, but are also identical with it. . . . So all that is one is also many, and the one is neither absolute identity nor absolute difference' (Dasgupta 1975, Vol. 3: 6). Where Bhaskara sharply differs from Shankara is in his treating the waves as much a reality as the sea, and not as *mithya* as Shankara does. 'Bhaskara maintained that there is no *maya*, and that it was Brahman which by its own powers, underwent a real modification' (Dasgupta 1975: 2). Brahman is both an efficient and material cause of the world. It is both the creator and the material of creation. Everything is Brahman, but at the same time it is diverse, and the diversity is not an illusion but a reality. Another important difference between Bhaskara and Shankara is in the former's emphasis on karma (Sharma 1985: 26). We fulfil the purpose of our Creator through our work, and not by spiritual knowledge or jnana alone. Bhaskara was not averse to Vedic rituals, but by karma, he mainly meant doing our duties to the society of which we are members. His preference was for a combination of both jnana (through meditation) and karma (*jnana-karma-samuchchaya*) (Sharma 1985: 28). There is no personal God in Bhaskara's theory and thus no place for bhakti or divine grace (Harshananda 2008, Vol. 3: 522). Probably, that is why he could not be popular, since common people want a personal God whom they can worship and pray to. Even Shankara's philosophy had a personal God, at least as a stepping stone to full realisation of the Supreme. The acharyas who came later also met this need in their system of philosophy. Though Bhaskara is not as well known today as the other commentators, maybe for this or other reasons, he could not be ignored by them. While the other three commentators established their own *mathas* and ensured a following for their doctrines, Bhaskara did not seem to have bothered about it. Not much is known about his life, and there are no available biographies on him.

Ramanuja

While Bhaskara tried to correct the balance in the interpretation of the Gita in favour of karma and acknowledging the reality of the world, the task of restoring it in favour of bhakti was performed by Ramanujacharya (Ramanuja in brief). Swami Harshananda observes in this context: 'India seems to have a special knack of producing great saints almost on a "made to order" basis, as per the needs of the time' (2008, Vol. 3: 56). Though according to tradition, Ramanuja lived for 120 years from 1017 to 1137 CE, according to another account, he lived for 80 years from 1077 to 1157 CE (Tapasyananda – year not available: 1). There was already a tradition of Vaishnava Alvars in Tamil Nadu, known for their passionate advocacy of bhakti and composition of mellifluous songs in Tamil, from which Ramanuja drew inspiration (Ramakrishnananda 1959: 11–39). The Shrivaishnava sect was already established (to which Ramanuja belonged), with its main centre at Srirangam in Tamil Nadu.

Ramanuja was born in a Brahmin family at Sriperumbudur, about 48 km southwest of the present Chennai. Endowed with sharp intellect and prodigious memory, he had been well educated by the age of sixteen, thanks to his learned father Keshava Dikshitar and particularly to Kanchipurna, a great devotee of the deity Varadaraja of Kanchi temple, who used to visit the family of Ramanuja and teach him. Kanchipurna came from what was considered as a low Shudra caste, but Ramanuja had no hesitation in venerating him and even touching his feet as a teacher. The family, particularly Ramanuja, was liberal and catholic in spirit. Ramanuja was married at sixteen and shortly thereafter his father died. Ramanuja moved to Kanchipuram, a reputed centre of Vedic learning, and joined Yadava-prakasha, a reputed scholar in the Advaita tradition, as a student. The young student, however, was too sharp and open minded for the orthodox teacher, and after a few unsavoury incidents, Ramanuja left him for good. By this time, the fame of the young student had spread far, and the chief pontiff of Shrivaishnavas then, Yamunacharya of Srirangam, decided to name Ramanuja as his successor after coming to know of the latter's leaving the tutelage of Yadava-prakasha. He sent a word to Ramanuja to meet him, but by the time he reached Srirangam, Yamunacharya had just died. After the funeral of Yamunacharya, Ramanuja returned to Kanchipuram with his wife. His wife came from an orthodox family believing in rigid rules of caste and of purity and pollution. Ramanuja used to meet learned men and devotees of Kanchi Varadaraja from all castes, who used to visit his house also. This did not go well with his caste-minded wife, resulting once in humiliating the wife of a person whom Ramanuja greatly respected as teacher. This clinched the issue, and Ramanuja sent his wife to her parents, and became a *Vaishnava sannyasi* or a renunciate. This news reached Srirangam, and a respected representative came from there to press Ramanuja to come and settle there. Ramanuja was reluctant, but finally accepted the invitation.

An incident reported to have happened at this juncture, which reveals the greatness of Ramanuja. After reaching Srirangam, he was advised to take a holy mantra from a great Vaishnava saint, Goshtipurna. But this saint wanted to test the earnestness of Ramanuja and asked him to come again and again eighteen times. Ramanuja was persistent, and finally the saint obliged him and gave the mantra on condition that he should not impart it to others. He also told that it had tremendous potency and whosoever heard it even once is sure to go to heaven, and hence it was meant only for the deserving few. Delighted at this, Ramanuja, on his way back, saw a temple; climbing its *gopura* (tower), he shouted loudly inviting people around to gather and imparted the mantra to them. After Goshtipurna heard of this, he sent for Ramanuja and severely scolded him. He said that Ramanuja would go to hell for disobeying his instruction. Ramanuja calmly replied that he did not mind it at all if in the bargain it guaranteed heaven to so many. By this act, he conveyed a simple but noble principle that spiritual seeking need not be confined to a chosen few, but has to reach all.

After some further training under the senior disciples of Yamunacharya, Ramanuja took over as the head of the matha and the Sriranganatha temple at Srirangam. His discourses in Tamil on the life and teachings of Alvars, especially Nammalvar, and on Vaishnava philosophy made him very popular. His discourses on Nammalvar have been compiled together in a Tamil book by one of his disciples, Kurukesha or Pillan. Ramanuja was recognised in his own lifetime as a very learned and saintly teacher and became known as Yatiraj (king of monks). He began to attract many disciples and took into his fold of disciples even from the so-called low castes including untouchables and deplored caste distinctions in the realm of God (Seshadri 1996). He did not want the word 'pariah' applied to untouchables and called them as 'Tirukulattar' (which means people of noble descent) intending to impart to them greater dignity in society (as Gandhi did much later by calling them as Harijans). It is said that he used to spend hours in the hut of an untouchable devotee, discoursing on philosophy. The community of devotees of God which he built, known as Shrivaishnavas, had people from all castes and women, all of whom he treated with equal love and regard (Yamunacharya 1988: 36–38; Dasgupta 1975, Vol. 3: 104). Ramanuja wrote commentaries in Sanskrit on the *Brahmasutras*, the *Upanishads* and the Gita. He also travelled widely in the country, spreading his philosophy and winning debates.

However, as Swami Tapasyananda observes, the tenor of Ramanuja's life at Srirangam was disturbed by a policy of persecution of Vaishnavas under the Chola king, Kulottunga, a fanatic Shaivite, and Ramanuja had to flee to Melkote in Karnataka to save his very life. Melkote was under the Hoysala king Bittideva at that time, known for his generosity and open mind. He was a Jain. Ramanuja visited him and defeated several Jain scholars in debate. Bittideva was so impressed that he converted to Vaishnavism, taking a new name, Vishnuvardhana by which he became more famous. Ramanuja founded a *matha* at Melkote on a picturesque hilltop, which still attracts thousands of pilgrims. Ramanuja went back to Srirangam after the demise of Kulottunga, as the latter was succeeded by a more tolerant and liberal-minded ruler. Ramanuja spent most of the rest of his life there only (Tapasyananda: 19–20). Though he lived mostly in the south, he left an indelible impact in north India too. Ramananda who had the distinction of having eminent disciples like Kabir and Ravidas was a close follower of Ramanuja, not only in his theology and metaphysics but also in social philosophy of opposing caste discrimination and treating all as equals (Dasgupta 1975: 27–28).

Though the philosophy of Ramanuja is known as *Vishishta-advaita* (qualified monism), it is much closer to the *Dvaita* (dualism) philosophy of Madhvacharya (Madhva in brief) than to Shankara's Advaita. This is because the Supreme for both Ramanuja and Madhva is personal God with attributes (*saguna*), though they do not mind calling Him as Brahman as well. He is different from the insentient world and the sentient *jivas* (souls), though both the world and *jivas* are dependent upon God and supported by Him and both are real for both philosophers, though different from each other. In an individual living being, the insentient body becomes sentient because of the *jiva*. *Jivas* have consciousness (*chit*), which are different from the world because the latter is *achit* (not having consciousness). *Jivas* are also different from God in both these philosophies, because though *jivas* have consciousness, which is also an important characteristic of God, they do not share many other characteristics of God and are dependent on God. In both philosophies, the relationship between God and *jivas* is one of Master and servant (*sheshi* and *shesha,* respectively, in Ramanuja's words). God is accessible through bhakti; though both jnana and karma are also necessary, they are so only in so far as they lead to bhakti. For both these philosophies, bhakti is the most important and indispensable means of God realisation. *Jnana* and karma even when combined are not enough without bhakti.

According to Ramanuja, though God, nature and the *jivas* are different with different characteristics, they form a unity in the 'body' of God in a 'Pan-organistic system' as Tapasyananda terms it in his introduction to Svami Adidevananda's translation of Ramanuja's *Gita Bhashya* (Adidevananda 2014: 12). Nature and *jivas* cannot exist without God and His support, and it is in this sense that they are a part of the body of God. Ramanuja's school of philosophy is called as 'qualified monism' (*Vishishta-advaita*) precisely because as per this school, 'the unity of Brahman is qualified by the sentient and insentient things' (Yamunacharya 1988: 40). But these two are different from God, because while nature is insentient or jada, the *jivas* are subject to imperfections and suffering. By contrast, God is free from any such deficiencies (Radhakrishnan 1996, Vol. 2: 660). God is the creator of both these things which emanate from Him, who is the efficient as well as the material cause of both. The school is known as qualified monism also because its God is not a *nirguna Brahman* who is abstract, without attributes and indifferent to suffering humanity, but a God with attributes who responds to the love and prayers of his devotees. Ramanuja is eloquent in describing the numerous attributes of God. He calls Him as the storehouse of all beneficent qualities (*samasta-kalyana-gunakara*). He is one and absolutely so, and yet allows within Himself all the diversity comprising nature and *jivas*. His essential and eternal characteristics are that He is *sat, chit* and *ananda* (absolute existence/truth, consciousness and bliss). He is omniscient, omnipotent, omnipresent and immanent in the universe, which is His creation and his portion or part, and also transcendental. What is most important for devotees is that He is also accessible to them (*sulabha*). 'It is the manifestation as the Incarnate and as images that stand for the extreme accessibility of Narayana' according to Ramanuja (Tapasyananda: 49). Narayana as personal God is full of compassion and mercy for all, and loves His devotees and looks after them. He is just and fair to all equally. He is also indescribably beautiful, graceful and sweet (Yamunacharya 1988: 41). Ramanuja's emphasis on the personal God and His superlative attractiveness and goodness is consistent with the immense importance given by him to bhakti in God realisation. This personal and accessible God is not Ramanuja's invention, but is sourced from his reading of the Gita itself, apart from the various *Puranas* that preceded him and the rich devotional tradition of Alvars before.

Culmination of bhakti, according to Ramanuja, is *prapatti* – total surrender to God and His will. It is a state wherein the devotee does everything as service to God (*kainkarya*) and offers the fruit of all his acts or works at his feet. Self-interest is totally erased. The devotee is always conscious that everything is the abode and property of God, and he or she has no claims against or even prayers for wish fulfilment to Him. The entire burden of salvation of the devotee is put on God. This puts the devotee completely at ease, free from any stress (Yamunacharya 1988: 52–53). Doesn't the devotee then have any need to put in some effort to win God's favour? Two schools of thought emerged among the followers of Ramanuja in this respect: one, known as *markata-kishora-nyaya* (the logic of monkey's kid), would argue that just as the monkey's kid holds on to its mother, a devotee has to take some responsibility to win God's favour. The second, known as *marjala-kishora-nyaya* (the logic of kitten), argues on the other hand that just as the mother cat lifts its kitten by the neck and carries them to safety, God will take care of the devotee who surrenders completely to Him. To which of these two schools of thought did Ramanuja subscribe? It is said that when he wrote the commentary on the *Brahmasutras*, he subscribed to the former; but when he later on wrote the commentary on the Gita, he changed his stance and subscribed to the later view (Yamunacharya 1988: 105–6). Two verses in the final (eighteenth) chapter of the Gita lend support to the doctrine of *prapatti* and particularly to 'the logic of the kitten'. Translated, they read:

> Occupy thy mind with Me, be devoted to Me, sacrifice to Me, bow down to me. Thou shalt reach Myself; truly do I promise unto thee, (for) thou art dear to Me.
>
> (XVIII.65)
>
> Relinquishing all Dharmas take refuge in Me alone; I will liberate thee from all sins, grieve not.
>
> (XVIII.66) (Tr. Swarupananda 1982: 397–98)

Release or liberation or salvation (*moksha*) is, however, left entirely to the grace of God. It is for the devotee, however, to be worthy of this grace. How can this worthiness be attained? When can *jivas* expect to be granted liberation? The intrinsic nature of *jivas* is that they are blemish-free (*amala*) and also eternal. It is when they develop body-conscious ego, mistaking themselves with the bodies, that they attract blemish and become *baddha* or bound by their karma. God grants free will to the *jivas*, who become morally responsible for their acts. The first step in liberation consists in developing the knowledge of their true nature as parts of the Divine or Its sparks, and awareness that the body is only an instrument of the self in pure form and the sense organs of the body should be at the control of the self. The second step in liberation is being engaged in works but only as a *kinkara* or servant of God, with the fruits of works offered to Him. The third step is *bhakti* and then *prapatti*, as explained earlier. The final liberation comes when the *jiva* joins God, and that is after death. There is no rebirth for a liberated *jiva*. Ramanuja rules out *jivan-mukti*, that is, liberation even while living. The process of karma continues until death, but comes to an end with death in the case of a liberated *jiva* and continues even after death in the case of other *jivas*. In the liberated state, Ramanuja observes, however, that there is no full absorption of the *jiva* into God; the *jiva* enjoys only fellow-equality status and nearness to God but not complete absorption into Him. 'The released soul is conscious of itself as separate but yet united with the highest Brahman' (Yamunacharya 1988: 124). It amounts to saying that all *jivas* are in a process of moral or spiritual evolution ever since a dormant state in the distant past in the early phase of the evolution of life in the world, going then through a struggle for survival and progress in their embodied state, and ultimately to a state of liberated perfection in fellowship with God Himself. Not all *jivas* attain the heaven of perfection obviously, and bulk of them take birth again and again.

Kumarappa observes that the main contribution of Ramanuja, based on his interpretation of the Gita, lies in reconciling two seemingly opposite views of the Supreme – the impersonal *nirguna* Brahman and the personal *saguna* God, who loves and likes to be loved by the devotees. While the Upanishads and Shankara focused on the *chit* (consciousness) aspect of the Supreme, Ramanuja drew attention to the *sat* (being; benign or good) and *ananda* (blissful) aspects too, based again on the Gita. This reconciliation between the impersonal and the personal, and, *nirguna* and *saguna*, is not possible on the basis of dry reasoning, but only on the basis of mystic experience of an ardent devotee. Kumarappa feels that it was nothing short of a revolution on the part of the Gita, which was rightly highlighted by Ramanuja (Kumarappa 1979: 58, and Part II of the book exclusively on Ramanuja – esp. 164–93).

Though Ramanuja's *Gita Bhashya* is hardly polemical on the whole, his attack on Advaita is generally sharp. For example, he almost ridicules Advaita's rejection of difference between God and *jiva*, and between *jivas*. He asks if it were so, what was the point in the Lord's teaching to Arjuna? 'For no one who is not out of his senses would undertake to give any instruction to his own reflections in mediums such as a . . . mirror, knowing, as he does, that they are non-different from himself' (Adidevananda 2014: 65). Shankara's idea of two *satyas* or realities – ultimate (*paramarthika*) and practical (*vyavaharika*) – is not accepted either by Ramanuja or by Madhva. A social significance of Ramanuja's philosophy is that it means equality of all human beings, all having the dignity of being parts in the body of the same Divine. He understood this implication clearly and applied it in his life. He gave equal respect and love to all irrespective of whether they were so-called untouchables or high-caste Brahmins. In fact, Shankara's Advaita philosophy also has the same implication of equal dignity of all, but his distinction between the two truths – ultimate and practical – could permit (mistakenly at least) some dichotomy between philosophy and practice. In Ramanuja, there is no such dichotomy, since he makes no distinction between the two truths.

Madhva

The next great commentator is Madhvacharya, or Madhva in short. In his case also, there is no agreement among scholars about the date of birth and death. While S. Dasgupta thinks that he was born in 1197 CE and died in 1276 CE (Dasgupta 1975, Vol. IV: 52, 54), B.N.K. Sharma takes these dates as 1238 and 1317 CE respectively (Sharma 1986: xv). There is agreement, however, on the fact that he lived for seventy-nine years and was born in a Tulu-speaking Brahmin family in a village called Pajaka near Udupi in Karnataka. He was named as Anandatirtha by his Guru on taking *sannyas* and later also as Purna-prajna on taking the leadership of his *matha* or monastery. But he is more popularly known as Madhvacharya or Madhva. He was tall, muscular and had no compunctions in combining a little indulgence in sports like running races and wrestling along with his scholastic and spiritual pursuits at least in his early life. Like his main intellectual adversary

Shankara, Madhva also toured widely all over India both in the north and in the south, debating with scholars and defeating them. He too was a prolific writer, producing some thirty-seven works in Sanskrit, including two on the Gita – *Gita Bhashya* and *Gita Tatparya*, besides commentaries on the *Brahmasutras*, the ten principal Upanishads and the *Bhagavata Purana*. In his *Gita Bhashya*, Madhva does not comment on all the verses of the Gita, but only on those which in his view required comment or explanation. Thus, only 385 out of 700 verses of the Gita are commented upon (Sharma 1989: 2). Madhva's writings, known for precision and brevity, often required further exegesis. This was provided by his disciples, an important one being Jayatirtha who wrote *Nyayadipika* on Madhva's *Gita Tatparya* and *Prameyadipika* on his *Gita Bhashya* besides other works (Harshananda 2008, Vol. I: 562).

In introducing Madhva's philosophy, B.N.K. Sharma observes that at the time of Madhva, India was in turmoil facing critical times due to invading Muslims and a philosophy such as that by Shankara saying that the world is unreal or *maya*, needed to be fought first as a precondition to resisting the invaders.[3] This need was fulfilled by Madhva, and there could be no indifference to the problems of the world which all were facing, be it in the name of either *maya* or seeking *moksha*. Interestingly, Madhva recommended the unselfish continuation of one's duties in the world even after spiritual realisation or enlightenment, which he aptly called *jnanottara-karma* (post-realisation karma) (Sharma 1989: 20). Madhva, according to Sharma, strongly felt that *mayavada* was a source of inner weakness, as it undermined the role of one's duties to the world or society (Sharma 1997: 3). The notion of *mayavada* was attacked earlier by Bhaskara and Ramanuja too, as observed earlier, but Madhva gave a further impetus to this attack.

Madhva, however, distinguished between Independent (*swatantra*) Reality, which is the Supreme, and dependent (*a-swatantra*) reality, which is the world. Interestingly, this corresponds to a similar distinction made by Shankara between *paramarthika satya* and *vyavaharika satya* respectively. Madhva, however, would not accept any hint of the latter reality being illusory or unreal in any way. The world is absolutely – not just relatively – real, according to him, though it is entirely dependent on the Divine for creation, maintenance and dissolution. This dependence does not reduce its reality.

While the Supreme is One, the world is diverse and so are the souls or *jivas* in it. The *jivas* are different both from the Supreme and from each other. *Jiva* is also different from the body–mind–ego complex. The Gita mentions (XV.16, 17) two *Purushas*, one *kshara* (perishable) and the other *akshara* (imperishable), both being different from each other and also from *Purushottama* (the Supreme Person), who pervades all worlds and sustains them. This mention makes sense only in the context of Dvaita philosophy. Clearly the perishable *kshara purusha* refers to the body–mind–ego complex, while the imperishable *purusha* means the *jivas* which are many, and different from the *kshara purushas* as well as from Supreme Master, *Ishwara*. The Gita's support to Dvaita (and also Vishishta-advaita) philosophy is evident from several other verses also, as, for example IV.11, VII.21–22, IX.22, XVIII.55, 61–62, 65–66.

Madhva speaks about five types of differences or *pancha-bhedas*. They are as between God and the insentient world (*jada*), God and souls (*jivas*), the world and souls, the souls themselves, and insentient entities within the world. While the basic or ultimate reality for Shankara is unity, it is unity in diversity for Ramanuja, and diversity for Madhva. Nevertheless, there is in Madhva's thought a unifying or integrating principle even behind diversity in the world, which is provided by the dependence of all non-divine realities on the Divine. Despite the emphasis on the *bhedas* or differences, even in Dvaita, the reach of the Divine is everywhere, and in that sense, the Divine is immanent too. God is omnipresent in all the three philosophies. Both in Dvaita and Vishishta-advaita, the Divine is an intensely personal God, having all benign attributes particularly compassion for the devotees. In Advaita on the other hand, the emphasis is on the impersonal nirguna God, but in the practical (*vyavaharika*) world, God can be conceived as personal and responsive to the prayers and the love of devotees as a preparatory step to seeking nirguna Brahman. This has implications for bhakti as *sadhana* (means of spiritual seeking and liberation). In Vishishta-advaita and Dvaita, bhakti is the direct means of liberation. By contrast, in Advaita, though bhakti to a personal God is important and useful, it is a stepping stone to jnana, and it is jnana only which leads to final liberation. So it is with karma. Accepting one's moral responsibilities and doing duties unselfishly is certainly important and necessary, but it is after it leads to jnana that final liberation comes. In Vishishta-advaita and Dvaita, the spiritual seeker simply surrenders all fruits of works or karma at the feet of the Supreme and is thus freed from any attachment to fruits.

The social significance of Dvaita philosophy is the importance given to diversity or pluralism. In this beautiful and enormous garden of God, there is a great variety of plants, flowers, fruits and beings, each with its own beauty and role, and all coexisting harmoniously under the same Master who nourishes all without discrimination. To deny diversity and homogenise everything goes against the very spirit of God's creation. Despite diversity, there is also a stress on equality of treatment, since compassion to and equal concern for all, especially the weak, is the innate quality of God (*saguna Brahman*) in all the three philosophies. Human behaviour has to be harmonious with God's will and cannot afford to go against it, whatever be the philosophy.

Though there are differences (see table in the Appendix to the chapter) between the three schools of Vedanta, they are not so overwhelming as to be disharmonious. They are only different ways of conceptualising the relationship between the selves or souls and God, depending on one's inclination to the Divine. These inclinations are personal or individual, and cannot genuinely be community or caste based. They can not only vary between individuals but also change over time. There can be no doctrinaire rigidity about it. For example, the sum and substance of the three schools of Vedanta has been tried to be encapsulated in terms of three short Sutras in Sanskrit: Dvaita by *Tasmaivaham* or *Tasyaivaham*, Vishishta-advaita by *Mamaivasau*, and Advaita by *Sa evaham*. There is a verse in Sanskrit which says that all the three can be practised by a sadhaka:

> *Tasyaivaham mamaivasau sa evaham iti tridha /*
> *Bhagavat-sharanatvam syat sadhanabhyasapakatah //*
> (Original source unknown; quoted in Anandashram 2014: 7)

The verse means: '"I am His only", "He is mine only" and "He is me only," thus in three ways, one may surrender himself to God in the course of spiritual practice' (translation by the author).

D. V. Gundappa (popularly known as DVG), an eminent poet-philosopher from Karnataka, has quoted and explained these Sutras in his treatise on the Gita in Kannada in order to bring out the harmony (*samarasa* as he calls it) between the three schools (Gundappa 2001: 565). *Tasmaivaham* means that 'I belong to Him' or 'I am meant for Him', indicating complete surrender to God. It represents height of devotion or bhakti. Though there is Dvaita or dualism in the sense of separateness of the self from God, there is also at the same time awareness that the self is His. There is a feeling of being a servant of God. In *Mamaivasau* which means 'He is mine only', taken to represent Vishishta-advaita, the feeling is from the other side. It is the beloved's feeling for her lover or a child's possessiveness about its mother. Though there is some awareness of separateness, the dominant feeling is one of unity of both, a unity in diversity. In Advaita, there is complete identity, *Sa evaham*, which means 'He is me!'. Any separateness between the self and God is submerged under the consciousness of oneness. Intense bhakti is required in the initial stage, which when attained transcends any dualism, and the person becomes a 'realised one', a jnani, whom the Gita describes eloquently.[4] Gundappa terms these three states of mind respectively as *Svatah-samarpana* (self-surrender), *Svatah-sahabhaga* (the self as associate of God)[5] and *Svatah-vilayana* (the self as merged into God). The significance of Gundappa's interpretation of the three schools of thought, which have fought bitterly with each other at least on the debating plane and consider themselves as rigidly separate from each other, lies in the fact that the same persons can have these three states of mind at different times, and one state of mind can easily move to into another. He illustrates this with the example of a married couple in love with each other. There are some duties which they do separately in Dvaita state, and some they do together as part of family in Vishishta-advaita state. But when they are in their height of love and forget each other's separateness, they are in the Advaita state!

Others in the Sanskritic tradition

There have been several other commentators as well, apart from the three discussed earlier: Abhinavagupta (in the tenth to eleventh century) in the Kashmiri Shaiva tradition, Nimbarka, Vallabha, Madhusudana Saraswati, Raghavendra Tirtha, Chaitanya and more. Nimbarka (twelfth century) subscribed to the theory of *Dvaitadvaita* (dualism-cum-non-dualism), holding that the soul (*jiva*), the world (*jagat*) and God are different from each other, yet the existence and the activities of the soul and the world depend on God's will, all the three constituting one integrated system. He emphasised bhakti as the promising path to *moksha*. Vallabha (1473–1531) is a prominent Vaishnava philosopher who advocated *shuddhadvaita* (pure non-dualism or monism) as his philosophy and *pushti-marga* as the path to spiritual seeking. Vallabha does not consider Shankara's Advaita as pure, because it accepts *maya*, which negates non-dualism. Brahman is the only reality, and there is no secondary reality. According to Vallabha, *maya* is a part and real power of Brahman, and not a different entity. Pushti-marga is essentially bhakti, but based on unconditional love of God which wins His grace. It is different from formal bhakti based on rituals or worship. It is through the unconditional love that God realisation and final union with God takes place. There is, however, a logical problem in this philosophy. Bhakti involves a difference between the devotee and God – the object of devotion, though the ultimate goal is attaining unity between the two. Shankara gets over this problem through the concept of maya, under which alone there is this difference. But Vallabha rejects this concept as untenable. If, on the other hand, he accepts that under non-dualism the difference between the devotee and God is illusory, he would be indirectly resorting to *mayavada*.

Madhusudana Saraswati (1490–1580) is an Advaitin who simultaneously enriched the literature on Advaita philosophy as well as on bhakti. He did not see a conflict between non-dualism and devotion to a personal deity. His work on the Gita, *Gudhartha-deepika*, which reflects his philosophy is rated highly.[6] He declares that the core message of the Gita, as well as that of other scriptures, is self-surrender to God, which is the culmination of all spiritual practices.[7] This stand brings him close to other philosophies. According to him, the main theme of the first six chapters of the Gita is on karma-yoga (steadfastness in selfless action, in Gambhirananda's translation) and of the last six chapters is on the yoga of knowledge. But these two yogas are seemingly opposite and can be combined only through bhakti, which is the main theme of the middle six chapters of the Gita (Gambhirananda 1998: 21–22).Thus, there is coherence and a logical order in the *sadhana* (spiritual striving) commended by the Gita in M. Saraswati's view. Also, all the three yogas are necessary to attain spiritual liberation or *moksha*. What is recommended is a stepwise approach starting with the yoga of selfless action, going on to bhakti in God, both of which purify and prepare the mind of the seeker to gain knowledge or jnana. M. Saraswati says that the Gita is an enlightening guide for all those who want to overcome the sorrow, delusion and bondage inherent in mundane existence, and attain the blissfulness of liberation, which is the highest human goal or *purushartha* (Gambhirananda 1998: 26). Bondage is not a natural condition of the self, M. Saraswati clarifies. It is due to the limiting adjuncts of the mind, and the Gita helps the seeker of liberation in the right spiritual practice, which will gain for him or her the right knowledge which finally liberates (Gambhirananda 1998: 89–91). An interesting characteristic of Saraswati's work is that he honestly puts himself in the position of an opponent, raises objections and then rigorously replies to them, in the style of several classic works on philosophy in Sanskrit.

All of these great philosopher-sages contributed to disseminating the Gita in different parts of India and helped in its more nuanced interpretation, further enriching Hindu philosophy. All of them wrote in Sanskrit. Sanskrit not only played the role of a link language of the country until English took its place, but also assured a secure place in the long tradition of scholarship and spiritual knowledge. It thus became a storehouse of Indian philosophy.

The lives of the three great acharyas and their perspectives have been dealt with at some length in the earlier text because of the significant role that they played in making the Gita much better known among people. Their perspectives left an indelible impact on the development of philosophical thought in India, which is felt even today. Since the Gita itself does not include systematic discussions of philosophical issues, the contribution of the three acharyas in a logically rigorous and coherent manner helped a better understanding of the Gita itself, though put in alternative thought-provoking perspectives. These perspectives need not be taken as conflicting with each other. The Gita supports all of them in a way that does not suggest any conflict between them or their mutual contradiction with each other. The focus of the three acharyas as well as of others in the Sanskritic tradition was, however, on the theological and metaphysical aspects and on spiritual striving (*sadhana*) to gain liberation from bondage to the mundane worldliness (or *samsara*) and realise the Ultimate. Though they did not altogether ignore ethics, they tended to assign it only the role of being the means to purify mind and prepare oneself for *sadhana*. The issue of serving people or society at large and meeting larger social needs apart from the individual spiritual aspirations was rather sidetracked. It hardly received any noticeable attention of the classical commentators, though the Vedic prayers had the welfare of all people in mind and, what is more, had an honourable place in the Gita itself. It was with Jnaneshwar that the focus started becoming broader and more comprehensive, giving more attention to ethics and ways of making one's life in the world itself more meaningful.

Jnaneshwari – The Gita goes to people at large

Jnaneshwar, also known as Jnanadev and Jnanoba, is a unique saint. He introduced the Gita, probably for the first time, to common people in an Indian regional language. The earlier commentators wrote only in Sanskrit, though they gave discourses in Indian regional languages. Jnaneshwar wrote in old Marathi (prevalent in the thirteenth century) in the lyrical and easy-to-recite 'Ovi' metre.[8] He called his work *Bhavartha-dipika* (one which sheds light on the essence of the Gita).

But it became known popularly as *Jnaneshwari*. It is poetic and is not a mere literal translation, but more an explanation embellished with literary flourish like similes and illustrations. The ease with which he elaborates and interprets even some of the perplexing verses of the Gita is remarkable. A good translation of *Jnaneshwari* is available in English, made by M. R. Yardi (2011; first edition in 1991). *Jnaneshwari* was originally a series of discourses given to people by Jnaneshwar at a temple in Alandi, his native place near the present-day Pune where he was born. His elder brother and guru, Nivrittinath, used to be present during these discourses as an informal moderator, and questions and doubts from the audience were freely raised and discussed, all of which are recorded faithfully in the text. The dialogic form of the Gita was extended into a seminar in the *Jnaneshwari*, with Jnaneshwar being the main speaker of course.

Another uniqueness of Jnaneshwar, though at a personal level, was that he lived only for twenty-one years, born in 1271 CE (about 5 years before Madhva's death). He had two more brothers and one younger sister. They had a difficult childhood as the family – though Brahmin – was treated as outcaste by the society. Their father who had taken *sannyas* (a renunciant's vows) had returned to married life on his guru's orders.[9] It amounted to breaking established convention according to which a person having once taken *sannyas* could not marry and take to family life. Jnaneshwar's family was ostracised for this reason, finally leading to suicide by his parents by drowning in a river. But the siblings, under the eldest brother Nivritti's leadership, could manage to survive and even get a good education. Jnaneshwar showed extraordinary brilliance and became accomplished in the Vedas and Upanishads quite early. He was initiated into the *Nath* tradition of yoga by Nivritti and became an adept in this order of yogis. Besides the *Jnaneshwari*, he also wrote a highly acclaimed treatise titled *Amritanubhava* (Experience of Immortality) (also in old Marathi). He was equally in the order of bhakti *sants* and composed several devotional and philosophical *abhangs*, which are still popular and sung. He mixed freely with the saint-poets of the time in Maharashtra, who emerged from among the common people, and was highly respected by them. He decided, however, that by the age of 21, his life's mission was accomplished, and time was ripe to merge with the Immortal, leading to his taking *sanjivan samadhi* (sitting in meditation in his tomb until so-called death). The samadhi in Alandi is attracting pilgrims in thousands even now. He is counted among the first *sants* who launched the bhakti movement in Maharashtra. His work on the Gita, *Jnaneshwari*, reflects his dual background clearly, with an emphasis both on meditative yoga and on bhakti.

Jnaneshwar was an Advaitin, being a follower of Shankara. But he did not accept the *Jaganmithya* implication of Shankara's teaching. The world is real, and not illusory; it is a *chidvilasa* (a joyous play by the Supreme Consciousness or Brahman). Along with human beings in it, the world is a natural and joyous expression of the Supreme Reality. We, the humans, are all players in this cosmic play and have to do our duties in the world. Jnaneshwar does not accept Shankara's prescription of renunciation; his is considered as a 'partially activist' interpretation of the Gita (Agarwal 1993: 246), because his emphasis is much more on bhakti rather than on karma. He suggests *nama-japa*, repetition of God's name with devotion, as an easy form of bhakti, adding to the exposition of it in the Gita. He points to the mutual love of Krishna and Arjuna, as an essential part of the Gita while explaining the importance of bhakti. In fact, before ending his poetic presentation of the Gita, Jnaneshwar shows Krishna drawing Arjuna in close embrace, suggesting the union of the devotee with his God. An ardent devotee's experience of bliss surpasses that of even a *jivan-mukti* (a seeker who is liberated while living). A devotee (*bhakta*) can also be actively engaged in the world even while devoted to God. Moreover, as Jnaneshwar emphasises, the path of devotion is easily accessible to all, poor and rich, low caste and high caste, women and men. He also expounds on Patanjali's path of yoga and meditation for realisation of Brahman, which for him does not conflict with bhakti. Though Jnaneshwar considered himself a follower of Shankara and an Advaitin, he was not just a *knowing* or intellectual Advaitin, but also a *feeling*, inclusive and socially aware Advaitin, *experiencing* the same Divine in himself and all.

In Jnaneshwar's view, the world in its basic essence is no different from Brahman. Jnaneshwar often takes the example of gold and gold ornaments to illustrate his point. The important difference, however, is that we have consciousness and will, while ornaments do not have it. But this is natural because the Supreme Brahman is itself the principal centre and origin of consciousness, which we too are bound to have because we are created from it. There is an apparent contradiction between Krishna's statement in verse 4 of Chapter 9 (*matsthani sarva bhutani* – all beings are within Me), and his statement in the very next verse (*na cha mat-sthahni bhutani* – the beings are not in Me), and again in the next verse (*tatha sarvani bhutani mat-sthani* – all beings are within Me). Jnaneshwar explains it by saying that this is so because everything is basically Brahman. He says in Ovi (verse) 88 of Chapter 9 of *Jnaneshwari* that according to the Lord, the world is not different from Him nor is He different from the beings in the world (Yardi 2011: 123). Yet, bhakti – though involving dualism – is emphasised as a path to God realisation in several places, as in the original Gita and as with Shankara. This is because, once in this world as His players, we are subject to limiting conditions which Jnaneshwar calls as *upadhis*, and bhakti is necessary to transcend these limiting conditions and to realise one's own real nature.

Jnaneshwari has an important place in the history of the Gita. It is mainly because of *Jnaneshwari* that the Gita became popular among common people particularly in Maharashtra. According to Jnaneshwar, the Gita is meant essentially for the common people irrespective of caste and gender. In the last chapter (viz. 18) of his work, he observes in Ovis 1,456–1,460 that the Vedas were niggardly in imparting their knowledge restricting them only to the three upper castes, giving no 'elbow room' to women and Shudras, who equally needed this knowledge. But the Lord gave the Gita to the world so that everyone can have access to it (Yardi 2011: 349). Jnaneshwar could be said to have carried out the unfinished task of the Lord, because he made available the Gita, which was in inaccessible Sanskrit, to common people in lucid and simple Marathi. He thus launched the era of translations of the Gita in various languages of people.

No proper records are available to indicate when translations of the Gita appeared first in the various Indian regional languages. Kumaravyasa's poetic translation of the Mahabharata into Kannada, composed in the thirteenth century, contains a summary of the Gita as well. The next to follow Jnaneshwar, writing in the vernacular on the Gita as an independent text though after a long gap, was Akho (1591–1656), a Gujarati poet, who composed *Akhe-gita*. However, it was not a translation as such but his own formulation of themes in the Gita (Desai 2014: 9). It was Narahari (1611–63) who first translated it in Gujarati. Even before this, in the sixteenth century itself, the Gita was translated into Persian by Abul Fazl, a respected scholar in the Mughal emperor Akbar's court. The translation seems to have been done at the instance of Akbar himself. There have also been translations of the Gita in Hindi and Urdu in the medieval period itself. A palm leaf manuscript of a poetic translation of the Gita in Kannada by Nagarasa, titled *Karnataka Bhagavadgite*, was discovered towards the end of the nineteenth century and published in the early twentieth century. But details of when it was written are not available from it. It is written in the style of Kumaravyasa's Kannada Mahabharata in the same *Bhamini-shatpadi* metre, but linguist and lexicologist G. Ventatasubbaiah feels that its language is close to the spoken language of the eighteenth-century Karnataka (Anon 2011: vi). The style, spirit and approach of the work, however, are closer to medieval works on the Gita rather than of the modern works.

The foregoing interpreters of the Gita affirmed the authority of the Vedas and the Upanishads, but were more inclined towards the Upanishads. But they also transcended both, like the Gita, in their emphasis on bhakti. The consensus appeared to be on *jna̲na–karma–bhakti samuchchaya*, that is combining the paths of knowledge, action and devotion. The modern interpreters too continued this tradition. As observed earlier, what distinguishes the classical and medieval works on the Gita from the modern is that while the former focused on theology, metaphysics and *sa̲dhana̲* (the means of seeking God realisation), the modern works give more emphasis on ethical implications of the Gita and its social relevance without ignoring theology and *sa̲dhana̲*. This difference in approach would come out clearly from the next three chapters here.

Surprisingly, iconographic or pictorial representations of the Gita's Krishna and Arjuna engaged in dialogue have been rare before the modern period. Robert Minor mentions two such illustrations, one from a frieze in the Halebidu temple in Karnataka belonging to the late twelfth century and the other belonging to the fourteenth century in a temple at Pushpagiri in Andhra Pradesh (Minor 1991-a: 4). Though there were many commentaries and vernacular translations, the Gita did not appear to have been a noticeable part of *public* religious consciousness before the modern period starting from the second half of the eighteenth century. Krishna as the object of adoration by *Gopikas* had been more conspicuous in *popular* imagination in the medieval period than Krishna the teacher of the Gita. Nevertheless, the importance given to the Gita in the medieval period cannot be belittled. Almost every prominent traditional religious leader thought it to be a minimum duty to write a commentary on the Gita to establish his credentials as a spiritual leader and a scholar.

In any case, while the Gita was highly regarded mainly among the Sanskritist elite before the early thirteenth century, it started being established among the common people only after that, thanks to Jnaneshwar's trendsetting translation, and well before the eighteenth century, it came to be accepted as an important sacred scripture of the Hindus by a significant part of them. Modernity did not dent the fame and prestige of the Gita in any way, but on the contrary, only accelerated its popularity as never before, not only among Hindus but also among others. It was in the modern times that it came to be regarded by a majority of Hindus as *the sacred book* of Hinduism, like the Bible among Christians and the Quran among Muslims, though – paradoxically – it has hardly displaced other sacred texts of Hinduism.

Notes

1 In the *Padma-Purana, Uttara-khanda*, Chapters 171–189, there is a detailed description of benefits accruing from the study and recitation of the Gita. In the *Skanda-Purana*, there is an appreciative reference to the Gita in three verses (49–51) in the section on *Kartika-masa-mahatmyam* in its second chapter. According to Hayavadana Puranik, an authority on the *Puranas*, the source of the *Gita-mahatmyam*, given at the end in many publications of the Gita, is unknown, since the *Varaha-Purana* itself does not have it though attributed to it (Personal communication, 2 January 2015).

2 For Shankara's commentary, see Sastri (1977), Warrier (1983) and Gambhirananda (1984); for references to Bhaskara's, see Dasgupta (1975, Vol. 3: 6), Arvind Sharma (1985: 16–41, esp. footnotes 1 and 3 on p. 16) and Harshananda (2008, Vol. I: 287); for Ramanuja's, see Sampatkumaran (1985) and Adidevananda (1992, 2014); and for Madhva's, see B.N.K. Sharma (1989).

3 While explaining the Advaita philosophy, it has been pointed out earlier that the interpretation of *maya* as the world being unreal and denying our moral responsibility in the world is misleading, and Shankara never meant it in this negative sense.

4 This is done in Chapter 2, verses 54–59, while describing *Sthitaprajna*; in Chapter 14, verses 22–26, while describing a person who has transcended the three *gunas;* and again in Chapter 18, verses 49, 51–56.

5 *Svatah samarpana* or self-surrender (in the sense of *prapatti*) is emphasised in Vishishta-adavaita also.

6 The account about Nimbarka, Vallabaha and Madhusudana Saraswati is based on respective entries in the three volumes of Harshananda (2008), and also on Gambhirananda (1998) for Madhusudana Saraswati. *Gudhartha-deepika* by Madhusudana Saraswati has been translated by Swami Gambhirananda, with an Introduction by Swami Atmaramananda (Gambhirananda 1998). An interesting thing about Madhusudana Saraswati narrated in the Introduction is about his founding a militant order of sannyasis, called the Naga sect, to counter frequent attacks on Varanasi by Muslim militant clergy. Thus he was not just a philosopher, but quite a worldly man too who rose to the occasion as required. This narration is based on a research by Prof. J. N. Farquhar (1925).

7 Cf. 'Introduction' by Swami Atmaramananda in Gambhirananda (1998: 18).

8 An *Ovi* has four *padas* (legs or steps), the first three with six letters each and the last having only four, together making twenty-two letters. This is shorter than the verses in the Gita, most of which have thirty-two letters in

four *pa̲das* of eight letters each, and some verses are larger still with each *pa̲da* having eleven letters. While the Gita has 700 verses, the *Jnaneshwari* has some 9,000 *Ovis* spread over eighteen chapters corresponding to the respective chapters of the Gita.

9 It was mandatory to have the approval of one's mother (if unmarried) or wife (if married) for taking *sannyas*. Jnaneshwar's father had not informed his guru that he had not obtained his wife's approval for it. Once his guru came to know about it, he ordered him to return to his wife and family life.

APPENDIX

The three Acharyas and their philosophies

	Shankara (eighth century)	*Ramanuja (eleventh to twelfth centuries)*	*Madhva (twelfth to thirteenth centuries)*
Name of the philosophy	*Advaita* (monism)	*Vishishta-advaita* (qualified monism)	*Dvaita* (dualism)
Nature of the Supreme	Impersonal (Nirguna)		Personal (Saguna)
Nature of the system	Unity*	Unity in diversity	Diversity
Nature of the world	Relatively real, ultimately unreal	Absolutely real (leela or play of God)	
Relation of the *jivas* to the supreme	Basically oneness, separateness illusory	Servant–master; part of one pan-organistic system	Basically separate but dependent
Concept of maya	Veil or projection on the basic oneness	Magical/creative/mysterious power of the Supreme; conditioning in *samsara* due to which God is concealed/forgotten	
Means of liberation	Ultimately only jnana, *but bhakti and karma can lead to jnana*	Only bhakti aided by jnana and karma, or directly through prapatti (total and unconditional self-surrender to God)	
Guiding principle	*Sa evaham* (He is me!)	*Mamaivasau* (He is mine only)	*Tasmaivaham* (I am meant for Him!)
State of mind of the seeker (*a la* D. V. Gundappa)	*Svatah-vilayana* (self merged into God)	*Svatah-sahabhaga* (self as associate of God)	*Svatah-samarpana* (self-surrender to God)**

(*Continued*)

(Continued)

	Shankara (eighth century)	*Ramanuja (eleventh to twelfth centuries)*	*Madhva (twelfth to thirteenth centuries)*
Nature of liberation	*Sarupya* (realisation of oneness) (possible when living)	*Sayujya* (joined with God)*** (possible after death)	*Samipya* (nearness or living with God)*** (possible after death)
Supportive verses from the Gita (examples only)	IV.24; VI.31; X.20; XIII.22, 32; XV.12–15.	VII.21–22; IX.22; XV.12–15; XVIII.55, 62, 65, 66	VII.21–22; IX.14, 15, 22, 34; XV.16–17; XVIII.62, 65, 66

*Only unity is real in a fundamental sense in Advaita, diversity being only relatively or apparently real.
**Relevant to Ramanuja also.
***With separate identity of the *jiva*/self retained.

Note: The table here presents only an approximate view; see the text of the chapter for a more nuanced presentation of differences as well as harmony between the three.

3

THE GITA GOES GLOBAL

Wilkins's English translation, impact and reactions

We can discern three stages in the spread and growing acceptance of the Gita. The first was when Shankara wrote his *bhashya* (commentary) on the Gita. Though there were a few commentaries on the Gita earlier and it was endorsed by a few *Puranas* which helped its popularity, it was after Shankara's bhashya and his tireless travel all over the country that the Gita came into the mainstream of Hinduism with a bang. Several more commentaries followed it, not only by Ramanuja and Madhva, but also by others mentioned in the last chapter. There may have been differences in interpreting the Gita, but it was agreed by all that it was a very important and authoritative religious text. Its position as a sacred text was consolidated. The second stage came in the thirteenth century, about five centuries after Shankara, when Sant Jnaneshwar liberated the Gita from the confines of Sanskrit and wrote his *Bhavartha-dipika* on it in people's own spoken language, Marathi. It launched the era of translations into vernacular, making the Gita more popular among common people. This trend continued well into the modern period and shows no signs of a slowing down.

The third stage began with the direct translation of the Gita from the Sanskrit original into English by Sir Charles Wilkins (1749–1836), at the instance of Warren Hastings (1732–1818), the then Governor General of India, published in London in 1785. It was titled: *Bhagavad Geeta or the Dialogues of Kreeshna and Arjoon, in Eighteen Lectures; with Notes*. Hastings, who encouraged and supported it, had to justify its printing and publication before the Court of Directors of the East India Company. Though he may have done so on the grounds of the need to know the culture and religion of the people who were ruled by the British, Hastings had a genuine interest in India's cultural heritage and was sure that the Gita 'will survive when the British in India shall have long ceased' (quoted by Desai 2014: 10). Hastings argued that 'reading the Gita would help a British public overcome its previous prejudice about Indian savagery, and acquire a more generous and true estimation of native dignity as well as accomplishment' (Davis 2015: 94). He also believed that the British should govern the Indian territories under its control, 'not according to British law but according to the laws and customs of the local residents' (Davis 2015: 76). Knowing their religion was a part of this policy. The choice of the Gita was because, as Wilkins wrote in his preface to his translation, 'The Brahmans esteem this work to contain all the grand mysteries of their religion' (Davis 2015: 79). Wilkins had located himself at Benares (Varanasi) to study Sanskrit and Sanskrit texts. The translation of the Gita was a result of collaboration between him and Sanskrit pundits there, particularly with the pundit Kashinatha Bhattacharya. Davis notes that there were no Sanskrit–English dictionaries then, and Kashinatha prepared a 10,000-word vocabulary and a list of Sanskrit verb roots to help Wilkins and William Jones, who was also deeply interested in translating Sanskrit texts (Davis 2015: 79). A flood of translations of other texts followed Wilkins's Gita (1785) – *Hitopadesha* (1787), *Shakuntala* (1789), *Gita Govinda* (1792), the *Laws of Manu* (1794) with many more to follow (Davis 2015: 76). William Jones took a sustained interest in Sanskrit, founded the Asiatic Society in Calcutta in 1784 and, apart from translating several Sanskrit texts, published a critical edition of *Amarakosha* in 1808. Jones is considered as the father of Indology, which emerged as a separate discipline by itself devoted to Indic studies. It interested many in Europe particularly in Germany. It gave rise to the idea that ancient Sanskrit could well have been the source of Indo-European languages. Wilkins's Gita was thus a trendsetter.

For Wilkins, the significance of the Gita did consist neither in showing the paths to liberation as interpreted by the earlier Indian commentators, nor in being a moral guide for living, but in the religious reforms it proposed within Hinduism. Davis quotes him in this regard:

> It seems as if the principal design of these dialogues was to unite all the prevailing modes of worship of those days; and by setting up the doctrine of the unity of Godhead, in opposition to idolatrous sacrifices, and the worship of images, to undermine the tenets inculcated by the *Veds*; . . . the design was to bring about the downfall of Polytheism; or, at least,

> to induce men to believe *God* present in every image before which they bent, and the object of all their ceremonies and sacrifices.
>
> (as quoted in Davis 2015: 81–82)

Obviously, Wilkins did not know that the religion of the Vedas and Upanishads had no idolatry or image worship, and they already had the concept of the unity of Godhead. He or Hastings hardly knew about the Vedas and the Upanishads, except being aware that such texts existed. Wilkins saw the Gita from a Christian perspective and interestingly saw coherence and consistency between his own faith and the teaching of the Gita. This was a notion which helped later in perceiving the universality of the Gita.

There were two younger contemporaries of Warren Hastings, evangelical Christian Charles Grant (1746–1823) and utilitarian James Mill (1773–1836), both of whom were quite opposed to Hastings's outlook and Orientalist enthusiasm for India and Sanskrit texts including the Gita. For both of them, India was scarcely above savage level in the 'evolutionary scale of civilisation'. This was not because of racial differences, but due to 'political and cultural despotism' from which India suffered. Only a profound transformation of society could save India. While Grant would allow a great role for Christian missionaries in this transformation, Mill would vouch for the secular process of modernisation (Davis 2015: 94–95). 'In Mill's view', Davis explains, 'religion ought to provide a depiction of the cosmos as a connected, perfect system governed by general laws and directed toward benevolent ends' (Davis 2015: 97). Mill points out at the account of Arjuna's awe at Krishna's all-encompassing form and observes that this is a 'monstrous exhibition' of a guilty cosmology. Mill also says that yogis (as per the Gita) are required to renounce all moral duties and affections, which is a torture that the religion of the Hindus requires. Davis rightly observes here that Mill failed to notice that the Gita on the contrary requires yogis to work in the world as per dharma, which includes both moral duties and affection. Davis concludes on Mill by the observation that his 'selective decontextualizing method of reading set the horizon of expectations for other colonial period English readers approaching the Gita and other classical works' (Davis 2015: 99). The attack by Grant, Mill and the like hardly however checked Orientalist enthusiasm for things Indian and the Gita. It also hardly halted the global spread of the Gita in and beyond Europe. As if to spite such criticism, one more direct translation appeared in English by

J. Cockburn Thomson in 1855 (though after a long gap after Wilkins), with more to follow.

Wilkins's Gita was not the first cross-cultural translation of the Gita; that credit probably belongs to Abul Fazl, who translated it into Persian at the instance of Emperor Akbar in the sixteenth century. There was also a Latin translation of the Gita by an Italian Jesuit missionary, Fransisco Benci, in the sixteenth century, from which a re-translation was done into Polish by Stanislaw Grochowski in 1611 (Brockington 2002: 100). Yet, Wilkins's Gita proved to be an important landmark in the history of the Gita. More than others before, it induced translations into other European languages, and its copies crossed the Atlantic and stimulated the curiosity of many in America and even impressed them. For the East India Company, which got it published, it proved to be a good investment well beyond its expectations.

Wilkins's translation had a greater impact abroad than the earlier Latin and Polish translations. Several English poets were influenced by the Gita as a result, like Robert Southey, William Blake, Wordsworth and Coleridge in Britain, and Ralph Waldo Emerson and Henry David Thoreau in America (Brockington 2002: 102). Thoreau (1817–62) was a leading American poet, philosopher, transcendentalist and environmentalist, whose work on Civil Disobedience was to influence Mahatma Gandhi later. Thoreau saw in the Gita a powerful advocacy of the discipline of a *muni* (sage), 'preferring the cultivation of wisdom through contemplation but not excluding action in the concentration on knowledge', and believed that the Gita epitomised the best of Eastern spirituality and that the West could learn much from the text (Robinson 2013: 104). Thoreau observed further that 'the New Testament is remarkable for its pure morality; the best of the Hindoo scripture [the Gita], for its pure intellectuality' (Robinson 2013: 105) and hinted that they were thus complementary to each other. Elsewhere, however, Thoreau does appreciate the 'moral grandeur and sublimity' of the Gita (Robinson 2013: 106). Robinson observes that 'the Bhagavadgita was hailed [by Thoreau] as an important work worthy of the widest possible readership, while its impact on his own ideas was [also] considerable' (Robinson 2013: 107). Both T. S. Eliot and E. M. Foster were particularly fascinated by the Gita's message of disinterested action, which was reflected in some of their works (Robinson 2013: 145).

Sir Monier Monier-Williams (1819–99) was another admirer of the Gita. He did not need Wilkins's translation to understand it. He was a professor of Sanskrit at Oxford University and known for his

Sanskrit–English Dictionary and a book on *Indian Wisdom* (1875), among others. The book shows his familiarity with other Hindu texts also like the Vedas, Upanishads, *Brahmanas, Smritis*, the six systems of philosophy and the two major epics – Ramayana and Mahabharata. In *Indian Wisdom*, he speaks of the Gita as 'one of the most interesting and popular works in the whole range of Sanskrit literature' and as representing the 'Eclectic school of Indian philosophy' (Monier-Williams 2001: 145). The Gita reconciles, in his view, the conflicting views of different systems by attempting to 'engraft the Sankhya and Yoga upon the Vedanta doctrines'. While the order of creation and cosmogony of the *Sankhya* is retained, 'the paramount sovereignty of the Supreme Soul of the universe as the source and ultimate end of all created things, and yet independent of all such creations', is also asserted (Monier-Williams 2001: 146). The author of the Gita, 'finding no rest for his spirit in any one system of philosophy, . . . was led to make a selection . . . so as to construct a composite theory of his own'. Monier-Williams adds that this was done with 'great perspicuity and beauty of language' (Monier-Williams 2001: 148). He considers the Gita as a pearl embedded in the Mahabharata, and yet quite independent of the great epic (Monier-Williams 2001: 147). Although finding several parallels between the Gita and the New Testament, he says that he would hesitate to concur with the view that the author of the Gita had any access to the New Testament, as the probability of contact between India and the Christian religion then could not have been high. Monier-William presumes that the Gita was composed sometime during the first two centuries of the Christian Era, though he does not try to explain the basis of this presumption. He adds however that there were such parallels between Roman philosophers and the Christian scriptures, and yet there is no ground whatever to suppose that the pagan writers of Italy derived their ideas from either Jewish or Christian sources, though the probability of contact between them was greater than in the case of India (Monier-Williams 2001: 166–67).

In spite of his admiration for the Gita, Monier-Williams finds a shortcoming in it as compared with the Bible. On the basis of his other writings, Robinson says that according to Monier-Williams, the devotion to personal God in Krishna is subordinated to the knowledge of an impersonal absolute – the Brahman. Thus theism in the Gita is undercut by pantheism. Pantheism is a bad word in Christianity. 'Monier-Williams is doubtful of the possibility of any real relationship between human and divine when both merge into the impersonal absolute' (Robinson 2013: 45–46). Monier-Williams is uncomfortable with any idea of a personal God (who in Christianity is the Supreme), being only an emanation of the impersonal Absolute in the Gita and also in Hinduism in general. This, in his view, makes Hinduism unable to meet the challenge of Christianity. Though from his Christian perspective, it constitutes a weakness of Hinduism, a Vedantin would consider it as its great strength. The idea of Brahman is intellectually more profound and rational and, when combined with a personal God, is emotionally satisfying and wish-fulfilling. Indian philosophers, saints and mystics found no conflict between a personalised conception of the Supreme and the Absolute – the Brahman. They are sure that both ensure spiritual success and realisation and liberation.

An important significance of Wilkins's translation is that it launched a trend of 'objective' and 'critical' scholarship with perspectives of history and comparative religion on the Gita. This new genre of scholarship on Indian sacred books was separated from the veneration of the Gita, which had characterised the earlier commentators in the Vedic tradition, though it was also often combined with critical appreciation. Not that earlier classical commentators of the Gita were uncritical, but their critical outlook was directed only against rival interpreters. The new trend of scholarship on Indian classics and sacred books influenced even Indian scholarship, promoting a dispassionate study of the Gita and critical discussion on it. K. T. Telang's translation of the Gita into English with a critical and detailed introduction (published in 1882, discussed further later) is an early example of such Indian scholarship. When 'objective' scholarship tended to be overcritical and prejudiced, when there was some tendency to view the Gita as no more than an inert given piece of historical material, resulting in distorted interpretations, both Indian and Western admirers of the Gita rose to the occasion coming up with more informed and deliberated response than would have been possible otherwise. The literature on the Gita thus became more thought-provoking and balanced, helping a better understanding of it. The role of Western scholarship, on the whole, has thus been positive and constructive.

Reception in Germany

Wilkins inspired many more translations including other European languages, some 300 in English alone, bringing the Gita on to the stage of the world at large. Brockington (1882) has given a fairly comprehensive account of the many translations of the Gita, helpful in knowing its global journey, and has been used in writing this section.

A French translation of Wilkins's appeared just two years later, a Russian translation a year further and a German in 1802 (1882: 103). The German philosopher and the first German Sanskritist, Friedrich von Schlegel, translated extracts of it directly from Sanskrit into German in 1808, while another Schlegel from Germany – Wilhelm von – translated it in Latin in 1823, giving along with it the original in Devanagari script. This Latin translation was considered to be not only accurate but also of high literary quality (1882: 104). This was followed by further translations into German in 1826 and 1834 (the latter being the first direct translation in German), French in 1846, Greek in 1848, Italian in 1859, Dutch in 1861 (not the full Gita but selected parts) and Czech in 1877 (1882: 104–5). What is more, in each language, there were several translations, particularly in English and German.

As Davis notes, the most enthusiastic reception to the Gita took place in Germany. He says that even before Sanskrit works appeared in Europe, Johan Gottfried Herder (1744–1803) had been portraying India as the cradle of civilisation. He translated portions of Wilkins's Gita into German, along with two other Indic texts in 1792. He declared the Gita to be a great unitary premise of pantheism: One in all, and all into One. He saw it as a theological principle with compelling ethical ramifications: all humans are energised by the one World Spirit, and human life should therefore be led by rational reflection and conscientious action. He believed that the Gita taught a universal principle as applicable to the eighteenth-century Germany as in ancient India. Friedrich Schlegel (1772–1829) is another important German deeply interested in India. He proclaimed that 'everything without exception has its origin in India'. Schlegel was an eminent 'romanticist' poet, philosopher, philologist, Indologist and a literary critic. He pioneered Indo-European studies on comparative linguistics and showed grammatical connection between Sanskrit and Indo-European languages. Schlegel was particularly interested in the *Jnana-yoga* preached by the Gita, the intellectual concept of Godhead, and 'the human quest to find union with the divine'. If India was the birthplace of human civilisation, the Gita came to be regarded as the earliest philosophical expression of the original wisdom with ideas that would remain relevant for centuries to come (Davis 2015: 84–87, 90). Friedrich Schlegel's contemporary, Wilhelm von Schlegel (1767–1845), did not share the former's 'romanticist' enthusiasm for the Gita but preferred its critical study from a Christian perspective, identifying 'good parts' that cohere with Christian doctrines and dismissing the remainder as myth or superstition (Davis 2015: 92).

Wilhelm Von Humboldt (1767–1835), the founder of Humboldt University in Berlin, gave two lectures on the Gita in Berlin in 1825 and 1826 respectively, which were subsequently published. He proclaimed the Gita as 'the most beautiful, presumably the only philosophical poem of all known literatures' (as quoted in Davis 2015: 101). His assessment was challenged by philosopher Hegel (1770–1831), who argued that yoga required withdrawal from the world leading to a passive immersion into the Brahman. Brahman is an inert conception, in contrast with the Christian God who engages in the world process. According to him, the introverted and static aspirations of Hinduism articulated in the Gita consigned India to a backward status (Davis 2015: 102–4). Hegel completely ignored the activist and intervening concept of God very much evident in the Gita, particularly in the idea of *avatar*, and also the Gita's conception of yoga as active but selfless work in the world. He had a misunderstood and distorted version of Advaita philosophy as represented in the Gita. The criticism from James Mill, Hegel and Christian missionaries stopped neither more Sanskritists from emerging, nor the spread of the Gita even among others including poets and other intellectuals.

F. Max Müller (1823–1900) was a leading Indologist from Germany, whose six-volume edition of the Rigveda along with translation and Sayana's commentary was a pioneering and major contribution to the knowledge of Sanskrit literature in the West. It proved to be valuable also to educated Indians who did not know enough Vedic Sanskrit to understand the Rigveda. His main interest, however, was in the Vedas and Upanishads, rather than in the Gita, and considered the Gita as less significant than the former particularly from the point of studying the history of religion. His major concern was 'to discover how and what he called Aryan religion began and developed', and in this task, the Gita did not interest him much (Robinson 2013: 39). Nevertheless, he commissioned K. T. Telang to edit and translate the Gita as a part of his project of publishing multi-volume *Sacred Books of the East*. More about this later.

Richard von Garbe (1857–1927), a noted Indologist, translated the Gita and proposed the theory of its multiple authorship. According to him, the original Gita was written in the second century BCE as a theistic tract, and in the second century CE, it was adapted by the upholders of Upanishadic monism. He says: 'These two doctrines – the theistic and the pantheistic – are mixed up with each other, and follow each other, sometimes quite unconnected and sometimes loosely connected. . . . [T]he two beliefs are treated of almost throughout as though there was no difference between them, either verbal or real' (as quoted in Radhakrishnan 1996, Vol. I: 530). Radhakrishnan meets this criticism by suggesting that a living warm religion of personal religion does not eschew the spiritual idealism of the Upanishads (Radhakrishnan 1996: 530). Some of the sants of the bhakti movement were known to have had the mystical experience of the immanent Brahman through intense devotion. The kind of criticism Garbe makes is a result of a purely scholastic or academic approach which divorced from any experiential attempt at gaining knowledge. Paul Deusen and Leopold von Schroeder separately opposed Garbe's views on the multiple authorship of the Gita (Brockington 2002: 105).

Rudolf Otto (1869–1917), Garbe's pupil, supported his teacher on the issue of multiple authorship or interpolation. He was, however, attracted by the charm of the Gita and was not concerned with using it for proselytising Hindus.[1] He took the Gita as an example of the literature of the 'numinous' or the holy, and valued its theistic and mystical content. He also considered it to be an eclectic work, evolved through different stages of composition, and tried to identify the 'original Gita' (see Note 5 to Chapter 1). He said that the original Gita was 'Krishna's own voice and deed, referring directly to the situation in which Arjuna finds himself, intended, however, not to proclaim to him any transcendent dogma of salvation, but to render him willing to undertake the special service of the Almighty Will of the God who decides the fate of battles' (quoted in Robinson 2013: 46). According to Otto, the rest of the Gita added later, which included *Sankhya* and yoga philosophies, was meant to accord divine authority to various ideas. Yet, he was impressed by the devotional theism of the Gita, much of which is in those parts of it which he did not regard as 'original'. Robinson says that Otto's refusal to regard the Gita as a unitary work representing a synthesis gained him many detractors (Robinson 2013: 47).

Otto had studied Shankara's commentary on the Gita and observed that 'the impersonal Brahman rests here also on a theistic basis, and this is not unimportant for the perception of the Brahman itself'. This affirmation of the lower level of truth associated with personal deity, an affirmation arising out of a developmental rather than an oppositional model of knowledge of Brahman, meant that he described Shankara's thought as 'super-theism', not 'anti-theism' (Robinson 2013: 47). Shankara, according to him, 'conflated the qualities of the personal deity with the impersonal Brahman' and applauded it because it did not trivialise devotion to a personal deity (Robinson 2013: 48).

An interesting contribution of Otto is his comparison of the Gita's religion with Christianity. He notes striking similarities particularly in theism, but also 'the most profound difference of all'. He explains: 'The difference consisted in the contrast between grace that releases a soul from sin and guilt in the case of Christianity, and grace that releases a soul from the bonds of *samsara* (the wheel of existence) in the case of Indian religion' (Robinson 2013: 48). Otto asserted that 'the Indian notion of sin and related concepts such as repentance and confession were not as developed as they were in Christianity and that conscience was not as central' (Robinson 2013: 48). However, Swami Vivekananda turned the table against such criticism by observing that Hinduism did not consider humans as born in sin, regarding them in their basic essence as the children of Immortal (*Amritasya putrah*). Sin arises out of ignorance and sentimental attachment (*moha*), according to Hinduism; it is not innate, inherent or inevitable. The concept of repentance (*paschattapa*) and atonement (*prayaschitta*) is quite present and popular in Hinduism as well, which is not possible without a concept of conscience. In any case, the Christian concept of salvation is different from the Hindu concept of liberation or *moksha*, and this is highlighted by Otto. A Hindu can also confidently claim that the Hindu concept of liberation as more sophisticated than the Christian concept of salvation. However, it is unfair to regard one of them as less developed or inferior to the other. Each has its own distinct background and justification.

Further spread

Interestingly, it is not the Hindus who first took the trouble to take the Gita beyond the cross-cultural frontiers, but others. A cross-cultural translation presents special problems, of which Hastings was quite aware. He duly appreciated the difficulty of doing so which in his view was due to 'the subject itself, which is highly metaphysical, to the extreme difficulty of rendering abstract terms by others exactly corresponding with them in another language, to the arbitrary combination of ideas in words expressing unsubstantial qualities, and more to the errors of interpretation' (quoted by Desai 2014: 10). However, it is to the credit of Western scholars who crossed the cultural barriers and came out with so many translations of not only the Gita but many other Sanskrit texts as well. As a result, the Gita acquired the label of 'Hindu Bible' much before the end of the nineteenth century. Hindus started translating the Gita into English only in the second half of the nineteenth century, and by the twentieth century, there were many who did so. By then, English hardly remained a foreign language, as Indians had made it their own. Several eminent Swamis went abroad, particularly to Britain and the United States, beginning with Swami Vivekananda's trip to Chicago in 1893, to give discourses on Hinduism and the Gita in English, which in due course were compiled in book form. Interestingly, many of the prominent translations into English were first published either in Britain or the United States, followed by less-expensive Indian editions. Several translations of the Gita along with the commentaries of Shankara, Ramanuja and Madhva also became available in English. Many Indians, paradoxically, started studying the Gita through these translations in English, which thus played an important role in popularising the Gita even in India. It is not necessary to list all the translations of the Gita even in English here, there being others who have done so fairly comprehensively (see, e.g. Kapoor 1983; Brockington 2002; Davis 2015). There were also many translations in every major Indian language by the first half of the twentieth century. There is no need to list them in this chapter, the purpose of which is only to indicate how the Gita went on to be seen as a sacred book at the global level. What is noteworthy here is that globalisation of the Gita went ahead simultaneously with its accelerating popularity within India.

The first translation into English *by an Indian* was by K. T. Telang, which was published in 1882 as the eighth volume under the series on *Sacred Books of the East*, edited by Max Müller and published in England. Max Müller by then had acquired the reputation of being an authority on India and oriental studies and, apart from being respected by scholars both in the West and India, was also popular among the public in both places.[2] The inclusion of the Gita as a part of the *Sacred Books of the East* gave a stamp of international recognition to its already known status. It also made the Gita better known in the West than before. Telang had a little earlier published a translation into English in verse in Bombay (now, Mumbai). The 1882 edition, however, was in prose and included *Anu-Gita* and *Sanatsugatiya*. Telang also wrote a scholarly introduction to it in the true spirit of the new discipline of Indology, which was becoming popular.

Sir Edwin Arnold (1832–1904), already a reputed poet being the author of *Light of Asia* (1879) and known for his interest in the Orient, particularly India,[3] went through Telang's translation of the Gita. He did not very much like it and observed that it lacked 'the dignity and the grace of the original' (quoted by Yardi 1991: 9). Arnold gave his own translation in verse form, calling it, *The Song Celestial*, published first in 1885. It was not a literal translation; instead it tried to bring out the essence, dignity and grace of the original in verse. It is said that Arnold aimed at bringing the original closer to the readers, rather than bringing the reader to the original, as Goethe had suggested as a principle to be followed while translating (Sinha 2010: 307). Great in literary quality, *The Song* helped the Gita to enter into public consciousness in the West. Between 1785 when Wilkins's translation came out and 1885, there was a lot of change in readers' perception of the Gita. A reviewer of Wilkins's translation had observed that its primary function was to satisfy readers' curiosity about the exotic East; a hundred years later, a reviewer of Arnold's *The Song Celestial* saw it as 'a book for a spiritual truth-seeker, irrespective of religion and culture', and yet the poem is 'also simultaneously read as a text whose pleasure lies in its value as an aesthetic object' (Sinha 2010: 308). Thus, from its status as a sacred book, the Gita acquired in public consciousness of the West the eminence of being a literary work, besides being a storehouse of universal values. Mahatma Gandhi was introduced to the Gita by his theosophist friends in England through Arnold's rendering of it. It impressed him a lot and inspired him to not only study the Sanskrit original, but also make his own translation and commentary (which we will take up later). By a significant coincidence, 1885, the year of publication of Arnold's poetic rendering of the Gita, was also the year when the Indian National Congress was founded. The year marked the birth of Indian nationalism, and the Gita was to play a crucial role in it as we would be observing in the next chapter.

More translations followed Arnold's, not only in English but also in other languages. Owing perhaps to his influence, there was a shift from literal to free translations, with greater concern for content than to form (Brockington 2002: 115). There was a Hungarian translation in 1887, and two translations in to Spanish – one published in Buenos Aires, Argentina, in 1893, and another in Barcelona, Spain, in 1896–97. Early in the twentieth century, a direct and complete translation into Dutch was made by J. W. Boissevain in 1903 at Amsterdam; and M. L. Kirby and C. Jinarajadasa brought out a translation in Italian together with the commentary by Shankara in 1905. A free verse translation in Russian by A. P. Kasnacheyeva came out in 1909. Two Polish translations were published in 1910, one at Warszawa by Stanislaw Franciszek Michalasky, an able Sanskritist, and the other by Bronislaw Olszewsky at Brody. There were thus so many translations of the Gita by 1920 that Max Weber remarked in his work, *The*

Religion of India, that the Gita had been 'translated into almost all the languages of the earth' (quoted in Desai 2014: 12).[4] The steady trend of translations along with erudite introductions continued thereafter too, to justify Max Weber's remark even if he had somewhat exaggerated. Translations came out in Japanese by J. Takakushi in 1921, in Swedish by Nino Runeberg in 1922, Icelandic by S. K. Petersson in 1924, Serbian by P. Jevotic (extracts) and Rumanian by D. Nanu in 1932 (Brockington 2002: 117).

Further translations appeared in English, significant for their insightful introductions, some of which may be noted here. They were respectively by Franklin Edgerton (an eminent American Sanskritist and linguistic scholar) published in 1944 at Cambridge Mass, by S. Radhakrishnan with commentary based on Shankara's published first in 1948 at London and by R. Zaehner in 1969 at Oxford. Radhakrishnan's proved most popular, which has been continuously reprinted ever since its publication, never going out of stock. In terms of the enormous circulation, Radhakrishnan's seems to have been overtaken now by the translation by A. C. Bhaktivedanta Swami Prabhupada, *Bhagavad-Gita as It Is*, published by the International Society of Krishna Consciousness (ISKCON) first in English in 1968 at Los Angeles, which has subsequently gone into many reprints and further translations into other languages. The contributions of Radhakrishnan and Prabhupada will be discussed in greater detail in Chapter 5.

R. C. Zaehner (1913–74), apart from discussing the Gita in his other books on Hinduism and Hindu scriptures, wrote one specially focused on it (Zaehner 1969). Advocacy of devotion to a personal deity and related mysticism was the most significant contribution of the Gita according to him. He attributed the subsequent rise of devotional Hinduism to the influence of the Gita. He rejected the notion that devotion was just one of the paths, because knowledge and action could hardly be differentiated 'from the life of love and devotion to God' (quoted in Robinson 2013: 50). He felt that according to the Gita, only divine grace could liberate a living being to become one with the Brahman. According to him, Ramanuja was a better interpreter than others because he 'was nearest to the mind and the author of the Gita' (Robinson 2013: 50). He upheld theism over monism in his reading of the text, not only because devotion to a personal deity was the ultimate means and the end, but also because it was easier and open to all irrespective of class, caste and gender. He thought that the Gita changed India's religious history. However, he also pointed out that 'the type of devotion it inculcated was not the impassioned self-abandonment later to characterise the bhakti movement but detached dutiful service' (Robinson 2013: 51). Zaehner accorded a pivotal position to the Gita, as providing a basis for dialogue between religions, as it contained different standpoints of all religions of the East and the West, ranging from 'immanent pantheism' to 'transcendental monotheism' to 'atheistic mysticism' (Robinson 2013: 52). He considered it not only as 'the most influential text within the Hindu tradition', but also as 'the most significant sacred text in the whole history of religion' (Robinson 2013: 52).[5]

Many swamis went abroad, particularly to the United States, United Kingdom and Europe, to preach Hindu philosophy and gave series of well-attended lectures on the Gita, which were also published in book form soon including the original with the translations and commentaries. Among these, some of the notables are Purohit Swami (1935), and more recently, Sri Sri Paramahamsa Yogananda (1995, 2002), Swami Chinmayananda (1996) and Swami Dayananda Saraswati (to be distinguished from the founder of Arya Samaj of the same name) (2011). Chinmayananda and Dayananda Saraswati, based mainly in India, have done wonders both in *dharma-prachar* and social service there, though they also went abroad. Eknath Eswaran, not a swami as such, also did remarkably well in contributing to a better understanding of the Gita through a free translation in beautiful verse in four volumes. Their work is taken up in the subsequent chapters.

Translations continued in other languages too. Among them, noted by Brockington, are the translations in Russian by B. L. Smirnov in 1956, Hebrew by I. Olsvanger in 1956, Japanese by M. Hattori first in 1959 and another by Naoshiro Tsuji in 1980. There were three in Italian respectively by Juan Mascaro in 1962, by Giulio Cogni in verse form in 1973 and by Raniero Gnoni with Abhinavagupta's commentary in 1976. There was Estonian by Linnart Mall in 1980 (2011: 117). Meghnad Desai mentions at least four recent translations of the Gita into Chinese: 'first in 1985 by Yang Feihua, then in 1989 by Zang Baosheng and within the last few years by Xu Fanshang in 2009 and Huang Baosheng in 2010' (Desai 2014: 24). Desai further refers to a long tradition of Sanskrit learning in China. It implies that there may have been some translations earlier too, though traditionally China had more links with Buddhism than with Hinduism in the past.[6]

The emergence of Indology as a scientific discipline in its own right has been briefly referred to earlier while discussing Wilkins's first translation into English. It needs a little more attention because of the important role it played in promoting a critical understanding of India's history, art and literature, not only abroad but even among Indians themselves. It included a critical study of the Gita too. There was indeed the tradition of commentaries (*bhashyas*) on the Gita, but they ignored historical aspects and approached the Gita from the perspective of a given doctrine which may not be considered as quite objective. Indology helped a better appreciation of the Gita and its strengths and of the precautions to be taken in interpreting it. Telang's long introduction to his English translation referred earlier is a testimony of how Indian scholars too were influenced by the analytical tools developed by the new discipline. The birth of Indology owes greatly to the enthusiastic interest and pioneering efforts of both Wilkins and William Jones (1746–94), who had come to Calcutta as a judge when Hastings was the Governor General. Basham remarks that Jones was a linguistic genius who had not only mastered the important European languages but also learnt Arabic, Persian, Turkish and even had a 'smattering of Chinese'. After coming to India, he learnt Sanskrit with the help of Wilkins (Basham 1967: 5). Jones pioneered the idea that the ancient classical languages of Sanskrit, Greek, Latin and Persian had a common root. He labelled this family of languages Indo-European (Desai 2014: 11). Translations of several classics from Sanskrit into English and other European languages were made around the same time. Jone's translation of Kalidasa's play, *Sacontala or the Fatal Ring* (*Shakuntalam*), published in 1789, became even more popular for a while than Wilkins's Gita and whetted the appetite for knowing more about India and its culture (Sinha 2010: 302). The publication of translations of the Upanishads by the French Jesuit priest philologist Abraham-Hyacinthe Anquatil Duperon in 1802–04 into Latin (*Oupnek'hat*) further added to this appetite (Sinha 2010: 302). Sanskrit began to be taught in European universities. A new breed of scholars known as Orientalists or Sanskritists emerged. Institutions like the Asiatic Society (started first in Calcutta, and then in London and Bombay) and Écoles des Langues Vivantes (Paris) were started to promote research in Indian languages, culture and history. Dictionaries of Sanskrit into English, German and French started being published. Basham has described in some detail the exciting period of the emergence of Indology and its rich outcome in terms of a much better understanding of India's past, in a book he fondly titled as *The Wonder That Was India* (1967: 4–8). All these activities boosted the self-confidence of Indians making them proud of their past and stimulated in turn social reforms and India's freedom struggle – an impact which was not even dreamt of when Hastings encouraged Wilkins to translate the Gita.

Though curiosity about the things Indian was a major factor behind the spread of the Gita abroad initially, there was a qualitative change in the perception about it by the end of the nineteenth century. The publications respectively of Duperon's *Oupnek'het*, Max Müller's *Sacred Books of the East* and Arnold's *The Song Celestial* gave the Western public access to a new dimension of spirituality which they were seeking. A further landmark was the six lectures by Swami Vivekananda at the Parliament of Religions at Chicago in 1893, followed by many more lectures in America and Europe on Hinduism and its philosophy.[7] In his first address itself on 11 September, the Swami referred to the traditional tolerance of Hinduism towards different faiths and its acceptance of multiple paths of spirituality, and quoted the Gita's famous verse (IV.11), translating it as: 'Whosoever comes to Me, through whatever form, I reach him; all men are struggling through paths which in the end lead to Me' (CWSV 2000, Vol. I: 4). The way he began his first lecture addressing the audience as 'Sisters and Brothers of America', which received standing ovation for a few minutes, signified the basic philosophical spirit of Hinduism. Here was an exponent of Hinduism who knew about all the religions and could impress the representatives of various faiths about what made Hinduism so special and outstanding. In his 'Paper on Hinduism' presented on 19 September at the same Parliament, he told the audience that humans are not sinners, but they are the 'Children of the Immortal Bliss' as proclaimed in the Vedas. He told them, you are not matter, you are not mere bodies, you are the masters of matter; matter is your mere servant. Hinduism is not just a set of beliefs or doctrines, but shows the ways of realisation; it consists not in believing, but in being and becoming (CWSV 2000: 11–13). His lectures strengthened the awareness about the potential of Hinduism and the Gita to help in spiritual pursuit and to help overcome new problems of excessive materialism created by industrialisation. A feeling that the philosophical knowledge and spiritual wisdom of Hinduism, particularly as found in the Upanishads and the Gita, was not meant for Hindus alone, but is relevant for all humanity, began to spread. One did not have to convert to Hinduism to study or even follow the Gita and the Upanishads. Whatever be one's cultural or geographical background, their relevance seemed universal. This growing belief in the universality of the Gita was a major factor behind the success of the Gita in its global journey. Interestingly, the particular context of the Gita – that of the war and its teaching to Arjuna to fight in a declared and just war and not mind killing even his own people in the process – hardly became a hindrance in the global march of the Gita. This was because, not only Gandhi but also other interpreters like Aldous Huxley[8] considered the war background of the Gita as only an allegory (Sinha 2010: 304). Far from teaching violence, both Gandhi and Huxley interpreted the Gita as pacifist, teaching nonviolence. As Sinha points out, this transformation in the perception of the Gita was an outcome of a dialogic or dialectical process between the Western and Indian spiritual interpreters (Sinha 2010: 299, 304). It culturally enriched both India and the West.

In any case, the nineteenth and twentieth centuries played an important role in the history of the Gita. It received the widest recognition in the world during these two centuries as never before. This also deepened its recognition within Hindus, even contributing to their identity. The remarks of Jaqueline Hirst are noteworthy in this regard:

> It would be quite wrong to insinuate that the *Bhagavadgita̱* was an insignificant text before the interaction of Europe and India in the modern period. Its place in the triple foundation of Vedạnta is clear and it acted as a model for other texts, the *Ishwaragita̱* being one example. However, its prominence in neo-Hindu thought in the nineteenth and twentieth centuries cannot be abstracted from a context in which western academics stressed the textual basis of religions, Christian missionaries preached on social ethics and Hindu Indian nationalists looked for inspiration to their own heritage as justification for diverse approaches to obtaining Independence.
>
> (Hirst 2000: 49)

Notes

1 The account about Otto here is based on Robinson (2013: 46–49).

2 Between 1879 and 1910, forty-nine volumes of the *Sacred Books of the East* were published. Sinha informs that the cost of this 'extraordinary and expensive project' was met by the Oxford University Press and the British Government in India (Sinha 2010: 305).

3 Sir Arnold was in India before he became eminent in Britain. He was the principal of Government College, Poona (now, Pune). After returning to England, he became a successful journalist and became the editor-in-chief of the *Daily Telegraph* (Sinha 2010: 307).

4 This book was first published in German in 1920 and in English in 1958.

5 The account about Otto's contribution is based on Robinson (2013: 49–52), which in turn is based on most of Otto's books on Hinduism and Hindu scriptures.

6 Sinha (2010: 299) has referred to Kapoor's Bibliography of the Gita, which has listed almost all the translations of the Gita into various languages of the world between 1785 and 1979 (Kapoor 1983). There have of course been further translations too.
7 Swami Vivekananda's lectures and writings are included in *The Collected Works of Swami Vivekananda* (CWSV), first published in 1907 under four volumes, with the ninth volume (the last thus far) added in 1997, in continuous editions or reprints ever since (Vivekananda 1997–2001).
8 See his Introduction to Prabhavananda and Isherwood (1944).

4

MAKERS OF MODERN INDIA AND THEIR INTERPRETATIONS OF THE GITA

The exposure to Western education and ideas had a significant multidimensional impact on India. Social and religious leaders emerged one after the other who absorbed the new ideas and values of modern Renaissance in Europe and, in that light, examined India's social, economic and political conditions. Though rooted in Indian culture and proud of it, these leaders could also see that India's conditions cried for drastic improvements in almost all spheres of life. They became acutely aware of mass illiteracy and rampant superstition prevailing in the country, associated with the exclusion of the bulk of people from education. Colonial exploitation and destruction of indigenous industries had produced mass poverty. Subjugation under foreign rule had also made people docile and submissive. There was a need to awaken and energise the masses, make them aware of the social evils and yet restore their self-confidence. Most of the modern leaders did not feel that they had to reject the old scriptures wholesale either as hindrance or as irrelevant in this task, but found on the contrary that many of them were quite useful if only re-interpreted consistent with the Renaissance ideals of liberty, equality and fraternity. They found that these values were very much there in Indian scriptures, but were obscured by some of the later developments like the caste system and suppression of women. Basic teaching of sacred books had to be rediscovered, while unnecessary accretions of irrational and false religious beliefs could be rejected. The modern Indian leaders produced their own version of Indian Renaissance, without which India could not have become a modern nation in the comity of nations in the world and make its presence felt.

The modern leaders were essentially makers of modern India. They made their thrusts on three fronts simultaneously and in interrelated way, sometimes the same leader (especially Gandhi) operating on all of them. The first was social reforms particularly for emancipating Indian women, eradicating social evils like untouchability, breaking down the hierarchy of the caste system and imparting education to the masses. The second was achieving renaissance within Hinduism and reviving it in a reinvigorated form, and ridding it of its major weaknesses – superstition, irrational but not so amusing ideas of purity and pollution, and above all the obstinate belief in a hierarchical caste system. And the third was mobilising the masses for a freedom struggle to throw off the yoke of colonialism and make a transition to a democratic, egalitarian, sovereign republic.

Interestingly, most of the leaders made use of the Gita in important ways in operating on these three fronts, investing new meanings into the old text in this task. They found the Gita inspiring in their work, whether it was in social reform, reforming Hinduism, nation building or in freedom struggle. As Minor observes, 'the exhortation to action from Krishna suited the aspirations of Indian nationalists in their struggle for *swaraj*, independence from British sovereignty' (1991-a: 6). Further, 'they regarded Krishna as the karmayogin *par excellence*, working unceasingly and with total selflessness' and as an inspiration for engaging in social action and reform (1991-a: 6). The spirit with which the modern leaders used and interpreted the Gita conveyed at least three important messages: one, that the Gita was relevant not merely in purely spiritual pursuit, but also in mundane and secular matters; two, it was relevant not merely in the case of private life of individuals, but also in nation building and reforming the society; and three, it was relevant not merely to Hindus alone but also to all people all over the world, without in any way implying either that it was an exclusive guide in all matters or that it was necessarily so important or dominating that it subjugated all other sources of guidance and authority. In other words, even while importance was given to it, there was no fanaticism about it, and no overarching dominance ever given to it. In his daily public meetings of prayers and *bhajans*, Gandhi insisted on combining recitation of selected verses from the Gita with the sacred books of other religions too.

The modern interpreters of the Gita are divided for the purpose of presentation in this book into two broad categories: the first consisting of early modern interpreters who were very much engaged in the task of making of the modern India particularly in the national freedom struggle and social reforms, and found the Gita quite useful in their task; and the second consisting of the more recent interpreters whose main focus was on providing spiritual and moral guidance and on adapting Hinduism to the challenges of modern times. The first group, which played a major role in the renaissance of both India and Hinduism, is presented in this chapter itself, and the second group in the next. These eminent persons are taken in the chronological order of the year of their birth within each of the two chapters. Many of them worked both in India and abroad, though a few focused mainly on India. A few others concentrated on providing spiritual guidance to Hindus abroad, incidentally also acquainting not merely scholars but even common people among non-Hindus there with Hinduism and its scriptures, thus building valuable cross-cultural bridges and taking Hinduism and the Gita even beyond Hindus.

Raja Rammohan Roy

The pioneer in the work of renaissance in India is undoubtedly Raja Rammohan Roy (1772–1833).[1] He is for this reason known as the father of Indian renaissance, and the Maker of Modern India. He was well versed not only in English and Sanskrit, but also in Persian and Arabic. At Varanasi, he studied the Vedas, the Upanishads, the Gita, and the Shastras. He visited Tibet to study Buddhism first-hand. He acquired a wide scholastic vision and a broad mind spanning different cultures. He helped the Mughal emperor in getting his pension from the British increased, for which Rammohan had to visit London. It was the Mughal emperor at Delhi who gave him the title of Raja. He held a good position in the East India Company Government, but gave up his job in the interest of scholastic pursuits and social work.

Two incidents in his life left a lasting impression on him and firmed up his special soft corner for women and his resolve to improve their condition. He was deeply opposed to idol worship, and he openly expressed his views about it while in Tibet. The enraged lamas there who wanted to assault him, but was saved in time by Tibetan women who hid him. The second incident was when his elder brother died, his wife wanted to commit *sati* or have concremation with her husband's body. Rammohan tried his best to dissuade her but failed. However, when she climbed onto the funeral pyre, she could not bear the burning heat and wanted to rush out of it. To the horror of Rammohan, the group gathered there pushed her back into the fire with bamboo poles and she was burnt to death. Rammohan resolved then and there that he would not rest until he put an end to this horrible practice.

The practice of *sati* prevailed more in Bengal than in other parts of India and that too among propertied elite than among the working classes. More than the keenness to ensure heaven for the deceased and his wife, or the backing of the Shastras, the husband's relatives were interested in usurping the property which otherwise would have gone to the wife. They used to subtly encourage the wife to commit *sati*. Rammohan began his work of ending the practice both by requesting the government to do it and by promoting public opinion against it. Since the practice had a social backing, the government could not instantly act in the matter in spite of being convinced by Rammohan's arguments. There had to be public debates between Rammohan on one side and pundits on the other who backed the practice by quoting from the Shastras in their support. Rammohan argued based on his deep knowledge that no Shastra had made it mandatory for a woman to commit *sati* and that it was entirely voluntary, and rare or occasional even in the past. The pundits agreed but argued that the practice of *sati* ensures heaven not only to the couple but also to several generations on both sides and is a noble practice. They argued that while a widow does not enjoy a respectable status, the woman who commits *sati* – who is not regarded as a widow – is highly honoured; and that a woman from a noble family desires this honour rather than the disrespect shown to a widow, and why should she be prevented from exercising her choice? Rammohan countered saying that while the arguments of the pundits were based on quotations from some of the later Smritis, his own arguments are based on the philosophy of Shrutis and the Gita, which undoubtedly had a higher status as authorities in matters of religion and its practice. He said that the Gita despised the desire for going to heaven through rituals, and *sati* was a horrible and cruel ritual, but praised a life dedicated to selfless work and devotion to the Lord. He further argued that the contemporary society attached false value to *sati* and despised the widows, but this attitude had no approval of the Hindu sacred books. Above all, the practice imposed horrible pain on the woman for no fault of hers, and amounted to extreme cruelty, and needed to be stopped forthwith. He quoted from the Gita profusely in his support. He pleaded that the society should instead respect widows and allow them to lead a pious life. In reply to the pundits' argument that women may not be capable of such a life and fail, he replied that the Gita does not send such people failing in piety to doom and instead promises that no sincere effort in spiritual pursuit goes in vain even if done imperfectly. Ultimately, Rammohan's arguments prevailed, and the Governor General, William Bentinck (who had come to India in 1828), declared the practice of *sati (Suttee)* illegal in 1829.

Rammohan had a far-sighted vision about imparting education to people of India at large. He sent a letter to Lord William Amherst, the Governor General of India during 1823–28, requesting the British government to take initiative in starting Western or English education in India for people at large, through which Indians can learn modern sciences, history and geography in English medium at higher levels. This general education was to be made available to both boys and girls from all classes of people. He also backed the idea of some financial support from the government to traditional educational institutions so that the traditional languages and knowledge systems do not go extinct due to official neglect. In other words, he appears to have envisaged two systems of education in India operating simultaneously. Rammohan's initiative came well before Macaulay's famous Minute on Education in 1835. Rammohan pursued the issue with Lord Bentinck, who was the next Governor General (1828–35), but it was adopted as a policy for implementation only after Macaulay's Minute, that is, unfortunately after Rammohan's death. Rammohan also wanted to reform Hinduism; he was particularly opposed to idol worship and ritualism, which had dominated Hinduism. In this again, he had the support of the Gita since there was no idol worship in the Gita and it was also opposed to ritualism. He founded the Brahmo Samaj in 1828 to show a way of practicing genuine Hinduism based on the Upanishads, the *Brahmasu̲tras* and the Gita, ridding Hinduism of false beliefs and unnecessary rituals.

Bankimchandra

The next important leader of Hindu Renaissance was Bankimchandra Chattopadhyay[2] (Chatterjee, as per British spelling) (1838–94), a pioneering Bengali novelist and poet, noted for his strong nationalist inclinations. He is famous as the author of the national song – *Vande Ma̲taram,* which for the first time perhaps conceptualised India as the mother, a powerful concept to mobilise people in the national cause. He wrote a commentary on the Gita in Bengali, titled – *Shri̲madbhagabadgita̲*, parts of which were published in his journal *Pracha̲r*, between 1886 and 1888. The rest of the book remained as manuscript, until it was posthumously published in 1902. An English translation was, however, published only in 2001, edited with an introduction by Hans Harder. But even this book contains his commentary only on the first three chapters of the Gita and a half of the fourth chapter. Harder attributes this to Bankimchandra's heavy preoccupations including other literary works, but Gowda feels that perhaps Bankim felt satisfied that his another work *Dharmatattva* did justice to the remaining parts of the Gita and kept aside the former work unfinished.

Bankim believed in the historicity of the Mahabharata and tried to demonstrate it scientifically. It implies that he also believed in the historicity of the Gita, though he did not try to separately prove it. He also firmly believed that Krishna was a historic person, an ideal man and an *avatar*, but he admitted that the depiction of his story suffered in the hands of later romancers. Bankim argued that Krishna not only preached but also *acted* to actually establish dharma and eliminate *adharma* as claimed in the Gita. Bankim gave a fresh meaning to the term, *dharma*, by describing it as humanism, involving the culturing of human beings and their faculties – physical, mental, executive and aesthetic – to the fullest possible extent. He believed that both bhakti-yoga and karma-yoga are needed in realising this full potential, but bhakti involves not merely unwavering devotion to God, but also incessant love and benevolence towards the distressed, backed by appropriate action like selfless social service (Gowda 2011: 26–27). This is where Bankim's nationalist cause becomes relevant. In his view, the dismal state of the country then was due to ignoring this basic teaching of Krishna about engaging in karma combined with bhakti in the cause of people and their welfare as one's duty (Gowda 2011: 27). This is where Krishna's concept of *swadharma* becomes relevant.

Bankim argues that just as karma does not mean sacrifices and mere rituals as per the Gita, its concept of *swadharma* does not just mean following caste- or *varna*-assigned duties. The concept is based on equality, not inequality. Following *swadharma* on the contrary means following the process of realising one's fullest human potential according to one's aptitude, even if it means going outside one's *varna*. It may have a specific context as when one has to do one's duty as required by circumstances, but selflessly, without prejudice to the overall goal of achieving people's welfare or *loka-hita*, a term used by the Gita itself. Selfless service, or *nishkama karma*, is worship of God, and as the Gita says, it has to be done with dedication and also efficiency. But it is not purposeless and has to be directed at achieving certain defined goals. In that sense, it is not desireless. Non-attachment similarly does not mean lack of dedication, and even a certain amount of passion may be needed in dedication. Non-attachment emphasised by the Gita means only avoiding selfishness (Gowda 2011: 28–35).

Regarding nonviolence and violence, Bankim takes the stand that the Gita teaches nonviolence as an ultimate value and condemns violence when it is not according to or required by dharma. But sometimes, adhering to nonviolence in specific or special circumstances may vitiate against achieving overall nonviolence, or limited acceptance of violence in special cases may prevent overall or larger violence. In the act of self-protection, resort to violence may sometimes be required. Defending oneself or one's property and livelihood against aggression or oppression is neither selfishness nor violence; it is dharma or *dharma-yuddha*. This complexity is recognised and appreciated by the Gita, according to Bankim.

Regarding idol worship, in Bankim's view, the material objects of worship are irrelevant for the Gita; a true devotee, even if he starts with idol worship, has to transcend it soon and has to conceptualise the Supreme, which is beyond all forms. He thinks that the Gita is basically monotheistic, and polytheism such as there in practice is only secondary, a mere aid to a variety of people to access God. The Gita is not fanatical about it and reconciles different forms of worship with the One Supreme. He did not consider idol worship as an essential part of Hinduism. Thus, Bankim takes a sympathetic, to some extent a condescending, view of idol worship, but does not go the extreme of rejecting it as was done by Rammohan and his Brahmo Samaj.

In his essay on Bankim, Gowda says that Bankim felt troubled by the 'debilitating passivity of India in thought and action, a kind of sentimental paralysis that made Arjuna drop his famed Gandiva [bow] in the battlefield' (Gowda 2011: 45). He took it as a metaphor for the condition that India was in then. But Bankim did not take the metaphor too far and did not suggest taking up arms against the British for a freedom struggle. His call to Indians was only to realise the social and political realities in the country, and to appropriately respond to them, and to 'remember that love for one's country is the highest dharma and ranks above all else' (quoted in Gowda 2011: 45).

Theosophical Society and Annie Besant

Bankim's contribution soon complemented and further developed by the Theosophical Society and its movement, which did a lot by giving a new allegorical interpretation of the Gita both through its Indian and through Western followers. It was officially formed in New York City of the United States in 1875 by Helena Petrovna Blavatsky, Henry Steel Olcott, William Quan Judge and others.[3] Olcott became the first president and remained so until his demise in 1907. The theosophical movement had started even earlier in the United States and India, with several followers among intellectuals. Olcott and Blavatsky moved to India and established the international headquarters of the Society in Adyar at Madras (now, Chennai) in 1882, which became quite active with significant Indian following. Neufeldt has presented in some detail the contribution of theosophists, both Indian and Western, to the interpretation and modern understanding of the Gita (1991: 11–33). A few highlights of this contribution are briefly given later.

A pioneer among these theosophists was an Indian, Subba Row, who gave four lectures at the annual convention of the society at Adyar in 1886, published in 1888 as a book, *The Philosophy of the Bhagavad Gita*, republished later in 1921. For Row, the Gita is a practical guide for man in the evolutionary path towards realising the essential immortality. He adopts a fourfold classification of cosmic principles, *Parabrahman* being the first cause, eternal and omnipresent. From this springs *Logos*, which is individualised or personalised principle of the first or ego of the cosmos. It is represented by Krishna, an instance of the *Logos* descending to the human plane for the benefit of humanity. *M<u>u</u>laprakriti* is the veil over *Parabrahman*, its material manifestation in the cosmos. *Daiviprakriti* is the light of the Logos, acting on the *M<u>u</u>laprakriti*, and everything that occurs in the cosmos owes to this process. Arjuna represents the human monad in the process of evolution, struggling through conflicts and confusions. There is no loss of individuality at the end of the evolution; there is only eternal bliss and no re-entry into the cycles of rebirth and death.

The next Indian theosophist was Mohini M. Chatterjee, who gave both a translation and a commentary of the Gita in *The Bhagavad Gita or The Lord's Lay*. The date of its first publication is not known, but an edition of this was current by 1888, which may have come out earlier. Arjuna's predicament is described by Chatterjee as follows: 'Whenever a man loses faith, these three evils, grief, fears, and weakness, attach him, and he begins to delude himself into the belief that it is fruitless to persevere on the upward path' (Chatterji 1960: 26; as quoted by Neufeldt 1991: 16). The concern of the Gita is to help man to overcome these internal weaknesses. An interesting feature of Chatterjee's work is its frequent referring to the Bible, particularly the New Testament, trying to bring out parallels and commonalities in ethical content between the two sacred books.

A further work comes from A Brahmin, F.T.S., based on a series of lectures at the Kumbhakonam branch of the Theosophical Society, published in 1893 under the title, *Thoughts on the Bhagavad Gita*. According to it, the Mahabharata symbolises the battle between divine and gross elements, or what takes place between higher and lower selves. The exhortation to fight does not mean an injunction to literally kill people, but to fight in the cause of justice in a spirit of renunciation and perform duties consistent with human evolution to a higher plane. The emphasis on sacrificial action means an obligation to work for others to relieve their grief.

A few studies came thereafter by Rajendra Lal Mukerji, published under the pseudonym, Dreamer, between 1902 and 1904. He considers the Gita as a timeless guide on the path of non-attachment, service, love and sacrifice, and says, 'the Ego's progress . . . lies in recognising itself as merely an aspect of the Divine energy instead of being a separate centre by itself' (quoted by Neufeldt 1991: 22). Following *swadharma* means in the Gita following the most efficient lines appropriate for individual development. *Avatar* appears when conflicts grow so much as to threaten the evolutionary progress, which then restores the equilibrium.

According to the interpretation by Pandit Bhavani Shankar, as given in his lectures between 1914 and 1925 (published in 1966), Advaitins are wrong because they reject individuality while Krishna teaches the perfection of individuality. He advises activity which leads to progress, not passivity. Individuality, however, is not rejected by Advaita at the *vyavaharika* (practical) level, and thus there is no question of requiring individuals to be passive as a part of spiritual pursuit, as has already been clarified earlier.

Among the Western theosophists, Neufeldt first takes up William Q. Judge, an American, who interpreted the Gita through a series of essays in the last quarter of the nineteenth century, published together much later in 1969 along with a recension. Judge felt that focusing on the Gita as historical material, as Western scholars do, overlooks the Hindu psychological system underlying the work (Judge 1969: 108; Neufeldt 1991: 23). The Kurus represent the material side of existence, while the Pandus represent the spiritual. The blindness of Dhritarashtra, the father of Kurus, 'represents the fact that the material body has no inherent power of sight or feeling; rather, it is the Self which is the final support of every phase of consciousness and form' (Judge: 112–14; Neufeldt: 23). Arjuna represents the human being standing at the threshold of higher development. The battle is between the material and spiritual forces in every individual, and the battle is necessary for evolutionary progress. According to Judge, 'The Bhagavad-Gita tends to impress upon the individual two things: first selflessness, and second, action' (Judge: ix; Neufeldt: 24).

With Annie Besant[4] (1847–1933), we move into an active and accelerating phase of renaissance in India and Hinduism. She is the most well known of theosophists at least in India and an outstanding figure in quite a few ways. Born in England, the country of India's rulers then, she came to India in 1893 as a theosophist in search of truth and soon adopted the country as her own as if she was born into it. As Neufeldt observes, 'while she was a Westerner, she identified thoroughly with India and Indian causes' (1991: 25). After her entry into Indian politics in 1913, she started mobilising Indians to fight for what she called home rule or self-rule and freedom from the British. She was the president of the Indian National Congress in 1917 and was interned by the British government for three months in the same year for her political activities. More than her political role, her contribution to Hinduism and its renaissance – which started even much earlier – has been immense and enduring, no less significant than that of others born as Hindus. She wrote more than 200 books and pamphlets, including particularly on Hinduism, Buddhism, Jainism, psychology, yoga, and social problems such as women's issues. Through her writings, she tried to make Indians aware of their glorious spiritual heritage and goaded them to rise above their present status and conditions. She was an excellent orator and travelled through the length and breadth of India for the purpose. She also campaigned for women's rights and for spreading education including higher education for all. She founded the Central Hindu School and College at Varanasi (Benares, as the British called it) in 1898, which later became the nucleus of Benares Hindu University. She also started two colleges in the south, one at Madanapalle (Andhra Pradesh) and another at Adyar. She became the second president of the Theosophical Society in 1907 after Colonel Olcott and developed the headquarters of the Society at Adyar. The society played an important role through its many publications and branches spread in various parts of India, in promoting a philosophical and cultural understanding of Hinduism in non-sectarian and non-ritualistic ways, suitable to modern times. Mrs Besant was the main inspiration behind these activities.

Mrs Besant had joined the Theosophical Society in 1889, after her disillusionment with free or secular thinking in which she had played an active role. She was close to Madame Blavatsky, who had pioneered the theosophical movement. Mrs Besant helped the theosophical movement to spread in England. Gandhi when in England was introduced to them by friends who were in this movement. He informs in his autobiography that it was these friends who had introduced him to the Gita first – to Arnold's *The Song Celestial*. Gandhi also read Madame Blavatsky's *Key to Theosophy* (1889), which stimulated him to take more interest in Hinduism. Theosophists thus played a crucial role in Gandhi's life and the development of his thoughts.

Annie Besant has the distinction of first interpreting and applying the Gita explicitly as a weapon in India's freedom struggle, before others like Tilak and Aurobindo did it. Her book in which she did it, *The Bhagavad Gita or the Lord's Song*, was first published in 1907, based on her lectures at Adyar in 1905. It played a pioneering role in the nationalist discourse on the Gita and gave a fillip to India's freedom struggle. Though Bankim was aware of this potential of the Gita and also had hinted at it earlier, he was not so explicit and forceful in this task. Mrs Besant 'used her allegorical reading of the text [of the Gita] in the service of her political commitment constructing an ingenious parallel between the Mahabharata war and the Indian freedom struggle' (Sinha: 312). The war in the Mahabharata became a struggle by Arjuna 'to destroy a usurper who was oppressing the land; it was his duty as prince, as warrior, to fight for the deliverance of his nation and restore order and peace' (Besant 1907: iv; Sinha: 312–13). For Mrs Besant, action is the central teaching of the Gita – action with optimism, skill and sacrifice (Neufeldt: 27). In addition to the special significance of the Gita as a source of inspiration for India's freedom struggle, theosophists, including Mrs Besant, acknowledged its universal spiritual significance as relevant to all humanity. For her, the Gita was 'not a Hindu text, nor even an Indian text, but a universal text' (Neufeldt: 25). Viewed thus, as Sinha observes, 'the Gita became a central text of Theosophy and through its intercession the Gita could reach a transnational, transcultural audience, acquiring new, spectacularly effective, forms and meanings in the West as well as in India' (2010: 313). Interestingly, an allegorical interpretation of the Gita is common to all theosophists, and they deliberately did not look upon it as a mere historical material. All human beings are in the place of Arjuna on the evolutionary path to spiritual progress, and as Subba Row put it, 'We are each of us called upon to kill out all our passions and desires . . . [and] establish ourselves on the higher planes' (Row 1934: 4; Neufeldt: 32). It was the genius of Mrs Besant that she successfully built a bridge between the universal significance of the Gita and its application to the specific situation of India's freedom struggle. Just as individuals, nations too are on the evolutionary path of moral and spiritual development, and she found the teaching of the Gita pertinent to them too.

Bal Gangadhar Tilak

Bal Gangadhar Tilak[5] (1856–1920) dominated the Indian political and intellectual scene like a titan before the entry of Gandhi. Around his time, two groups were identified among nationalists, the 'moderates' and the 'extremists'. The former, like Gopal Krishna Gokhale, were content with greater autonomy within the British Empire, and focused more on social reforms, educational and economic progress, addressing illiteracy and poverty rather than full political freedom. On the other hand, the first and immediate priority of the 'extremists' was on attaining swaraj or full freedom from the British. Tilak was a prominent leader of this latter group. He is famous for his public assertion in 1908 for the first time: 'Swaraj is my birth right and I shall have it.' Though at times, he also used the term 'home rule', he meant by it only swaraj or full independence. Tilak wanted the social reforms to be introduced and implemented by the Indians themselves through their own government rather than by the British. This stand of his was sometimes misunderstood as when he opposed the Age of Consent Bill (1891) aimed at ending child marriages. He got his own daughters married much above the minimum age envisaged in the Bill, showing that he was not opposed to the reforms as such but only to their being introduced by a government which was not responsible to the people as in a democracy.

Tilak was already established as a popular journalist by the age of 25, when he owned and edited two weeklies, one in Marathi, called *Kesari*, and the other in English, called *Mahratta*. Both were openly nationalistic and aimed at spreading awareness about the need to secure independence from the British rule. Tilak was imprisoned twice, and both times, it had a connection with the Gita (Agarwal 1993: 102–13). The first time was in 1897, when in a public speech, taking support of the Gita, he had defended the killing of Mughal General Afzal Khan by Shivaji. Tilak argued that Afzal Khan had invaded upon Shivaji's land and people, and the killing was not in his personal interest as such but for getting rid of an aggressor in the interest of the society. It was, therefore, moral according to the Gita, argued Tilak. A few days later after this speech, one Chapekar shot dead a British officer, Rand, who had become notorious because of his insensitive and oppressive handling of anti-plague measures. He was so dreaded that people felt that plague was better than Rand! The British government assumed that Chapekar was incited by Tilak's speech, though they could not establish any link between the two. Chapekar was hanged, and Tilak was sentenced for eighteen months in jail. Thanks to the intervention of Max Müller and others in England who appealed to the Queen, Tilak was released six months before the completion of his jail term.

The second imprisonment of Tilak was ordered in 1908 in the wake of the partition of Bengal by Lord Curzon, announced in 1905 on the grounds of administrative efficiency. It became extremely unpopular with Indians, and strong agitations against it were launched in various parts of the country. Tilak supported this agitation and called for non-cooperation with the government, and for Swadeshi, that is, boycott of British goods and British education and replacing it by national institutions of education (Agarwal 1993: 109). He reiterated his demand for full independence. It was in this context that Tilak asserted for the first time at Akola in 1908 that Swaraj was his birthright and he would have it. Interestingly, Tilak's weapons of non-cooperation and Swadeshi were to be later used by Gandhi also. But what actually occasioned Tilak's imprisonment in 1908 again was the incident in Muzaffarpur involving Khudiram Bose. Bose threw a bomb at a carriage which he thought was occupied by the chief presidency magistrate who had earlier got some young men flogged for a minor offence. The bomb killed a British woman and her daughter instead. Bose was caught and hanged. Though no connection of Tilak with this incident could be established, he was charged with sedition particularly for two of his editorials in his popular Marathi daily, *Kesari*. Tilak pleaded his own case eloquently and said that as an editor it was his duty to speak his mind on topical issues without fear of reprisal. Wolpert saw in his defence an echo of *swadharma* doctrine of the Gita (Agarwal 1993: 111). The jury found Tilak guilty, and he was sentenced for six years in Mandalay jail. But the connection between Tilak's second imprisonment and the Gita was of a different nature. It was in Mandalay jail that he wrote his *Gita Rahasya* ('The Esoteric Import of the Gita') in Marathi in less than five months from 2 November 1910 to 30 March 1911. As Desai observes, 'Tilak wrote what is the first complete modern treatise on the Gita written by a political activist who was also a Sanskrit scholar' (2014: 19).

Tilak had been thinking of the Gita for several years already and had given a few lectures on it earlier in 1902 at Nagpur, but his active journalistic and political work had not given him the needed time to write in detail his thoughts on the Gita. The jail sentence made it possible now. He titled his work as *Shri Bhagavadgita Rahasya athava Karmayoga-shastra*. In the first volume of this work, Tilak provides a holistic and general account of the Gita in terms of his perspective in fifteen chapters, followed by scholarly appendices and indexes. One of the indexes is on the words used in the Gita, which can be very useful to scholars working on the Gita. The first volume constitutes the main contribution of Tilak's *Gita Rahasya*. The second volume contains original Sanskrit verses of the Gita and their translation. As Stevenson observes, 'Tilak's *Gita Rahasya* is very much a combination of the "traditional Indian" and "modern scholarship"' (1991: 49). Tilak's book in Marathi was published in two volumes first in 1915 at Poona and was translated soon in other Indian languages. Hindi and Gujarati translations came out within two years in 1917; Kannada, Tamil and Telugu in 1919; Bengali in 1924 and English in 1935–36. It has gone into many reprints thereafter in all these languages. It turned out to be the most popular work on the Gita before India's independence.

Tilak starts by explaining in his preface why he wrote the book. He was exposed to the Gita since childhood, but was troubled by a doubt as to why the Gita should contain detailed exposition of how to obtain the release (*moksha*) through the path of knowledge (*jna̲na*) and devotion (*bhakti*), when the main issue was how to induce Arjuna to fight in the war. So he tried to study the Gita independent of all commentaries such as by Shankara and probe what the original Gita taught. He came to the conclusion that the original Gita did not teach the philosophy of renunciation (*Nivritti*), but taught energism (karma-yoga) instead, and where the term 'yoga' was used, it meant only karma-yoga. Though Tilak admits that the Gita also taught about how to obtain release through *jna̲na* and *bhakti*, he asserts that it is not its principal subject matter. The Gita basically propounds the way of ultimately obtaining release by performing action without incurring sin. The earlier commentators missed this point because they had a preconceived doctrine to propound by using the Gita. Though Tilak follows Shankara in matters like the concept of Brahman, he rejects Shankara's prescription of jna̲na (knowledge) through renunciation as the only means to liberation. The Gita does not preach renunciation of the world, but only of the desire for fruits of action for oneself. According to Tilak, the Gita is openly emphatic about karma-yoga, which stares in the face of anyone who approaches the Gita with an open mind. He feels that the Gita is essentially about ethics, ethics of action, and the question of ethics arises when one acts or decides to act or not to act. Often we face a deadlock arising from mutually conflicting principles resulting in confusion, but the Gita shows a way out of this deadlock and confusion. We cannot prevent ethical problems from emerging by deciding not to act. Avoiding action is not an option according to the Gita, because, willy-nilly, we are ever engaged in some action or the other as long as we are in this world alive. But we have the option of making our action meaningful, moral and liberating, by making it unselfish and aimed at the welfare of the world (*loka-sangraha*, as said in the Gita), carried out in a spirit of non-attachment and without any desire for personal appropriation of the fruits of action.

Tilak says that according to the Gita, even a realised *jnanin* (one who has attained knowledge) like Janaka did not give up worldly life. A person who seeks only a personal release or *moksha* for oneself alone is selfish and destructive of the society. Therefore, even sannyasis should be engaged in action for the welfare of the society at large, and this is the clear message of the Gita. As for bhakti, according to Tilak, it is recommended by the Gita only as an easier option to attaining jnana or knowledge of the Brahman, whatever be the form of devotional worship. True bhakti leads invariably to the knowledge of the Brahman. If a jnanin cannot avoid action, a bhakta too cannot and has to be engaged in action in the world as a form of worship to God. A bhakta offers the fruit of his action at the feet of the Lord as his tribute. Work done as service to God is also a form of devotion. Thus, even jnana and bhakti are consistent with and help karma-yoga, but cannot be substitutes to it. They are actually subservient to karma-yoga as preached in the Gita (Tilak 1936: xxv).

The ideal person according to the Gita, in Tilak's view, is a *sthitaprajna* ('mentally steady and balanced'), who is not only unattached, even-minded, egoless, calm and cool, but also actively engaged in the welfare of the world without any selfish motive. Such a person is sinless, and karma does not attach him. In the course of being engaged in action, such a person honestly follows the principles of non-violence, truth, non-stealing and justice. But in the course of being so engaged, if exceptions are made at times, entirely in the interest of people or society or welfare of the world, then sin does not attach such a person. This is a teaching of the Gita, in Tilak's view. This is how Tilak defended Shivaji's killing of Afzal Khan. Stevenson observes in this context that 'It is disturbing for ethical theory for it asserts that some men are above the law' (Stevenson 1991: 58). These exceptions are particularly disturbing if we take note of the fact that Tilak wanted the leaders of a nation to have the qualities of a *sthitaprajna*. He desired that leadership of a country should be in the hands of such ideal persons or moral elite. By providing exceptions to them, Tilak could not have meant that leaders can be corrupt and opportunistic on the excuse of acting in national interests. Even a genuinely honest leader may at times commit a mistake or impropriety as judged by others, but in good faith. However, Tilak's ethics, at least as he meant, can be dubbed neither as ethical relativism, nor as moral hypocrisy. Exceptions to moral principles are subject to severe controls and cannot be indulged in by all sorts of people for all sorts of reasons in all sorts of circumstances. Even Gandhi who had absolute faith in truth and non-violence conceded exceptions to them under severe controls, and even common law recognises them. Otherwise, life would be impossible. Absolute non-violence is an impossibility. Even a single step of walk upon this earth involves killing countless germs or life forms. In the cases of a conscious act, law recognises that killing a person in self-defence in the face of a murderous assault cannot be considered as murder. A soldier killing enemies in a legally declared war and according to norms of just war cannot also be accused of murder. Though in principle Tilak was not against using violence as the last resort against cruelty and oppression, at no time he advocated it as the preferred path in the freedom struggle. He proposed instead *swadeshi* and non-cooperation as weapons for it. Ruling out violence altogether and absolutely would in Tilak's view eliminate in the oppressor's mind any fear of reprisal by the oppressed and could encourage tyranny. Gandhi was on the other hand totally opposed to the use of violence in the freedom struggle, but used the legacy of Tilak's peaceful methods of swadeshi and non-cooperation.

Tilak was not the first to declare a socially oriented karma-yoga as the central message of the Gita. Perhaps that credit goes to his younger contemporary, Swami Vivekananda. The young Swami had become quite well known by the end of the nineteenth century, well before Tilak's writing down his own treatise on the Gita. But Tilak was probably the first to do so in a rigorous, scholarly, and systematic way. Anyhow, Tilak's activist reading of the Gita contributed to energising the whole country and gave a further momentum to the freedom struggle. It helped Gandhi too to take the country further ahead towards India's independence. Tilak can be said to have prepared the ground for Gandhi in more than one way. Tilak's *Gita Rahasya* also influenced many subsequent commentators of the Gita including the contemporary, in giving more importance to karma-yoga in the form of social service. Social service got a boost as a result. In the discussions on the relative merits of alternative paths of God realisation or means of *moksha*, the balance was now irreversibly tipped in favour of socially engaged karma-yoga as never before. The *Gita Rahasya* played an important role in this.

Swami Vivekananda

Swami Vivekananda[6] (1863–1902) was born seven years later, but died eighteen years earlier than Tilak. But the Swami accomplished a great deal in less than forty years of his short life and left a long-lasting impact on India and Hinduism, which is cherished even today. Born in a highly cultured Bengali Kshatriya family, Narendranath Dutt (Naren, for short, the Swami's earlier name before *sannyas*) had a good Western-type education in Scottish Presbyterian College at Calcutta. Even while in the college, he had come under the magnetic influence of Shri Ramakrishna Paramahamsa. He asked Ramakrishna a straight question, 'Sir, have you seen God?' And Ramakrishna also gave an equally straight answer, 'Yes, my son, I have, just as I see you before me, only much more intensely.' He went on, 'God can be realised. One can see and talk to Him as I am seeing and talking to you. But who cares?' The sincerity of his reply left Naren tremendously impressed (Disciples 1989, Vol. I: 77). The association between the two became closer and profound, and Naren even began to experience spiritual trances. As French says, 'The combination of paths which the Gita speaks seems to have been experienced personally by the young Vivekananda, as his relationship with Ramakrishna unfolded' (1991: 132).

It was not just the spirituality of Ramakrishna which Vivekananda imbibed, but also his deep compassion for humanity. Once when Vivekananda implored Ramakrishna to show the way to *nirvikalpa samadhi*, the state of ultimate release and bliss, the latter rebuked him. 'Shame on you!' he said, 'I never thought you to be so mean as to be anxious for your own salvation only, whereas you have the powers to do so much good to mankind' (French 1991: 144). It influenced Vivekananda to make his monastic order to be responsive to the needs of the society, particularly of the poor and downtrodden. After Ramakrishna shed his earthly body in 1886, his disciples got together to establish the Ramakrishna Math and start the Ramakrishna Mission with the aim of carrying forward the ideals and philosophy of Shri Ramakrishna. Both the math and the mission have since grown worldwide with many branches or centres, doing exemplary work in health care, education, famine and disaster relief, and providing homes, besides disseminating basics of Indian culture and philosophy. In this philosophy, an activist compassion for humanity is an intrinsic part of spiritualism. Vivekananda's interpretation of the Gita was a reflection of this philosophy.

Vivekananda did not write any systematic treatise or a commentary with the translation of the Gita as many others did, for he had no time for it. But many of his lectures and discussions are replete with references to the Gita. He gave a discourse particularly on the Gita in Bengali at Calcutta in 1897 (*Thoughts on the Gita*, CWSV 1998, Vol. IV: 102–10), and three lectures at San Francisco in 1900 (*The Gita I, II, and III*, CWSV 2000, Vol. I: 446–80). Further, his lectures on karma-yoga (CWSV 2000: 25–118), bhakti-yoga (CWSV 2001, Vol. III: 31–100; CWSV 1998, Vol. IV: 3–60), jnana-yoga (CWSV 1999, Vol. II: 57–288) and other topics draw significantly from the Gita. He was leaned in most of the scriptures, but had a special fascination for the Gita. Referring to it, he said, 'no better commentary on the Vedas has been written or can be written'; 'that wonderful poem, without one note in it of weakness or unmanliness' (Disciples 1989, Vol. II: 203, 361).

For Swami Vivekananda, the historicity of the Gita or of its characters was not a pertinent issue. It was composed at a time when no importance was given in India to assigning dates and authorship. What is pertinent in the Gita for all time is its teaching, not history. The universal value of the Gita hardly depends on its history, he felt. Citing a parable of his guru, he said that if you go to a mango garden full of luscious fruits hanging down the trees, you should savour the mangoes, rather than waste time in counting the leaves and branches or estimating the age of the trees. Nevertheless, the Swami agreed that historical research may be useful in identifying unnecessary accretions to the texts, which distort the basic teaching. But he considered the Gita an intrinsic part of the Mahabharata, taking into account the similarity both in the teachings and in the style, and not as an interpolation (Gowda 2011: 94–98).

Swami Vivekananda thought that the teaching of the Gita was most pertinent in achieving the main task before him. Awakening national consciousness among Indians and making them sensitive to the appalling poverty and backwardness of the masses constituted his main task. This is reflected often in many of his lectures and letters. He asked whether there is any reason why India should lie in the ebb-tide of the nations of the world. 'Is she inferior in intellect? Is she inferior in dexterity? Can you look at her art, at her mathematics, at her philosophy, and answer "yes"? All that is needed is that she should de-hypnotise herself and wake up from her age-long sleep to take her true rank in the hierarchy of nations' (CWSV 1997, Vol. V: 227). In this task, he found two verses of the Gita in which Krishna exhorted Arjuna as not only very pertinent, but also constituting its central message to India, placing India in the position of Arjuna. When Arjuna cast away his bow and arrows, and sank down in the seat of his chariot, distressed and full of tears, Krishna addressed him thus in two most powerful verses (The Gita II.2–3):

> *Kutastva kashmalam idam vishame samupasthitam /*
> *Anaryajushtam asvargyam akirtikaram Arjuna //*
> *Klaibyam maasma gamah Partha naitad tvaiyupapadyate /*
> *Kshudram hridaya-daurbalyam tyakvotthista Parantapa //*

> ('In such a strait, whence comes upon thee, O Arjuna, this dejection, un-Aryan-like, disgraceful, and contrary to the attainment of heaven? // Yield not to unmanliness, O son of Pritha! Ill doth it become thee. Cast off this mean faint-heartedness and arise, O scorcher of thine enemies!'
> – Tr. by Swami Vivekananda, CWSV 1998, Vol. IV: 107–8)

The Swami says, 'If one reads this one Shloka – *Klaibyam . . . Parantapa* – one gets all the merits of reading the entire Gita; for in this one Shloka lies imbedded the whole Message of the Gita' (CWSV 1998: 110). What he meant was that India should arise and fight poverty, ignorance and other such weaknesses among its masses. He observed, 'The one thing that is at the root of all evils in India is the condition of the poor. . . . The only service to be done for our lower classes is to give them education, *to develop their lost individuality*. . . . Every nation, every man, and every woman must work out their own salvation' (CWSV 1998: 362). He put great emphasis on educating the poor, and said, 'If the poor boy [or girl] cannot come to education, education must go to him [or her]' (CWSV 1998: 363). He advised volunteers, including sadhus and sannyasis, to go from village to village or even door to door and provide education, where there were no schools, or where poor children were not attending schools. He deplored the practice of child marriage and advocated providing proper education along with character building both to boys and girls. He ridiculed orthodox religious leaders who opposed the Age of Consent Bill raising the age of marriage and asked them whether religion consisted in making a girl become a mother at the age of twelve or thirteen (CWSV 1997, Vol. V: 341–42). But he did not favour preaching religion to the poor before their problems of hunger and constant anxiety about bare existence are solved (CWSV 1997: 380).

Now, such a social service to the poor and needy should be provided without ego, arrogance and any selfish motive. And that is where the

Gita's *nishkama-karma* (desire-free or selfless work) becomes relevant for the Swami. His preference for karma-marga over jnana and bhakti comes out clear and loud. He said, 'If you want any good to come, just throw your ceremonials overboard and worship the Living God, the Man-God – every being that wears a human form' (French 1991: 143). Further, 'You think Jnana is dry knowledge to be attained by a desert path, killing out tenderest faculties of the heart. Your Bhakti is sentimental nonsense which makes one impotent. . . . Who cares for your Bhakti and Mukti? . . . I will go to hell cheerfully a thousand times, if I can rouse my countrymen, immersed in *Tamas* [darkness, lethargy], and make them stand on their feet and be Men, inspired with the spirit of Karma-yoga' (French 1991: 144). The Swami did not, however, altogether cast aside the other paths taught in the Gita, so long as the importance of karma-yoga is not undermined. In a sense, he saw no conflict, since karma-yoga can be made more effective by combining it with knowledge and devotion. In fact, he gave several lectures both in India and abroad on the other paths taught in the Gita also, but he firmly believed that India's destiny lies in following karma-yoga, whatever may be the value attached to other paths by individuals for their personal spiritual progress.

According to the Swami, a karma-yogi should resist any temptation to choose only work of 'higher' status and avoid 'lower'. Each is great in his own place, he declares, and advises that each should respect his or her own work, for no work is inferior. One should never despise or hate oneself (CWSV 2000, Vol. I: 36–51). *Swadharma* in the Gita does not necessarily mean caste-duty. In the course of our life, we have to perform different roles with corresponding duties, that of a student, teacher, parent, husband, wife, a soldier, a judge, a doctor, a sanitary worker and so on, which fall to our lot sometimes by choice and sometimes without. But, 'Duty of any kind is not to be slighted. A man who does the lower work is not for that reason only, a lower man than he who does higher work; a man should not be judged by the nature of his duties, but by the manner in which he does them' (CWSV 1997, Vol. 5: 241).

An important characteristic of karma-yoga, which the Swami stressed, is that it is not for the elite alone, but meant for everyone irrespective of the level of education and wealth. It is an equaliser. Karma-yoga, in the sense in which the Swami meant (and not in the sense of rituals), does not need any priest as an intermediary between the individual and God. The Swami rejected caste and other hierarchies, and underlined the egalitarianism of the Gita, by pointing out to verses 27 and 28 in its Chapter 13, which said: 'He who sees the Supreme Lord dwelling equally in all beings, the Imperishable in things that perish, he sees verily. For seeing the Lord as the same everywhere present, he does not destroy the Self by the Self, and thus he goes to the highest goal' (Gowda 2011: 93). Realisation of the Supreme is open to all, and one can achieve this through dedicating one's work and fruit thereof to the Supreme with a pure mind, sincerity and skill. And this is the secret of karma-yoga, according to the Gita.

The manner in which we perform our work shapes our character. The Swami says:

> Karma in its effect on character is the most tremendous power that man has to deal with. Man is, as it were, a centre, and is attracting all the powers of the universe towards himself, and in this centre is fusing them all and again sending them off in a big current. Such a centre is the *real* man. . . . Good and bad, misery and happiness, all are running towards him and clinging around him; and out of them he fashions the mighty stream of tendency called character and throws it outwards. As he has the power of drawing in anything, so has he the power of throwing it out.
>
> (CWSV 2000, Vol. I: 29–30)

A karma-yogi cannot be flippant and should not fritter away his or her energies. The Swami reminds that according to the Gita, yoga is doing work with skill and cleverness. He says, 'by knowing how to work, one can obtain the greatest results. You must remember that all work is simply to bring out the power of the mind which is already there, to wake up the soul. The power is inside every man, so is knowing; the different works are like blows to bring them out, to cause these giants to wake up' (CWSV 2000: 31). This is how karma-yoga helps spiritual development. A karma-yogi, explains the Swami, can find serenity and peace of mind amid most intense activity; stress or tension does not affect his soul. The key to success of karma-yoga as a spiritual discipline lies in introspecting over the motive of our work and keeping it pure and noble (CWSV 2000: 31–35).

The secret of success in karma-yoga lies in working through love according to the Swami. Referring to a verse in the Gita (III.22), he quotes Krishna: 'Look at Me, Arjuna! If I stop working for one moment, the whole universe will die. I have nothing to gain from work; I am the one Lord, but why do I work? Because I love the world.' His teaching is work like a master, not as a slave; work with a sense of freedom. Selfish work, work without love, is slave's work, the Swami explains. Working with love brings its own happiness, which is a reward in itself (CWSV 2000: 57–58). He clarifies further that working merely with a sense of duty is not enough, because even a slave may do that. It brings no joy. The Gita stresses due performance of one's duties without attachment for the sake of society's welfare. But unless one begins to take pride in one's duty skilfully done and with love, it may not be effective and will not bring happiness either to the individual or to the society. That is why good work is possible only in an environment of freedom, not compulsion, nor slavery. Inculcating a sound work ethic is crucial to the character building of an individual and also to what the Gita calls *loka-sangraha*, or people's welfare or nation building. He wanted a modern India, strong and self-confident, freed from poverty and squalor, built on the foundation of a work ethic provided by the philosophy of karma-yoga. Developing such a work ethic has been the most important contribution of Swami Vivekananda, which energised the whole country as well as Hinduism and continues to do so.

Lala Lajpat Rai

Lala Lajpat Rai (1865–1928) was one of the three prominent members of the Indian National Congress, before its domination by Gandhi, bracketed as Lal-Bal-Pal. Like the other two, Lajpat Rai also demanded full freedom, and not just autonomy under British supremacy. He studied law at Government College, Lahore. He became a follower of Swami Dayananda Saraswati, the founder of Arya Samaj. He was known as Punjab Kesari, or the Lion of the Punjab, for his bravery in leading the struggles in national cause. He too found Lord Krishna and his Gita a great source of inspiration and motivation in his movement. Like many educated Indians, Rai also found the Puranic Krishna problematic. The *Puranas* had shown him as a seductive lad, indulging even with married milkmaids' amorous games and dances. Jayadeva's *Gitagovindam*, though acknowledged as great in literary and lyrical qualities and a favourite work with professional classical singers and dancers, was particularly a source of headache for those who wanted to depict Krishna only as a great teacher and a yogi. Rai felt that these devotional poets 'have so pierced him with the arrows of their petty and vulgar imaginations that his personality has totally changed'. Like Bankim, Rai tried to probe into the true historical Krishna, stripped of his romantic image created by Puranas and other later works, and in this attempt published *Yogiraj Shri Krishna* in 1900 (Davis 2015: 121).[7]

According to Rai, Krishna was a warrior and a ruler during the early Vedic period and took part in the great Mahabharata war as a friend of Arjuna and presented his teachings to the latter, which formed the core message of the Gita. Rai describes Krishna as 'a great teacher, a great warrior, and a man of great learning' (quoted in Davis 2015: 121). In his view, later additions turned Krishna into a divine incarnation, and still later accounts created his romantic image during his childhood and teenage years. However, Rai believes that Krishna was indeed a 'model human being', living a life as taught in the Gita. This meant that the Gita represented a lived experience of its teacher and held valuable lessons relevant to the Indian youth of Rai's time and beyond. 'What Lajpat Rai has in mind is that Indian youths should commit themselves to opposing British colonial rule, even if that involves risking their lives – as he did' (Davis 2015: 124).

Lajpat Rai was leading widespread peasant's agitations in the Punjab and was therefore deported without even a trial to Mandalay in Burma in May 1907. But Lord Minto decided that there was not enough evidence against Rai, and he was thus allowed to return in November the same year. During his incarceration, much like Tilak (who wrote his *Gita Rahasya* later, also from Mandalay), Lajpat Rai wrote a lengthy article on 'Message of the *Bhagavad Gita*', published later in *Modern Review*.[8] According to his interpretation, the primary purpose of the Gita was to persuade Arjuna to fight, all else – discussions on jnana, bhakti and so on – being secondary. 'Dharma or duty should be the supreme law of one's life, and once one recognises that duty, no consideration of self-interest, love, or mercy should distract one from it. As such, Krishna above all advocates the path of karma-yoga' (as summarised in Davis 2015: 125). Rai found this message greatly relevant to India of his time. Referring to the concluding verse in the Gita attributed to Sanjaya about the beneficial presence of Krishna and Arjuna, Rai said: 'A nation's prosperity and success depend upon wisdom like that of Krishna and bravery like that of Arjuna' (quoted in Davis 2015: 125).

Lajpat Rai died at the age of sixty-three in 1928 following a police attack on him during a demonstration. He was a martyr to the cause of India's freedom struggle, inspiring many more to join the freedom movement. There was no doubt that he highly adored Krishna as well as his Gita. But he saw Krishna as a highly evolved human rather as an *avatar*, which hardly diminished the significance of the Gita in his view.

On the contrary, since as he argued, Krishna lived the life he taught and bade Arjuna also to follow, his teaching had the backing of experience and was amenable to being put into practice. Yes, Rai put aside aspects of Krishna's teaching other than karma-yoga as secondary and could be considered to have attenuated its scope and significance in the bargain. But he was in the thick of freedom struggle, and his sharp focus on karma-yoga was a product of the time and circumstances he faced. Karma-yoga, however, is relevant in other circumstances too (like fighting poverty, promoting social welfare) as many interpreters found. While Rai may not have brought out the universality of the Gita, his interpretation of the Gita acted as powerfully as Swami Vivekananda's and Tilak's in awakening India's national spirit, urgently needed then.

Mahatma Gandhi

Mohandas Karamchand Gandhi (1869–1948) made no secret of his tremendous admiration and love for the Gita. In a letter to Gulzarilal Nanda in 1927, he wrote: 'though I am reading many things, the Bhagavad-Gita is becoming more and more the only infallible guide, the only dictionary of reference in which I find all the sorrows, all the troubles, all the trials arranged in the alphabetical order with exquisite solutions' (Iyer Ed. 172). He considered it as his eternal mother and an inspiring source of his ideas, which he applied not only to his daily life but also in leading the freedom struggle. He declared, 'I somehow or other fancy that "my philosophy" represents the true meaning of the teaching of the Gita' (CWMG Vol. 26: 140). He said that some of his key principles like mental equipoise, *swadharma*, equality and even the idea of non-cooperation came from the Gita (Gowda 2011: 198n). More than understanding the literal meaning of the Gita, Gandhi strove to get at its inner significance and implications for problems faced in life. He observed:

> The Gita is not an aphoristic work; it is a great religious poem. The deeper you dive into it, the richer the meaning you get. It being meant for the people at large, there is pleasing repetition. With every age the important words will carry new and expanding meanings. But its central teaching will never vary. The seeker is at liberty to extract from this treasure any meaning he likes so as to enable him to enforce in his life the central teaching.
>
> (Desai 1946: 130–31)

Gandhi was first introduced to the Gita in 1889 while in England through Sir Edwin Arnold's *Song Celestial*, which fascinated him instantly. But it was only later while in South Africa that he took it seriously enough to study the original and even learn Sanskrit to understand it properly, which he continued after returning to India in early 1915. By 1919, he felt confident enough to make his own interpretation of the Gita. When he called for a *hartal* and suggested people to observe fast and read the Gita, some people questioned him as to how the Gita was relevant since it preached violence. Gandhi responded by explaining that the war was only an allegory, which the Gita seized to draw attention to the war going on within ourselves between the forces of good and forces of evil (represented respectively by the Pandavas and Kauravas), and that he was saying this on the basis of experience and not just as an argument (Jordens 1991: 89). Jordens observes that by 1925, Gandhi had a fully worked-out definitive approach to and interpretation of the Gita, which was evident from a six-page article he wrote for *Navjivan*, on 11 October 1925, on the 'Meaning of the Gita' (Jordens 1991: 89) (CWMG Vol. 28: 315–21). Even before this, he used to refer often to the Gita in his speeches and letters ever since 1890 (Gowda 2011: 169). In 1926, he gave as many as 218 lectures on the Gita at the Satyagraha Ashram at Ahmedabad during morning prayers over nine months. They were mostly simple translations of the Gita (Gowda 2011: 169, 199n) They have been collected and published as *Discourses on the Gita* (CWMG Vol. 32: 94–376) and also as a separate book (Gandhi 1980). His more systematic translation and commentary articulating his interpretation of the Gita as *Anasakti-yoga* appeared in Gujarati in 1930. It was translated into English with an introduction by Mahadev Desai (1946) and published with a foreword by Gandhi, titled as *The Gospel of Selfless Action or The Gita according to Gandhi*.

Gandhi took the stand that while determining the meaning of a text like the Gita, 'one should not stick to the letter, but try to understand its spirit, its meaning in the total context' (CWMG Vol. 28: 318; Jordens 1991: 95). The literal text is a product of the times and circumstances in which it was written, but its basic message may well outlast those times, and the real task is to explore and determine that enduring message. That is why there is a need for interpretation in a way that one can transcend the literal translation, whether it pertains to a given word or even the text as a whole. Gandhi pointed out that the author of the Gita himself did so by 'extending the meaning of words' like 'karma', 'sannyasa' and 'yajna'. He therefore felt justified in following the footsteps of Vyasa, by observing that 'We shall do no injustice to Vyasa by expanding the meaning of his words. Sons should enrich the legacy of their fathers' (quoted in Jordens 1991: 95). Gandhi further felt that, in the task of interpreting such texts, more than mere scholarship, 'one must have a well-cultivated moral sensibility and experience in the practice of their truths' (Gandhi 1980: 10). He considered himself well qualified from this point of view even if he might not be a scholar like B. G. Tilak (Jordens 1991: 97).

Tilak's advocacy of karma-yoga and acceptance of violence if needed for a noble and selfless cause was interpreted by revolutionaries as justifying its use in the freedom struggle. Gandhi did not agree with the use of the Gita as an ideological support for an armed struggle against the British. He made it a point to show that the Gita and the Mahabharata stood for non-violence, about which he was firmly convinced. Gandhi's first step in this task was to stress that the background of war in the Gita was only an allegory, indicative of the ceaseless spiritual struggle going on within all of us. Had it been only an advice to Arjuna to fight his adversaries, the Gita would not have attained such widespread popularity and significance. The purpose of the Gita, Gandhi argued, is not to narrate history, but to teach something of a universal and everlasting value. Motivating to kill could hardly have been such a teaching. Gandhi points to the Gita's description of the characteristics of a perfected man, a *sthitaprajna*, in the last eighteen verses of its second chapter and says: 'I do not see any to correspond to physical warfare. Its whole design is inconsistent with the rules of conduct governing the relations between warring parties' (Desai 1946: 124). It is not inconceivable for such a person to choose *himsa* as his means of solving problems, Gandhi suggests. The Gita does not of course teach non-violence of a coward, and Gandhi made it clear that faced with a choice between cowardice and violence, he would choose the latter (Iyer Ed. 1993: 237). For the same reason, by non-violence, Gandhi did not mean compromising with the evil. He observed in an article in *Young India* (of 4 August 1920) that 'the Bhagavad Gita is a gospel of non-cooperation between forces of darkness and those of light' (Iyer Ed. 1993: 330). Taking the Gita as a whole, Gandhi had no doubt that it advocated truth and non-violence, the foundational values for human life and spiritual progress according to him. He thought that this was true not only of the Gita but also for the Mahabharata as a whole. According to Gandhi, 'Vyasa wrote his supremely beautiful epic to depict the futility of war. What did the Kauravas' defeat and the Pandavas' victory avail? How many among the victors survived?'

(quoted in Jordens 1991: 99). The epic demonstrated the utter futility of war and its violence. Gandhi took the epic essentially as anti-war, and the Gita stood at its centre.

The object of the Gita, Gandhi said, was to show 'the most excellent way to attain self-realization' (Desai 1946: 125).[9] The key to self-realisation is *anasakti*, which literally means disinterestedness or detachment, but Gandhi took it as indicative of desireless action, or renunciation of the fruits of action, with as much emphasis on action as on detachment. It cannot be renunciation of action because, according to the Gita, renunciation of action is not possible. 'There must be action where there is a body. (But) every action is tainted, be it ever so trivial. . . . How can one be free from action, i.e. from the taint of sin? The Gita has answered the question in decisive language: By desireless action; by renouncing fruits of action; by dedicating all activities to God, i.e. by surrendering oneself to Him body and soul' (Desai 1946: 125). Gandhi's prescription thus is selfless work. Renunciation does not mean indifference to the outcome of action. It also does not mean a want of fruit to the renouncer; in fact, 'he who renounces reaps a thousand-fold' (Desai 1946: 128). Gandhi explains that leaving the outcome to God contributes to efficiency in work and improves outcome. 'He who is ever brooding over result often loses nerve in the performance of his duty. He becomes impatient and then gives vent to anger and begins to do unworthy things; he jumps from action to action, never remaining faithful to any' (Desai 1946: 128). Gandhi does not undermine the role of jnana and bhakti, but only in combination with selfless action; they can make action meaningful and effective. Jnana ensures that the action is meaningful and purposive, and bhakti ensures that action is pursued with the whole heart in it. But jnana and bhakti or either of them devoid of action amount to self-indulgence, according to him. Jnana and bhakti have to stand the test of renunciation of the fruits of action (Desai 1946: 126, 127). There is thus no conflict between the interpretations of Tilak and Gandhi; the former's karma-yoga and the latter's *anasakti-yoga* amount to one and the same, and both make jnana and bhakti subordinate to action. The crucial difference between the two was in respect of the attitude to violence and non-violence. While unselfish violence for a noble cause would be permitted by Tilak, Gandhi was quite reluctant about it. While an armed struggle for freedom was consistent with the Gita's teaching in Tilak's view, it was not in Gandhi's. According to Gandhi, the central teaching of the Gita, viz. *anasakti*, is inconsistent with violence. Though he admitted that 'the Gita was not written to establish *ahimsa*', he pointed out that while following the central teaching of the Gita, one is bound to follow truth and *ahimsa* (Desai 1946: 129). He added emphatically that 'after 40 years' unremitting endeavour fully to enforce the teaching of the Gita in my own life, I have, in all humility, felt that perfect renunciation is impossible without perfect observance of *ahimsa* in every shape and form' (Desai 1946: 130).

In Gandhi's view, non-violent means of freedom struggle were more potent than the violent; what is more, as he said, he derived the former directly from the Gita. He wrote: 'The Bhagavadgita's intention [is] that one should go on working without attachment to the fruits of work (*anasakti*). I deduce the principle of Satyagraha from this. . . . As far back as 1889, when I had my first contact with the Gita, it gave me a hint of Satyagraha and as I read it more and more, the hint developed into a full revelation of Satyagraha' (CWMG Vol. 15: 312–13; Gowda 2011: 176). Gowda explains that for Gandhi, satyagraha was the positive form of *anasakti,* and non-cooperation its negative aspect. Gandhi believed that he derived even his belief in the spinning wheel (*charkha*) and *swadeshi* from the Gita. *Swadeshi* was inspired by the concept of *swadharma* in the Gita (Gowda 2011: 176, 200n).

Gandhi emphasised the paramount importance of performing one's own duties in life, as advised by the Gita. The question, however, is how duties are determined. He translates the first half of verse 8 in Chapter 3: 'Do thy allotted task (*niyata karma*); for action is superior to inaction.' Commenting on this, he takes *niyata karma* as synonym for *swakarma* or one's own task, *swadharma* or one's duty, *swabhava-niyata karma* or work determined according to one's nature, and also for *sahaja karma* or 'work to which one is born' – the words used in Chapter 18, verses 45, 47 and 48. Gandhi adds then: 'What falls to one's lot does not therefore mean work imposed upon one, but work which one has found out to be in accordance with one's own nature, one's bent, the law of one's being' (Desai 1946: 172). The added comment clearly implies that according to Gandhi, *swadharma* does not mean caste duty based on one's birth. A hurdle is his translation of *sahaja karma* as 'work to which one is born'. But this is too literal a translation, and Gandhi was emphatically critical of any literal translation when applied to interpreting the Gita as supportive of violence even for a selfless or a patriotic cause. *Sahajam* also means *swabhava-niyatam* or natural or one's bent, not necessarily determined by birth. Lord Krishna was well aware of non-Kshatriyas fighting in the Mahabharata war like Kshatriyas, and he hardly had an objection to it. Gandhi too was aware of it. And yet, when it comes to commenting on the famous verse *Chaturvarnyam maya sristam guna-karma-vibhagashah* ('the four *Varnas* were created by Me according to *guna* and *karma*' – Chapter 4, verse 13), Gandhi says, 'The Gita does talk of *Varna* being according to *guna* and *karma*, but *guna* and *karma* are inherited by birth. The law of *Varna* is nothing if not by birth' (Desai 1946: 196). Gandhi was surprisingly conservative and orthodox in taking such a stand. It is accepted that *guna karma*, means work as per one's aptitude, which need not necessarily be based on birth. By declaring that varna is according to one's calling and aptitude, the Gita demonstrated only its intention to reform and democratise the society and religion. Gandhi's interpretation of birth or heredity determining one's duty is inconsistent with his own explanation that it is not work imposed, but found according to one's own nature and bent. It is inconsistent also with his emphasis on equal treatment of all work and occupations, and denial of any hierarchy in this, for which also he found support from the Gita (verses 29–32 in Chapter 6). He believed in according the same status to a scavenger as to a lawyer or a doctor. Gandhi was certainly not against elevating the social and economic status of downtrodden castes, particularly of untouchables. But how could he ignore the connection between elevating their status and freedom necessary to break out of traditional caste-based occupations and move to new jobs? The verse 47 in Chapter 18 may have appeared to Gandhi as being against such freedom. His translation of this verse is: 'Better one's own duty, though uninviting, than another's which may be more easily performed; doing duty which accords with one's nature, one incurs no sin' (Desai 1946: 374). He comments on this further by saying that if one follows the Gita's principle of doing one's work with detachment, there is no room for preferring another's work. But there is no reason why the verse should necessarily refer to hereditary caste duty.

It is important to note, however, that Gandhi changed his stance subsequently and in his later writings was clearly against the caste system based on birth. He said: 'The caste system as it exists today in Hinduism is an anachronism. It is one of those ugly things, which will hinder the growth of true religion. It must go if both Hinduism and India are to live and grow' (CWMG Vol. 79: 384). Gandhi moreover was forthright and consistent throughout in condemning and completely rejecting untouchability. There was no support for untouchability in the Gita directly or indirectly. On the other hand, Gita called for equal treatment of all, as Gandhi stressed. He warned: 'If untouchability is not removed root and branch, Hinduism is bound to perish, for no religion can nurture itself on the degradation of its votaries' (CWMG Vol. 56: 194). He worked sincerely for eradication of untouchability in India,[10] for which he found justification from the Gita. Gandhi's philosophy of *anasakti*, selfless and detached work for the good of the country, could hold no room for hierarchical social relations, because cornering any privileged position in society is totally opposed to this philosophy.

Aurobindo Ghose

Sri Aurobindo Ghose (1872–1950) was a slightly younger contemporary of Gandhi, born three years later and died two years after him. By a significant coincidence, his birth date, namely, 15 August, was also the date when in 1947 India became independent. On the first day of independence, he had just completed seventy-five years. Sri Aurobindo was a revolutionary politician, teacher, social analyst, philosopher, visionary poet and a mystic all rolled into one. He became a highly respected spiritual leader only after he transcended nationalism and started looking into the spiritual problems of the humanity as a whole. Born in Calcutta, he had a highly anglicised upbringing and was sent to England for education when he was only seven. He spoke only in English as a child and started learning Bengali when he was eighteen. He appeared for the Indian Civil Service examination under pressure, passed it, but did not want to go into it. He, therefore, deliberately neglected horse riding due to which he was not finally selected. He returned to India in 1893 when he was twenty-one and joined the administrative service of the Maharaja of Baroda. Soon he changed to the educational service of the state by serving in the Baroda College and became its vice principal. It was in Baroda that he acquired a thorough knowledge of Bengali and Sanskrit and studied the Upanishads and other Indian ancient texts. It was also at Baroda that he had started his yogic practices in 1904 and had deep spiritual experiences, initiated into them by a Maharashtrian yogi, Vishnu Bhaskar Lele. But drawn also into the nationalist struggle in the wake of the partition of Bengal, he resigned from his service in Baroda in 1906 and went to Calcutta as the principal of a newly started Bengal National College. There, he was enrolled by the eminent nationalist leader Bipinchandra Pal to write regularly for the English newspaper *Bande Mataram*, which had become the mouthpiece of nationalist movement. At that time at least, Aurobindo did not believe in Gandhi's path of peaceful resistance, but in violent resistance. His association with revolutionaries who plotted a bomb blast led to his imprisonment in Alipore in May 1908, but was acquitted for lack of evidence and released in May 1909. While in jail, he had series of deep spiritual experiences. In one of them, he felt that the Divine placed the Gita in his hands and that he became a faithful and selfless instrument of the Divine. Out of jail, he started two journals in 1909 – *Karmayogin* in English and *Dharma* in Bengali, 'in which he propounded the philosophical basis of nationalism and important features of Indian culture' (Pandit 1998: 12). In both the journals, he also began expounding the yoga of the Gita. Soon, however, he had to entrust the responsibility of running the journals to others. For, it was at this time that he had a spiritual urging to go to Chandernagore (a French enclave then) in February 1910 and then to Pondicherry in April 1910. Pondicherry being under the French at that time, he could escape from regular harassment from the British government there and pursue his spiritual path in peace. He spent the rest forty years of his life there, making Pondicherry internationally famous because of his presence and his Ashram there.[11]

Sri Aurobindo saw India's independence as necessary not only for its political and socio-economic emancipation, but also for its spiritual rejuvenation. He believed that the Gita justified even violence if needed for attaining India's freedom, but he viewed it mainly as a text to guide us on the path of spiritual progress. In his later writings on the Gita from Pondicherry, this spiritual aspect of the Gita became most important, rather than it being a source of inspiration for the freedom struggle. He would not express the main spiritual goal of man as merely breaking the cycle of births and deaths, and liberation from *samsara*. The main goal in his view was spiritual perfection, and this goal was as much relevant to humankind as a whole as to individuals.

Essays on the Gita is one of the well-known works of Sri Aurobindo, a few of the many others being *The Life Divine, Savitri, The Secret of the Veda, The Upanishads, The Synthesis of Yoga, The Foundation of Indian Culture, The Human Cycle*, and *The Ideal of Human Unity*. He wrote *The Essays on the Gita* during 1916–1920, in two series, the first consisting of twenty-four essays on the first six chapters of the Gita and the second also with twenty-four essays on the remaining twelve chapters of the Gita. They were published first as a series of articles in the monthly *Arya*, which he started at Pondicherry. *The Essays* together (with nearly 600 pages) constitutes Volume 13 of Sri Aurobindo Birth Centenary Library (brought out by Sri Aurobindo Ashram, Pondicherry, in 1970) and is available as an independent book too (Aurobindo 1996). His another much larger work (with more than 900 pages), *The Synthesis of Yoga*, is also based on the Gita. It is an elaboration of the yoga, which in his view was taught by the Gita. It began to appear as a series of articles in the same *Arya* from 1914, but stopped before completion when the journal ceased publication in January 1921. His last article for the same series, 'The Supramental Consciousness', was published as the last chapter of the work along with the rest of the articles of the series in one book, only after his death. *The Synthesis* constitutes Volumes 20 and 21 of Sri Aurobindo Birth Centenary Library and is available online (surasa.net/aurobindo/synthesis/). Both these works are useful in understanding Sri Aurobindo's thoughts on the Gita.

Sri Aurobindo had regarded the Gita very highly even before his departure for Pondicherry. In his journal, *Karmayogin*, he had declared that the Gita is our 'chief national heritage, our hope for the future, our great force for the purification of the moral weaknesses that stain and hamper our people' (quoted in Minor 1991-a: 61). During the time he was busy in the nationalist movement, he drew support from the Gita for active resistance to the British rule. The titles of the two journals that he published from Calcutta, *Karmayogin* and *Dharma*, were inspired by the Gita. He had derived this activist understanding of the Gita from his Baroda days (Minor 1991-a: 65). He also saw universal value of the Gita apart from its being a source of inspiration in the nationalist struggle, for he declared in his journal, *Dharma*, that 'the Gita will become the universally acknowledged Scripture of the future religion' (quoted in Minor 1991-a: 71). However, it was really at Pondicherry that he devoted more of his philosophical reflection and writing on the Gita, from which emerged both *The Essays* and *The Synthesis*, as mentioned earlier. For, he had started his practice of the 'yoga of the Gita' (as he called it) soon after reaching Pondicherry.

Sri Aurobindo called the yoga of the Gita by various terms – *purna-yoga* (complete yoga), 'integral yoga' and *adhyatma-yoga* (Minor 1991-a: 77). In his view, the yoga of the Gita was an integral combination of different paths – jnana, karma, bhakti and self-perfection. They are all harmonised in the Gita without conflict. The yoga of the Gita is meant basically for experiencing, practicing and living it, rather than merely for arriving at an intellectual understanding. Sri Aurobindo was not a karmayogin of popular Bankim–Tilak brand. His position is much more nuanced and much above the mundane and ordinary. In his essay on 'The Core of the Teaching [of the Gita]', he explains: 'The argument of the Gita resolves itself into three great steps by which action rises out of the human into the divine plane leaving the bondage of the lower for the liberty of a higher law.' Briefly, the first step is the renunciation of desire for fruit and doing the works only as a sacrifice to the Supreme. The second step is to give up not only the desire of the fruit, but also the claim to be the doer of works. All works in the world are to be understood as simply the operation of the universal force of the nature–soul, *prakriti*, the only unequal, active and mutable power. The third and the last step is to see the Supreme Self as the Purusha (Purushottama, or the highest or supreme Purusha) as governing this *prakriti*, or the nature–soul, which is a partial manifestation of the highest Purusha, and by whom all works are directed through nature. It is to this highest Purusha that all love, adoration and sacrifice of works are to be offered (Aurobindo 1996: 37–38).

Sri Aurobindo then explains:

> The first step is Karmayoga, the selfless sacrifice of works, and here the Gita's insistence is on action. The second is Jnanayoga, the self-realisation and knowledge of the true nature of the self and the world; and here the insistence is on knowledge; but the sacrifice of works continues and the path of Works becomes one with but does not disappear into the path of Knowledge. The last step is Bhaktiyoga, adoration and seeking of the supreme Self as the Divine Being, and here the insistence is on devotion; but the knowledge is not subordinated, only raised, vitalised and fulfilled, and still the sacrifice of works continues; the double path becomes the triune way of knowledge, works and devotion. And the fruit of the sacrifice, the one fruit still placed before the seeker, is attained, union with the divine Being and oneness with the supreme divine nature.
>
> (Aurobindo 1996: 38)

Aurobindo does not thus consider 'disinterested performance of duty as the highest and all-sufficient law'. It is necessary but not sufficient. He admits that 'an inner situation may even arise, as with the Buddha, in which all duties have to be abandoned, trampled on, flung aside in order to follow the call of the Divine within. I cannot think that the Gita would solve such an inner situation by sending Buddha back to his wife and father and the government of the Sakya state. . . . The Gita does not teach the disinterested performance of duties but the following of the divine life, the abandonment of all dharmas, *sarvadharman*, to take refuge in the Supreme alone' (Aurobindo 1996: 32–33).

Nevertheless, Aurobindo does not recommend renunciation as the general path for spiritual progress for all and admits that the Gita prefers action to renunciation. He says, 'God in the world and you in the world are realities, the world and you are true and actual powers and manifestations of the Supreme. Therefore, accept life and action and do not reject them. One with God in your impersonal self and essence, an eternal portion of the Godhead turned to him by the love and adoration of your spiritual personality for its own Infinite, make your natural being what it is intended to be, an instrument of works, a channel, a power of the Divine' (Aurobindo 1996: 577).

In *The Synthesis of Yoga*, Sri Aurobindo (1999) not only further elaborates the three paths of 'divine works' (karma-yoga), 'integral knowledge' (jnana) and 'divine love' (bhakti) in the first three parts of the book respectively, but also discusses 'the yoga of self-perfection' (raja-yoga or dhyana-yoga) in the fourth and final part. As the other three, the last one also is taken from the Gita. Here again, this path is not shown as a substitute, but as complementing the first three, together making the *sadhana*, or spiritual striving, a more perfect one. Aurobindo distinguishes two stages of this path. In the first, the mind is disciplined, purified, stilled, concentrated and directed towards the Divine. In doing so, he clarifies, the 'Hatha-yogic methods of disciplining the body, can be dispensed with, but there is no objection to their partial use' (Aurobindo 1999: 612). The main effort has to be directed at the mind, rather than the body. An obsession with the body can be an obstacle, but a disciplined and healthy body is certainly a help. Once the mental motives are raised above the ordinary and spiritualised, and the disciplined mind is directed to the Divine on a stable basis through one's own will, the next stage is self-surrender to the will of the Divine. 'A greater perfection can only be arrived at by a higher power entering in and taking up the whole action of the being. The second stage of this Yoga will therefore be a persistent giving up of all the action of the nature into the hands of this greater Power . . ., until the Divine to whom we aspire becomes the direct Master of the Yogic efforts' (Aurobindo 1999: 619). This does not mean that such a yogi abstains from the society and its work, or from service to fellow beings or suffering humanity. The only difference is that such a work is done by the yogi as an instrument of the Divine and as willed by the Divine.

It is difficult to label Sri Aurobindo in terms of Advaita, Dvaita and so on. According to him, the ineffable Brahman is the Supreme Soul, and all individual souls are tireless flames of this one Soul (Aurobindo

1996: 578). The Supreme has manifested in the world or nature from out of His own infinite existence and spiritual essence, and this world is not an illusion but a reality. As in Vishishta-advaita and Dvaita, he emphasises love or bhakti towards the Supreme, combined with an attitude that one is only an instrument in the hands of the Divine. The individual souls are different from the Supreme only in a transitional phase when they are in pursuit of perfection, that is, before they realise their true essence. The transitional phase itself has a function or purpose, for it is in this phase that the individual souls can experience the joy of their love and of the striving for oneness with the Supreme. It is the destiny of every soul to attain this oneness sooner or later.

Swami Sahajananda Saraswati

Swami Sahajananda Saraswati (1889–1950) is a creative interpreter of the Gita. The Swami was no ordinary monk confined to spiritual pursuit. He was a polymath, a highly learned person, having a good knowledge of sociology, Marxism, history, linguistics, grammar, apart of course from Vedantic philosophy. He was an ascetic, a peasant leader, a nationalist and a revolutionary. Yes, many modern Hindu monks have engaged themselves in social work, but mostly of a non-adversarial nature without unduly disturbing the powerful established vested interests. Though Swami Sahajananda set out as an earnest *sadhaka* at the age of eighteen itself, he came under the influence of Gandhi in around 1920 and until 1930 was active in the Congress party and its struggles (Agrawal 2004: 93). He took up the cause of downtrodden peasants and led their movements in Bihar during the 1930s and 1940s against powerful zamindars or landlords who were mercilessly exploiting them. The mobilisation of these peasants had been initiated earlier by another monk, Swami Vidyananda during 1919 and 1920. After taking over the leadership of the movement, Swami Sahajananda started the Bihar Province Kisan Sabha in 1929 first, and then the All India Kisan Sabha (AIKS) in 1936 along with other luminaries like N. G. Ranga, E.M.S. Namboodiripad and Jayaprakash Narayan. The Swami was elected as the first president of AIKS at its Lucknow session in 1936. The peasants sought nothing less than a complete abolition of the zamindari system. The movement also demanded minimum wages to agricultural workers through legislation (Das 1982: 48–87). Notably, the Swami was born in the same caste to which the majority of zamindars belonged, but that was no problem for the Swami, whose conscience commanded him to struggle against even his own caste in favour of the oppressed. Unfortunately, the Swami had to leave the AIKS, which he founded and nourished due to ideological differences with the communists who increasingly came to dominate it. While the Swami was a staunch nationalist as well as a peasant leader and did not want either the nationalist or the peasant struggles to abate, the communists wanted to moderate, probably sedate them, as the British along with the Soviet Union were fighting fascism in World War II. He had left the Congress earlier and later left the communists as well. He was a more serious revolutionary in supporting the peasant cause, than either the Congress or the communists, and both disappointed him. Yet his fascination for Marxism continued.[12]

Both Swami Vidyananda and Swami Sahajananda were steeped in traditional discourse but were also sensitive to social issues (Agrawal 2006). They saw no contradiction between their being monks and peasant leaders at the same time. Once the landlord leaders got together and asked Swami Sahajananda how he being a sannyasi could get involved in such temporal issues as peasant problems. He told them, quoting a Sanskrit verse: 'Mendicants are selfish, living away from society, they try for their own salvation without caring for others. I cannot do that. I do not want my own salvation apart from that of many destitutes. I will stay with them, live with them, and die for them' (Saraswati 2000: 171).[13] To the Swami goes the credit of extending the meaning of the word, *moksha*, to mean not individual liberation from the cycle of births and deaths as in the traditional religious sense, but the liberation of the oppressed from poverty, exploitation and illiteracy (Agrawal 2004: 94). For this, he depended on his own interpretation of the Gita.

When imprisoned along with numerous others for participating in the Freedom Movement of 1942, the Swami completed his commentary on the Gita in Hindi, under the title *Gita Hridaya*. It was first published in 1948 and has been republished recently under the collected works of the Swami as Volume 3 (Saraswati 2003). The heart of the Gita, the Swami contends, lies in activist spiritualism, which gets manifested in the love for humanity and active participation in relieving the humanity, particularly the oppressed and the poor, of the burden of injustice, exploitation and oppression. Indeed, Raja Rammohan Roy and others also had used the Gita for their social reform projects, but Swami Sahajananda Saraswati used it in his fight against economic and social exploitation. In the preface to *Gita Hridaya*, he takes the stand that there is no conflict between the dharma enunciated in the Gita and that of Marxism (Saraswati 2003: 4–5). At least two verses in the Gita strongly support equity as much as Marxism, though the Gita is theistic while Marxism is atheistic. The two verses are: 'He who sees Me in all things and sees all things in Me, never becomes departed from me, nor am I lost to him' (VI.30). Again, 'he who judges pleasure and pain in others by the same standard as he applies to himself, that yogi is the highest' (VI.32). The Gita praises *sarva-bhutatma-bhutatma* (one who realises the self in all beings as his own self, V.7) and *sarva-bhuta-hite ratah* (engaged in the welfare of all beings, V.25; XI.4). The Swami asks who can be truer Marxist than a *sarva-bhutatma-bhutatma* and *sarva-bhuta-hite-ratah?* (Saraswati 2003: 5).

The Swami explains further that social work needs the Gita's yoga, which insists on doing the work without expecting any personal reward, without attachment and arrogance, but with dedication, skill and enthusiasm, leaving the outcome into the hands of the Divine, facing with equipoise both success and failure, and with the feeling that the doer is only an instrument of the Divine will (Saraswati 2003: 27–37). Lord Krishna may have meant this yoga for following in everyday living, but all ordinary economic activities are carried out with some motivation of a gain, through which one can make a living. But there can be no doubt that the Gita's yoga is particularly relevant and necessary in social and political work. Such work has to be fully directed at helping others, not at making a personal gain. The reward will come on its own, without one having to stressfully striving at it.

Explaining why he considers that there is no conflict between the Gita and Marxism, the Swami observes that there is really no strict opposition to atheism in the Gita (Saraswati 2003: 56). The emphasis instead is on selfless work for the benefit of humanity. There is no problem for an atheist Marxist or a socialist in becoming a karma-yogi. In fact, a genuine socialist *has to be* a karma-yogi. Just as the Swami does not take a narrowly religious view of the Gita, he does not also take a narrow view of Marxism, as being necessarily opposed to religion, which after all is a personal matter. He quotes Lenin to say that the Marxist opposition to religion is not absolute or valid in all times and circumstances; the opposition arises because leaders of religion have always in the past supported exploiting classes at the expense of exploited classes. Religion need not necessarily act as an opium for the poor; it has helped the poor in being optimistic. He also quotes Lenin, who advised against splitting the working class into atheists and believers (Saraswati 2003: 71). He quotes Stalin also, who told the dean of Canterbury: 'Religion cannot be stopped. Conscience cannot be stilled. Religion is a matter of conscience and conscience is free. Worship and religion are free' (Saraswati 2003: 67). As for the class struggle, the Swami tried to show that religion is and should be supportive of the downtrodden rather of the powerful propertied class.[14]

Agrawal points to the liberation theology movement of the 1970s in Latin America. The church there took the stand that it should be on the side of the exploited and oppressed in the class struggle, and Christ was seen as the liberator. Swami Sahajananda launched a similar idea in India in the context of Hinduism and the Gita over four decades earlier (Agrawal 2004: 93). If one takes into account the peasant struggle launched by Swami Vidyananda in 1919, the date of religious leaders taking up the cause of the exploited classes against their oppressors goes backwards even more. However, neither of the two Swamis led their struggles under the flag of Hinduism, unlike the liberation theology movement which was church-led. Nevertheless, Swami Sahajananda did not fail to point out, both by teaching and by acting, how the Gita is fully supportive to the cause of the exploited and the poor in their struggle against exploitation and oppression.

Jawaharlal Nehru

This chapter concludes with an account of how Jawaharlal Nehru (1889–1964) viewed the Gita. This chapter has dealt with how the makers of modern India viewed and used the Gita, which had become global by their time. Yet they also saw something in the Gita which was vitally relevant to designing their approach to solving the problems of India and modernising it. Nehru was the most conspicuous of the makers of modern India. He certainly did not claim that he used the Gita as a guide in formulating his approach to modernising India, which was the main task he undertook. Neither did he write any verse-by-verse commentary on the Gita. Yet, he had some insightful and interesting observations on the Gita, particularly in his book, *The Discovery of India*, written when he was in Ahmednagar Fort prison, during five months, April to September 1944, and first published in 1946. His observations are mostly in a special section devoted to it, 'The Bhagavad Gita' (Nehru 1981: 108–10), apart from stray references elsewhere.

Nehru begins by noting that the Gita's 'popularity and influence have not waned ever since it was composed and written in the pre-Buddhist age, and today its appeal is as strong as ever in India. . . .

In times of crisis, when the mind of man is tortured by doubt and is torn by conflict of duties, it has turned all the more to the Gita for light and guidance' (Nehru 1981: 109). He also notes, however, that its interpretations have differed widely, some like Gandhi basing his belief in non-violence on it, while others have justified violence and warfare for a righteous cause. This seems to be a problem with all sacred books, and the propriety of the interpretation lies more in the person interpreting rather than in the book. The Gita itself calls for using one's own critical faculty (XVIII.63) and desisting from taking a one-side view of the problem at hand deluding oneself that everything concerned is taken into account (XVIII.22). Most misinterpretations or wrong decisions arise because of failure to heed this advice of the Gita. That is how Godse, who murdered Gandhi, tragically misread the Gita, though ironically both Gandhi and Godse claimed to follow it. Nehru observes that according to the Gita, its call for action has to keep the spiritual background and the larger purpose of the universe in mind (Nehru 1981: 109). Any action or decision is always subject to the advice of the Gita to use one's critical faculty and to take a holistic view. Nehru is in full agreement with the interpretation of the Gita's karma-yoga as one aimed at social betterment and social service, and based on altruism. One can fight for a righteous cause, but the mental frame should be one of non-violence and spirituality.

Nehru characterises the message of the Gita as 'not sectarian', and as 'universal in its approach for everyone, Brahmin or outcaste', and thus 'found favour with all classes and schools' (Nehru 1981: 110). He adds:

> There is something in it which seems to be capable of being constantly renewed, which does not become out of date with the passing of time – an inner quality of earnest inquiry and search, of contemplation and action, of balance and equilibrium, in spite of conflict and contradiction. . . . Its temper is one of supremacy over the changing environment, not by seeking escape from it but by fitting in with it. During the 2500 years since it was written, Indian humanity has gone repeatedly through the process of change and development and decay; . . . but it has always found something living in the Gita, something that fitted into the developing thought and had a freshness and applicability.
>
> (Nehru 1981: 110)

We now go, in the next chapter, to modern interpreters who saw the Gita in universal terms, beyond the immediate relevance to India, and more into its spiritual significance like the ancient and medieval interpreters. This was in keeping with the global appeal of the Gita, which emerged since modern times. The next chapter can also be viewed as an extension or continuation of the present one. While these interpreters used the earlier commentaries, they also added something of their own, further enriching the expanding literature on the Gita.

Notes

1 The account here of the Rammohan's life and work, and of he used the Gita, is based mainly on Agarwal (1993: 3–48) and to some extent on the website en.wikipedia.org/wiki/Ram_Mohan_Roy downloaded on 17 January 2015.
2 The account of Bankim's work here is based mainly on Gowda (2011: 9–49); also see Ajit Ray's chapter on Bankim, in Minor (Ed.) (1991: 34–43).
3 Source: en.wikipedia.org/wiki/Theosophical_Society, downloaded on 26 January 2015.
4 The account of Annie Besant's life and work here is based on Neufeldt (1991: 25–28), Sinha (2010: 311–13) and www.ts-adyar.org/content/annie-besant-1847–1933, downloaded on 20 January 2015. Also see Jinarajadasa (1996).
5 The account of Tilak's life, work and philosophy here is based on Tilak (1936), Stevenson (1991), Agarwal (1993: 89–135) and Gowda (2011: 50–89).
6 Apart from CWSV (see Note 5 in Chapter 3), two volumes of *The Life of Swami Vivekananda* by 'His Eastern and Western Disciples' (referred simply as 'Disciples'), sixth and seventh editions (1989 and 2001 respectively) have been used here. French (1991), Agarwal (1993: 49–88) and Gowda (2011: 90–123) were also quite useful.
7 Writings of Lajpat Rai have been published together in *The Collected Works of Lala Lajpat Rai* (CWLLR), edited by B. R. Nanda, 2003, Delhi: Manohar. *Yogiraj Shri Krishna* is in Vol. I. The account about Lajpat Rai here is based on Davis (2015: 120–28), and to some extent on www.britannica.com/EBchecked/topic/328063/Lala-Lajpat-Rai.
8 Included in the CWLLR (op. cit.), Vol. 3, 329–53 (as per Davis 2015: 219n-10).
9 For Gandhi, as in the Hindu tradition, Self-realisation is God realisation. He did not believe in a personal God existing beyond the universe. Gandhi's concept of God or cosmic spirit is presented insightfully by Bhikhu Parekh (2001: 35–41).
10 For details of how Gandhi worked for eradication of untouchability, see Nadkarni (2013: 141–42).
11 The brief life-sketch here is based on Minor (1991: 61–67), Agarwal (1993: 137–62), Pandit (1998: 1–27), Diwakar (1999: 1–80), Heehs Ed (1999: xiii–xviii), and Gowda (2011: 124–26). A few of the other books on his life and work are A. B. Purani (1978), *The Life of Sri Aurobindo*,

Sri Aurobindo Ashram, Pondicherry; Peter Heehs (1989), *Sri Aurobindo: A Brief Biography*, Oxford University Press, Delhi; Nirodbaran (1990), *Sri Aurobindo for All Ages*, Sri Aurobindo Ashram, Pondicherry.

12 For more details, see Hauser (1995), Saraswati (2000), and Das (2008).

13 Sahajananda Saraswati devotes a lengthy section on *Marxava̱d aur Dharm* (Marxism and religion) to prove his point that Marxism is compatible with religion (Saraswati 2003: 67–79).

14 Sahajananda Saraswati devotes a lengthy section on *Marxava̱d aur Dharm* (Marxism and religion) to prove his point that Marxism is compatible with religion (Saraswati 2003: 67–79).

5

CONTEMPORARY INTERPRETATIONS

Swami Ramdas

In this chapter are presented a few selected modern interpreters of the Gita who were focused more on its general ethical and spiritual content rather than its nationalistic and social implications. Even while dealing with the spiritual content of the Gita, these interpreters also brought out its relevance as a guide for day-to-day living in a morally acceptable and psychologically satisfying way. This helped in re-establishing the Gita as a text of universal significance. These interpretations aimed at bringing out the Gita's teaching in helping man (or woman) find a higher purpose and sustainable and deeper happiness. There have been several more interpreters than those presented here, but some had to be excluded so that repetition of overlapping ideas is minimised and also because enough material on them was not available. Some of the contemporary interpreters are referred to in succeeding chapters, though separate sections are not earmarked for them.

Swami Ramdas (1884–1963) was a modern mystic who could convey his teaching in simple and lucid English as well as in Hindi, Malayalam, Kannada and Konkani (his mother tongue). Born as Padukone Vitthal Rao in Kanhangad, then a part of the South Kanara district, now in Kerala, he became a *sannyasi* in 1922, renouncing family life and business, and took a new name – Ramdas, a servant of Ram. He also took three vows: 'I am no more Vitthal Rao', 'this body is servant of Ram and shall always be in His service alone' and 'all women are mothers to me'. His Ram was not the son of Dasharath and king of Ayodhya, but the unborn formless Immortal Ram who is within us all, the same Ram to whom Kabir and Gandhi were devoted. After taking *sannyas*, Ramdas met Ramana Maharshi and received his grace. The Maharshi blessed him through his glance – 'Be filled with Joy', and he was. A smiling, benign and compassionate expression never left Ramdas since then. With the mantra of 'Om Shri Ram Jaya Ram Jaya Jaya Ram' ever on his lips and in his heart, he set out literally 'In Quest of God', wandered for a few years all over India and the Himalayas, in a frenzy of God intoxication. He finally returned to his native place, Kanhangad, set up an ashram there ('Anandashram') and started his spiritual teaching. He went on a world tour in 1954, giving discourses to his admirers in several countries. His books are all in English, *In Quest of God, In the Vision of God, God Experience, Swami Ramdas on Himself* and *Gita Sandesh (Message of the Gita).*

Gita Sandesh, published first in 1966 after his demise, is based on the discourses that Swami Ramdas gave, having eighteen chapters, each on the eighteen respective chapters of the Gita (Ramdas 1976). Ramdas interprets Arjuna's predicament as one of overcoming *moha* or emotional attachment to a narrow circle of relatives, family and possessions. *Moha* arises from identifying 'I' with the body and 'mine' with only those near. The Gita holds forth the goal of liberation from all limitations and enjoying the bliss inherent in a state of expansive immortal self. This requires overcoming *moha*, which is the source of bondage. Like Arjuna, everyone faces the conflict between aspiring for the vaster vision and 'the crystallised selfishness of an individualistic view of life' (Ramdas 1976: 2). Ramdas observes further that *moha* has its own ways of defence against the development of a higher and expanded vision, which are reflected in Arjuna's arguments for unwillingness to fight (Ramdas 1976: 2–3). Krishna's call to Arjuna to fight is not to be interpreted literally to kill relatives, but to overcome his narrow attachments and to realise his larger universal purpose. Altruistic service to humanity taught by Krishna is not possible otherwise. *Moha* throws a person only into darkness, delusion and selfishness, overcoming which is the basic requirement to spiritual progress, according to Ramdas's interpretation of the Gita.

The way to transcending *moha*, Krishna tells, lies in discriminating between what is transient and what is permanent, between what is perceived by senses and what is beyond, between what is particular or individual and what is universal. One has to understand one's true self as the eternal spirit present in all, and not as the perishable body, and thus get on to a higher level fixed in the bliss of the Universal Atman. In this state, one does not have to – in fact, should not – desist from being engaged in action in the world. Being in such state helps one to do work effectively and enjoy it too and, what is more, to judge with fairness what is a right action and what is wrong. What one should desist from is any desire to appropriate the fruit of action and arrogance of being the actor. It means a complete surrender of all actions and their outcomes to God. This is real karma-yoga. Swami Ramdas clarifies that sannyas is not necessary for this or any type of yoga. He emphasises, however, that the Gita advises strict discipline and self-control in one's life, particularly in eating and sex, also overcoming anger, jealousy and such mental weaknesses, as an aid to control attachment and desire. Spending some time regularly every day in *japa* (recitation of a holy mantra or of even the syllable OM or AUM in the proper way) and *dhyana* (meditation) is quite helpful in this task. A person practicing the Gita's yoga, combining detached work with right knowledge, and devotion, would always be in perfect poise and peace. A karma-yogi treats all people with equal respect and love and is compassionate even to animals.

Swami Ramdas points out to three kinds of doers of action, as explained in the Gita. A *satvik* doer performs his work without any selfish desire for personal reward, but effectively, efficiently and calmly without being ruffled by success and failure. A *rajasik* doer works for a personal reward and is emotionally attached to the outcome, ruffled by success and failure. A *tamasik* doer is lazy, slow, irregular, deceitful and quarrelsome, doing a mess of his work. Only a satvik doer can be a karma-yogi (Ramdas 1976: 102). A karma-yogi is freed from karma only when he transcends egoism completely, that is the sense of 'I am the doer!', and dedicates all credit for action and its outcome to God. This requires combining work with complete devotion and surrender to God. This is the highest stage of *sadhana* or spiritual seeking, which the Gita has shown.

The central message of Swami Ramdas's interpretation of the Gita is to get rid of *moha*, that is emotional attachment to a small circle of oneself, one's family and friends, and possessions only. *Moha* is the source of selfishness, corruption, violence and all evils. Though he teaches this in the context of spiritual seeking, it seems to be equally – probably, more – relevant in social and even political work. Social workers and political leaders have to be karma-yogis to be credible, effective and efficient. Eradicating *moha* does not mean destroying the spring of love in oneself, but extending it to cover the larger world, making it more general and universal, instead of confining it to a small circle.

D. V. Gundappa (DVG)

D. V. Gundappa (1887–1975), popularly known as DVG, is a big name in Kannada literature. An eminent philosopher-poet-journalist, adept equally at both prose and poetry, he was simply prolific, with fifteen collections of poems, two book-size-long poems on moral wisdom (*Manku Timmana Kagga* and *Marula Muniyana Kagga*, the latter being an extension of the former), a book on the Gita and several other books on political science and journalism, biographies, memoirs and books for children. He founded the Gokhale Institute of Public Affairs in 1945 in Bengaluru.[1] He gave a series of lectures in Kannada on the Gita at this Institute, which were tape-recorded, transcribed and serially published first in a Kannada weekly, *Prajamata*, between February 1963 and July 1964. They were then put together, checked and edited by DVG himself and published in 1966 as a book, with a preface and an introduction by him. The book in Kannada was titled as *Shrimad-Bhagavad-Gita-Tatparya Athava Jeevana-Dharma-Yoga* (*Essence of the Bhagavad-Gita or The Dharma of Living*, Gundappa 2001). It won the Sahitya Akademy Award in 1967.

DVG's work on the Gita is one of the most thorough-going, well-reasoned, refreshing and at the same time lucid books on the subject in any language. It is immensely enjoyable to read with apt examples and witty expressions, and at the same time enlightening. The beauty of its prose makes it difficult to translate into English, but a modest attempt is made here to bring out the essence of this great book or at least its salient points. This is done in my own way, not necessarily in the same order as in the original.

In his introduction, DVG explains how his approach to the Gita is different. First, while the great acharyas saw the Gita only as a *moksha-shastra* (the science of liberation), his work sees it as a guide for living. The key to a happy, honourable and stress-free living lies in following the Gita's dharma. We need a source of confidence and courage in the turbulent journey of life, and the Gita provides it. The rigours of life's journey are thus lightened by the Gita.[2] Second, his book steers clear of theological controversies on Advaiata, Dvaita and so on and indicates the possibility of harmonising them. Third, DVG also sees complementarity between different paths of *sadhana* like *jnana, karma-yoga and bhakti*. Fourth, while the great acharyas relied more on the authority of the Vedas and the Upanishads to support their arguments, DVG relies more on critical reasoning. Fifth, the book is not addressed to the followers of the Vedic religion alone, but is non-sectarian and universal in approach; nor is it addressed to pundits but to common men and women who are keen to solve riddles of God, soul, dharma, faith and destiny, written in a conversational style (Gundappa 2001: 22–23, 33).

DVG explains that what may seem as a lack of coherence in the Gita is due to the fact that it was an informal dialogue between friends, though on a serious theme (Gundappa 2001: 26–27). As to how a serious and long dialogue could take place in a battlefield, DVG observes that wars at that time had certain rules and disciplines to follow, and though the war was declared earlier, there was still time for actual commencement. Around the time that the Gita-dialogue was taking place, Yudhishthira (the eldest of the Pandava brothers) was entering the enemy camp unarmed to pay respects to the elders and teachers like Bhishma and Drona (he also came out unharmed), and thus there was time enough for a serious dialogue to take place (Gundappa 2001: 28).

As to the question of whether Arjuna was right in his refusal to fight or whether Krishna was right in insisting that Arjuna should, DVG observes that Arjuna was only sentimental, and his grief was more an impulse of the moment rather than one based on reasoning. DVG insists that even compassion cannot be irrational and has to be based on dharma. The war was earlier tried to be avoided by the Pandavas and Krishna himself, and the Kauravas had rebuffed every such move by further humiliating them. It was now a question of honour, and any move on the part of Arjuna to withdraw at that juncture was bound to be judged as cowardice. Compassion is good no doubt, but even compassion has to be justified by dharma or justice. One cannot refrain from punishing a murderer or a rapist out of compassion for him. It does not mean that a criminal does not deserve any compassion. Even a heinous murderer should not be subjected to stoning by death or such other undue torture to match his crime. Dharma is based not on momentary impulses, but on long-term considerations of ethics and moral duty. If there is a conflict between the two, dharma should prevail since otherwise the world cannot function in an orderly way (Gundappa 2001: 63–74).

According to the Gita, there is no conflict between dharma and pursuit of *moksha*. There can be no *moksha* without following dharma, says DVG. A primary requirement for following the Gita's dharma is to keep one's mind pure, cleaning it of arrogance, lust, jealousy, emotional attachment and anger, and similar other mental weaknesses. One needs also a sense of discrimination between the everlasting and momentary, and between right and wrong. One has to cultivate self-control, endurance (*titiksha*) and equipoise in the context of ups and downs, and also *shraddha*, translated approximately as faith. *Shraddha* does not mean being credulous and giving up critical reasoning, but a faith in oneself, in the basic goodness of others and in God. It also means faith in the goodness and joy of living. Life is a manifestation of the energy of God, and one should respect it both in oneself and others. Without *shraddha*, one cannot do anything in life; one cannot even travel from one place to another without some faith that one would reach the destination safely and on expected time. Precautions may be necessary, but one should also have faith (Gundappa 2001: 33–53).

The Gita says, DVG points out, that no person can avoid action. Action is both nature induced and deliberate. Deliberate action binds all persons to the law of karma and the cycle of births and deaths. The way to circumvent the law of karma is to do work without desiring its fruit and with an honest attitude that 'I am not the doer'. DVG clarifies that one cannot escape from moral responsibility for one's action by merely telling oneself hypocritically that 'I am not the doer'. The action should be genuinely selfless and done with utter humility and as an offering (Gundappa 2001: 168, 181). The action also should not be done thoughtlessly without heed to consequences; it should be based on a discrimination between desirable and undesirable action, the former promoting the welfare of the world (i.e. consistent with dharma) and the latter harmful to the world (i.e. against dharma). A helpful criterion, a golden rule, which the Gita provides here, is contained in verse 32 of Chapter 6: 'Judge the pleasure or pain in others by the same standard as you would apply to yourself.' Having done accordingly, one should not worry about the outcome, but leave it to God. Accept the outcome with equanimity, says the Gita. All these together, with all the given conditions or riders, constitutes karma-yoga. According to the Gita, DVG points out, it is easier to follow karma-yoga and be effective, if one follows *swadharma*, what comes naturally to oneself based on aptitude (Gundappa 2001: 126–51, 332–35).

Chapter 16 of the Gita lists what it considers as divine or godlike and demon-like qualities. Among the former are included fearlessness, purity of heart, generosity, self-control, uprightness, non-violence, truthfulness, kindness to all, modesty, forgiveness, cleanliness and such other qualities (verses 1–3). Among the demonical are included ostentation, arrogance, anger and self-conceit (verse 4). DVG asks, why did not the Gita talk about human qualities? That is because the same qualities can be found in the human beings themselves. He considers life as an adventure sport of climbing a greasy pole, constantly striving to climb up from the base demonical qualities to the godlike qualities (Gundappa 2001: 404). A success in this sport has its own rewards, apart from the thrill of adventure. It gives us a great peace of mind, fearlessness, moral confidence, a sense of freedom and ever being in a state of happiness, in spite of all vicissitudes of life.[3]

DVG points out at another type of distinction made in the Gita in the seventeenth and eighteenth chapters, between *satvika* (good, upright), *rajasika* (pleasure loving, emotional) and *tamasika* (dull, lethargic) *gunas* (qualities), which too has a great relevance to practical issues. Applying the distinction to voters' attitude in elections, DVG says that a voter who does not mind the trouble of going to the booth irrespective of sun or rain, takes into account who is the most deserving and votes accordingly is a *satvika* voter. A fair-weather voter who avoids going if there is hot sun outside, or goes to vote only if he or she gets a free lift, is *rajasika*. One who is indifferent, forgetful and too lazy to go to vote is the worst type – a *tamasika* voter (Gundappa 2001: 452).[4] A given person may not exclusively be of one *guna*, but can be *satvika* in one respect, *rajasika* in another and *tamasika* in yet another respect. All are combinations of the three in different degrees.

In the concluding chapter, DVG points out at four challenges to the interpreters of the Gita in modern times. They are (i) significant loosening of the caste system; (ii) growing complexity in the nature of livelihoods; (iii) women's status, rights and duties; and (iv) a significant questioning tendency (Gundappa 2001: 524). As to the first, DVG says that the 'mixing of castes' (*varna-sankara*) is inevitable and will continue, though castes may not altogether disappear. In the olden days, the economic system was simple and caste system was clear and conspicuous, and *swadharma* could have been taken simply to mean caste duty. Not anymore. It can now be taken only to mean dharma based on one's aptitude, inclination and training. Regarding women's issues, there is hardly anything in the Gita which throws light on them, but DVG seems to have raised it mainly to express his opinion. He welcomes women stepping out of the kitchen and working alongside men to earn an income of their own, provided the vocation is such that it does not compromise the dignity and status of women. However, as to the women's right to choose their own husbands particularly outside the community or caste, DVG does not give a straight answer. He only insists that a marriage is not to be seen only as a union between two individuals, but as a coming together of two families, and the happiness of the couple and the families depends on mutual regard and affection. He also hints that there is no question of the husband being dominant and the wife being just obedient in married life, because the relationship is one of unity, solidarity, cooperation, mutual trust and equality. As to the fourth point earlier, DVG observes that a questioning tendency is not new in Indian culture and religion; otherwise, there would not have been so many philosophies. The Upanishads are a strong evidence of the questioning tradition. In the Gita itself, Arjuna was not to be convinced at one stroke; he kept asking questions. The questioning attitude poses no threat to the Gita or its following, believes DVG (Gundappa 2001: 552–53). At the same time, faith has its own role and scope, just as critical reasoning has, particularly in matters like acceptance of the idea of Atman and Brahman. Even for a person who has no faith in the idea of Atman or Brahman or *moksha*, who regards the Gita teaching on spiritual pursuit as irrelevant, it can still be a guide in leading a stress-free, enjoyable and morally honourable life.

Swami Sivananda

Swami Sivananda (1887–1963) was one of the most leading yoga gurus of the twentieth century. A prolific writer in English, he has to his credit some 340 books and pamphlets on yoga and philosophy, including several on the Gita. Born in Tamil Nadu, with Kuppuswami as his earlier name, he studied medicine in Tanjore and began his medical practice in Malaysia in 1913. He became popular as a kind, hardworking and selfless doctor, known particularly for helping poor patients with not only medicine but even with food and money. A spiritual urge took him back to India leaving lucrative medical practice. He became a wandering mendicant for a while, until he found his guru at Rishikesh and became a sannyasi in 1924. He started an ashram and a free dispensary for the poor there. He began lecturing and writing on spiritual matters since 1929, founded the Divine Life Society at Rishikesh in 1936 to publish books, conduct seminars and conferences, and disseminate spiritual education. He was also the main inspiration behind Yoga Vedanta Centres worldwide. He observed no caste distinctions and admitted both men and women from all castes and classes to his order.[5] He has summarised his teaching in six words: serve, love, give, purify, meditate and realise.

According to Sivananda, the Gita is the 'cream of the Vedas' and the 'essence of the Upanishads' (Sivananda 2013: xi), and it 'alone is sufficient for the purpose of *Svadhyaya* (scriptural study)' as 'you will find a solution here for all your doubts' (Sivananda 2013: xiii). Its appeal is for all mankind (Sivananda 2013: xiv). There is a yoga here for every type of a spiritual seeker, jnana-yoga for a rational or intellectual temperament, karma-yoga for the active and bhakti-yoga for the emotional, and there is harmony between them (Sivananda 2013: xv). *Moksha* can be attained in this very life by annihilating the ego, by overcoming *raga* (likes) and *dvesha* (dislikes), and through selfless active work (Sivananda 2013: xvii).

Sivananda admits that there are conflicting verses in the Gita. One should not, therefore, go by the literal meaning of one verse alone, but relate them to others and get an overall message. For example, in verse 33 of Chapter 3, Krishna says that everyone behaves as per one's nature and asks 'what can restraint do?', but in the very next verse, as Sivananda points out, Krishna also adds that one must nevertheless try not to yield to senses and get them under control (Sivananda 2013: xxv). Taking another example, Sivananda points out (Sivananda 2013: xxvi), Krishna says that he dwells in the hearts of all beings and controls them as if they are mounted on a machine (XVIII.61). Yet, he also advises that one must raise the self by the self and not allow it to be destroyed (VI.5). In the very advice that one must do one's own natural duty rather than someone else's (XVIII.47), there is an assumption of freedom of will and action. The overall sense is that human beings do have some freedom, but it is not absolute and unconstrained. However, whatever freedom of discrimination and action one has should be exercised and exercised wisely and with moral responsibility and humility.

What is heartening about the Gita is the series of assurances one after another given by the Lord, out of kindness and love to the spiritual seekers and devotees. Sivananda puts the concerned verses together – at least eight of them – and calls them together as *Pratijna Gita* (Promising Gita).[6] (Sivananda 2009: 11, 12). In one of such verses, the Lord assures that a seeker should not feel frustrated and fear about the waste of effort and that even a little effort goes a long way (II.40). 'No one who does good, will ever perish' (VI.40). 'I am easily attainable to those who remember me all the while' (VIII.14). 'I will take care of devotees who have set their minds on Me' (IX.22). These verses increase one's self-confidence.

In the Gita, moral and spiritual progress go together; there can be no gap between the two. Sivananda says: 'An ethically disciplined, morally purified and spiritually illumined soul is the goal of Gita-ethics. To attain this, the Lord exhorts the Man to spiritualise his entire personality' (Sivananda 2009: 50). He explains further that to do this, the Gita ethics requires one eradicate *tamas* in oneself, wisely control *rajas* and add to the *satvika* in all possible ways. A great thing about the Gita's ethics is that it does not demand extreme austerity; it is practical and teaches moderation. Neither starvation diet nor overindulgence in food is advised; neither sleeping too little nor too much is recommended. Even in spiritual seeking, there is insistence on self-effort so as to avoid insincerely or lazily leaving everything to God's will (Sivananda 2009: 28–29). Sivananda insists that merely avoiding evil ways is not enough; one should positively cultivate virtue and the divine qualities insisted upon in the Gita (in Chapter 16) (Sivananda 2009: 41).

To teach the values of self-control, self-reliance, selfless service, virtuousness and mental equipoise, Sivananda says that the Gita should be taught as a part of the curriculum in all schools and colleges in India and even the world at large (Sivananda 2013: xxvii). Since the Gita is not the only religious text which teaches these values, students should also be exposed to the highlights of moral teachings from the sacred texts of all religions which are relevant for solving the problems of our times. Avoiding religious parochialism is itself a moral value to be taught, and the Gita's tolerant outlook to differences in religious paths is particularly pertinent. There is no doubt a great necessity to develop students' moral personality and their self-confidence, and the Gita can play an important role in this task also.

K. M. Munshi

Kulapati Dr K. M. Munshi (1887–1971) was a prolific writer in Gujarati, English and Hindi, an eminent lawyer, an outstanding political leader and an educationist. He is remembered, among other things, for founding Bharatiya Vidya Bhavan, which has now grown into a worldwide institution for promoting Indian art, culture, literature and values. A major project finished by the Bhavan is a monumental eleven-volume venture on *The History and Culture of the Indian People*, which was a brainchild of Munshi, nourished by his indomitable energy. He was a member of the committee which selected the National Flag and also of the committee which drafted the Constitution of India. He took the initiative and leadership of the project for reconstructing the historical Somanath temple in Gujarat, inaugurated in 1951 by Dr Rajendra Prasad, the then president of India. As a member in Nehru's Cabinet for a brief period during 1952–53, he is known for launching the *Vana-mahotsava* movement for increasing the forest cover. Due to differences with Nehru, he left the Indian National Congress in 1959 and joined C. Rajagopalachari's Swatantra Party.[7]

Munshi wrote some twenty-one novels and three plays in Gujarati and Hindi and nine books in English. Among the latter is *Bhagavad*

Gita and Modern Life, published first in 1947. It was revised and enlarged from time to time until 1969 (two years before his demise) and reprinted several times thereafter (Munshi 1988). It is an inspiring, elegantly written and thoughtful book on the Gita.

In the introduction, Munshi discusses various ways in which the Gita is read or studied and how it is best approached. Some recite it expecting a material gain, some for *punya*, some view it merely as a textbook on morals and some see it as a piece of literature meant for criticism, dissecting and analysing it with no love for it. Such people miss the mystical charm of the Gita and the pure joy of reading and reciting it. It has to be approached with reverence and due humility. He advises that we must 'read the Gita to see the Light which burns within us' (Munshi 1988: xiv).

> When you read the Gita again and again, as all scriptures should be read, the words begin to grow in you; the nervous system is stimulated; the constant repetition of some appealing verse transforms our minds and makes our spirit more articulate. Then it is woven into the texture of our mind and spirit. If we feel down-hearted, one of the oft-repeated verses rise to the surface in the shape of a mandate and we find in ourselves a new hope.
>
> (Munshi 1988: xiii–xiv)

Munshi does not belittle the moral significance of the Gita. He says that as we recite the Gita everyday at least for some time, taking its meaning to heart, we become purer, more patient and forgiving, develop more compassion for the poor and the deprived, and become more active in helping the desolate. In brief, we become more noble and strong at the same time (Munshi 1988: xiv). He adds: 'It [the Gita] is not a scripture of the next world, nor of asceticism, nor of inaction. It is an intensely human document; a guide for every human situation. It urges man in the thick of life's battle to shed his limitations' (Munshi 1988: 19).

Dharma, as taught by the Gita, is neither a religion, nor a dogma, according to Munshi (Munshi 1988: 20). It is a universal law of becoming, also a law of moral causation and is all pervading. It is as ineluctable as the law of gravitation. Munshi spells out this law:

> If anyone achieves Truth, his work shall bear fruit.
>
> If anyone achieves Non-violence, men shall come to him shedding their hostility.

> If anyone achieves Non-stealing, wealth shall come to him.
> If anyone achieves Non-waste, he shall obtain the vigour that does not fade.
> If anyone achieves Non-possession, he shall know the end and meaning of life.
> When this Law is followed, however little, attachment, fear, and wrath begin to give way to truth, beauty, and love.
> The Law of Moral Causation is the Law of Freedom.
> (Munshi 1988: 21–22)

Yoga is another concept which occurs in the Gita throughout. Munshi defines yoga as 'the one comprehensive process by which man ascends in the scale of life by performing acts which are the expression of a dynamic personality based on the complete co-ordination of all his powers' (Munshi 1988: 39). Based on verses 17 and 18 in Chapter 3 of the Gita, Munshi says that 'to be a yogi is to be oneself' (Munshi 1988: 43). A personality has to be enriched from within by developing inner power. Therefore, he says, a yogi is greater than what he does. 'To "be" is nobler than to "do".' For example, 'there was something greater and nobler in Gandhiji himself than in anything he said or did' (Munshi 1988: 45).

Karma- , jnana- and bhakti-yogas are not substitutes, exclusive from one another. Munshi says, 'Action brings to knowledge its true fulfilment. Knowledge gives the true direction to Action' (Munshi 1988: 81). Bhakti is a divine emotion. He observes that knowledge and action without emotion would amount to 'cold-blooded activities', untouched by love and inspiration. They would serve no purpose. 'Action in search of the self-realisation which the Gita envisages is illumined by Knowledge and inspired by Devotion. It is an offering to be made at the feet of the Lord with love and humility' (Munshi 1988: 81). Munshi clarifies that knowledge that the Gita speaks of is not just worldly knowledge, but knowledge which burns our fetters, frees us from delusion and makes our mind purer and nobler.

An important question in karma-yoga is to decide what work to pursue. Krishna's answer, stresses Munshi, is to follow one's nature and aptitude. Though repression of one's nature is fraught with danger, it can be transmuted through careful training (Munshi 1988: 102). One can begin with the task which circumstances dictate, then find a task to which one is best suited by trial and error and perform it with detachment without aspiring for its fruits. No task, however, is to be considered as inferior or low.

Munshi explains why we should not worry about results but be detached. This is because otherwise anxiety, impatience and restlessness will disturb our attention; steady flow of concentration necessary for achieving results is not possible. Mental energy gets dissipated (Munshi 1988: 106–7, 109). Work, however, needs to be performed seriously as a yoga in pursuit of truth. That is why performing the task as a worship is stressed. It follows that once a task is chosen, the difficulties and pains involved have to be faced cheerfully and with *titiksha* (endurance). In fact, this is true in facing life in general. Munshi clarifies that one does not have to practice sleeping on a spiked bed to develop endurance, for the Gita advises against such methods which torture oneself. Endurance is a mental attitude of being tough. It has to be developed not by repressing one's mind, making it only more rebellious, but by practice and exercising imagination (Munshi 1988: 114–20).

Munshi declares that 'if Yoga means anything at all, my ordinary life has to be transformed by conscious effort into a life which can ultimately lead me to discover God in me' (Munshi 1988: 226). However, he also says that all conscious striving ceases when one submits to the will of God. Then the path becomes clearer, anxiety vanishes and frustration ends (Munshi 1988: 238). Munshi thus sees in the Gita more than moral discipline. It shows a way out from the oppression of materialism of modern life and shows a path of peace and progressive pursuit of reaching the Divine, without having to abdicate one's responsibility to the world.

S. Radhakrishnan

Dr Sarvepalli Radhakrishnan (1888–1975) is a modern acharya who, like the earlier ones, translated and wrote commentary on the *Prasthanatriya* – the *Upanishads*, the *Brahmasutras* and the *Bhagavad-Gita*. He did more. Through several scholarly books, he interpreted Hinduism for the modern times, defending it against unreasonable criticism. He showed that Hinduism is essentially rational, humanistic and ethical, besides being deeply spiritual. For him, Vedanta was 'not a mystical flight into other-worldly experience, but a rational system of thought deserving the name "philosophy"' (Minor 1991-b: 424). He will be remembered much more for this contribution than for the fact that he was India's second President during 1962–67, an uneasy and critical period when India's first prime minister, Jawaharlal Nehru, passed away. Apart from his books on the *Prasthanatriya*, among his well-known books are the two-volume *Indian Philosophy* (1923), *The Hindu View of Life* (1927), *An Idealist View of Life* (1932) and *Eastern Religions and Western Thought* (1939). His birthday, September 5, is celebrated every year in India as the Teachers' Day.

Apart from references to the Gita in other works, Radhakrishnan dealt directly with the Gita in two works. The first is a substantive chapter on 'The Theism of the Bhagavadgita' in Volume 1 of his *Indian Philosophy*, published first in 1923 (Radhakrishnan 1996, Vol. 1: 519–80). The second is a full book, *The Bhagavadgita*, first published in 1948 (Radhakrishnan 1993). His accurate translation, along with commentary, an insightful scholarly introduction, apt references to other commentaries and sacred books in the scholarly notes, has all made his book a classic and a standard reading on the Gita. In the beginning of the book, he gives a brief account of different commentaries on the Gita, from Shankara to Vallabha, and concludes it by observing that even if seemingly conflicting, the different views about the ultimate reality are held to be complementary in the Hindu tradition (Radhakrishnan 1993: 16–20).

Radhakrishnan observes that for the Gita, the world is the scene of an active struggle between the good and the evil, and an intervening personal God 'pours out his wealth of love in helping man to resist all that makes for error, ugliness and evil' (Radhakrishnan 1993: 25). The Gita's emphasis is on the Supreme as the personal loving God, who resides in the heart of every being (XVIII.61). He stirs our hearts to devotion and grants our prayers (IX.24) (Radhakrishnan 1993: 25). He also leads us to right conduct if we listen to His voice in us. Humans, however, also have freedom of will or choice, which entangles them in the law of karma. The Gita, therefore, suggests ways of overcoming binding karma, through karma-yoga. This is at the individual level. At the social or aggregate level, God intervenes whenever there is a grave crisis or deadlock between forces of good and evil. When felt necessary, He takes birth again and again to renew the work of creation on a higher plane (Radhakrishnan 1993: 33). Radhakrishnan clarifies: 'The avatara is the demonstration of man's spiritual resources and latent divinity. It is not so much the contraction of Divine majesty into the limits of the human frame as the exaltation of human nature to the level of Godhead by its union with the Divine' (Radhakrishnan 1993: 32).

According to Radhakrishnan, the Gita is specially suited to address the problem of reconciliation of mankind, as 'it attempts to reconcile varied and apparently antithetical forms of the religious consciousness and emphasises the root conceptions of religion which . . . belong to the very flesh of humanity, past, present and future' (Radhakrishnan 1993: 8). It is addressed to 'pilgrims of all sects who seek to tread the inner way to the city of God.' Radhakrishnan explains further that the contribution of the Gita lies in reconciling different currents of thought, the Upanishadic teaching of the transcendent Brahman, the *Sankhya* dualism, the yoga of meditation, action and devotion, into an 'organic unity', and shows how these different lines of thought converge towards the same end (Radhakrishnan 1993: 14). The reconciliation is achieved in a way that 'sets forth in precise and penetrating words the essential principles of a spiritual [and universal] religion which are not contingent on ill-founded facts, unscientific dogmas or arbitrary fancies' (Radhakrishnan 1993: 11). Radhakrishnan believes, therefore, that the Gita represents no particular sect of Hinduism but Hinduism as a whole, and 'not merely Hinduism, but religion as such in its universality, without limit of time and space' (Radhakrishnan 1993: 12).

Radhakrishnan explains further how the Gita has been creative in achieving a synthesis between different schools of philosophy. For example, there is a dualism between *purusha* and *prakriti* in *Sankhya* philosophy. Prakriti or nature does not have its own consciousness or awareness, and yet its activities are purposive and serve the purpose of gaining freedom of the soul. On the other hand, the individual purushas or souls are merely passive experiencers; they have consciousness but they do not act. This seems unconvincing and inconsistent. The difficulty is solved by the Gita by bringing in Purushottama, the Supreme Soul, who provides the three-way integration between Purusha, Prakriti and Itself (Radhakrishnan 1996, Vol. 1: 528–29). Another example of a creative synthesis is that the Supreme can be viewed as an impersonal immanent Absolute (Brahman) or as a personal God amenable to devotion, or both. Through the Gita, the reflective or contemplative idealism of the Upanishads can be combined with emotional demands of human nature. 'The Gita attempts a spiritual synthesis which could support life and conduct on the basis of the Upanishadic truth, which it carries into the life-blood of the Indian people' (Radhakrishnan 1996: 531). A spiritual pursuit of realising the Brahman need not be dry; it can provide room for devotional love, faith, prayer and service, in terms of the Gita's teaching. Radhakrishnan admits: 'Of course the Gita does not tell us of the way in which the absolute as impersonal non-active spirit becomes the active personal Lord creating and sustaining the universe. The problem is considered to be *intellectually* insoluble. The mystery clears up only when we rise to the level of intuition' (Radhakrishnan 1996: 539; emphasis added). All problems are not amenable to logical reasoning. Some can be solved only experientially and through intuition. As Radhakrishnan rightly observes, 'When devotion is perfected, then the individual and his God become suffused into one spiritual ecstasy, and reveal themselves as aspects of one life. Absolute monism is therefore the completion of the dualism with which the devotional consciousness starts' (Radhakrishnan 1996: 565). In spite of this emphasis on experiencing and intuition, Radhakrishnan uses reasoning too. Referring to Ramanuja's commentary on the Gita, Radhakrishnan suggests that an impersonal immutable Absolute could not have created the Universe and the beings in it. It is only a personal manifested God who could do so. *Maya* is the mystic creative power of this God, as told in the Gita (VII.25) (Radhakrishnan 1996: 543).

The central purpose of the Gita, according to Radhakrishnan, is to solve the problem of life and stimulate the right conduct (Radhakrishnan 1996: 532). It is thus an ethical treatise, a yoga-shastra. Yoga is 'the discipline by which we can train ourselves to bear the shocks of the world with the central being of our soul untouched. . . . We can train our will so as to make our whole life one continuous divine service' (Radhakrishnan 1996: 532). There cannot be a void between righteous living and spiritual pursuit. They nourish each other. The search for truth is both an ethical and spiritual endeavour. The Gita thus provides 'an intellectual search for truth as well as an attempt to make the truth dynamic in the soul of man' (Radhakrishnan 1996: 533).

Ethics are relevant only if the world and changes therein are held to be real. According to Radhakrishnan, the Gita repudiates the view that 'the world is untrue, without any fixed basis, devoid of any ruler, brought about by union caused by lust and nothing else' (XVI.8) (Radhakrishnan 1996: 548). Ishwara is the ruler of the world, about whose welfare He is deeply concerned; He incarnates Himself as an *avatar* to save the world from crisis whenever the need arises. He combines within Himself the immutability of the Absolute, as well as the mutation of becoming for the sake of the world (Radhakrishnan 1996: 546–47).

According to the Gita, points out Radhakrishnan, Ishwara as personal God can be approached and worshipped through any of His aspects or forms, which makes Hinduism tolerant of differences in faiths. It promoted a spiritual culture of allowing that the one truth can have many sides and can be approached in many ways. Consistent with this stand, there is no question of which of the different paths among jnana, karma, bhakti and meditation is superior. The Gita tends to leave it to the choice of the individual (Radhakrishnan 1996: 575) and the individual's aptitude, nature and circumstances. There is no conflict between them, and they can also be combined. From the point of view of the welfare of the world, however, the Gita tends to emphasise action or work more than others. Radhakrishnan observes: 'the Gita recognises that it is through work that we are brought in relation with the rest of the world. The problem of morality has significance only in the human world' (Radhakrishnan 1996: 566). The Gita does not support the ascetic ethics of abandoning the moral responsibilities to the world (Radhakrishnan 1996: 567).

Though Radhakrishnan says that the Gita asserts the truth of Advaita or non-dualism (Radhakrishnan 1996: 537), he is not a rigid follower of Shankara's commentary. Here and there, there are appreciative references to the views of other schools. *Moksha* or release in Advaita is the full realisation of the identification of the individual soul with Brahman, and there remains no separate individuality. But Radhakrishnan says that *moksha* or *mukti* is 'not an obliteration of individuality for all eternity, but a state of blissful freedom of the soul with a distinct existence in the presence of God' (Radhakrishnan 1996: 577). In this state, the individual soul is in continuous enjoyment of being in God's presence. Quoting Krishna ('My devotees come to Me', VII.23, IX.25, IV.9), Radhakrishnan says that the 'author of the Gita seems to believe in a continuance of conscious individuality even in freedom [*mukti*]' (Radhakrishnan 1996: 577). Radhakrishnan also refers to the other view of *mukti* where the freed soul loses itself in the impersonality of Brahman and attains a peace beyond worldly strife, and says that it depends on how one applies the idea of the Absolute Brahman. If one believes firmly that the Absolute reveals Itself as a personal God who enjoys our love and whose love we can enjoy, the individuality would remain (Radhakrishnan 1996: 578).

Radhakrishnan thus interpreted the Gita not only as the basis of Hinduism, but also as a spiritual religion of universal relevance, as stressing inclusiveness and accommodation of different currents of thought, an activism with a social purpose and meeting the demands of ethics as well as the emotional needs of persons to be loved by a caring God, without depriving them of a mystical experience of the immanent Divine. He never attempts to assert the superiority of the Gita over the scriptures of other religions. His scholarly and insightful contribution will be long remembered.

Sri Sri Paramahansa Yogananda

Sri Sri Paramahansa Yogananda (1893–1952) is a very eminent name in exporting spiritual wisdom and yoga from India, who became a celebrity in bringing together the people of India and the United States. His movement covered mainly the Americans, and not just the Indian diaspora in the United States. Born in a Bengali family in Gorakhpur as Mukunda Lal Ghosh, he came under the influence of eminent Yoga Guru Sri Yukteshwar, whose disciple he became. At the instance of his guru, he went to the United States in 1920, but kept in touch with India. He founded Yogada Satsanga Society in Ranchi in India and Self-Realization Fellowship in Los Angeles in the United States. He preached a specially developed method called kriya-yoga. He insisted, however, that yoga is not a question of mere technique, but something through which all selfish desires are consumed in the fire of love for the Divine. His *Autobiography of a Yogi*, first published in 1946, turned out to be one of the most popular autobiographies, next only perhaps to Mahatma Gandhi's.

Most of the commentators on the Gita have focused on karma-yoga, jnana-yoga and bhakti-yoga, to the relative neglect of raja-yoga, which also is an important teaching of the Gita. Yogananda, however, gave priority to the training of one's mind, without which the other paths or yogas meaningful cannot be meaningful. His two-volume book (with continuity in pagination), having a mouthful title, *God Talks with Arjuna: The Bhagavad Gita – Royal Science of God Realization – The Immortal Dialogue between Soul and Spirit – A New Translation and Commentary*, was published first in 1995 at Los Angeles, and then in India too (Yogananda 2002). It has been very well received both in the United States and in India and considered as a significant contribution.

Yogananda says that the real background of the timeless message of the Gita is not one battle a long time ago, but a continuous and universal conflict between various opposing forces – good and evil, life and death, knowledge and ignorance, health and disease, changelessness and transitoriness, self-control and temptations, discrimination and non-discrimination, soul and body, and spirit and matter (Yogananda 2002, Vol. 1: 1). The Gita intends to guide human beings in the onerous task of resolving these conflicts in a way that help them attain their spiritual goal and real and lasting happiness. The Gita teaches that it does not help one to be emotionally mired in these conflicts, but has to raise the level of consciousness to a higher plane of detachment to resolve them. So long as a human being is bogged down into the daily flux and is tossed about by changes, there will be restlessness. This *restlessness* has to change into *calmness* (but not depression). Yogananda classifies states of mind into four types: (i) always restless, never calm; (ii) restless part of the time, calm part of the time; (iii) calm most of the time, restless occasionally; (iv) always calm, never restless. He points out how the Gita explains that restlessness eclipses *buddhi* (discrimination, wisdom), leads to mistakes and further to more restlessness. One has to gradually try to reach the most ideal state of always being calm in spite of all vicissitudes, through a conscious effort (Yogananda 2002, Vol. 1: 34–36).

Yoga helps in this task by raising one's consciousness fixed on mundane matters to a higher cosmic level through various steps. First, by practicing guru-given meditation. The seeker would then be able to expand his narrow attachments confined to family and a narrow circle of friends to a larger level of all-inclusive love. The next step is to overcome constant body-consciousness and the identification of the self with the body, and focus on the Divine. Next is to achieve control on breathing and heartbeat, and direct attention and energy on the spinal centres (*chakras*) as described in the yoga-shastra. If this is achieved, the seeker can reach a state of super-consciousness and experience the Immanent Brahman (Yogananda 2002, Vol. 1: 37–38). Yogananda insists that yoga has to be practiced under the personal guidance of a guru. However, nothing is lost if one stops after achieving the first step, and the Gita assures that even persons practicing some level of spirituality and dharma are saved from fear and will find the strength to go higher (II.40). Everyone does not have to seek attaining the super-conscious state, but everyone – including the worldly – has to ponder over moving on to a higher plane of moral existence. That is how one can contribute to *loka-hita* (welfare of the world) preached by the Gita. Gurus like Yogananda think that if one sets aside even a little time regularly for meditation, it helps in spiritual, moral and material progress. They strengthen each other in a mutual way. Daily meditation helps in gaining 'self-control necessary to overcome the bad habits that constitute one's lower nature' (Yogananda 2002, Vol. 1: 178). That is how the Gita includes a chapter on dhyana-yoga as well, along with emphasising karma-, jnana- and bhakti-yogas.

An important teaching of the Gita which Yogananda highlights is about how to face death – one's own or of the dear ones. It has to be faced with equanimity. 'Grief is born of ignorance, attachment, and selfish love, because the ordinary man sees only the present frame of existence' (Yogananda 2002, Vol. 1: 240). The Gita says that for the immortal soul, death of the body is like giving up old clothes for a new one (II.22). It is a continuation of the same life process under which a child becomes an adult, and an adult becomes old (II.13). Yogananda observes: 'In sleep every night an individual discards the consciousness of the tired body and mind and so finds peace; in the greater sleep of death, a man forsakes the disease-torn body and the attachment-corroded mind for a restful state of joy' (Yogananda 2002, Vol. 1: 219). It does not mean that the Gita approves suicide or going about killing others on the plea that the soul cannot be killed. It is because the Gita also wants that as long as one lives according to God's will, one owes it to the world to perform one's duties and allow others as well to do so. A man has no right to violate the God-ordained circuit of life. Yogananda also clarifies that the Gita does not teach us to be heartless. A yogi, a person of perfect equilibrium, is 'neither hyper-sensitive nor stoically heartless'. During a bereavement caused by the loss of a loved one, he or she understands, feels the loss and even expresses it in a natural way. But the person will not allow the loss to emotionally devastate his or her life. Death of a loved one should teach us that one's emotional attachment should not be confined to a tiny little circle, but expand to cover all mankind (Yogananda 2002, Vol. 1: 240–44).

Like other interpreters, Yogananda also considers that the central message of the Gita is to get actively and selflessly engaged in the world to help others with a sense of detachment. Nevertheless, he adds that 'the worldly man should seek out a meditative man and create his own inviolate inner environment of God-communion. . . . Only when he has thus strengthened himself can he be of help in uplifting others' (Yogananda 2002, Vol. 2: 1042). The inner spiritual development of a person is necessary, according to him, to be an effective karma-yogi. That is why the Gita provides a holistic and comprehensive course for such a development. Yogananda's interpretation of the Gita has much to help a mentally troubled world; that is why he was so popular in the West. However, he did not show the same acute sensitivity which Swami Vivekananda had to social problems of underdeveloped countries like poverty and deprivation, where also the Gita had something useful and inspiring to say, which Vivekananda brought out clearly even in his brief writings on the Gita.

Vinoba Bhave

Among a few rare persons who would strictly qualify to be called as karma-yogis, dedicating their entire life to the selfless service of humanity, there is undoubtedly Vinoba Bhave (1895–1982). He is considered as the spiritual successor to Mahatma Gandhi. He took a vow of *brahmacharya* (celibacy and highly disciplined life) early in his life and lived up to its ideals to the end. He did not take *sannyas*, but took the whole world as his family (*Vasudhaiva kutumbakam*) literally. He coined a slogan, *Jai Jagat* (Victory to the World!), to reflect his cosmopolitan and inclusive philosophy. He left his college studies in 1916, burnt his certificates and joined Gandhi in his freedom struggle and national reconstruction work. Gandhi placed him in charge of his Wardha Ashram and also sent him to Vaikom in Kerala to oversee the struggle for entry of Harijans (untouchables) to a temple there. Vinoba was jailed several times by the British. It was during one of the stints of imprisonment that he gave his famous 'Talks on the Gita' to fellow prisoners at Dhule in 1932, published first in Marathi (under the title *Gita-pravachane*) and later into many other Indian languages. The English translation came out in 1958. Vinoba also started the *Sarvodaya* (uplift of all) movement in rural areas even before independence. After independence, being moved by the plight of landless rural labour, he started the Bhoodan movement in 1951, beginning with Andhra Pradesh. He declared *Sab bhoomi Gopalaki* (all land belongs to God) and coaxed thousands of large landholders to donate their some of their lands for the landless. The movement was hardly a great success, since not much land was donated, and even the donated lands were mostly inferior, which needed investment of time and money to make them productive. This was not feasible for the poor landless. The Bhoodan movement spurred him to launch another rural movement called *Gram-dan*, wherein an entire village would pool all the productive resources together, managing and working the rural economy collectively, and distribute the output or income equally to all based on their needs. Remarkably, over a thousand villages came under this movement. He used to actually *walk* from village to village covering vast stretches of the country, addressing people, and move on, as part of these movements. In spite of his tireless work, he attracted a lot of criticism, including personal attacks for his idealism and idiosyncrasies. His support to Emergency declared by Indira Gandhi in 1975 attracted a strong criticism; he was nicknamed *Sarkaari sant* (Government's saint) by the media because of this. He had welcomed

Emergency as *Anushasan Parva*, that is time for law and order, and discipline, which he felt India needed very much. However, he wanted such discipline not only among the ruled but also among the rulers. (But who would discipline rulers under a dictatorship?) He was reverentially called as acharya (spiritual teacher-scholar) by his followers. He was the first recipient of Ramon Magsaysay Award for community living in 1958 and posthumously honoured with Bharat-Ratna by the president of India in 1983.[8]

His *Talks on the Gita* (Bhave 1964) could be said to be based broadly on Gandhi's ideas, with a great overlap in views. Like Gandhi, Vinoba also emphasised truth and non-violence and selfless service of humanity by setting a personal example. He tried to live according to the principles preached by the Gita. Both were opposed to cow slaughter and meat-eating, as an expression of following the principle of non-violence. Like Gandhi again, Vinoba considered the Gita as his spiritual mother.

Vinoba explains that it was not the fear of battle which made Arjuna reluctant to fight, not even the fear of causing violence in principle; but it was only his emotional attachment to his own people which made him despondent. That is why Krishna had to teach Arjuna that he had to place dharma or duty above attachment to some chosen people. One may come across similar situations in life, where moral duty requires a certain action, but there is a temptation to avoid it because of the fear that it may hurt one's near and dear ones. From the point of view of the Gita, ethics of duty should prevail over attachment to relatives and friends. Vinoba emphasises that according to the Gita, one does not have to wonder what duty to perform; it is *swadharma*, a duty which comes naturally to oneself. Vinoba does not, however, go deeper into this question though he reverts to it now and then almost throughout his *Talks*. He tells, however, that swadharma need not be something which is fixed for all life for a person, but can change based on thinking and experience (Bhave 1964: 8).

According to Vinoba, the right way to worship God is not to decorate His stone or metal images with diamond and gold, nor to engage in rituals like *abhisheka* (pouring water or milk on the idols), but see Him in the humanity at large and serve Him by serving people (Bhave 1964: 121), an advice which he followed himself in practice. He suggested that a farmer who toils all day to feed many is a greater spiritual seeker than others who do not work but engage themselves in rituals (Bhave 1964: 127). However, he recommended reciting the name of God (*japa*) even while working as a way to spiritual advancement.

This way, all life can be filled with God. He had tremendous faith in the power of God's name (*naam*), just like Gandhi.

Nevertheless, Vinoba did not oppose image worship as idolatry. He considered it as an aid to spiritual seeking and respected a devotee who sees in the little image she or he adores the beauty, holiness and power of the Supreme who pervades the whole cosmos (Bhave 1964: 162). The Gita may not have endorsed image worship explicitly, but its endorsement is clear in the assurance of the Lord that he would accept all different ways of worship done with a pure heart. Vinoba considers the debate on *saguna* (God with attributes) and *nirguna* (God without attributes) as pointless, because God is both (Bhave 1964: 172–74). It is a matter left to devotee's own convenience and perception. Nevertheless, Vinoba feels that a devotee who sees God everywhere in all humanity and works for the welfare of all is the ideal (Bhave 1964: 176). He says that without nirguna, saguna worship is defective if God is seen only in the image and nowhere else. Similarly, without the love of a saguna devotee for humanity and without active work for the welfare of all, nirguna worship becomes dry and dreary (Bhave 1964: 177–78). Thus, in Vinoba's view, both saguna and nirguna are complementary.

The significance of Vinoba's interpretation of the Gita is that, as in Gandhi's case, he actually lived his life as taught by it. He thought like Gandhi, dressed like Gandhi, lived an austere life like Gandhi and spent all his life in the selfless service of others like Gandhi. He is perhaps the last Gandhian of his stature.

A. C. Bhaktivedanta Swami Prabhupada

Abhay Charanaravinda Bhaktivedanta Swami Prabhupada (1896–1977) is one of the most successful among swamis who went to the West to spread Hinduism, though a particular brand of it. He left for New York from Calcutta at the age of sixty-nine in 1965, and what he achieved thereafter in the last twelve years of his life was monumental both literally and metaphorically. He started his work alone at a storefront in New York chanting Krishna's name. His mantra to everyone until the end was simply *Hare Krishna Hare Krishna, Krishna Krishna Hare Hare, Hare Rama Hare Rama, Rama Rama Hare Hare*. His musical chanting and dancing with complete abandon attracted several including derelicts. Soon he gathered a large following, bulk of which consisted of drug addicts who had lost their purpose in life and were desperately seeking an alternative. Krishna chanting worked like magic on them and led to a complete transformation of their lives. Soon he attracted many more including intellectuals and spiritual seekers. Simultaneously Prabhupada edited and translated with commentary *Srimad-Bhagavatam* (30 volumes) and wrote many other books – about sixty, *Bhagavad-Gita as It Is*, being one of them. His book on the Gita was first published in 1968, followed by an expanded edition in 1972. The second edition came posthumously in 1983. Swami Prabhupada travelled widely, and with the help of his numerous followers, he built 108 temples all over the world. They turned out to be centres not only of spreading Krishna consciousness, but also of rendering social service. Their huge project of providing midday meals to school children has attracted many poor children to schooling in India. He started the International Society for Krishna Consciousness (ISKCON) in 1966 in New York – within a year of his arriving at the United States, which has now many branches all over the world.[9]

According to Swami Prabhupada, though many have interpreted the Gita, most of them projected their own views rather than of the Gita itself, and his purpose was to project the Gita as it really was. Hence the title of his book *Bhagavad-Gita as It Is* (Prabhupada 1983). He asserts: 'We must accept Bhagavad-gita without interpretation, without deletion and without our own whimsical participation in the matter' (Prabhupada 1983: 15). After translating a verse, therefore, he does not give a 'commentary', but gives its 'purport'. Interpretations, in whatever name, are necessary because we cannot literally apply every word or sentence to a different time and context. For example, Prabhupada explains verse 19 in Chapter 2, by saying that merely because the soul cannot be killed and Krishna spurs Arjuna to fight, it does not mean that people can be killed wantonly. Prabhupada cites the Vedic injunction – *Ma himsyat sarva-bhutani* ('Never commit violence on anyone') – in support and opposes even animal slaughter on this ground (Prabhupada 1983: 100). Obviously, his advice for caution against irresponsible interpretation is well intentioned. Having read the Gita many times and also many interpretations of genuine sages and scholars, I cannot, however, really say that these interpretations are not based on the Gita and only Prabhupada's is genuine and authentic. Nevertheless the claim about the Gita 'as it is' helped marketing Prabhupada's Gita worldwide, backed by the unbounded energy which Prabhupada infused into ISKCON. It is considered as 'the largest selling, most widely used edition of the Gita in the Western world' (as claimed on the back cover). It has been translated into many languages – Arabic, Bengali, Chinese, Dutch, French, German,

Gujarati, Hindi, Italian, Japanese, Portuguese, Russian, Spanish, Swedish and many more (Prabhupada 1983: vi).

If you go by the word of the Gita, Prabhupada says, Krishna is the 'Supreme Personality of Godhead'; He is also the Paramatma, the Supreme Soul, or Ishwara, or Bhagavan, who lives in everybody as the controller. He is pure, free from all blemish, unborn and eternal. He is all grace, full of kindness and responds to the prayers of his devotees. He is just, sees all as equals (though having a soft corner for devotees). He is equally accessible to all irrespective of class, caste or gender. He intends to take his devotees to a higher level of spiritual development bringing them closer to Him. He not only controls all the *jivas* (living beings), but also helps them all in their spiritual evolution. The Supreme, as per the Gita, in Prabhupada's view, is not the impersonal Brahman. He does not deny the existence of an impersonal aspect of the Supreme, but it is in the form of 'shining rays of the Supreme Personality of Godhead' and is incomplete by itself and subordinate or secondary to the latter. Only the Supreme Personality of Godhead is complete. He elaborates: 'Impersonal Brahman realization is the realization of His *sat* (eternity) feature. Paramatma realization is the *sat-chit* (eternal knowledge). But realization of the Personality of Godhead, Krishna, is realization of all the transcendental features: *sat, chit*, and *ananda* (eternity, knowledge, and bliss) in complete *vigraha* (form)' (Prabhupada 1983: 14). Prabhupada thus tries to resolve the debate about how the Gita reconciles the two opposite perspectives of the Supreme – the impersonal and personal – and leaves us in no doubt about which is higher and fuller.

Prakriti, or material nature or universe, is controlled and run by the Supreme. It is of two kinds – superior prakriti comprises all life or living beings and inferior prakriti is purely material with no life as such. The *gunas* or 'qualities' – *satvika, rajasika and tamasika* – are attributes of living beings in superior prakriti, especially in human beings (Prabhupada 1983: 9). Manifestation of prakriti may be temporary, but it is not false. It is like a cloud, which appears and disappears, but cloud is not false merely because it is transitory. The cycle of manifestation and dissolution of prakriti takes place through phases of time, but the cycle itself is eternal. The material nature is the manifestation of energy of God, and He is above it. Prakriti is a part of Him, but He is not a part of it (Prabhupada 1983: 10, 865). Prabhupada is totally opposed to *mayavada*, which regards the world as an illusion and denies individualities. He thinks that individualities of living beings or their souls are retained even after *moksha*. He appreciatively quotes Chaitanya, who had forbidden reading commentaries based on *ma̱ya̱va̱da*, as it could spoil a correct understanding of the Gita (Prabhupada 1983: 89–90).

There is, however, a problem in Prabhupada's philosophy. According to him, all beings, including humans, are under complete control of the Supreme. 'If a living entity says that he is not controlled but that he is free, then he is insane' (Prabhupada 1983: 8). Krishna is the owner of all senses and also their director (Prabhupada 1983: 46–47). However, if God is in complete control, how can the question of karma, or of *pa̱pa* (sin) and *pu̱nya* (merit), arise? How can moral obligations arise if human beings are considered as having no freedom of will and are merely cogs in a machine run by God? However, Prabhupada is forced to modify his stand when it comes to explaining verse 63 in Chapter 18, where Krishna asks Arjuna to ponder over what all he had said and then decide what to do. Prabhupada admits here that 'God does not interfere with the little independence of the living entity' (Prabhupada 1983: 848).

The sum and substance of Prabhupada's interpretation of the Gita can be stated in his own words: 'Factually we are related to the Supreme Lord in service. The Supreme Lord is the supreme enjoyer, and we living entities are His servitors. We are created for His enjoyment, and if we participate in that eternal enjoyment with the Supreme Personality of Godhead, we become happy. We cannot be happy otherwise' (Prabhupada 1983: 20).

Swami Ranganathananda

Swami Ranganathananda (1908–2005) became a monk in the Ramakrishna Math order at the age of twenty-five and rose to become the president of Ramakrishna Math and Mission in 1998. He was a great orator, and it is said that having listened to his lecture on Islam, Mohammad Ali Jinna exclaimed, 'Now I know how a true Muslim should be!' The Swami has authored more than fifty books, including the famous *Eternal Values for a Changing Society* (1971). He had a scientific temper and was open to learning from natural and social sciences. He had a simple way for assessing spiritual progress. He said: 'Are you growing spiritually? Can you love others? Can you feel oneness with others? Have you peace within yourself? And do you radiate it around you? That is called spiritual growth, which is stimulated by meditation inwardly, and by work done in a spirit of service outwardly.'[10]

Apart from referring to the teachings of the Gita in other works, Swami Ranganathananda wrote a special three-volume book on the Gita itself – *Universal Message of the Bhagavad Gita: An Exposition of the Gita in the Light of Modern Thought and Modern Needs* (2000). The book contains not only a translation of each verse of the Gita, but also a lucid commentary on each of them. Like other interpreters, he explains the different paths of spiritual growth along with moral lessons of the Gita, but the way he does it appeals to modern minds. For example, while explaining verse 18 of Chapter 4, he says:

> Work is no work at all. It is a question of agency and attachment. When these two are not there [with agency attributed to God], work ceases to be work, it becomes play, it becomes spontaneous, it becomes natural. . . . [W]ork comes when there is effort, struggle, tension. When you become thoroughly detached, then all that tension goes away. You are working, but you don't feel you are working. . . . [T]oday's industrial civilization is teaching that work is a drudgery. Joy must be found outside work. . . . As soon as Friday evening comes, millions of people are running out for a holiday. These five days were all drudgery.
>
> (Ranganathananda 2000, Vol. 1: 431)

Swami Ranganathananda is certainly not against taking a few holidays to enjoy a quiet change in routine, but not because work is drudgery. Working with detachment does not mean indifference or non-seriousness. It is not loafing. One has to work sincerely and express one's personality through work. It can then be a spiritual experience (Ranganathananda 2000: 432).

Quoting Shankara's commentary, Swami Ranganathananda says that the human society needs to move on an even keel balancing both *pravritti* (material advancement) and *nivritti* (spiritual pursuit). Through *pravritti*, a welfare society has to be established, where no one goes hungry and without education, home and health care. This can be achieved only alongside a value-based life and spiritual strengthening of every person, ensuring dignity for all. There has to be peace between individuals and social groups, and also peace and self-confidence within each. A healthy society can be achieved with proper co-operation, co-ordination and understanding and not by each fighting against the other. Progress has to be achieved together both fronts, material and moral, with everyone included and covering the villages too (Ranganathananda 2000: 26–35).

Swami Ranganathananda's commentary is unique in emphasising environmental implications of the Gita, which have been ignored by other interpreters. The relevant verses on which his commentary is based are tenth to sixteenth in Chapter 3 of the Gita. The Swami says that according to these verses, the whole world – even the whole cosmos – is based on the concept of *yajna*, with give and take going on everywhere. Everything is related to everything, and there is great interconnectedness. Unknowingly birds carry seeds from place to place and propagate plant life; unknowingly again, they control pests affecting plants by eating them and rendering them harmless. Wastes are turned into manure. Earthworms toil ceaselessly, upturn the soil and make it nutrient rich. The nature uses them all and maintains ecological balance. Unfortunately, man in his ignorance and short-sightedness breaks this interconnectedness, violates the yajna of nature and endangers his own and others' lives. The Gita's advice is 'nourish and support each other and reap the highest' (*parasparam bhavayantah shreyah paramavapsyatha*, III.11). This is as much true for the natural resource environment as for the social world. If you only take from nature and not give it back to nourish it, it amounts to abusing it and would be breaking the natural ecological cycle that sustains the world. Verse 13 in the same chapter (the third) (*Yajna-shishtasinah . . . atmakaranat*) can be interpreted thus in this context: those who eat or use sustainably only what is left as *prasada* (grace) from the nature's yajna are blameless, but those who exploit God-given natural resources unsustainably and greedily for themselves eat only sin. The Gita condemns unsustainable exploitation of nature (including its use as waste-sink) and wants the cycle of life and natural regeneration to continue unbroken. The Gita supports sustainable use of nature in another way too, by exhorting us to curtail our wants and avoiding unnecessary luxury and wasteful consumption (Ranganathananda 2000: 265–78).

According to Swami Ranganathananda, '[e]very word in this Gita is meant to make people better, [and] civilization richer and purer, whether it is East or West' (Ranganathananda 2000: 444). He says that the Gita of course is the essence of the Upanishads, but the further essence of this essence is verse 55 in Chapter 11, which he translates as: 'One who does work for Me alone, and has Me for his or her goal, is devoted to me, is free from sensory attachment, and bears no enmity towards any being – he or she attains to Me, O Pandava!' (2000, Vol. 2:

513). In explaining this verse, the Swami clarifies that detachment is not being apathetic and lack of love. *Nirvaira* (no enmity) is not just a negative concept, but it means positive love for all. It is not enough not to hate anyone; one should have love for all, indicates the Swami. To say or feel 'Children are weeping there. I don't care. I have no attachment' is not detachment. He explains, it is expansion, not contraction of mind and love, expressed in helpful action. 'No hatred towards anybody; only love for all; with a detached mind.' That is the Gita, says the Swami (Ranganathananda 2000: 514). His interpretation of the Gita is one of the most inspiring, arousing the noblest human emotions and building a society of mutual concern and harmony – not focused just on individual salvation. He showed that individual salvation lies in fact in contributing to building such a society.

Eknath Easwaran

Eknath Easwaran (1910–99) has been respected worldwide as one of the most profound and inspiring writers and orators on religion and spirituality. Born in Kerala, he had higher education at Nagpur University, where he also served as a professor of English. He went to California University in the United States as a Fulbright Scholar in 1959, lectured on meditation in San Francisco Bay Area in 1960 and met his wife Christine there first. He returned to India in 1961 and went back again to the Bay Area in 1965. He settled in California thereafter. He developed a way of meditation, which he called Passage Meditation. Essentially, it is a silent repetition of a memorised inspirational passage from the books of any great religion of the world. He founded the Blue Mountain Center of Meditation and Nilgiri Press in North California, which has published most of his books. He wrote many books on Hindu, Buddhist and Christian sacred texts and also on Gandhi and Badshah Khan – known as Frontier Gandhi in India (whom he called as the 'Nonviolent Soldier of Islam'). Many of his talks are available in audio and video format.[11]

His two works on the Gita have been critically acclaimed, the first being a three-volume book on *The Bhagavad Gita for Daily Living* (Easwaran 1997). Its first volume, *The End of Sorrow*, came out in 1975; the second, *Like a Thousand Suns*, in 1979; and the third, *To Love Is to Know Me*, in 1984. The first volume, based mainly on the first six chapters of the Gita, is focused on the individual; it shows how one can find one's own self and transform one's life through meditation and selfless service. An interesting highlight of this volume is the detailed teaching on how to meditate. The second volume based mainly on the next six chapters of the Gita, projects the basic and indivisible Unity governing all creation, which has implications for relationships between individuals that can heal the divisions in society. The third volume mainly based on the last six chapters of the Gita deals chiefly with how each one of us can make a difference in the world today and how to find fulfilment through bhakti. The other book on the Gita by Eswaran, *Essence of the Bhagavad Gita – A Contemporary Guide to Yoga, Meditation and Indian Philosophy* (Easwaran 2012), was edited by his long-time students and close associates as per his instructions given less than a year before his death, published posthumously. It is based on the transcripts of his talks and informal sessions with his close students and is considered as the distillation of his teaching on the Gita in his own words. The following account of Easwaran's main contributions to the understanding of the Gita is based mainly on this second book, as it draws not only from the first book but also from his subsequent insights. However, the first book is no less essential for a full understanding of the Gita.

Easwaran regards the Gita as a text not so much on Hinduism as on *sanatana dharma*, 'which is the bedrock of reality, the eternal principles or changeless values on which life is based, regardless of creed, country, culture, or epoch,' and 'the whole point of sanatana dharma is that religion must be based on personal experience'(Easwaran 2012: 13). According to Easwaran, 'the central message of the Gita is that life is an indivisible whole – a concept that contemporary civilization flouts at every turn'. It is only when we realise this that we can live in harmony with others and with ourselves. He adds: 'The Gita doesn't ask us to take this on faith. It simply offers a frame of reference through which we can look afresh at what we see around us, scrutinize the plans and promises offered by contemporary politics and economics, and judge for ourselves how useful any approach can be that does not begin with the essential unity of life' (Easwaran 2012: 18).

The Gita has to be seen more as 'a practical manual for daily living' than as a text on philosophy or as mere poetry, emphasises Easwaran (1997, Vol. 1: 11). That is why the title *The Bhagavad Gita for Daily Living* for his major book on the Gita (1997). To convince us about the practicality of the manual, we need some exemplars who lived out their lives on it. There have been many of them in the Hindu spiritual tradition with unbroken continuity, says Easwaran (Easwaran 2012, Vol. 1: 13). '[T]o grasp the meaning of the Bhagavad Gita, we need look no further than Mahatma Gandhi, who made it a guide for every aspect of daily living' (2012: 8). Gandhi certainly has not been the last in this line, since such eminent exemplars like Vinoba Bhave, Swami Chinmayananda and Swami Dayananda have followed him.

Easwaran says that it is his surmise that 'the Gita was originally an Upanishad which has been inserted into the Mahabharata, its first chapter serving as a bridge' between the two (1997, Vol. 1: 14; 2012: 15–16). The colophons at the end of every chapter, calling the Gita as an Upanishad, confirm this, he adds. Even accepting the Gita as an integral part of the epic, Easwaran agrees with Gandhi in treating the battlefield background as an allegory. He says that the names themselves support this. 'Dhritarashtra' means 'one who has usurped the throne'. The names of his sons all begin with *'du'*, which means 'evil'. 'Duryodhana' means a 'dirty fighter'. Krishna tells Arjuna that emotional weaknesses like lust and anger are enemies which must be fought. Easwaran, therefore, agrees with Gandhi in treating the battle as symbolic of a fight between the 'good' and the 'evil', which takes place right within us (2012: 16–17). He points out that the Gita presents this basically as 'a conflict between a lower self and a higher one' (Easwaran 2012: 27). The lower self is the ego or *ahamkara* (the 'I-maker'), which is a cage of separateness, and identifying oneself with this narrow self is 'the source of insecurity, friction, disrupted relationships, and mounting dissatisfaction' (Easwaran 2012: 27–28). Easwaran says that according to the Gita, 'in every one of us – by virtue of being human – there is an upward surge to evolve, to grow in humanity day by day, and a downward pull to remain engaged in conflict as separate creatures set against the rest of life' (Easwaran 2012: 29). He sums up the message of the Gita: 'gradually we can choose to throw more and more weight behind the pull towards our higher nature and away from the drag of separateness and conditioned behaviour' (Easwaran 2012: 31).

Meditation, according to Easwaran, is an important means of discovering the basic reality or the common ground of being within us and outside, which the Gita recommends. It cannot be realised through our sense organs tuned to the external world. The Upanishadic sages found that when we withdraw our attention from the senses, we can stand apart from the thought process and observe it objectively. 'Awareness then becomes absorbed in the world within' (Easwaran 2012: 38). He explains that 'as concentration deepens, thought merges in one titanic inquiry beyond words: "Who am I?" Finally, this inquiry itself dissolves and the mind remains completely still – yet awareness remains; we are immeasurably more awake than when the mind and senses are active'. It is then that we become aware that we are not separate creatures (Easwaran 2012: 39). Life finds its fulfilment when we know the common divine ground of existence, which is the Supreme Reality. This can be found within our lifetime; one does not have to wait for death (Easwaran 2012: 43–44). There are practical benefits also of this realisation. We can concentrate better, apply our mind more effectively and become better beings. Lower emotions like anger and hatred get dissipated and give way to compassion and goodwill for all. 'When we meditate every morning we are putting an armour for the day's battle against our own impatience, inadequacy, resentment, and hostility' (2012, Vol. 1: 46).

Easwaran cautions that meditating for some time in a day and then letting the mind do as it likes the rest of the day defeats its purpose (1997: 134). It should have an enduring impact on taming the mind and help self-realisation. Once we realise that we are not separate egocentric petty creatures and feel oneness with the real self, it marks the end of sorrow, according to the Gita, says Easwaran. He points to verses 21 and 22 in Chapter 6 of the Gita, which say: 'Having attained that abiding joy, there is no more to desire. You cannot be shaken even by the heaviest burden of sorrow' (1997: 65). Easwaran tells that the resulting profound peace in your heart spreads around you, and highest happiness comes to you (1997: 144). However, the Gita is careful to point out that this need not mark the end of action. 'Full inside, you don't need anything, but you are restless to give, to serve' (1997: 65). You continue to be sensitive, not to your own sorrow, but to the pain and suffering in others, and therefore work to mitigate it selflessly (1997: 66). Seeing the connection between self-realisation, development of compassion and love for all, and action, Easwaran comes up with an inspiring message based on the Gita's teaching: 'To know is to love, and to love is to act' (1997: 119). He gives his translation of verses 54–56 in Chapter 18 in support:

> United with Brahman, ever joyful, beyond the reach of desire and sorrow, they have equal regard for every living creature and attain supreme devotion to me. By loving me, they come to know me truly; then they know my glory and enter into my boundless being. All their acts are performed in my service, and through my grace they win eternal life.
>
> (1997: 119–20)

Like other interpreters of the Gita, Easwaran also explains the different paths of spiritual pursuit in his own insightful way. The advantage of emotional detachment from outcome or results even while working hard for a great cause selflessly is that we can then work without anxiety and with confidence and peace of mind. It does not mean we should be indifferent to expected consequences of our action. But we don't lose our nerve when things go wrong and can take corrective steps calmly. An important requirement of karma-yoga is to avoid work which may harm others (1997: 122–25). Bhakti, which means devotion or love, is a precious capacity and is a part of being human, says Easwaran. It is 'forgetting completely in the welfare of all' (1997: 125). This implies that bhakti is combined with work and is not a mere sentiment. He cautions against the 'absurd idea that love has anything to do with the body or senses'; it is 'a state of consciousness'. He adds that love is the 'opposite of self-will' through which one tries to manipulate and subordinate (1997: 126). Easwaran admits that Krishna at times seems to prefer one path over the others, which confuses Arjuna (III.2), but Easwaran advises that to avoid confusion, the Gita is to be taken as a whole and 'follow a way of life in which the three paths are combined'(1997: 127).

According to Easwaran, *Homo sapiens* represent a stage in evolution, which is halfway between our biological nature and what we can become. We have the capacity and choice to take up the evolutionary duty of taking our destiny as individuals into our own hands and guiding life to its fullest potential (1997: 206). As an example, he says that when somebody is angry with us and we remain calm instead of retaliating, we break a link with the animal and rise a bit higher on our personal ladder of evolution (1997: 208). The way we reflect the three *gunas – sattva, rajas and tamas* – explained in the Gita determines how we evolve. He translates verses 11–13 from the fourteenth chapter of the Gita in support:

> When sattva predominates, the light of wisdom shines through every gate of the body. When rajas predominates, a person runs about pursuing selfish and greedy ends, driven by restlessness and desire. When tamas is dominant, a person lives in darkness – slothful, confused, and easily infatuated.
>
> (1997: 210)

Sattva helps the evolutionary process, as when we render selfless service or forgive. At the opposite end is tamas, which pushes us down the ladder of evolution, as when one gets a feeling of 'who cares?' or 'not my problem'. Easwaran says, 'we can draw upon rajas to transform tamas, and then channel and harness rajas to transform it into sattva. . . . sattva is the platform we must reach in order to move beyond the gunas altogether into unitary consciousness' (1997: 213). In our evolutionary struggle, our real self or the higher self is our friend, and the ego is the enemy. Easwaran quotes two key verses from the Gita in this context (VI.5–6), which say 'Raise yourself by yourself, and don't demean yourself'. He says, 'we don't have enemies outside, but we have the fiercest enemies inside if we undermine our will'. The Gita, according to Easwaran, puts the responsibility for our evolutionary rise and emancipation on our own shoulders, through these two verses (1997: 226). He elaborates: 'As long as we try to prop ourselves up with possessions and people, we have no freedom, and the props are guaranteed to fail. Sooner or later we have to learn to rely on the Self alone' (1997: 242). Life is thus a struggle, and Easwaran says that it is significant that the Gita does not end with victory, but with a resolution (by Arjuna) to fight until the war is won.

Easwaran is one of the most readable authors. Both of his books on the Gita are so full of wisdom and so charmingly written that it is tempting to quote every sentence. I have selected, however, a few from just one chapter (1997, Vol. 1, Chapter 1), given here, to bring out the flavour of his writing.

> One of the best definitions of confusion is doing what is unnecessary and failing to do what is necessary.
>
> (p. 32)

> We have been so conditioned to search for happiness in sense-pleasure that defying these urges appears to be a denial of life itself. . . . As we progress on the spiritual path, . . . we discover that we have been pursuing agitation instead of joy and accumulation instead of security.
>
> (p. 33)

> [I]t is the non-violent person who cannot be frightened; the violent person can always be threatened with greater violence.
>
> (p. 35)

> [W]hat lasting joy there is in trying to complete one another rather than compete against one another.
>
> (p. 38)

> When we fight others, we are harming everyone; when we fight all that is base and self-willed in us, we are benefiting everyone.
>
> (p. 43)

> Unfortunately in our day anger is considered to be part of expressing oneself. . . . We have anger groups, called by other names, and we have anger seminars, called by other names, in which people agitate one another and send each other out as harmful influences into their homes and society. We have anger books, anger plays, and even films glorifying the angry man.
>
> (p. 44)

Swami Chinmayananda

Swami Chinmayananda (1916–93) is well known as one of the most inspiring and knowledgeable exponents of the Gita, who contributed to popularising it both in India and abroad in many countries. He was born in Ernakulam, Kerala, as Balakrishna Menon, in an influential and religious family. He joined Lucknow University for higher education, but left it to join the Freedom Movement and was jailed. When down with typhoid and high fever, he was dumped on a roadside in Delhi to avert death in prison. Fortunately, an Indian Christian lady took him home and nursed him back to recovery. He later completed his masters in English literature with Honours. He was a firebrand agnostic and socialist in his views then and chose to become a journalist. To do a story on Swami Sivananda and to 'expose' him if possible, he visited Rishikesh in 1947. The visit and his experience there transformed his life. He stayed on there and chose the spiritual path and to become a monk. Swami Sivananda was not in a hurry and asked Balan (as he was then called) to wait and make up his mind and consult his parents. He made up his mind and, at the age of thirty-three, took sannyas initiated by Swami Sivananda. He stayed on to continue the study of Vedanta and practice of intense meditation, until his guru asked him in 1951 to go into the wider world and teach.

Swami Chinmayananda started conducting Gita Jnana Yajnas, which were attended by all classes of people and became very popular. He soon gathered around him a lot of disciples all over India, who started the Chinmaya Mission in 1953. The Swami took interest in initiating a world organisation to protect the interests of Hindus and Hinduism in all countries, and with the support of like-minded people, Vishwa Hindu Parishad was started in 1964, with him as its first president. In 1965, he set out on a world tour giving lectures covering thirty-nine cities in eighteen countries. Chinmaya Mission became an international organisation with more than 300 branches worldwide. The Swami laid emphasis on social service too, and the Chinmaya mission has established seventy-six schools and seven colleges. He also started Chinmaya Mission Hospital in Bengaluru in 1970, which is now a major landmark of the city, catering to the medical needs of the poor specially.[12]

The Swami was not parochial in his views and supported inter-faith dialogue and harmony. He deplored the caste system and attracted disciples from all castes and classes to his movement. He often used to say that his mission was to convert Hindus to Hinduism! He felt that many Hindus had lost their roots, and religion was falsely identified with superficial rules and practices. He wanted to promote a greater sense of social responsibility and duties particularly to the disadvantaged, as per the teachings of the Gita.

The Swami was prolific in his writings, with more than sixty books to his credit, including several especially for children. His two main works on the Gita are *The Art of Man Making* (Chinmayananda 1978), being a compilation of 114 short talks on the Gita, and *The Holy Geeta* (Chinmayananda 1996), which includes a brief introduction, translation and detailed commentaries on the verses of the Gita. There are two more books on the Gita by the Swami, one a rendering in prose and the other for children. Though only ten out of eighteen chapters of the Gita are covered in the first book (1978), it contains many of the Swami's general insights on the Gita.

Swami Chinmayananda drew attention to the staggering difference between the respective backgrounds of the Upanishads and the Gita. The former were composed in the serene *ashrams* in forests, while the Gita had the background of a tumultuous, noisy, dusty battlefield. And yet the essence of the two is the same, the Swami says. What the Gita did was to transform a teaching which was supposed to be meant for quiet spiritual pursuit in a secluded corner to what is relevant to face the day-to-day battle of living. It teaches that what is needed to lead a successful, satisfying life in the world without stress – even in 'marketplace' – is not very different from what one needs for spiritual pursuit. One can, and has to, reconcile both the pursuits (Chinmayananda 1978: 21–22). The Swami says that religion is meant to advance perfect living in the world. It is a process which brings forth an effective person from out of even a state shattered by despair, as

Krishna did successfully in the case Arjuna through the Gita (Chinmayananda 1978: 18, 23). This reconstruction of personality has to be through dedicated self-effort, which the Gita prompts. 'The spirit of challenging yourself by yourself is the secret of self-improvement and personality unfoldment' (Chinmayananda 1978: 36).

The Swami says that the Gita is specially addressed to the young, who have a lifetime ahead to act and express themselves in the world. The Gita asks the youth not to run away from problems. Krishna tells Arjuna, 'This war has been thrust upon you. Face it as a welcome challenge as befits a soldier.' The young should face the challenges cheerfully and shoulder their responsibilities and solve the problems of the society, country and the world (Chinmayananda 1978: 44–45). This has to be done with a steady mind (*stithadhih*), without attachment, fear and anger (*veeta-raga-bhaya-krodhah*) (II.56) (Chinmayananda 1978: 51). The Swami devotes several talks (18–23, 52–70) to describe the 'Man of Perfection' (*sthitaprajna*) as in the Gita. He thinks that the description of the 'Man of Perfection' is a unique contribution of the Gita. Karma-yoga, which the Gita strongly recommends, can be followed only by turning oneself into a person of such perfection. The Swami explains: 'When any action is undertaken with ego and ego-centric desires – "I" and "I want" attitude – that action leaves its impression as a *Vasana* in us, prompting a repetition of the same action' (Chinmayananda 1978: 72), which binds a person more and more tightly in karma. A person becomes a criminal with even one murder, while a soldier who may kill many in a legitimate war is not a criminal (Chinmayananda 1978: 72). The secret of eliminating *vasana* while doing dedicated and selfless work as a duty for the benefit of the world is karma-yoga (Chinmayananda 1978: 73). Avoiding work is no way to eliminate *vasana*. To live is to work. 'To escape work is to escape "life" and run into "death"; it is suicidal' (Chinmayananda 1978: 77).

The Swami adds that since total detachment is an impossibility, the spiritual seeker first withdraws narrow attachments from worldly things (even while working) and attaches himself or herself devotedly to the Lord. This attachment to the Lord is inclusive of, and expressed as, love for all and enmity for none (1996: 752–53). The Gita thus focuses on the essentials and does not require rituals for spiritual progress, marking an important break from the Vedas. The path shown by the Gita develops the moral and spiritual content of man, while the rituals may not do so. The Swami says, 'The ritualist gets involved in the means, without aspiring for the Real Goal' (1996: 108).

Self-control is a crucial aspect of man-making both for a successful life and for spiritual progress, which is well emphasised by the Gita. The Swami explains, however, that to control is not to forcefully suppress. It is instead 'an inward blossoming, an inner growth and development by which one's earlier fields of enjoyments through the senses, drop out and make room for the perception of a newer field of ampler joys and more satisfying Bliss' (1996: 142). Happiness does not depend on the amount of consumption, the Swami says. According to him, happiness is a quotient, with the desires fulfilled divided by the total number of desires entertained by the same individual (or community). The clue to increasing happiness (without cost) lies in reducing the desires entertained! (1996: 154–55).

The Swami says that 'sin in Hinduism is a mistake of the mind in which it acts contrary to its essential nature of the Self' (1996: 95). An important contribution of the Gita is its reply to Arjuna's question as to what prompts us to sin, sometimes even against our wishes (III.36–37). According to the Gita, the explanation lies in our excessive desire or lust and anger born of *rajas*, which is our greatest enemy if not properly controlled. 'Any act of sensuousness which the mind pants for in the world of objects . . . creates necessarily within itself more and more agitations' resulting in sin (1996: 95). The Swami says that the Satan or Devil is not an external person with a tail and horns, but is something in our own animal urges. Untamed desire and anger is the cause of sorrow not only for individuals but also for communities and countries, as the Swami adds (1978: 113–15). Desire is so powerful that in unguarded moments, it can cloud our wisdom (III.38–39). We need, therefore, to be alert against temptations and keep awake our sense of discrimination all the while. The Swami says, 'Don't sleep at the steering wheel of life's vehicle' (1978: 120).

There is hope for all in the Gita, points out the Swami. There is no question of eternal damnation for anyone. Even the most sinful can cross across all sin by the raft of jna̲na (IV.36); all karmas are reduced to ashes by the fire of jna̲na (IV.37). This is reiterated again in Chapter 5, verse 17. What is this jna̲na which is so redeeming? The Swami explains that jna̲na consists in shedding one's ego completely, cultivating love for everyone in the world, engaging in selfless activities for the benefit of others, overcoming anger and lust, identifying with the Divine Light within oneself and having complete faith in God. Repentance as a requirement is not explicitly stated but very much implicit. What is required is much more than repentance (1978: 154–60). One who has attained jna̲na not only is cleansed of all sins, not only will not repeat the sins, but also attains spiritual liberation (*Brahma-nirvanam*) (V.24–25) (1978: 193–98). What is involved is more than getting cleansed of the sins; the goal is not less than the realisation of the Supreme through jnana, selfless work, devotion and meditation, or combining these ways, as suggested in the Gita. The Lord assures, however, that one need not worry about a shortfall in this effort, for even a small but genuine step can free one from fear; but with practice and determination, it is possible for all (1978: 236–47).

Another important contribution of the Gita is its positive, soothing and consoling perspective on death. That is why Gita has been considered as the most effective balm on the minds of the bereaved in facing the loss of their dear ones. One can mourn and give a vent to the emotion, but not to the extent of allowing the death of a dear one to devastate the life of the bereaved. The key verse in the Gita in this regard (II.22) says that for the immortal soul, death is like throwing out worn out clothes for new ones; it is a process of renewal. Without death, there can be no change, no renewal. The Swami says that when there is an increase in population beyond the means to sustain it, people get worried. How unimaginably disastrous it would be if death were not there, and all people who were born since the beginning of creation were to survive. There could have been no births in fact if there were no deaths. Life is the purpose of death. The Gita does not mean, however, that one can indulge in wanton killing, as that would amount to *himsa*, which has to be avoided by all means. Life cannot be stubbed out whimsically; it has to be respected by all means (1996: 653–54).

Swami Chinmayananda is emphatic that the Gita is explicitly against the traditional caste system based on birth. When it refers to the four *varnas*, it refers to classes based on the nature of their work (IV.13). Every advanced society has these classes – those doing white-collar jobs, soldiers and political class ('rulers'); those engaged in business like trade, agriculture and industry; and lastly the blue-collar workers. India had a pretty advanced economy even in those days, and naturally had these classes, but there was social mobility, and the *varnas* were not based on birth. There are many examples like Vyasa himself who rose from humble origins and rose to the highest stature. The Lord has an illuminating presence in every bosom without distinction of caste, class and gender, according to the Gita, asserts the Swami. The Gita teaches equality (1978: 136–39).

Swami Chinmayananda has an important place in the history of popularisation of the Gita. His hundreds of lectures on the Gita all over India and abroad were attended by thousands and were highly admired. It was not just because he made the audience spellbound by his oratory, but also because he inspired many to take up the study of the Gita seriously with a modern perspective, leaving an enduring impact. He showed that the Gita is a living text, which is of no less relevance as a guide to life than it was in the past. He attracted all sections of people, not just the leisure class but also active youngsters irrespective of caste, creed or gender. He inspired his listeners to be generous and service oriented, making their lives meaningful by being helpful and affectionate to others. The Chinmaya Mission, which he founded and breathed his very life and philosophy into it, endowing it with his enormous energy, is a huge international organisation today. It has been doing excellent work not only in propagating the teachings of the Gita but also in doing valuable social and educational work. Its work has spread not only to major cities but also in the interiors of India, showing its broad-based character.

Swami Dayananda Saraswati

Swami Dayananda Saraswati (1930–2015) is to be distinguished from the founder of the Arya Samaj of the same name. The Swami being presented now is from south India, born as Natarajan in Tamil Nadu on 15 August 1930, sharing the birth date with Sri Aurobindo, coinciding with India's Independence Day too. He started his career as a journalist and was soon attracted by Swami Chinmayananda's lectures and joined the Chinmaya Mission. He was initiated into sannyas by his icon in 1962. After a stint of editing the Mission's magazine, *Tapovan Prasad*, he left for Rishikesh for deeper study of Vedanta and for further *sadhana*. After three years, he started working on his own, travelling widely and giving discourses. He is known for profundity and deep insights, and he soon attracted plenty of followers. He established four centres for the teaching and dissemination of Vedanta philosophy under the name, Arsha-vidya Gurukulams, at Coimbatore, Nagpur and Rishikesh in India, and at Saylorsburg in Pennsylvania in the United States. He believes that Vedanta is a means of knowledge (*pramana*) rather than a fixed system of thought. This stand enabled him to creatively apply Vedanta to new situations and problems. The Swami was a gifted orator and established good rapport with both small and large audiences with remarkable ease. He travelled widely over the globe, lecturing on Vedanta philosophy. He was a prolific writer with more than sixty books to his credit, which are all marked by deep analysis as well as profound holistic insights, besides being quite inspiring.

A distinctive contribution of the Swami is his starting All India Movement for Seva (AIM for Seva) in 2000. The organisation reaches out to underprivileged sections of people particularly in far-flung areas as in forests and backward regions, by providing them health care and, what is more, education to the children through a chain of well more than hundred free student homes spread across some fourteen states of India. In these homes, children of the poor are housed, fed, clothed and educated with care and affection. The dropout rate of these students is reported to be below 1 per cent, and the rate of passing in Board examinations is 100 per cent. Swami Dayananda wanted to cover every district in India under this project within the next few years. This is financed entirely by donations from his admirers and followers. He has also started Veda Pathashalas for training in the study and recitation of Veda and Agama mantras, so that this precious heritage is preserved intact.[13] He was thus an ideal karma-yogi cum jnana-yogi combined with dedication and love for both people and the Supreme, consistent with the Gita's teaching.

Swami Dayananda has written at least four books on the Gita, one of them, *Bhagavad Gita – Home Study Course* (Dayananda 2011, new edition), with a detailed introduction, explanation and commentaries on the verses. He follows Shankara's *bhashya* closely in this book, referring to it often and adding his own commentary on it. He does not hesitate to depart from Shankara where necessary.[14] This book is the longest (with the main texts alone spread over nine volumes containing more than 1.2 million words in 3,974 pages!) and one of the most penetrating commentary on the Gita so far, yet enjoyable to read, logically leading from one point to another, with stories and anecdotes thrown in between. His other books on the Gita are compact – *The Teaching of the Bhagavad Gita* (1989, first edition), *Value of Values* – a treatise on ethics based mainly on the Gita (2007-a, revised edition) and *Srimad Bhagavad Gita* (transliteration and translation in English along with the original, 2007-b, first edition). Though the Swami is an Advaitin, there is much in his writings which may be acceptable to other schools of philosophies too.

The Swami provides a remarkable summary of the Gita's contents in the blurb for his nine volumes on the Gita (2011). It says: 'The Bhagavadgita gives a view and a way of life. The view is that the self is free from any blemish that inhibits self-approval. In reality, the self is the whole. While unfolding this truth, in seventeen chapters [second to the last], it also helps one with a way of life, making one a mature person in terms of self-management, to receive this vision – I am the whole.' This is a charming way of succinctly explaining that the Gita is both a *brahma-vidya* ('a view') and a *yoga-shastra* ('a way of life'). The Swami explains further that *brahma-vidya* means the knowledge of 'what is'. It answers questions like: 'What is Brahman? What is Ishwara, the Lord? What is the reality of the world, *jagat*? What is the nature of the individual, *jiva*? What is the truth of oneself, *atma*? What is the relationship between the *jiva*, the *jagat* and Ishwara?' (Dayananda 2011, Vol. 1: 45). The Swami's interpretation of the Gita's answers to these questions is in terms of Shankara's *Advaita* philosophy, which is rigorously argued throughout the nine volumes, guessing what objections the opponents would raise and replying to these objections one by one. Even those who may not accept Advaita philosophy in its full measure can enjoy the intellectual treat of the rigour of Indian philosophical debates from these nine volumes, particularly the last.

Contrary to the popular notion that that there is only one way in which the Ultimate reality is conceptualised in Advaita, the Swami presents two different standpoints (Dayananda 2011, Vol. 7: 1–4). One is to visualise It as *nirguna* (attributeless) and *chaitanya* (pure consciousness). Another way is to visualise the same Brahman as wielding the creative power of *maya*, and as the Creator (*srishti-karta, jagat-karana*), who can also be a *saguna* personal God, who can be prayed to and worshipped. The Gita permits both these conceptualisations, and there is no question of one being tenable and another nontenable.

About the question of how to gain *Brahma-vidya*, the Swami says that *karma-yoga* provides the answer (Dayananda 2011, Vol. 1: 45). He clarifies, however, that karma-yoga by itself does not *directly* lead to *moksha* or the release; karma-yoga qualifies and helps one to acquire the knowledge (*jnana*) of Brahman through purifying the mind and preparing it, and it is this *jnana* alone which leads to *moksha*.

The Swami distinguishes the Vedantic concept of *moksha* from the Christian concept of salvation. According to the latter, human beings are born in sin, and they need to be saved from sin, and this saving is salvation. In Vedanta, on the other hand, the self, the real one, is *Atman*, which is *chit* or pure consciousness (not the 'I-maker' – *ahamkara* – of the body–mind–senses complex), is blemish free and pure. The self is by its essential nature *sat* (existential, absolute Truth), *chit* (pure consciousness) and *ananda* (blissful and compassionate). It is beyond *gunas* (attributes). *Sat, chit* and *ananda* are not attributes but its *svabhava*, very nature. Now, this is also the nature of Brahman, and the basic teaching of Advaita is that Atman is the same as Brahman – *Tat tvam asi* (That thou art). *Moksha* is just realising that one's real self is this pure self, which/who is also absolutely free and eternal, and which is also Brahman. *Moksha* literally means release or freedom, and it is freedom from bondage to the mundane world due to *avidya*. *Avidya* is ignorance about the true nature of one's own real self. *Moksha* can come in one's lifetime itself, and not necessarily after death. What is more, a person who has gained it can carry on day-to-day activities of pursuing other *purusharthas* – *dharma, artha* and *kama* (Dayananda 2011, Vol. 1: 17–18). He or she can continue to practice karma-yoga as before. But there would be a difference between a *jnani* (one who has gained the knowledge of oneness with Brahman) and other ordinary humans. A jnani works not only with detachment and a pure mind, but also with the conviction that he or she is not the doer and with a feeling of complete freedom and fearlessness, knowing that his or her real self, the Atman, is no less than Brahman. Since the fruits of karma do not bind such persons, there is no rebirth for them. The Swami emphasises that the Upanishadic *mahavakya* (great saying) does not say that you will become (*bhavishyasi*) *Tat* (That) (Brahman), but you are (*asi*) already That (Dayananda 2011, Vol. 6: 1). One has to just know or realise this. Once this realisation takes place deep within oneself, all sorrows and anxieties are removed, and all sins or karmas are gone. *Moksha* is freedom from being a wanting person, from fear and insecurity, because Atman is free of these inadequacies. Once gained, *moksha* is permanent, there being no question of forgetting the self-realisation.

The Swami raises a question here (on behalf of an imagined opponent) whether the presumption of two selves here is tenable – one who seeks and the other who is sought (Dayananda 2011, Vol. 6: 94). The former is the *jiva*, the confused self, which has not yet realised its oneness with the Brahman, and the latter is Atman, which is the Brahman itself. The Swami answers by saying that as long as there is confusion or ignorance about the identity of the *jiva* with the Atman/Brahman, the duality persists, and there will be a difference between the seeker and the sought. The seeking self is a part of the creation, the *samsara*. The creation is a manifestation of the Brahman taking names (*nama*) and forms (*rupa*), which are not eternal and independent, but dependent on Ishwara, the Lord who possesses the creative power, who is the Brahman itself. The Swami gives the analogy of clay (analogous to Brahman) and clay pot (analogous to the world of names and forms). He observes:

> . . . what we call an existent thing, like a pot, is neither non-existent nor existent. It is not independently existent because

> it has no existence apart from the clay, nor can we dismiss it as totally non-existent because it has a functional reality. It is something in between, which we call *mithya*. This is the status of the whole creation. What is independently existent is real, *satya*, and what is dependent on it is called *mithya*.
>
> (Dayananda 2011, Vol. 9: 224)

He clarifies further that the only thing that does not depend on anything else is Atman or Brahman. The pot cannot be taken as false; it is not non-existent. But it is not a fundamental reality as compared with clay. *Maya* then is what makes clay appear as pot; *maya* is nothing but the creative power of the Brahman. However, unlike the clay involved, Brahman does not undergo any transformation or change. According to Advaitins, the creation is an appearance superimposed on the Brahman, as when a rope is mistaken in dim light as a snake. The creation being the result of *maya* is *mithya*, which means relatively real/unreal, because it is transitory and dependent, and not fundamentally real or eternal and independent. Only Brahman is fundamentally real and eternal. And so is Atman, which is the same as the Brahman. While *Atman* is real, the mundane self which identifies itself with the body–mind–senses complex is only relatively real. It depends on the *Atman*, for the mundane self is nothing if it does not have consciousness.

There is a problem, however! One may reconcile with the idea of the individual self, being in the nature of pure consciousness, being *akarta*, but not with the idea of the Creator being *akarta*. The Swami clearly says that Ishwara is both the efficient and the material cause of creation. In other words, he created the universe out of his supreme intelligence and power, which is also his material manifestation. And yet He is said to be *akarta* (Dayananda 2011, Vol. 9: 178). Moreover, if Ishwara is *akarta*, why should devotees pray to Him for help? But the Lord in the Gita is also presented as a personal deity to whom worship and the fruits of their works are offered, which he lovingly accepts and reaches out to them. The Brahman in Advaita is totally indifferent. The Swami argues, however, following Shankara, that from the point of view of Brahman, the *Sat Chit Ananda*, there is no creation; it is all pure *chaitanya* or energy ultimately. But names and forms, which constitute creation, cannot be completely false, which the Swami himself admits.

To understand the viewpoint of Shankara's Advaita, which the Swami upholds, a distinction between two types of truths or *satyas* – *Adhyatmika* (*paramarthika*) and *vyavaharika* – made by Shankara is relevant. The former is the fundamental or spiritual truth, and the latter is the truth of the mundane world under the veil of *maya*. The latter cannot be dismissed as pure illusion or ignorance or falsehood. Otherwise several problems arise. For example, if Atman is *akarta* (non-doer), for whom is meant the injunction of the Vedas to do certain rituals? Who has to practise karma-yoga? Who has to follow the ethical values commended by the Gita itself? The Swami is well aware of such questions and in fact raises some of them himself as possible objections by opponents in the debate (Dayananda 2011, Vol. 7: 261–344, and, Vol. 9: 399–553). If the world is *mithya*, why was the Swami himself engaged so much in social work to uplift thousands of poor and deprived children in neglected interiors all over India with total seriousness? Moreover, who is doing all this valuable, well-thought-out and organised work, if the Swami is *akarta*, his associates are *akartas* and even the Great Brahman Himself is *akarta*? Of course, *akarta* in the Gita is also one who is engaged but has no attitude or feeling of doership. In an abstract, transcendental or *paramarthika* reality wherein all dualities are resolved, and there is One Absolute, there is neither doer nor non-doer. The answer to all the earlier questions lies basically in acknowledging that even *vyavaharika satya* has its own validity, its own meaning and its own values, and it has also to be taken seriously. Without this, an equally important part of the Gita, *yoga-shastra*, will have no meaning, as it is meant for the people in the world. If the world and the people in it are all false, all unreal, where is the need to teach them anything?

Usually, it is believed that the type of path chosen for spiritual striving or *sadhana* depends on one's conception of Ishwara. If Ishwara is taken as a personal deity, the path of bhakti is taken along with karma-yoga including rituals associated with worship. If on the other hand, Ishwara is taken as the ultimate reality in terms of an impersonal Brahman, the path of *jnana* and meditation is taken, with much less emphasis on bhakti and karma. Swami Dayananda Saraswati does not accept such a notion of *sadhana*. According to him, though *moksha* is gained only through *jnana*, it does not come without preparing the mind for it through conquering our passions, attachments, hatred, jealousy and the like. A purification of mind on these lines is possible only through karma-yoga, which means doing all that one ought to do, without aspiring for the fruit of one's work for oneself, remembering that the giver of the fruit of work is only Ishwara and surrendering to His will. Having desires is no problem, the Swami clarifies, but having desires that bind you, with which you are obsessed, is a problem. The attitude to the desired outcome of work should be: 'If you get it, you will enjoy it; but if you do not get it, you are not going to be unhappy' (Dayananda 2011, Vol. 9: 329). Further, the work should be done without any *ahamkara*, that is, without any notion of '*I* am doing this'. Karma-yoga cannot be a yoga without such an attitude, and without absolute faith in and devotion to Ishwara. Choosing to do only what one enjoys doing, or only what is very easy to do, instead of doing what ought to be done, is not the spirit of karma-yoga, though it does not mean that one should not enjoy what one is doing. Compulsions of situations or circumstances may often determine what one ought to do in that context. The Swami explains: 'by doing my own *karma, svakarma*, what is appropriate at a given time and place, I am worshipping I̱shwara' (Dayananda 2011, Vol. 9: 185). The work has to be done with devotion, thoughtfulness and detachment. Meditation or contemplation on the Divine or on the Atman helps, but without abandoning karma-yoga. The Swami explains the dilemma of choice which Arjuna faced between abandoning work (*karma-sannya̱sa*, as he thought) and karma-yoga, but the Lord tells him that doing work by surrendering its fruit to the will of God itself amounts to *karma-sannya̱sa* and karma-yoga, and that one cannot desist from action. Can an atheist be a karma-yogi? The Swami says that 'an atheist can be an ethical person, but not necessarily a yogi, because *karma-yoga* means recognising I̱shwara' (Dayananda 2011, Vol. 9: 187). Thus, what the Swami interprets as the message of the Gita for spiritual striving is a combination of the paths dominated by karma-yoga. He clarifies, however, that it is not tenable to say that karma is the means of *moksha*, because *moksha*, being *nitya* (eternal), is not *produced* as such. The knowledge of the *nitya a̱tma* alone is *moksha*, and *karma* only facilitates this knowledge (Dayananda 2011, Vol. 9: 398).

There is a verse in the Gita, verse 66, in the last chapter (eighteenth), wherein the Lord tells Arjuna, which literally translated means: 'Giving up all *dharmas*, take refuge in me alone. I will release you from all sins, do not grieve'. This verse is liable to be misinterpreted. Can one give up all moral duties (*dharmas*), and just take refuge in God, and be released from all sins and derelictions of duties? Swami Dayananda Saraswati says that by 'dharmas', the Lord meant karmas, and the karmas are given up – not by abandoning work or duties – but by leaving the outcome to the Supreme, and not entertaining any notion of self-agency or *kartritva* (Dayananda 2011, Vol. 9: 370–71). The swami raises another question about this verse. By asking Arjuna to 'take refuge in me alone' is Lord Krishna showing himself as a jealous

God? 'No,' replies the Swami. 'When Bhagavan says, "Me", we are to understand that as the one who is of the nature of all' (Dayananda 2011, Vol. 9: 373), the One who is all pervading and all-inclusive.

It is impossible to do justice to all the writings of the Swami, even on the Gita alone. What is attempted earlier is to convey his main ideas briefly and to give a flavour of his valuable contribution to the understanding of the Gita. I conclude this summary of his contribution by pointing out how, according to the Swami, Advaita can make a difference to the psyche of a person: 'Since the basic problem is one of self non-acceptance [non-acceptance of the Self], acceptance is possible only when a person discovers the self to be free from any lack, in other words, complete. And the self happens to be complete. Discovering this fact releases the individual from his erroneous sense of imperfection' (Dayananda 2011, Vol. 8: 156). He believed in the equal dignity of all, and the right of all to dignified treatment. He put this in practice through his All India Movement for Seva, opening student homes and schools for the children of the weak and the neglected, assuring them of dignified life.

Notes

1 For a list of DVG's works, and books on DVG, see Gundappa (2001: 638–39).
2 There is another more recent book, *Lokayatre*, in Kannada by G. S. Amur (2013), but on the *Mahabharata* as a whole, which brings together the moral wisdom for day-to-day living as in the numerous dialogues one finds in the epic like the Gita.
3 See 'Why ethics?' in Nadkarni (2014: 10–15).
4 The threefold classification of qualities or *gunas* can be similarly applied to several other things. For a tabular representation, see Nadkarni (2013: 59–60).
5 For more details of Swami Sivananda's life and work, see Nadkarni (2013: 277–78).
6 The concerned verses are: II.40; IV.36; VI.40; IX.22, 31; XII.7; XVIII.65, 66.
7 For details of his life and work, see en.wikipedia.org/wiki/Kanaiyalal_Maneklal_Munshi.
8 This account about Acharya Vinoba Bhave here is based mainly on en.wikipedia.org/wiki/Vinoba_Bhave. It is given in some detail, not only because he was an important follower of Gandhi and known for his work for the rural poor, but also because his 'Talks on the Gita' is among the most popular commentaries available in most of the Indian languages.
9 This account is based on Prabhupada (1983: 867–68) and Nadkarni (2013: 274–75). Also see prabhupada.krishna.com.
10 See en.wikipedia.org/wiki/Swami_Ranganathananda; downloaded on 22 April 2015.

11 For further details, see the opening page about the author in Easwaran (1997, any of the three volumes), and en.wikipedia.org/wiki/Eknath_Easwaran (downloaded on 24 April 2015).

12 For more details, see Patchen (2003), Nadkarni (2013) (279–81) and en.wikipedia.org/wiki/chinmayananda_saraswati (downloaded on 24 April 2015).

13 This account is based on Nadkarni (2013: 281–82).

14 For example, in the verse *Karmanyevadhikaraste* (II.47), while Shankara interprets karma narrowly as Vedic rituals, Dayananda takes the word to mean any work (as other modern interpreters have also done) (Dayananda 2011, Vol. 2: 238). In the verse (II.49) again, while Shankara interprets *kripanah*, as *dinah* or 'helpless weaknings', Dayananda takes the word to mean 'misers' who amass money but have no heart to spend it (Dayananda 2011, Vol.2: 288–89). The latter makes better sense in the context.

6

PHILOSOPHY OF THE GITA

The Gita and the pursuit of happiness

Many interpretations of the Gita have been reviewed above. What do they all add up to? What does the text itself say? What follows is not an attempt to present yet another interpretation different, but an attempt to arrive at my own understanding of the Gita's philosophy with openness, without sentimental attachment to any particular established school of philosophy (following the Gita's advice to be detached in this respect too!). Such an intellectual detachment can also impart some freshness.

The whole purpose of the Gita can be said to be to show how to obtain lasting happiness, after basic needs are met. If basic needs of food, shelter, clothing, health and some education are not met, there is no question of obtaining higher happiness. Though the main concern of the Gita is with higher happiness beyond the satisfaction of basic needs, it is not indifferent to people's need for welfare or well-being. It explicitly advises that one should have adequate food and sleep, not eat too little (nor too much), and it calls upon all those who have enough to eat and have a surplus, to rise to meet the basic needs of others through its emphasis on *loka-sangraha* (III.20,25) or people's welfare. Since it says there is divinity in all beings, it emphasises the value of loving respect for all and selfless service. This is the philosophy of the Gita expressed in the concepts of *karma-yoga* and *loka-sangraha*. Gandhi was inspired by this philosophy and developed his concept of trusteeship. To follow this teaching is to help not only others but also one's own self in spiritual advancement. However, the main focus of the Gita is on guiding people to attain higher levels of happiness well beyond animal existence, without detriment to satisfying basic needs. Even after the basic needs are met, relentless pursuit of further happiness through sensual pleasures can be endless and frustrating (apart from being environmentally unsustainable). The Gita points to better and more satisfying alternatives of real and higher happiness.

This section on the Gita's approach to human pursuit of happiness not only introduces but also integrates the rest of the next three sections in this chapter. The themes of the following sections, namely, ethics, the concept of God and the world, and *sadhana*, are of interest to us only because of our pursuit of happiness. Indian culture and literature recognise that 'all beings act with the motive of attaining happiness and getting rid of unhappiness' (*sukham me syat dukkham me ma bhut iti loka-pravrittih*, quoted in Banavathy and Choudry 2014: 146, fn. 12). The Gita is read by many people as it is believed to be a guide to happiness both in this world and beyond. According to the second verse in the *Gita-Mahatmyam* ('Greatness of the Gita'), a person burdened with karmic baggage would feel lightened, liberated and happy through the study and practice of the Gita's teaching. How?

First, in the pursuit of happiness, we need the guidance of ethics which the Gita provides. Acting in an immoral way merely to get some momentary pleasure cannot really give happiness because such a person will be burdened with bad conscience, complications in personal relationships, possibly even having to face legal consequences, apart from adding to one's karmic junk, which is not easy to dispose of. Suffering takes over the moment goodness departs. On the other hand, goodness imparts happiness (*Sattvam sukhe sanjayati*, XIV.9). A person burdened with a guilty feeling cannot really be considered as happy. Happiness should therefore be consistent with ethics. Second, the Gita recognises several types and levels of happiness, and tries to take us from lower levels of momentary happiness to higher levels of more enduring and lasting happiness. This is what leads to God and *sadhana*. The Gita is not against happiness, not even against mundane happiness, but does not want us to stop at or confine ourselves within the narrow sphere of sensual pleasures, but rise above. We are certainly welcome to enjoy the beauty of the rising and setting Sun against the backdrop of birdsongs, the comforting company of our loved ones and the soothing and lifting tunes of music. In addition to having many such small and harmless but invigorating pleasures, which indeed make our life happy, we also have to think how to make our more life worthwhile and meaningful on the whole. The teaching of the Gita can provide valuable guidance in this task.

Unlike sensual pleasures which can be accessible only to the rich, one does not need to be rich to pursue higher levels of happiness, once the basic needs are met. This is because the higher happiness which the Gita points to is not something which is caused by external stimulus but by internal contentment. This is emphasised in several verses. For example, verse V.21 says that the Yogi realises the joy within his own self, not obsessed with external objects. This requires that passions for external objects are controlled (V.24). Such a person becomes *prashantatma* (peaceful at heart) and *vigatabhih* (fearless), finds the inner light easily and realises absolute bliss (VI.14). A real yogi is always in a state of happiness, without any apparent external reason to make him or her happy. This does not mean that such persons are insensitive to the suffering of either one's own or of others. But such suffering or sorrow, instead of depressing or destroying them, makes them rise to the occasion and do their duty to help as *karma-yoga*. It does not end either their composure or their selfless activism. The composure is combined with activism. It is obvious from this that from the point of view of the Gita, happiness is not a state of constant excitement. By its very nature, excitement stimulated by external objects is bound to be momentary, and if one is after constant excitement, one can land into depression. The Gita, on the contrary, points to stable, sustainable or lasting happiness, which comes from controlling desires for external objects and finding inner light. Like the Buddha, Krishna also teaches in the Gita that the sure way of finding lasting happiness is to control passions or desires. The path of *karma-yoga* is itself based on this precept, since its activism is without desire for personal gain.

It follows that happiness cannot be captured by one word. The Gita is fully aware of it and uses many words which have a bearing on it, ranging all the way down from *bhoga* up to *nirvana* or *brahmi-sthiti*. It is clear that these words are not synonyms. The Gita's approach to happiness is nuanced and sophisticated. It is worth having a look at the variety of these words and note where they appear in the Gita. They are listed here arranged approximately – but not smoothly – in the ascending order of their spiritual or moral value from the Gita's perspective:

Bhoga – Sensual enjoyment (I.32; II.5, 43, 44; III.12; and V.22).
Priti – Pleasure (I.36).
Harsha – Cheer, rejoice (I.12; XII.15; XVIII.76–77).
Abhinanda – Rejoice (II.57).
Tripti/Tripta – Satisfaction/Satisfied (III.17).
Tushti/Tushta – Cheerful satisfaction/ cheerfully satisfied, contentment (II.55; VI.20; X.5).

Santushti/Santushta – Well satisfied, quite content (III.17; XII.14, 19).

Shubham – Good (II.57).

Shreya – Good, beneficial, morally desirable (II.7; III.11, 35).

Hita – Well-being, welfare (as in *Bhuta-hita or loka-hita*) – (V.25; X.1; XII.4).

Utsaha – Enthusiasm (XVIII.26)

Yogakshema – Meeting the needs, providing security (IX.22).

Arama – Relaxation (V.24).

Prasanna-chetas – Tranquil mind (II.65).

Prashanta – Peaceful at heart, calm and composed (VI.14).

Sukham – Pleasure/Happiness (I.32; II.15, 38, 56, 66; IV.40; V.3, 13, 21; VI.7, 21, 27, 28, 32; XII.13,18; XIII.6, 20; XIV.6, 9, 24; XVIII.36–39).

Vigatabhih – Fearless (VI.14).

Prasada – Tranquillity, coolness, composure, good temper, well-being (II.64–65).

Siddhi – Perfection (III.4).

Shanti – Peace (II.70–71; IV.39; V.12, 29; VI.15).

Shrirvijaya – A combination of success, prosperity, welfare and moral perfection (XVIII.78).

Nirvana/Brahmi-sthiti/Brahma-nirvana/Moksha – A state of perfect or highest and eternal happiness; union with the Divine; release from the cycle of births and deaths (II.72; V.25–26; VI.15).

Most of the these words are in the context of individual or personal happiness, but words like *hita, yogakshema, shanti, sukham* and *shrirvijaya* are applicable both at the personal and at the community/country level. The Gita is concerned with happiness both at the personal and at the community level, but the former gets greater attention. *Sukham* is a general term, denoting varieties of happiness, and is used most often. Sometimes the Gita specifies what type of *sukha* is meant in a particular context. It distinguishes between three kinds of *sukhas* or happiness in three verses (XVIII.37–39): *sattvika, rajasika* and *tamasika*, in diminishing the order of moral value. The first, *sattvika*, is unpleasant in the beginning, involving hardships and sacrifices, but is like nectar at the end. Though the Gita specifically refers to the happiness arising from realisation of the self to illustrate this kind of happiness, we know many examples at a mundane level: a farmer, after back-breaking work and investment on his farm, getting a good harvest and a good return; scientist, after painstaking and long research, coming out with an important discovery or a research paper; a student putting in long hours of study with concentration, getting a good rank; and so on. The second type of happiness which the Gita mentions here, *rajasika*, comes mostly from contact with senses, which seems like nectar in the beginning, but results in sorrow at the end. A student who spends all the time in getting fun and frolic but ignoring studies is an apt example of such a type. The third type, *tamasika*, is illusory happiness, for there is no happiness here both at the beginning and at the end. It is based on delusion and ignorance. The Gita itself mentions examples of this type: laziness, over-sleeping and miscomprehension or miscalculation. Complacence and non-seriousness in work can also be considered as *tamasika*. The main point of this classification is the stress on taking a long-term view of things, and not to be tempted only by short-lived momentary pleasures as they cannot provide happiness in the long run. The Gita cautions particularly against reckless indulgence in sensual desires, as they are insatiable and lead to frustration, anger and delusion (XVI.10; II.62).

The important Upanishadic word for highest happiness or bliss, *ananda*, does not figure in the earlier list, as it is not used in the Gita. The word is used, however, as part of prayer both in the *Gita-Dhyanam* and in the *Gita-Mahatmyam* as an epithet of Krishna, the Divine. In the Upanishads, the essential nature of Atman is described as one of *ananda* or blissfulness, along with two other epithets of Atman – *sat* (existence, truth) and *chit* (consciousness). Its essential nature of blissfulness is masked or eclipsed because of *maya* or involvement in *samsara*. The aim set before everyone is to realise one's essential blissful nature, for which the Gita shows the way through *sadhana*. The Gita does use the concept underlying *ananda*, employing words for it such as *sukham atyantikam* (highest/infinite happiness, VI.21) or *brahmi-sthiti* (II.72). The Gita observes that such a happiness, which is beyond sense perception, can be gained while living, and after gaining it, no sorrow disturbs the person enjoying this bliss and no sensual pleasures or material gains hold any attraction (VI.22). In this state, there is no grief and no desire anymore (XVIII.54). Such a person who is one with Brahman (*Brahmabhutah*), is also called as *Prasannatma*, since his Atman is in absolute bliss (XVIII.54). This bliss is felt within (*Atmani tushyati*, V.20) and does not come from outside. In fact, it comes from focusing the mind on the Atman and attaining quietude by withdrawal of senses from outside through meditation (V.20). The person experiencing it attains *Brahma-nirvana* (V.24). According to the Gita, when such a spiritual peak and height of happiness is possible, it makes no sense to be bogged down to petty pleasures. However, for success in this, mental discipline for years is necessary as advised by the Gita. Though meditation helps in this task, it is not enough, and one should consciously strive to control one's mind keeping it free from immoral temptations and other weaknesses of mind.

Does it mean that the Gita teaches one to be only an obsessive introvert, cutting off from any interaction with others, and spend all the time concentrating on the tip of one's nose? This may not be the concept of happiness for most of us. This is not the concept of happiness in the Gita either. Had it been so, Krishna would not have taken so much time and trouble to persuade Arjuna to fight the war. He would then have agreed with Arjuna to drop his weapons and go to a forest as a recluse. It stands to reason to deduce that such practices like meditation and withdrawal of senses from external objects are to be confined only to limited periods (though to be practiced regularly for a long time), *after* fulfilling one's duties in the world. The Gita clearly and explicitly rejects renunciation of the world and duties to the world as a way to gaining the ultimate or infinite happiness, as is evident from its second chapter. The Gita is not concerned only with personal happiness and stresses one's duty to contribute to the happiness (*hita*) of all beings (*sarva-bhuta-hita*) and people (*loka-hita*). Its recommendation of *loka-sangraha* (taking care of people) also suggests this (III.20, 25). But how is it consistent with the goal of *moksha* or *nirvana*? The Gita shows the way.

The way shown by the Gita is Karma-yoga. The charm of this concept in the Gita is that one can be an active participant in and contributor to the affairs of the world and, at the same time, in the very process, achieve the final goal of moksha. What is more, the advice to do one's work or perform one's duties unselfishly or unattached to the fruit of work does not mean that one cannot enjoy doing so. On the contrary, the Gita recommends doing one's work with enthusiasm (*utsaha*) and efficiency. A work can be done efficiently only if done with enthusiasm and pleasure. All genuine social workers know this. They derive immense happiness and spiritual satisfaction working for a noble cause unselfishly. This happiness is their reward, for which they do not mind facing risks and undergoing hardships. Karma-yogis may sacrifice many a mundane personal pleasure, but they do not have to sacrifice the happiness of doing work unselfishly. They love doing it so much that even the goal of *moksha* holds no attraction for them, and they pray that they be born again and again if only to serve the people in dire need. As we saw, many interpreters of the Gita have stressed this teaching of the Gita as its main contribution.

It is not that the Gita is absolutely against other sources of happiness. It allows even *vishaya-sukha* (sensual pleasure) but within limits, and it urges moderation. Notably, sensual pleasure is considered as *rajasika*, appearing in the middle of the hierarchy of *sukhas*, and not at the lowest end. It is certainly inferior to the *sattvika sukha* of spiritual happiness, but is not considered as contemptible as lolling in lethargy which is considered as *tamasika*. After all, *kama* (sensual desire/pleasure) is accepted as one of the four *purusharthas* (basic human goals) in Indian philosophy including the Mahabharata, and the Gita is not against it. The Gita is also not against pursuing another mundane human goal, *artha* (wealth and power), and enjoying it. This is clear from Krishna's call to Arjuna to enjoy the wealthy kingdom which he (along with his brothers) would gain after winning the war (*bhunkshva rajyam samriddham*, XI.33). The Gita only insists that pleasures should be indulged in a way which is not against dharma or ethics. While describing how the Divine is identified with what is good and glorious in all the things, the Gita includes sensual desire unopposed to dharma among them (VII.11).

Indian tradition since ancient times has also commended aesthetic pleasure (*rasasvada*), and enjoyment of *kavya* (poetry), *natya* (drama), *sangita* (music) and other arts. There is not a word in the Gita indicative of disapproval of them on the ground of their being inconsistent with religious pursuit. On the contrary, verse X.35 is appreciative of music, and poetry. While the Gita has warned against excesses in the enjoyment of sensual pleasures, no such deterrent is expressed against aesthetic pleasures. The ancient Indian tradition has effectively developed these arts both on a religious and on a secular basis. It has been recognised that these arts can be used also for spiritual progress. A question that arises here is where to draw the line between sensual and aesthetic pleasures, since aesthetic pleasures like music can be had only through senses. Adopting the Gita's approach, one could say that the criterion can be on the basis of which of the pleasures stops at a merely physical level, and which, by contrast, is morally acceptable, soul-filling and spiritually uplifting. Even sexual pleasure with one's spouse out of spontaneous love and without force can be soul-filling and provide spiritual ecstasy. A pleasure should not make one feel guilty, as that is a sign of unhappiness. This may be a subjective criterion, but is nevertheless useful. After all, happiness is itself subjective. The Gita would add, however, that sexual pleasure, or enjoyment of power, however ecstatic and intense, and free from guilt, would not be everlasting, and if one is obsessed with it or makes them the dominant or ultimate goal of one's life, it would come in the way of spiritual liberation and blissful peace. But such a blissful and everlasting peace can come only through sincere *sadhana*.

A significant teaching of the Gita is that there are both happiness and unhappiness in the world, and that we should not lose our head on gaining some happiness, nor should we allow ourselves to be devastated or destroyed by sorrow (*duhkha*). The Gita's wise person rises above this duality of *sukha* and *duhkha* both of which are momentary, treating both with a certain maturity, detachment or equanimity, and aims at making his or her life meaningful and worthwhile on the whole. Some may find this worthwhileness in gaining *jivan-mukti* (liberation while living); to some it may consist in unselfish service to suffering humanity; and some may be wise enough to combine both of these effortlessly and effectively. The Gita can be a guide for all the three types.

Ethics in the Gita

A problem in presenting the philosophy of the Gita is to decide the sequencing of the three main aspects – ethics, theology and metaphysics, and *sadhana* or yoga. The three issues are expressed in terms of three questions respectively: 'What ought I to do?' 'What can I know?' and 'What may I become?' (Srinivasachari 2009: 36). Which of these three questions has the utmost primacy? The problem arises in *sadhana* too – which comes first, which is basic, between being ethical, understanding the ultimate reality, karma-yoga as selfless action or bhakti? Can one be ethical without having to know the Ultimate and without *sadhana*? Is the Gita relevant to such a person too, or only to those who are earnest about all these aspects? Is it possible to arrive at the knowledge of the ultimate reality without striving for it, without *sadhana*? Or is *sadhana* possible at all without some notion of the Ultimate? What will inspire *sadhana* in one who has no notion of It (*Tat*) – the Ultimate or the Supreme? We begin in any case with ethics first as a starting point, but without isolating it from the other two questions, since all the three are interrelated. A remarkable thing about the ethics of the Gita is a near unanimity about its content and approach among its many interpreters, in spite of differences on other questions particularly related to theology and metaphysics.

The first issue which arises philosophically in ethics is who is the moral agent or moral self? Which self is it that is responsible for moral conduct or behaviour? Interpreters of the Gita, particularly Advaitins, emphasise that *Atman*, the real Self, is *akarta*, a non-doer; being Pure Consciousness, it does not act. It is only a witness, *sakshi*. Gandhi interpreted it as the inner voice. Atman is simply the Divine presence in all beings. This presence is not responsible for our *punya* (merit) or *papa* (sins). There is someone else who is responsible for them. The Gita actually talks of *three selves* – the embodied and empirical self or *dehi*, the subtle self or *jiva* and the real spiritual and eternal Self or the *Atman*. *Dehi* is 'I-maker' or *ahamkara* which acts in the mundane world and also feels that it acts. It has the power of free will, though within certain limits. It has the three mental faculties of cognition, conation and feeling. It is responsible for karma and receives its fruit (*karma-phala*). It is also the one which pursues the *purusharthas* – human ends or purposes or ideals. It is clear, therefore, it is *dehi* in this sense who is the moral agent. After death, it is not an active doer any more, but its subtle body, the *sukshma-sharira* or the *jiva* carries the fruit of the *dehi*'s *karma* as a repository. In essence, *dehi* and *jiva* are one and the same, the distinction lies in the former being embodied and the latter after death has only a subtle body or *sukshma-sharira*. To 'enjoy' the fruit of karma, after death, it either goes to heaven or hell as the case may be, or takes rebirth. Even if they go to heaven or hell, they return to the mundane world through rebirth, after the fruit of karma (be it *punya* or *papa*) is exhausted. There is no eternal damnation. Freedom from the cycle of death and rebirths is gained only when the *dehi* realises that its real self is not the embodied mundane self of the body–mind complex but the Atman, the non-doer. In Gandhi's perspective, there is liberation when there is perfect harmony between the moral agent and the inner voice. *Moksha* can simply be viewed as freedom from the bondage of the *dehi* from the trap of narrowness of mind, its weaknesses and limitations, such as infatuations, obsessions, hatred, jealousy, arrogance and greed. When the mind is freed from such limitations, it becomes one with the Pure Self, the Atman. Liberation can take place during one's own life. What the Gita teaches is not liberation from the world, but liberation in the world. But after death, there is no rebirth for the *jiva* identified with the Atman, unless there is a deliberate attachment to the world from the point of contributing to its welfare as an instrument of God. Such persons, having no desire for even *moksha* in its traditional sense, may be reborn for the good of the world. The Gita, however, is not quite consistent in the use of these three terms – *dehi*, *jiva* or *sukshma-sharira*, and *Atman*, in the strict sense indicated respectively for them, often using the terms *dehi* and *jiva* for the *Atman*. But if we try to arrive at consistency and coherence in their use, they have to be interpreted in the way explained earlier.

One of the most profound ethical teachings of the Gita is contained in verse VI.5, which emphasises the moral responsibility of the self and the freedom of will it enjoys to shape its own destiny. The verse is as follows:

> *Uddharet atmana atmanam na atmanam avasadayet /*
> *Atma eva hi atmanah bandhuh atma eva ripuh atmanah //*
> (VI.5)

A literal translation of this verse is that the self should uplift itself by its own self. Never let the self destroy itself. The self is the only friend of oneself; it can also be its only enemy.

Though the word used here for self is Atman, what the Gita means by it is the moral agent having the power of free will. Easwaran, therefore, translates the verse as follows: 'A man should reshape himself through the power of the will. He should never let himself be degraded by self-will. The will is the only friend of the Self, and will is the only enemy of the Self' (Easwaran 1997, Vol. I: 340). This does not mean that we cannot count on God at all, but that even to gain God's help, we have to first exercise our own will, and make our own efforts, since we are not inert matter but are sentient spirits endowed with free will, expected to shape our own destiny. A thinking person can certainly have bitter conflicts within oneself, and it is God's presence within as Atman that resolves them. The Gita makes it evident where the self can itself be one's own enemy in verses like III.37, that is, when the mind is overtaken by lust and wild temper and loses self-control.

The moral responsibility or obligation of individuals, and their freedom to carry it out is acknowledged by all interpreters of the Gita. Moral obligations are expressed by the term 'dharma', which is basic to the ethics of the Gita right from the beginning to the end. It can be said to be the central principle of the Gita. It makes a beginning with the word *dharma*. The world is itself a *dharma-kshetra*, mentioned in the very first verse of the Gita, which means the ground on which our moral obligations are played out, resolved and reconciled. The word, 'dharma', occurs in most of the chapters of the Gita, since it is a principle stressing the significance of which can be taken as the main purpose of the text. Dharma is so important that preaching and promoting it is the very rationale of Krishna's *avatar*, as two popular verses in the Gita itself declare:

> *Yada yada hi dharmasya glanirbhavati Bharata/*
> *Abhyutthanam adharmasya tadaatmanam srijamyaham //*
> (IV.7)

> ('I bring forth Myself, Bharata [Arjuna], [into the world] whenever there is a decline of dharma and an ascent of *adharma* [immorality].')

> *Paritranaya sadhunam vinashaya cha dushkritam/*
> *Dharma samsthapanarthaya sambhavami yuge yuge //*
> (IV.8)

> ('To protect the good and destroy evil, and [thus] to establish *dharma*, I take birth in the world from time to time.')

The verses have a double significance. On the one hand, they clarify that the essence of dharma in the sense of ethics or moral order is to promote the good and eliminate the evil. Second, dharma is so important that the Lord Himself takes responsibility to uphold it in the world. He is the very abode (*pratishthaham*) of Eternal Dharma (*shaswatasya dharmasya*) just as He is abode also of Absolute Bliss (*aikantikasya sukhasya cha*) (XIV.27). The Gita affirms God's moral responsibility in several places and also clearly suggests that humans follow His way (*mama vartmanuvartante manushyah Partha sarvashah*, IV.11). In the very act of following the Divine moral order of dharma, human beings fulfil the purpose of the Divine and come close to It or identify with It (*madbhavam agatah*, IV.10).

Unfortunately, the Gita itself does not explicitly define dharma anywhere, though its content is implied as we see here. But in *Karna-parva* of the Mahabharata (Chapter 69, verse 58), which comes after the Gita (in *Bhishma Parvan*), dharma is clearly defined thus:

> *Dharanat dharma ityahuh dharmo dharayate prajah/*
> *Yat syat dharana-samyuktam sa dharma iti nishchayah//*

> ('Dharma is so called as it upholds. It upholds people [society]. Whatever has this [moral] quality of upholding may be considered as dharma.')

The importance given to dharma in the Gita and in the Mahabharata as a whole stimulated more discussion of it in later writings particularly in the *Dharma-shastras*. Dharma is mentioned as the first and foremost of the four *purusharthas*, human goals, in all the *Shastras*. The other human goals, *artha* (acquisition of wealth and power, earning livelihood), *kama* (satisfying sense objects and one's emotional needs) and *moksha* (explained earlier), are all subject to first satisfying *dharma* – the moral conditions or the moral law. It is the moral responsibility of *dehi* to reconcile any conflicts that may arise between dharma on the one hand and other purusharthas, without sacrificing dharma. This is because the world will not run smoothly otherwise. The dominant need for dharma led the *Manu Smriti* to famously declare that when dharma is protected, it protects us in turn (*dharmo rakshati rakshitah*, VIII.15). The *Dharma-shastras* took up the task of explaining to people that we cannot just live in a society where *adharma* (immorality) prevails, where anybody can cheat, rob and attack anybody with impunity, and that dharma is the basis of law and order which even kings should follow. A lot of story literature like the *Panchatantra*, the *Hitopadesha* and *Katha-saritsagara*, and *Puranas* also developed to make the same point especially to impress young minds and common people. Thus, the Gita and the Mahabharata can be said to have given a big boost to literature on ethics.

However, what upholds people or the society? The people, and with them the society as a whole, are upheld, and their collective welfare taken care of when everyone or at least the bulk of them follow their dharma by carrying out their duties or moral obligations scrupulously. Dharma means both common morality and duty. But is dharma universal or relative? Is dharma suited only according to occasions and circumstances? Does it vary according to *varna* (profession), *kala* (time), *kula* (family) and *ashrama*? Is this what the Gita commends? The stress in the Gita on *swadharma* (one's own dharma) has led to a lot of controversy. The *Dharma-shastras* distinguish universal or common dharma (*samanya dharma*) from the specific or relative dharmas like *varna* and *ashrama* dharmas. The *samanya dharma* is mandatory for all and at all times, and consists in following a whole lot of various values or virtues commended in the Gita quite explicitly in several chapters, particularly, e.g. the twelfth chapter in verses 13 and 14, the thirteenth in verses 7–11, and 13–14, and in the sixteenth in verses 1–3 as divine qualities and again in the seventeenth in several verses as characterising the *satvika* (the gentle and the good) particularly in verses 14–17. These are not relative, but absolute values to be respected and followed in common, and are more crucial to upholding the society than the relative dharmas. These values are well known and also many and, include, in the words of the Gita itself purity of mind and body (*sattva-samshuddhi, shaucham*), truthfulness (*satyam*), non-injury or non-violence (*ahimsa*), absence of hatred (*adveshta*), compassion to all beings (*daya bhuteshu, mardavam*), uprightness (*arjavam*), forbearance (*kshantih*), steadiness (*sthairyam*), fortitude (*dhritihi*), self-control (*atma-vinigrahah*), humility or absence of egoism (*amanitvam, anahamkarah*), unpretentiousness (*adambhitvam*), charity or generosity (*danam*), control of senses (*damah*), fearlessness (*abhayam*), forgiveness (*kshama*), studiousness *(svadhyaya-abhyasanam*), austerity (*tapah*), tranquillity and absence of anger (*shantih, akrodhah*), aversion to fault-finding (*apaishunam*), non-treacherousness (*adrohah*) and so on. The Gita also advises that one should see the presence of God equally among all (XIII.27) and cause no harm or injustice to any one including one's own self (XIII.28, 13). The Gita expects all to speak the truth without causing vexation and in a way which is beneficial (XVII.15). It is a long list indeed, but it shows the seriousness of the Gita about the need for virtuous conduct. In listing such virtues, the word, dharma, may not have been mentioned, but we are left in no doubt that they constitute the common dharma. The significance given to these values also explains why dharma is considered as the very first or basic of the four *purusharthas* – human goals (others being *artha, kama* and *moksha*). Dharma is meant for everyone to aim at, at being virtuous, without exception. This is clear from the fact that everyone wants to be judged as a good person by the society and by God. Dharma is a human goal not only for individuals but also for every society or state (*rajyam*), because without it no society or state can be happy and liveable. Gandhi, in his *Hind Swaraj*, thought that the quality of even a civilisation is to be judged in terms of its moral development, and not in terms of the level of comforts and conveniences. He said, 'Civilisation is that mode of conduct which points out to man the path of duty' (in Parel Ed. 2009: 65).

In immediate response to Arjuna's declared unwillingness to fight the war, Krishna does not, however, appeal to any of these earlier values, but to *swadharma* – his own duty under the circumstances. In the same breath, he reminds him that he is a Kshatriya – a fighter, a soldier – and as such, he should not desist from fighting a just or righteous war (II.31). When Arjuna talks about renunciation or becoming a monk, thus escaping from all the evils of a war, Krishna says that he cannot do so by avoiding his own duty: 'Better to stick to one's own dharma even with a shortcoming, than to perform someone else's duty well; better to die doing one's dharma, since doing others' duties is (more) risky' (III.35). These two verses have been interpreted by some as casteist – an allegation which is made even against the Gita as a whole. The criticism about the Gita being casteist will be addressed in the next chapter, but we stick here to explaining the real meaning of *swadharma* which can make good sense even in the present times.

Swadharma does not mean caste duty or *jati-dharma*, but only the duty of one's profession or *varna* which is most relevant in the given circumstances. Varna cannot be translated as caste, and the Gita certainly does not talk about caste or *jati*. Every country in the world has these four professional classes – the intelligentsia; the class of soldiers, security and police; the business class; and the class which depends on manual labour. They are referred to as the *varnas* in the Gita, the Kshatriyas coming under the second of the four classes. Krishna clarifies that the classes are divided on the basis of aptitude (*guna*) and work or profession (*karma*) (IV.13) and *svabhava* (natural disposition, XVIII.41). They are not necessarily based on birth, though in the course of history, they came to be determined by and large on birth and became castes. This was because there were no professional schools except for teaching the Vedas and the art of governance and fighting in wars, and children simply adopted the work of their parents and were taught by them. But the system was hardly rigid, and in the Mahabharata war, there were many in the armies of both sides who were not born Kshatriyas. There was nothing casteist in Krishna's asking Arjuna to fight like a Kshatriya, a warrior. Krishna also does not commend hierarchy in the *varnas*, but on the contrary preaches equality. The Gita declares that the one who sees own self among all beings everywhere, treating all as equals (*sarvatra samadarshinah*), is a yogi (VI.29). Krishna endorses this further by saying that 'one who sees Me [God] in all and all in Me, is never lost to Me, nor am I lost to him' (VI.30). Consistent with this philosophy, no *varna* or profession or work has superiority over others. The advice is that whatever be one's work or profession, it has to be done as a yoga or *sadhana*, and attain spiritual fulfilment. The Gita clearly implies that a belief in the presence of God in all the beings means equal dignity of all the beings and their equal right to dignified treatment. It endorses equality, not inequality.

The advice to follow one's duty (*swadharma*) rather than someone else's (*paradharma*) is not meant to bar professional mobility but to insist that once a job is chosen, it must be performed sincerely. The wisdom of the advice to follow *swadharma* and shun *paradharma* comes out hilariously clear from a cartoon by R. K. Laxman. The cartoon shows a minister telling his peon who is shown sitting comfortably and reading the files near the door to the minister's chamber: 'You may be a graduate, but bring the papers and files to my desk first!' Nothing can prevent a peon from becoming a minister, but as long as he is a peon, he should do a peon's duty, and not start reading the files and passing orders in them even if he may be more educated than the minister. Matters can hardly be so hilarious, if, for example an army chief tries to take over the duties of the civilian president or prime minister on the plea that he can perform the task of governance better than the latter. 'Swadharma' just means own sphere of duty, and nothing more. There is nothing to prevent a change in one's sphere of duty when circumstances change, subject to universal ethics or *samanya dharma*.

Why swadharma cannot necessarily mean the dharma inherited from parents is illustrated by A. Parthasarathy with the example of an established physician with a well-equipped clinic and lucrative practice, trying to persuade his son or daughter to follow the same career (Parthasarathy 2011: 252). But the physician may not succeed in this. His children may be interested in some other career. For them, medical practice would be a *paradharma*, not *swadharma*.

Swadharma is important as a starting point on one's spiritual path, according to Eknath Easwaran, and relevant even now. He observes:

> On the spiritual path, we start from where we stand by fulfilling our present responsibilities, on the campus, at the office, or in the home. This *svadharma* may change as our spiritual awareness deepens. Later on, as our capacities grow, our responsibilities and opportunities for service will become greater. What is the right occupation now may not be right later on, but as long as it is not at the expense of others, our job or profession can be made a part of our *sadhana*. . . . By using the word *svadharma* Sri Krishna is saying not to try to follow a profession because someone else is following it. It is much better for you to learn to know yourself, to know your assets and liabilities, to remember your training and follow the career which blends with your *sadhana*, than for you to compare yourself with others and what they are doing. . . . It is a very enjoyable thing to be oneself, to stop acting.
>
> (Easwaran 1997, Vol. I: 197–98)

The Gita often uses the words *swadharma* and *svakarma* as synonyms, since own *duty* (dharma) and own *work* (karma) are expected to be the same. The advice to stick to one's dharma in the third chapter (verse 35 referred earlier) is given again in Chapter 18 in verse 48, saying that one should not give up one's natural work (karma) even if it has a shortcoming (*sahajam karma Kaunteya [Arjuna] sadosham api na tyajet*). In both these verses, it is clearly added that dharma has to be followed, work has to continued, even if it is found to be defective or imperfect or short of one's ideal (*vigunah* in III.35; *sadosham* in XVIII.48). This is a very practical advice not only for the smooth functioning of a society or economy, but also for a peaceful, tension-free, complex-free individual living. A college teacher may feel that he or she is better suited to become the principal of the college, and it may also be true. But as long as she or he is only a teacher, it is better to do that job honestly and then catch the opportunity of becoming the principal when it arises. Following swadharma does not mean going against social and occupational mobility. Two other important verses in the eighteenth chapter, verses 45 and 46, are also clear examples of *swadharma* and *svakarma* being used as synonyms. The actual word used is karma, but it means both dharma and karma here.

One should guard against the temptation of interpreting *swadharma* as purely relative or as so specially tailored to each individual's nature or *svabhava* that the common dharma could be ignored. Alf Hiltebeitel quotes Ravana telling Sita in the Ramayana (5.18.5) that 'making love to others' wives and even carrying them off by force is the *svadharma* of Rakshasas' (Hiltebeitel 2011: 532). Hiltebeitel does not of course approve of such an interpretation of *swadharma* and shows in a detailed footnote that the epics and the *Puranas* do not accept it (Hiltebeitel 2011: 533). The Gita itself terms some qualities as *asuree* or devil-like – qualities such as arrogance, ostentation, hot temper, harshness and ignorance – and says that they lead only to bondage and suffering (XVI.4, 5). Even if such qualities are 'natural' to some, it does not mean that they are therefore morally justifiable. On the other hand, the expectation is that all persons try to overcome them, by pondering over what ought to be done (*karya*) and what ought not to be done (*akarya*) (XVI.24). The Gita does of course provide for specific dharma, as, for example, for students, householders and other *ashramas* (stages in life), but they too are subject to the common basic moral codes. It is clear, therefore, that universal ethics or *samanya-dharma* prevails over even *swadharma*.

The opposite of *dharma* is *adharma*. The Gita is concerned with it also. While *dharma* is what promotes moral development and welfare of the world, *adharma* obstructs them. One could say that deliberately indulging in *adharma* is sin or *papa*. The Gita uses several words for it like *durachara, dushkrita* and *mogham*. They may not be exact synonyms, the first two conveying more heinous sins. In any case, they represent evil – evil in us as well as in others. The question is how the Gita treats evil. The Gita goes to great lengths in emphasising that we should eliminate or at least control evil within us, by controlling our anger, desires, greed, jealousy and so on. This is an essential part of *sadhana* or spiritual seeking. However, the question of dealing with evil in others is more problematic and raises the question of whether using violence to curb evil in others is justified. Tilak and even Sri Aurobindo, in his early phase, thought that according to the Gita, violence is justified in countering the evil and evil persons and evil regimes. Tilak finds support for this view from what Krishna says in the verse – *Ye yatha mam prapadyante tanstathaiva bhajamyaham* (IV.11). Tilak takes it to mean 'eye for an eye', while its usual translation by most is 'In whatever way people worship Me, I reward them accordingly'. Gandhi took the clear stand that the Gita is against using violence as a way of solving the problem of evil in others. There is no dichotomy between dealing with evil within us and dealing with evil in others according to Gandhi's perspective of the Gita. We have to appeal to the sense of what is good even in persons indulging in evil and help to change their heart. There is a battle within us between the forces of the good and evil, and Gandhi treats the Mahabharata war as only an allegory of this struggle. But even Gandhi did not believe in absolute non-violence, since some violence in self-defence in fending off an attack is justified. However, such violence cannot be extended as a long-term solution. He had faith in the power of non-violent resistance even against mighty oppression. He found the Gita supportive of this view, because of its stress on control on mind, equanimity, moral development and dharma, all of which indicate non-violence. Hannah Arendt, however, significantly observes (with which some would agree): 'If Gandhi's enormously powerful and successful strategy of nonviolent resistance had met with a different enemy – Stalin's Russia, Hitler's Germany, even prewar Japan, instead of England – the outcome would not have been decolonization, but massacre and submission' (1970: 53). A few lines later, however, she also observes that use of violence involves a very high price; 'for it is not only paid by the vanquished, it is also paid by the victor in terms of his own power' (1970: 53). Violence can never be a preferred option; it cannot also be a lasting solution, hence the emphasis of the Gita on cleansing one's mind and on appreciating others' problems by asking what we would have done if we were in their position (which is the purport of VI.32). This is Gita's solution to conflict resolution, not violence, on which Gandhi's reading of the Gita on violence as a way of dealing with evil is based. The Gita's attitude to sinners is not spiteful and violent; it gives a chance to them to realise their mistake and submit to God. This is evident from verses 30 to 32 in Chapter 9 (as explained further in another context at the beginning of the next section).

A great teaching of the Gita for which it is well known is about karma as a yoga. It is already discussed earlier under most of the interpreters since this has hardly been ignored by any of them. It is a means of spiritual striving no doubt, but it is also an important part of the social ethics of the Gita. It says that it is impossible to be without karma or work or activity, but one can make one's work more meaningful, purposive and efficient by doing it selflessly and without attachment, and for the welfare or maintenance of the world at large and all its beings (*loka-sangraha*, in III.20, 25; *sarva-bhuta-hita* in V.25, XII.4). Of the two means of liberation, renunciation and selfless activism, the Lord clearly shows His preference for the latter (V.2). Though the emphasis of the Gita on karma-yoga is hardly in doubt, a few verses in it do not *seem* to be consistent with it. In the verse XII.16, and again in XIV.15, Krishna says that a devotee who is *sarvarambha-parityagi* is dear to Him. Gandhi translates it as the one 'who indulges in no undertakings' (Gandhi 1980: 232). Many commentators have also translated it similarly as the one who has renounced every undertaking (Swarupananda 1982: 284) or one who has given up all initiative or initiation (of action) (Radhakrishnan 1993: 297; Dayananda 2007-b: 167; parentheses in original). Such a translation goes counter to the philosophy of karma-yoga. Palshikar has, however, pointed out that according to Oliville (1987: 16), the word *arambha* is also used in ascetic literature to mean ritual activities, which meaning seems to be more pertinent. *Sarvarambha-parityagi* would then mean 'the one who has given up all rituals' (Palshikar 2014: 10). Indulging in rituals does not constitute karma-yoga, as clarified by this verse. A real ardent devotee has no use for rituals, but she or he will continue to serve God through work for the love of God, and God likes it that way. That is the intent of the verse.

Karma-yoga advocated by the Gita is intended to raise the moral and spiritual status of the individual, as well as to take the society to a higher level of welfare, in a mutually fulfilling way. The Gita transformed the earlier concept of *yajna* as ritualistic offering of food in sacrificial fire or animal sacrifice into sharing with others what one has. The philosophy is that we have received from God everything that sustains us, and we repay our debt to Him through *yajna* by sharing with others, be it food, wealth, knowledge or simply labour or work. The Gita speaks of a virtuous cycle (*chakram*) of mutual help, which one should not break (III.10–16). Karma is mentioned as an important form of *yajna*. The word *shrama-da̲n* (gift in the form of free labour) may have been coined much later, but its basic principle is to be found in the Gita (Nadkarni 2013: 66). The makers of modern India like Raja Rammohan Roy, Swami Vivekananda, Lokamanya Bal Gangadhar Tilak and Mahatma Gandhi, whose role and interpretations of the Gita have been discussed earlier (in Chapter 4), were quick to recognise the social significance of the activism preached by the Gita and tried to put this teaching into practice. There is a whole book of 475 pages addressed to the social significance and role of the Gita by Satya P. Agarwal (1993). Agarwal observes that there are two stages of *loka-sangraha* in the Gita – the first according to dharma which is duty-bound and the second is spontaneous as a way of life (Satya P. Agarwal 1993: 351–84). The second is spiritually higher and more promising, and characterises spiritually and morally mature persons. Such persons are described in the fifth chapter, verse 25 of the Gita, which is translated by Easwaran as follows: 'With all their conflicts healed and all their sins removed, the holy sages work for the good of all beings, and attain the *Nirvana* of Brahman'(Easwaran 1997, Vol. I: 326). It does not mean that one has to wait until the person becomes perfect for spontaneity to emerge. It may well emerge naturally once the person is mentally attuned to selfless work. The performance of duties sincerely is itself a sure way to purification of mind leading to perfection (XVIII.45–46).

What distinguishes the two stages is the refinement of mental attitude. A given act like an act of charity (*da̲nam*) can be morally of a high order, middle order or a low level. An act of charity is morally highest or *sa̲ttvika*, only if done not only without expecting anything in return but also done with all humility without any conscious sense of doer-ship, and with a thoughtful propriety in the choice of the gift and receiver. An act of charity done with expecting something in return is of the middle order morally (*rajasika*). It can be of a low moral order even if done without expecting a return benefit, if done with contempt towards or to harm the receiver (XVII.20–22). Similarly, a doer or a performer of work (*karta̲*) is said to be *sa̲ttvika* if he or she is free from emotional attachment and egoism, but at the same time has steadiness, enthusiasm and equanimity about the outcome of work. If he or she is passionately attached to work and its outcome, and desirous of the fruit of work, such a doer is *rajasika*. If a doer is lazy, non-serious about work, haphazard or despondent, such a one is called as *tamasika* by the Gita (XVIII.26–28). It is thus clear that non-attachment commended by the Gita is not lack of interest in the work and its consequences. The Gita insists on efficiency in work (*yogah karmasu kaushalam*, II.50); further, a work done mindlessly without heeding to consequences (*anapekshya*) is called as *tamasika* (XVIII.25).

Ethical grading of several activities like work, devotion and *danam*, of mental traits like fortitude and happiness, in terms of *trigunas* (three *gunas*) – *sattvika, rajasika* and *tamasika* – is one of the most interesting contributions of the Gita. Actually, the Gita contains two ways of ethical grading. One is a simple two-way distinction between the divine (*daivee*) and devil-like (*asuree*) qualities in Chapter 16 (verses 1–4), referred to earlier. Human beings, however, are a varying mix of the two qualities. The path of spiritual or moral evolution lies in overcoming devilish qualities and acquiring the divine ones through deliberate effort at first. Then it becomes a spontaneous process. The purification of mind involved in the process leads one to freedom from bondage. What is even more interesting is the three-way classification into the three *gunas* in Chapters 14, 17 and 18. The Gita goes to great lengths here in discussing what is most ethical, what is less so and what is least ethical or plainly unethical. The rationale for this additional classification seems to be that no human is purely divine or devilish, and that it is better to spell out in some detail what makes a particular thing more ethical or less ethical. Moreover, when it comes classifying human nature and activities, there cannot be only pure white and pure black, but there is a vast grey zone in the middle. We cannot also say that *rajasika* is just a mixture of *sattvika* and *tamasika*, but has its own independent features.

The origin of the concept of the three *gunas* goes to the *Sankhya* system of philosophy, which is perhaps the most ancient of the six *darshanas* or schools of philosophy. Though Sage Kapila is considered as the father of this school, no text authored by him is available. There is a reference to him in the Gita as the most eminent among the perfected sages (X.26). A systematic exposition of *Sankhya* philosophy came after the Gita in *Sankhyakarika* by Ishwarakrishna of the second century CE. The Gita has taken some points from this philosophy as extant then and developed further, especially the ethical application of it. While Chapter 14 of the Gita explains the concept and significance of the three gunas, Chapters 17 and 18 apply the concepts to several things like action, renunciation and charity. The three gunas taken by the Gita as indicating psychological nature are *sattva* or *sattvika* (good, gentle, virtuous, truthful, wise, kind, productive of enduring happiness and enlightenment, benevolent – ethically at the highest level), *rajas* or *rajasika* (emotional, passionate, active, dynamic, energetic, outgoing, greedy – ethically at the middle level) and *tamasika* (or of the quality of *tamas* – darkness, indolent, dull, passive, apathetic, ignorant – ethically at the lowest level). The Gita indicates, however, that no person is purely of one type, but a combination of the three. In the same person, one nature may dominate at one time, and another at another time. But it helps if a person is aware of his or her nature[1] in each context, particularly to control passion and sloth, and strives to maximise one's material as well as spiritual well-being. A classification of various things in terms the three *gunas* is provided in Table 6.1, based on Chapters 17 and 18 of the Gita.[1]

Table 6.1 Trigunas – sattvika (truthful, sage-like), *rajasika* (emotional) and *tamasika* (dismal)

	Sattvika	*Rajasika*	*Tamasika*
Individual's nature	Kind, compassionate, generous, friendly, soft spoken, calm and composed	Emotional, energetic, active, easily provoked to anger, harsh and critical, passionate	Dull, sleepy, lazy, ignorant, passive
Bhakti (devotion to God)	With a pure heart, for the pure joy of loving God and feeling one with Him	Expecting some material reward	Without proper *shraddha*, half-hearted or reward expected in the form of harming enemy
***Shraddha* (commitment and faith)**	Essentially in the Divine and humanity	Essentially in acquiring wealth and power	Belief in evil spirits or witchcraft to acquire power to harm others, irrational, superstitious
***Karta* (agent, doer)**	Endued with *dhriti* (fortitude), enthusiasm, humility, detachment, commitment and equanimity in success and failure	Passionately attached to fruits of outcome, affected by elation or dejection with outcome, tendency to be aggressive	Indifferent, uncommitted, unskilled, dishonest, ignorant of consequences, malicious, lazy, slow

	S<u>a</u>ttvika	*R<u>a</u>jasika*	*T<u>a</u>masika*
Karma (work)	Done with detachment and for the good of all	Done with narrow selfish motive for the good of only oneself	Done with malice, with no heed to consequences, harmful to oneself and others, duties performed reluctantly
Tyaga (renunciation)	Renouncing the fruit of action for oneself alone	Renouncing work because it is difficult or unpleasant	Renouncing obligatory work out of delusion
Jn<u>a</u>na (knowledge)	Sees the unity behind diversity, synthesises, based on holistic perception	Focuses on diversity or multiplicity, based on analysis	Wrong knowledge that mistakes a part for the whole, indifferent to cause and reasoning, obstinate
Buddhi (intellect, discrimination, understanding, perception)	Knows what is to be done/not to be done, what is good and what is bad, the distinction between *pravritti* and *nivritti*, and what leads to liberation	Confused, quick to judge	Pervert in attitude, taking right as wrong and wrong as right ('Fair is foul and foul is fair', as in the *Macbeth*)
Yajna and other rituals	Done with faith, devotion and understanding of the significance, desiring nothing for oneself but for the good of humanity and world peace	Done for the benefit of oneself and family only and for power and ostentation	Done improperly and without faith, or for harming others, involving no charity
D<u>a</u>na (gift, charity, donation)	Given without expecting anything in return, given to the needy or deserving	Expecting something in return including power and fame, given reluctantly	Given to undeserving or at wrong place and time, with contempt for the receiver, or for manipulating and harming the receiver

(*Continued*)

Table 6.1 (Continued)

	Sattvika	*Rajasika*	*Tamasika*
Tapas **(penance, austerity)**	Performed with faith for the good of all	Performed to gain yogic powers, fame and honour, or for worldly things for oneself	Performed with self-torture and/or for harming others
Dhriti **(fortitude)**	High level of moral courage and resoluteness, self-confident, in full control of mind	Using resoluteness only for a selfish purpose and ready to compromise for it	Wavering, not resolute, given to grief, diffidence, depression and fear
Sukham **(happiness)**	Based on clear understanding, and clean/clear conscience, long term	Sensual, short term	Based on delusion or perversion
Ahara **(food)**	Soft and juicy, easily digestible, contributing to health, hygienic, adds to life and nourishment, feel-good type	Acidic, spicy, pungent, may be tasty but produces discomfort	Stale, tasteless, unclean, makes one sleepy and indolent, harmful to health

Note: Based on the interpretation of Chapters 17 and 18 of the Gita.

A few points need to be noted regarding the contents of this table, which throws light on much of the Gita's ethical philosophy. The first is that there can be cross-effects and interaction between things, reinforcing the influence of a particular operating quality on other things too. For example, the Gita believes that the type of food one eats can influence not only physical health but also psychology and the nature of individuals, which in turn can influence attitudes and actions. A *sattvika* food promotes a *sattvika* nature, a *sattvika* nature enables a *sattvika* knowledge and a *sattvika* knowledge leads to *sattvika* actions. A person is known after all by his or her actions, shaping the whole life of the persons concerned. The starting point in the whole process here is right food – a very mundane thing may be, but having a significant moral and spiritual impact! Fresh fruit, vegetables, whole grains, nuts and milk are considered as *sattvika* food by tradition, though not specifically mentioned as examples of the type in the Gita. Interestingly, there is also no explicit bar on meat or fish or eggs; they are not included either in *rajasika* or in *tamasika* list (see XVII.9, 10), nor are they recommended as healthy or nutritious (XVII.8). The Gita does not go into too much detail, but leaves the choice to people having clarified the criteria of classification.

The second point is the contemporary relevance of *triguna* analysis even in day-to-day living, and not just for spiritual progress. A *tamasika* nature can hardly be helpful for success even in mundane matters. One may feel that a *rajasika* nature is the one most workable in a highly competitive world of today. It all depends on what our real goal is. If it is just acquisition of endless goods and power, it may appear so. If it is enduring happiness or oneself and all those around, the relevance of *sattvika* becomes obvious. An aggressive executive will hardly be successful with those working with him or her. On the other hand, a sympathetic understanding executive will be far more successful in getting co-operation from colleagues and subordinates. It does not mean that one need not be strict in implementing the right standards, but an executive who has no respect for those working with him may hardly succeed in doing so. Similarly, an executive or even an ordinary worker, who has a certain amount of healthy detachment about the outcome, is likely to be more effective. The Gita does not commend apathy or indifference to the outcome or consequences of one's work or action, as that would be *tamasika* as it says. One should have efficiency (*kaushalam*) and commitment (*shraddha*)[2] in one's work. The Gita commends, however, that having worked sincerely, putting in one's best, leave the outcome to God, as He is the *karmaphala-data* (the dispenser of the fruit of action). The detachment about outcome makes a person free from anxiety and tension, which not only will make the work more efficient but also is good for the health of the person concerned.

The third point is that an analysis in terms of *trigunas* can be used as a tool of ethical assessment, with due discrimination, on a much a wider scale than what is explicitly envisaged in the Gita. It can, for example be applied to an economy, politics, a society or institutions. Just to illustrate, a *sattvika* economy can be said to be one which is organised and functions ethically, with no poverty, no conspicuous inequality, with safety nets to all especially to the weak and vulnerable to meet emergencies and adequate social security for all. It provides for all equitable access to education, health care, all amenities and infrastructure. It allows only moderate inflation, and only a sustainable use of natural resources, with pollution minimised to sustainable limits. It ensures employment to all. Even its private sector is not focused on maximisation of profits or shareholder wealth alone, but takes into account the interests of all stakeholders also. In other words, a *sattvika* economy is *sarva-bhuta-hite-rata*, that is engaged towards achieving the welfare of all beings. A *rajasika* economy is focused only on the maximisation of the growth rate of national income, with less attention to other concerns mentioned earlier. A *tamasika* economy has neither social justice nor economic growth, but only rampant corruption and illegalities in running both public and private sectors, with very ineffective or little intervention to improve the situation. A rider to such a classification of economies is that an actual economy will not be purely of any of the three types and may in actual fact have features of all the three, but it may be possible to broadly determine which type or nature dominates it more than the other two.[3]

Fourth point is that no one individual or an institution or an economy is permanently of one *guna*, and there is always a struggle to get to the higher ethical level because it is more satisfying. It need not necessarily be a hard task. Roopa Pai points to simple ways of changing one's state of mind.

> If you are feeling depressed and sluggish and Tamasik, force yourself into a state of Rajas, i.e. do something – go for a run, call a friend, pull out your to-do list and finish a couple of tasks on it. You will feel energized, happy, and have a sense of accomplishment at the end of it. If you are stressed from too much Rajasik activity, take a break. Sit down by yourself in a quiet place for 10 minutes, take a few deep breaths, and try and empty your mind of all thoughts. Or simply remove yourself from the scene of activity and sink into glorious Tamas – take a nap, flip channels on your TV, have a snack. It will help you to recharge, and you will soon be ready for Rajas again. From Rajas to Sattva isn't a long journey – any activity that is right and unselfish and good naturally leads to Sattva.
>
> (Pai 2015: 194)

Even *tamas* can be useful, as hinted by Pai, provided it is within moderate limits. *Sattva*, *rajas* and *tamas* need not always be momentary states of mind and can even characterise more enduring traits of one's personality. That is when *tamas* has to be minimised and *rajas* moderated. Those who are already *sattvika* will have to try to remain so, until it becomes their very nature. The Gita also talks about a state where one transcends all *gunas* and becomes *nirguna*, but that is when one's *sadhana* is ripe and the spiritual goal of liberation is attained.

The discussion of ethics in the Gita so far has been on one aspect, the most important one, that is, *dharma*, which is also the first of the four *purusharthas*, human goals or aspirations. The second *purushartha* is *artha* (desire for wealth and power), and the third is *kama* (desire for pleasure). The word, *kama*, has been used in tradition mainly to denote sensual pleasure, but it is also used in the wider sense of desire for any material thing in the Gita. For example, the Lord while identifying himself with whatever is best in the world says – *dharmaaviruddho bhuteshu kamosmi*, that is 'I am the desire in all beings which is not opposed to dharma' (VII.11). The Buddha considered desire as the source of all sorrow in the world. The stand of the Gita also is not very different, though in the verse just referred, it appears that desire is no problem if it is pure and well oriented. Nicholas Lash (Lash 2000: 4, 10 in n-13) raises the question of whether the Gita stands for the suppression of desire or only for its purification. He thinks that the Gita is ambivalent on this issue and refers to verse VII.11, which stands for purification of desire, and verses III.39 and 43, where the Lord advises Arjuna to kill desire, which is the formidable enemy of the soul (*Jahi shatrum Mahabaho [Arjuna} kamarupam durasadam* – III.43). In the verse III.41 also, the advice is to kill desire, which is the destroyer of knowledge and spiritual realisation, by controlling the senses. This verse suggests that Krishna wants only that desire to be curbed which goes against moral and spiritual development, not where it is consistent with dharma. After all, not all desires can be an enemy of the soul according to the Gita, and even according to the interpretation of Lash, there can be a desire for being virtuous (follow dharma) and desire for God or spiritual realisation (Lash 2000: 6). Even other desires such as for food and basic comforts need not necessarily be an enemy of the soul, in so far as they are necessary to keep oneself alive and well functioning to practice karma-yoga.

The Gita is practical enough to commend moderation; it is against extreme austerity. Here again, the Gita's stand is similar to that of Buddhism. The Gita says clearly that yoga is not for those who either overeat or starve, nor for those who sleep all the while or those who hardly sleep (VI.16). But one who is moderate in eating, in recreation, in work, in sleeping and in wakefulness, yoga is not difficult (VI.17). The key to yoga is the control over one's mind, like an oil lamp burning steadily where there is no disturbing breeze (VI.19). The Gita is not against gaining happiness; it is supportive of gaining happiness which is more meaningful, truly satisfying and lasting. The Gita is not against even recreation of mind so long as it is proper and not against dharma (*Yukta-cheshta* – VI.17). Overall, the basic advice of the Gita is not one of suppressing desires, but one of purifying the mind itself through freeing it from both *raga* (obsessive attachment) and *dvesha* (hatred), since it is these two enemies which stimulate uncontrolled desire, anger, greed, jealousy and the like and lead to moral decay. The Gita says that one can move among the objects of the senses without coming under their control, but keeping them under control. The importance of controlling *raga* and *dvesha* is emphasised now and then at least in three verses (II.64, III.34 and XVIII.51). Verse XVI.21 regards *kama* in the sense of lust, *krodha* (raging anger) and *lobha* (greed) as the enemy of the self, and hence to be rejected or avoided. As Swami Chinmayananda has emphasised, it is the essential purpose of religion 'to lift the limited and selfish human being from his passions, greed, and hatreds to a loftier vision of the world' (Thapan Ed. 2005: 33). That is the purpose of the Gita too.

However, desirelessness as an ideal comes prominently in the karmayoga commended by the Gita. It comes out clearly in several chapters from the second to the last. It is reiterated in the discussion of *trigunas* also. According to verse XVIII.9, a *sattvika karma* is that which is done without attachment and without desiring its fruit (*sangam tyaktva phalam chaiva*), but done based on an assessment of what needs to be done as duty under the given situation. This is a very difficult ideal. Put aside for a while the second requirement of working without desire for its fruit. But what does work without attachment mean? Can such a work be effective or good? One may not always be lucky enough to get work which she or he loves, but unless the person begins to love the work she or he gets to do, can it be meaningful and fruitful? An emotional attachment to the work one does is not bad, but has, on the contrary, beneficial effects. Isn't mother's loving care for her child not *sattvik* merely because she is emotionally attached to her child, though her care is certainly not selfish. Osho solves this problem by explaining that non-attachment is not its opposite – aversion. 'Even aversion is a kind of attachment – to the opposite of attachment' (2006: 532). Desirelessness is also not aversion, because aversion is a desire for the opposite. Osho says that 'a non-attached mind, according to Krishna, is one who accepts everything unconditionally' (2006: 533). Mothers loving care for her child is non-attached because it is unconditional and is therefore *sattvika*. Non-attachment is just another way of expressing absence of any narrow or selfish desire. It is not indifference.

Let us now attend to the second requirement, namely desirelessness. What does it mean for a modern economy or society? Workers work for a salary, business enterprises work for profit. Can a doctor or a lawyer work without expecting fees? What is implied by the Gita is that one can certainly work for a legitimate reward, but without greed. A health-care system where the doctors are rewarded by the government, but not by the patients directly, appears to be consistent with karma-yoga. Even under a system of private health care, a doctor cannot treat a more paying rich patient better than another less paying patient. A school teacher may be paid for doing evaluation work by the school or the concerned institution, but cannot expect a higher remuneration for giving higher marks. The direct link between work and reward can lead to problems in several situations, and an emotional detachment about the reward can increase both fairness and commitment. That is why the *Ishopanishad* in its very first verse tells us that the world belongs to God, and we have to take only what is legitimately ours, and not covet what is not ours. This is of course a general philosophical principle, and the question of how to decide what is legitimately ours and what is not ours can be decided only on the basis of goodwill for all in Gandhian spirit and if we avoid being covetous. This is the message of the Gita too. We may pursue our legitimate desires and work to satisfy them, but this has to be within moral limits, without resorting to dishonesty, hypocrisy and greed.

There is a great significance in the overall advice of the Gita to keep our desires in check, which would be good not only for one's moral and spiritual development, for curbing inequality in consumption and making more resources available for the needy and for environmentally benign and sustainable development. A situation where endless consumption is the prime engine of economic growth can lead us to environmental disaster. We thus gain guidance from the Gita not only about individual ethics, but also about social ethics and environmental ethics. A few thinkers distinguish between virtues which are 'self-regarding' or individual oriented, and altruistic virtues which benefit others also or the society at large (e.g. Yardi 1991: 111). Yardi puts virtues like fearlessness, control over senses and emotions, and modesty under the first category; virtues like truthfulness, kindness and generosity come under the second and promote social ethics. It is not possible to draw a neat line of distinction between the two, because if in a society most people are virtuous even in the 'self-regarding' or individual sense, it would have tremendous benefits to the society; and altruistic virtues on the other hand would also benefit the individuals concerned by contributing to their moral and social development. In any case, Yardi's intention is to show that the Gita upholds both the types of virtues and promotes both individual and altruistic or social ethics. We have in the Gita a synthesis of not only individual and social virtue ethics, but also deontological ethics and consequential ethics – all in a harmonious blend. Human rights may not be explicitly mentioned, but human duties are, and in the Indian approach, as Gandhi insisted, rights and duties are counterparts of the same coin. There is in the Gita ethics for soldiers in war, for workers in the mundane world, for devotees in love with God, for the wise who seek spiritual realisation through knowledge and even for ascetics who like to transcend the world. What we get from the Gita is holistic, comprehensive ethics, useful in leading our day-to-day lives meaningfully and also transcending it gracefully.

A tricky issue in the Gita is about the question of free will. There are certain verses in it suggestive of absolute control by God in all matters, there being no question of choice or free will. The picture of universal form of God in Chapter 11 shows human beings as merely His instruments, acting according to His will, with their destiny completely in His hands (verses 32–34). Krishna tells Arjuna that all on the opposite side of the army are already decided to be killed, and Arjuna will be a mere instrument (*nimitta-matram*) with no choice. Again in the last chapter, Krishna tells that the Lord who dwells in the heart of all makes them to revolve as if they are all mounted on a machine (XVIII.61). Yet, in the 63rd verse of the same chapter, Krishna gives a choice to Arjuna asking him to ponder critically over all that was said and then decide as per his wish. Was it a mere courtesy? Why does a mere instrument, a cog in the machine require courtesy? Further, why does a mere instrument lacking free will need all the teaching about *swadharma*, controlling desires, detachment and ethics in general? What is the meaning of the law of karma if human beings are all puppets? Karma has a meaning only if they are moral agents. If you take the Gita as a whole, there is no doubt that human beings at least have been granted the power of free will, though this power is not absolute and subject to limits. Perhaps the distinction between *vyavaharika satya* (relative or practical reality) and *paramarthika satya* (ultimate or absolute reality) made by Shankara may help in resolving the issue. There is free will subject to limits in the former, but no such question in the latter, where everything is fused in to one ultimate reality with no distinctions.

God and His world

The Gita expects us to go beyond ethics. It is important to be a good person, but it is not enough. One has to have a higher purpose in life to awaken to deeper reality and meaning of what we are and our relation with the Ultimate. The Gita goads us to rise above the mere mundane, find the Divine within and realise our full potential. The Gita in its essence is theistic, and its major purpose is to make us know ourselves and our Maker. Ethics, however, continues to be relevant. It is connected to God in two ways in the Gita. One is that by leading a virtuous and selflessly active life, the mind is purified, which leads to God realisation. Ethics are quite necessary for *s<u>a</u>dhan<u>a</u>*. But the Gita's God is kind even to a sinner (*sudur<u>a</u>ch<u>a</u>ro*) (IX.30). Even if a person falters in ethics, he will be saved by God and brought to a good path if only he takes refuge in Him with a right resolve. There is a heart-warming promise, 'My devotee will never perish' (IX.31). The whole tone of the two verses, X.30–31, is one of compassion to sinners who surrender to God, but not to sinners considered as incorrigible – too arrogant, lustful, hateful and obstinate (XVI.18–19). A distinction between two types of sinners – those having the potential for redemption and those who are incorrigible – is evident. This does not belittle the importance of ethics, but only enhances the significance of the role of God. If only a sinner turns to God, he becomes a *dharm<u>a</u>tm<u>a</u>*, a righteous person (IX.31), because it will make him repent and resolve that he will not behave badly again. 'God holds us, fallen though we be, by the roots of our being and is ready to send His rays of light into our dark and rebellious hearts. The very consciousness of our imperfection and sin betrays the pressure of the Divine on our hearts' (Radhakrishnan 1993: 251). The primary condition here is that one should give up ego and be open to the Divine, because then 'the Divine takes up the burden and lift the soul into the spiritual plane' (Radhakrishnan 1993: 251). The concept of God here is a personal deity. People need God not so much as an impersonal force running the universe at large, but as the father, mother, friend or all combined, with whom they can talk and confide, to whom they can pray for help and protection in an increasingly uncertain and vulnerable world, made so by man himself in no small measure. Faith in a personal God is a source of great emotional security, even if there may be occasions of disappointment. For a devotee, each disappointment draws him or her closer to Him, enabling not merely survival through a turbulent world but even motivating for success in it.

Lord Krishna himself is a personal God in human form, who according to the Gita itself is an *avatar* of the Supreme. But the Gita also speaks of the Supreme as a personal but formless God endowed with all good qualities necessary to take care of the world and His devotees. Even as He is the origin and the Lord of all the worlds (*sarvaloka-maheshwara*), He is at the same time the friend of all beings (*sarvabhutanam suhridah*) (V.29). This God is described as omniscient (*kavi*), ageless or ancient (*purana*), ruler of everything (*anushasitara*), minuter than an atom (*anoraniya*), sustainer of all (*sarvasya dhatara*), of no conceivable form (*achintya-rupa*), self-luminous like the sun (*aditya-varna*) and beyond darkness (*tamasah parastat*) (VIII.9) (Tr. Swarupananda 1982: 184). He is the One to be known, the Pure, Upholder, the syllable Om, the three Vedas (*Rik, Sama and Yajur*), the Ultimate Refuge and Abode, the [understanding and helping] Friend, the Witness and the immutable substratum too (IX.17, 18) (Tr. Swarupananda 1982: 207). The Supreme is said to have manifold manifestations due to His yoga power (X.7) and is thus the origin of all (X.8). Arjuna acknowledges that Krishna in human form is the same as the Supreme Brahman, the Unborn, the Eternal, to whom all sages have been devoted (X.12). He is the Highest of all beings, *Purushottama*, a concrete Divine Personality and also the Supreme Self, the *Paramatma*, who pervades and sustains all the worlds (XV.17).

The concept of personal gods goes back to the Vedas. Vishnu, Indra, Varuna and Agni, for example, were personal gods in the Rigveda. Vishnu was taken as pervading (*vish*) the whole universe and controlling and taking care of it. Krishna was identified with Vishnu (Radhakrishnan 1993: 26). The *Shwetashwatara Upanishad* too has a personal god – Shiva – but also identified with the Supreme Brahman (Yardi 1991: 91). The Gita similarly has Krishna as a personal god, also identified with the same Supreme Brahman.

A personal God can be worshipped in any form or even without form as per the inclination of the devotee, who should have the faith that his personal God is only the same Supreme who is the origin and protector of all. The Gita assures that whatever form any devotee wishes to worship with *shraddha*, the Lord strengthens that *shraddha* and grants his or her desires (VII.21–22). Moreover, in Hinduism, personal God can be One or several, though it is always insisted that all the personal gods are various forms of the One and the same Supreme. The Gita declares that the worship of different gods also goes to the same Supreme, even if this worship is not done systematically (IX.23). There is thus freedom to conceptualise a personal god as per one's inclination and find fulfilment. The form is not important, but the *shraddha* and devotion are.

It is clear in the Gita that this personal God, also the Ishwara of all the worlds, is *sagu<u>n</u>a Brahman* (the Supreme with attributes). He is identified with the essence, the most significant and the best of everything in the world. He is the radiance of the sun, the sapidity of water, the syllable Om of the Vedas, the life of all beings and intellect of the intelligent (VII.8–10). 'There is no end to the particulars of My manifestations' (*n<u>a</u>sti anto vistarasya*), as Krishna tells Arjuna (X.19) (Tr. Swarupananda 1982: 229). He is the *<u>a</u>tma* existing within all beings. Among the radiant, He is the sun. Among the priests, He is Brihaspati. Of the waterbodies, He is the ocean. He is the Himalaya among the mountains, the Ashwattha (peepul) among the trees, the Ganga among the streams, alphabet A among letters and so on. He is the knowledge of the knowers, and the power of the powerful. He is the knowledge of the Self among all knowledges. He exists supporting the whole world only by a portion of Himself (X.19–42). He is the strength of the strong which is devoid of desire and attachment. He is the desire among beings which is unopposed to dharma (VII.11). He is the very abode of absolute and eternal dharma (XIV.27). Being the father and mother and friend of all the beings (IX.17–18, V.29), He is also the source of limitless love.

Though Ishwara as the personal God is Omnipotent, with no limits to His power, He takes responsibility neither for anyone's sin nor for anyone's merit (*n<u>a</u>datte kasyachit p<u>a</u>pam na chaiva sukritam Vibhuh*, V.15). Radhakrishnan explains: 'If the universe consists of active choosing individuals who can be influenced but not controlled, for God is not a dictator, conflict is inevitable. To hold that the world consists of free spirits means that evil is possible and probable. The alternative to a mechanical world is a world of risk and adventure. If all tendencies to error, ugliness and evil are to be excluded, there can be no seeking of the true, the beautiful and the good' (1993: 24). Yet, the Gita's God is vitally interested in ensuring that in the conflict between good and evil, the good ultimately wins. 'He pours out His wealth of love in helping man to resist all that makes for error, ugliness and evil. As God is completely good and His love is boundless, He is concerned about the suffering of the world' (1993: 25).

As personal God, Krishna is not only our parent and friend, but also our Guru too. 'He is not a hero who once trod the earth and has now left it, having spoken to His favourite friend and disciple, but is everywhere and in every one of us, as ready to speak to us now as he ever was to anyone else. He is not a bygone personality but the indwelling spirit, an object for our spiritual consciousness' (1993: 31). A special significance of the personal God in the Gita is that He is 'declared to be available to all, irrespective of their social status, gender or rules of ritual purity', or even 'karmic luggage' (Malinar 2009: 7). The Gita can be said to have democratised religion in India as never before, because of this and also by providing easy means like bhakti accessible to all.

Though an important aspect of *saguna Brahman* is His fond personal relationship with all beings, He is also immanent and has a universal form – *Vishwarupa*. A whole chapter, the eleventh, is devoted to describing this form of the Supreme. In this form, He does not appear as a personal God, but as not only the one who pervades the universe, but also the fierce force behind its relentless and continuous dissolution and renewal. Arjuna wanted to have a cosmic vision of the Lord, His real form, and is given special divine eyes to visualise the magnificent cosmic spectacle of the immanence and unlimited raw power of the Supreme. The impact of this on Arjuna is one of profound awe and even fear. The whole universe is now seen to be the body of the Supreme, in which exist and move all things, sentient and insentient – from celestial bodies to smallest creatures. The cosmic form has the splendour of a thousand suns and hosts all the multiplicity of the world (*pravibhaktam anekadha*, XI.13). It is 'the very form of the Lord that includes all the forms', and there is nothing of the universe that is outside it (Dayananda 2011, Vol. 7: 11). Even though awestruck, with his hair standing on end, Arjuna breaks out into a spontaneous and a highly poetic praise of the Lord. He exclaims, among other things, in the form of an evocative verse:

> *Tvam aksharam paramam veditavyam*
> *Tvam asya vishwasya param nidhanam /*
> *Tvam avyayah shashwata-dharma-gopta*
> *Sanatanahstvam purusho mato mey //*
> (XI.18)

> ('You are the Imperishable Supreme, the only thing to be known. You are the great refuge of the whole cosmos, the undying Guardian of Eternal Dharma, and the primeval eternal Purusha as I see.'
> – Tr. by the author)

The essential idea conveyed by the *Vishwarupa* chapter is that the world is not separate from God, but is the body of God, though He may be much more than this body. Arjuna visually experiences that the whole cosmos is all one in the Supreme. There is no hint anywhere in the Gita that the cosmic form is unreal or an illusion, or that only the unmanifest is real. Interestingly, the idea of the Cosmos being the body of the Supreme corresponds with the related concept of the human body being the abode or the field (kshetra) of the *jiva*, who is the knower of the field (*Kshetrajna*, in the thirteenth chapter). At the cosmic level, the Supreme is the *Kshetrajna* of the whole Cosmos. Since He pervades it, He is also in us all. Easwaran remarks: 'The greatest wonder is that this tremendous radiance reflected throughout the cosmos shines within us too. As our spiritual experience grows, as our separateness goes and our ego dissolves, we will experience a tremendous effulgence spreading throughout our consciousness, which no experience of the senses can ever help us comprehend' (Easwaran 1997, Vol. II: 276). 'The deeper we probe into the nature of the universe, whether it is the vastness of space or infinitesimal world within the atom, the more we shall see the glory of the Lord revealed' (Easwaran 1997: 277).

With *nirguna Brahman*, or *Parabrahma*, one goes deeper into the quest for ultimate reality. *Brahman*, though an impersonal Absolute, as Radhakrishnan stresses, is not a mere abstraction in the Gita, for It is the very basis of all Reality, including the finite world (1996, Vol. I: 534). In contrast to the detailed description of the Supreme in His manifested cosmic form, there is not much in the Gita by way of explaining *Parabrahma*, the Unmanifest Supreme. This is understandable, because what is basically ineffable cannot be explained much; it has to be experienced or realised. Among the few verses which deal specifically with the Unmanifest or *nirguna Brahman* is the third in the twelfth chapter, where the Supreme is said to be *Akshara* (Eternal), *Anirdeshya* (Indefinable), *Avyakta* (Formless, Unmanifest), *Sarvatraga* (Omnipresent), *Achintya* (Unthinkable, Unimaginable), *Kutastha* (Immutable), *Achala* (Unmoving) and *Dhruva* (Firm, Constant, Permanent).

Surprisingly, there is explicitly no reiteration of the Upanishadic epithets of Brahman in the Gita – *Sat Chit Ananda* (truth/existence, consciousness, bliss), in personal, universal or even *nirguna* form. Indirectly, however, these epithets are clearly implied. The sixteenth verse in the second chapter says that what exists is *sat*, and the unreal does not and cannot exist. It is the very nature of truth that it alone exists, and falsehood (*asat*) can never. The second line of the verse says that persons of discrimination know what exists and what does not, what is real and what is unreal. The intention of the verse is not just to convey a truism that what exists, but to indicate that Brahman is *sat*, and Existence is

Its very nature. It is meaningless to call for a proof of the existence of God in the sense of Brahman, because Existence is what it is, and non-existence is its opposite – *asat*. The first half of the fifteenth verse in the fifteenth chapter, for example says that the Lord resides in the heart of all and is responsible for the memory and perception, as also their loss (*Sarvasya chaham hridi sannivishto mattah smritirjnanam apohanam cha*). Memory and perception are suggestive of consciousness or *chit*. Verses 27 and 28 of Chapter 6 clearly say that supreme bliss comes to the yogi who has realised the Brahman, the resulting happiness from the contact with the Brahman being simply extreme (*atyantam sukham*). This is clearly about the *ananda* aspect of the Brahman. The Gita also goes further. Not only is the Brahman of the nature of *sat, chit* and *ananda*, It is also the source of energy (*ojas*) which runs the world, whether the beings of the world are conscious of it or not. The Lord tells Arjuna, 'entering the earth with my energy I support all beings, and nourish all the herbs. . . . Abiding in the bodies of all beings as digestive fire, working with their very breathing, I absorb the fourfold food' (XV.13–14). Thus conceptualised, one does not have to seek God outside, be it in idols in temples or places of pilgrimage. The striving yogis find Him in themselves and, that too, firmly established (*yatanto yoginah chainam pashyantyatmani vyavasthitam*, XV.11).

There are several verses, especially in Chapter 2, which explain evocatively the nature of Atman, and in the Advaita philosophy, Atman and Brahman are the same. Atman or Brahman is that by which all this world is pervaded (*yena sarvam idam tatam*), which is indestructible (*avinashi, anashinah*), illimitable (*aprameya*) and immutable (*avyaya*) (II.17, 18). It neither slays, nor is slain; it is never born, nor does it die. It is not that not having been; it comes into being. It is eternal (II.19–21). Like discarding old clothes and wearing new ones, the *dehi* discards worn out bodies and takes up new ones (II.22). Weapons cannot pierce, nor can fire burn it. Water cannot soak it, nor can wind dry it (II.23). It is eternal (*nityah, sanatanah*), omnipresent (*sarvagatah*), constant (*sthanuh*) (II.24). It is unmanifest (*avyakta*), unthinkable (*achintya*) and unchangeable (*avikarya*) (II.25). Remarkably, the same epithets are thus used both for Atman and for Brahman in the Gita. A few verses leave no doubt that the indwelling Atman and Brahman are the same.[4] Take this for example:

Upadrishta Anumanta cha Bharta Bhokta Maheshwarah /
Paramatmeti cha api ukto dehesmin Purushah Parah //
(XIII.22)

> ('And the Supreme Purusha in this body is also called the Looker-on, the Permitter, the Supporter, the Experiencer, the Great Lord, and the Highest Self.'
>
> Tr. Swarupananda 1982: 301)

The remarkable similarity between epithets used for the Brahman and the Atman has been noted earlier showing them to be impersonal. Equally remarkably, the epithets of personal God are, however, different, the emphasis here being on His compassion, love for devotees, protective nature and so on, which are absent among the epithets for Brahman. The utterly impersonal nature of the Brahman, the ultimate reality, can be not only puzzling but also disconcerting to devotees in need of a personal God. The thirty-first verse in Chapter 13 states clearly: 'This inexhaustible Supreme Self, being without beginning and without qualities, does not act and is not tainted, though stationed in the body' (Tr. Radhakrishnan 1996, Vol. I: 535). It is merely a spectator, a looker-on and is not a doer (*akarta*). Radhakrishnan explains: 'The whole drama of evolution belongs to the object world. Intelligence, mind, senses are looked upon as the developments of the unconscious prakriti, which is able to bring about this ascent on account of the presence of spirit. The subject self is within us calm and equal, uncaught in the external world' (Radhakrishnan 1996: 535). The Brahman may be the source of our very existence and our consciousness. But to a devotee who needs an intervention to tide over the problems of the world, an impersonal non-doer God may serve little purpose. The impersonal God may appeal to a reasoning or rationalist mind, but not to a person who wants a listening and acting God.

We have thus different conceptualisations of God in the Gita, which can appeal to different types of persons. The Lord says in the Gita itself that four types of virtuous persons worship Him, the distressed (*artah*), seeker of knowledge (*jijnasu*), seeker of wealth (*artharthi*) and the wise (*jnani*) (VII.16). The Lord further says that the last, being singularly devoted and liberated [from pettiness, selfishness, etc.], is dearest to Him, just as the Lord is dearest to him or her above everything else in the world (VII.17). He clarifies further that though some of them have a narrower vision and discrimination, all these seekers are noble and good (*udarah*), and He fulfils their respective desires (VII.18–22). The important point made is that the Lord satisfies all His devotees according to their own respective conceptualisation and perception, some getting their earthly desires fulfilled, which means limited rewards, and some (like the *jnanis*) getting nothing less than oneness with the Lord Himself and gaining absolute bliss. Thus, the question of what form of God or ultimate reality is most relevant is decided by the devotees themselves according to their own perception and understanding. They get what they seek. If they seek only earthly titbits, their rewards may be limited, but they are their own making. If the seekers are spiritually more ambitious, and aim big, they also get as per their aspirations. We get the God we strive for.

Deepak Chopra observes in this connection, 'In our search for the one and only one God, we pursue the impossible. The issue isn't how many Gods exist, but how completely our own needs can be spiritually be fulfilled' (2001: 43). He says that in any case we need God, 'because without a source, our existence has no foundation at all' (2001: 7). But we select a deity based on our own perception or interpretation of our experience with reality. It is not as if our selection of a particular deity or concept of God is fixed and final. It evolves through stages, and Chopra identifies *seven stages*, with each stage meeting a particular human need. A person who needs protection from threat and danger needs a Protector God. This is the *first stage*. In the language of the Gita, it is the stage of *arta*, the distressed. Once the feeling of fear and insecurity of the first stage are transcended, the stage is set for seeking power and wealth – that of *artharthi*. This is *stage two*, where the seeker needs an Almighty God. The dominant emotion of stage two is awe about the power of God and the desire to accomplish much in the world with His blessings. In the *third stage*, we seek a God of Peace, detachment and calm. Life's challenge now is to be actively engaged and detached at the same time, enjoying the inner silence. The third stage can be said to be one of beginning with karma-yoga in the Gita's terminology. The spiritual seeking is no longer self-oriented. In the words of the Gita, the seeker is engaged in *loka-sangraha* and *sarvabhuta-hita*, the welfare of all beings. In the *fourth stage*, God is the Redeemer. We seek forgiveness and love of God. We need a loving and understanding God now. This is the stage of ardent devotion – *bhakti* in the words of the Gita. It enables the *bhakta* to get out of the coils of karma, having been aided by karma-yoga. It is still a stage where dualities persist.

In *stage five*, God is the Creator. In this stage, the sense of duality between the seeker and the sought God is reduced, and he or she joins God in a partnership of co-creation, participating in the continuous renewal and improvement of the world, enhancing its beauty and enjoyableness. One discovers one's creative self and gets engaged in creative expressions in art, literature, music and so on. In this stage, the seeker works with God, in harmony with His benign purpose. In *stage six*, we have a God of miracles – not in the usual sense of doing abnormal things breaking natural laws created by God Himself, but bringing about deeply transformative or epochal or paradigmatic shifts breaking with past trends. Several revolutionary changes have changed the world irreversibly, in which humans have partnered with God. The development of paper and printing technology in the past and of computers and Internet in the more recent times are examples of these changes. In this stage, the seeker is imbued with rich vision, drawing it from God. Many smaller miracles also take place in our lives, such as a recovery from what was regarded as a hopeless illness, often due to the strength of one's mind and faith. Miracles can and do take place at a spiritual level, when after years of effort, a sudden spiritual awareness dawns effortlessly and stays thereafter, transforming one's life. Such experiences have been recorded in the lives of several spiritual masters such Shri Ramakrishna Paramahamsa and Shri Ramana Maharshi. The stupendous achievements in the short lives of A̲di Shankara̲cha̲rya and Jnanadev are nothing short of miracles. The final stage, *stage seven*, is a culmination of spiritual striving, when the realisation of God as Pure Being, 'I am', takes place. Chopra says, 'The God of stage seven is holistic – he encompasses everything. To know him, you would have to possess a mind to match. . . . The God of stage seven is so intangible that he can be defined by no qualities' (2001: 155). He tells further that in the ancient Indian tradition, this aspect of spirit is defined only by negation – 'Unborn, Undying, Unchanging, Unmoving, Unmanifest, Immeasurable, Invisible, Intangible, Infinite' (2001: 156). As Chopra says, if this stage had been suddenly reached at the outset, one would not have realised the reality of God. 'You have to climb the spiritual ladder from one rung to the next', and once having reached the summit, no support is needed, not even of the mind (2001: 156). When you become one with the Pure Being, ordinary life, with all its activities, does not cease to exist, says Chopra. Until then, one's identity is 'wrapped up' in karma, in a cycle of desires that lead to actions, actions leaving impressions, which in turn lead to desires. In the final stage, one is freed from these cycles even while engaged in the world, for deep within, there is a genuine feeling of non-doer-ship, complete calm and detachment.[5]

We come now to the question of the relationship of God with the world, including the question of the reality of the world and of us all in it. The Gita does not anywhere say that the world is unreal or that it is an illusion. There is not a single verse suggestive of denial of the world as false or *mithya*. On the other hand, there are many verses which affirm the reality of it, though not as a reality independent of God. The Lord describes His lower *prakriti* as eightfold which includes the five elements including the earth, mind, intellect and the ego (VII.4), which are sustained by His higher *prakriti* [of *sat, chit* and *ananda*] (VII.5). The implication is that the world is a part of the same Divine, but dependent part. It is affirmed that God is both the origin and the cause for dissolution of the world (VII.6). There is a brief discussion of the different aspects of the Divine and its relation to the world at the beginning of Chapter 8 in verses 3 and 4, in response to an opening query by Arjuna made in verses 1 and 2. It sounds a bit complicated, but is significant. According to Krishna's reply, the Ultimate transcendental and imperishable reality is the Brahman, which at the same time imparts existence to everything and every creature in the universe. It exists also in the perishable bodies (*adhibhuta*) as the *adhyatma*, sustains everything as *adhidaiva* and receives all offerings (including actions, devotion) as *adhiyajna*. The different aspects of the Divine may have been given different names, but it is One, and there is no question of a lack of co-ordination! The verses could also be interpreted as speaking of three planes of reality – the perishable material world (*adhibhuta*), under the care of a personal God (*adhidaiva* and *adhiyajna*), both resolving ultimately into the impersonal and imperishable spiritual reality of *adhyatma* or Brahman. The whole universe is pervaded by Him (IX.4). He projects again and again into the whole multitude of beings (IX.8). As noted earlier, the whole universe is shown as within His body, in Chapter 11. He moves the whole universe and all the beings in it including plants through His energy (*ojas*) (XV.13). Yet, it is stressed that He is both doer and non-doer, and His actions do not bind Him, and He is unattached (IV.10–11). In other words, the moral responsibility for actions of at least the human beings does not belong to Him but to the humans alone. The Lord has provided them with a mind (*manas*), intellect (*buddhi*) and ego (*ahamkara*) of their own (VII.4). They have the freedom of choice or free will. It is clear from this that the whole world and all the beings in it are real, dependent on the Lord, and yet separate, with at least the human beings having a will of their own. But there is no question of absolute freedom for us, because we are subject to not only laws of nature, but also each other's freedom. Thus, the world of the Gita is one in which Arjuna and all beings are with enough freedom to operate and do their roles, and choose between good and bad, or between right and wrong. In Shankara's words, it is a world of *vyavaharika satya*.

Yet the Lord does not expect us to get bogged down to the mundane world (*samsara*) all the while and be burdened with its sorrows and problems until eternity. Though the world is His creation, having given free will to the humans at least, the Lord knows that this could land them into conflicts and even crises. Man needs freedom of will to realise his full mental and spiritual potential, but the karmic cycle is the side effect of this free will. The Lord expects humans to come out of the coils of karma, and thus transcend *samsara* or the world, and ultimately realise oneness with Him, and wake up to the ultimate reality, where there is no distinction between God and His world. Thus, the first verse in Chapter 15 compares *samsara* with the inverted peepul tree, with roots in the air and branches and leaves below, and expects the spiritual seekers to cut this tree down with the axe of detachment. This has to be done by each seeker individually, since the tree is perennial and when cut down by one seeker, it does not mean that it is cut down for others too. Significantly, the tree is stated as having its roots above (in the Lord himself) since the mundane world is also His creation only. But the fact that it can be cut down at the individual level when the spiritual development of the individual is ripe means that *samsara* can vanish in individual cases and the liberation from it is individual, not collective.

The world, thus, is not a completely objective fact, and its nature depends on individual seeker's perception of it too. It can vary with the level of one's spiritual development. Chopra sees seven stages in this regard too, corresponding to seven perceptions of God described earlier. In the first stage, the world is seen as full of misery and conflicts, and the response of a person to it is fight or flight. In the second stage, it is a world of competition and opportunities of satisfying one's ambition. In the third stage, it is one of inner self-sufficiency and calm, not by being an introvert but by being constructively and altruistically engaged in the affairs of the world and finding inner peace and fulfilment. In the fourth, it is a world of opportunities for insight and understanding, and further personal growth. In the fifth, it is one of providing scope for creative response through art, discovery and invention. The sixth stage is one developing a visionary response to the problems of the world. The seventh and the final stage is a transcendent world, where one sees beyond the world and gets to realise the ultimate reality of being one with the Pure Being (Chopra 2001: 177). The world thus is not just one of sorrow and struggle for survival, but is also one full of opportunities for self-development and fulfilment. The approach of the Gita to the world is not one of escapism, but one of active and constructive engagement, and ultimately gaining inner calm and fulfilment.

Sadhana: spiritual striving[6]

The literal meaning of *sadhana* is achieving or striving to achieve. Achieving anything requires dedication and commitment or *shraddha*, which are implicit in the term. The one who is on the path of achieving is called a *sadhaka* or spiritual seeker. Often the travel is more meaningful and exciting than the destination, and so it is with *sadhana*. The very task of spiritual seeking, when sincerely practised, purifies and ennobles us, imparts more confidence in us, strengthens our moral fibre, gives us peace of mind and lifts us above the ordinary, gross and mundane. And that is an achievement by itself.

Even then, it is the destination which inspires us and makes us undertake the arduous journey, and it is the destination which makes us choose the path. What is the destination of *sadhana*? The conventional answer is, by and large, *moksha*, which literally means liberation, and what is meant is liberation from the karmic cycle of births and deaths, taken as the highest human goal, or *purushartha*. This is also the ultimate goal set by the Gita – the goal of 'freeing oneself from the fetters of rebirth and reach that state which is beyond all evil' (*Janma-bandha-vinirmuktah padam gachchanty anamayam*, II.51). But not everybody may entertain such a distant goal, even if believing in rebirth. Most of us would be content with success in ensuring material prosperity and happiness in the present life itself, for which we may seek the blessings of the Almighty. The Gita does not deplore seeking *artha* and *kama*, but expects us not only to gain them through following the path of dharma, but invites us also to even go beyond and find greater, more meaningful and lasting happiness. The Gita does not think greatly of aiming at the goal of heaven and its pleasures, as they are also temporary like the pleasures of the world itself (II.43). It invites us to broaden and raise our concept of happiness itself. The beauty of the goal of liberation is that whether we believe in freedom from rebirth or not, the very path of achieving it promises freedom from bondage to narrow limitations of the world, and in the process, we find our self expanding in scope going beyond selfish interests and becoming so inclusive that we would be engaged selflessly in achieving the good of all (*sarva-bhuta-hite ratah*, V.25 and XII.4). Interestingly, in both verses, where there is a reference to those engaged in *sarva-bhuta-hita* (the welfare of all), there is either a promise of liberation (*brahma-nirvanam*) or uniting with the Supreme (*prapnuvanti mam*). Such persons are also described as freed from all blemish (*kshina-kalmashah*, V.25), with senses under control, and even minded (XII.4). The fact that *moksha* was not necessarily the preferred goal of *sadhakas* even in the past is clear from a verse in *Shrimad-Bhagavatam*:

> *Naham kamaye rajyam na svargam na cha apunarbhavam /*
> *Praninam dukkha-taptanam kamaye dukkha-nashanam //*
>
> ('I desire no kingdom, no heaven, not even freedom from rebirth [*apunarbhavam* or *moksha*] for myself. I desire only that beings afflicted by sorrow be relieved of it.'
>
> – Tr. by author)

The *moksha* that is sought here is the liberation from sorrow (*duhkha*) in others. It is freedom from poverty, illiteracy, homelessness and disease in others, not freedom from rebirth for own self, because that would be selfishness. The goal is expanding one's self into such an inclusive entity that it covers a concern for all the beings in the world. And that is genuinely uniting oneself with God, the ultimate reality, which is real *moksha*.

To avoid a possible misunderstanding that the goal of *sadhana* is escaping from the material world and seeking spiritual solace thereby, Jayant Kalawar prefers to define *sadhana* as striving to transcend the gross and seeking the subtle, and *sadhaka* as the subtle striver. He says that we are all material experiencers (*samsarika*) and at the same time subtle strivers (Kalawar 2012: 84–85). The value of the Gita's teaching lies precisely in reconciling the material with the spiritual and helping us to move from the gross to the subtle. G. S. Amur through his book, *Lokayatre* (in Kannada 2013), shows that not only the Gita but the Mahabharata as a whole does not teach us to reject the material and choose *instead* the other-worldly spiritual, but spiritualising our life and material experiencing itself. But what is gross and what is subtle? Kalawar explains that lemonade may be a gross matter, but its quality which we savour and enjoy – its aroma, sweetness and cooling effect – is subtle. What we seek is not matter per se, but this subtle quality. The material experience itself is *sukshma*, that is, subtle (Kalawar 2012: 17). The Gita of course goes much further, and by explaining the anatomy of the self, it shows how we move from the less subtle to the more subtle. It says in verses III.42 and 43: 'The senses are superior (to the body), the mind is superior to the senses, the intellect is superior to the mind, and that which is superior to the intellect is He (the Atman). Thus knowing Him who is superior to the intellect, and restraining the self by the Self, destroy, O mighty-armed, that enemy, the un-seizeable foe – desire' (Tr. by Swarupananda 1982: 94–95). *S̲adhan̲a* thus consists of striving to find the most subtle and important in us, the Atman, and realise our full potentiality. Stated in a different way, the goal is to find Krishna in us all as the witness, inner voice, energiser and protector.

An important part of *s̲adhan̲a* is preparing the mind for it, whatever path the seeker chooses. Being a virtuous person for its own sake, respecting moral values like truthfulness, compassion, generosity, in day-to-day conduct, totally avoiding hypocrisy, makes the mind pure and trains it for *s̲adhan̲a*. Closely related to this is the need for self-control – the conquest of the *s̲h̲ad̲vairis* (six enemies – lust, anger, avarice, conceit, infatuation and jealousy), and what is more, the conquest also over dualities like pain and pleasure, and whimsical likes and dislikes. Conquest does not necessarily mean full suppression or elimination of them; it only means being in full control of oneself and not losing one's balance by these disturbances. A mind prepared thus qualifies not only for spiritual striving, but also for social service and assuming leadership (V.25). As Parthasarathy says, a self-controlled person 'operates with his discriminating intellect rather than whims and fancies of his mind' (2011: 372).

Though apparently a number of alternative ways of *s̲adhan̲a* are indicated in the Gita – karma-yoga, jn̲ana-yoga, dhy̲ana-yoga and bhakti-yoga – there are interpreters as we have noted earlier who feel that all the yogas resolve themselves into an integrated one yoga only. However, there is no unanimity about what that one yoga is, or which of the different yogas mentioned in the Gita is the most important or decisive. The Gita starts with Arjuna's dilemma in this regard. He wants *nihshreyas*, the ultimate good, for himself and thinks that the best way of achieving it is renunciation of work or *sanny̲asa*. No, declares Krishna! The world is bound by action and driven by action, and there can be no escape from action. The choice lies not between action and inaction, but between more meaningful or ennobling action and selfish actions, or between action that secures us freedom and actions that bind us to karmic cycles. Work done with detachment, without a desire to appropriate the fruit of it for oneself, and further, done without a sense of agency or doer-ship, is the key to freedom, according to the Gita. This in brief is karma-yoga. The essence of the whole Gita can be said to have been captured by one *shloka*, which explains its unparalleled popularity. It prescribes karma-yoga and also defines it. It is:

> *Karma<u>n</u>yev<u>a</u>dhik<u>a</u>raste m<u>a</u> phaleshu kad<u>a</u>chana/*
> *M<u>a</u> karma-phala-heturbh<u>u</u> m<u>a</u> te sangostvakarma<u>n</u>i //*
> (II.47)

> ('You have a right only to work [to perform your duty], but not to its fruits. Don't think of yourself as the cause (*hetu*) of the outcome of work, but do not avoid work.'
> – Tr. by the author)

When one does not consider oneself as the cause of the outcome, because it is only God who produces it, there is no basis left to claim the fruit of work. When there is no link between one's work and getting its fruit for oneself, the karmic cycle is automatically broken. This is the rationale of karma-yoga. Malinar explains why this activity under karma-yoga is 'exempt from karmic retribution and conducive to a quest for liberation'. It amounts to 'equating one's actions with those of the cosmic cause of all activity (called *Brahman* or *prakriti*). Anyone who manages to substitute his own agency with "cosmic" agency for the sake of "welfare of all beings" can be liberated' (Malinar 2009: 5–6). Even a philanthropic or altruistic work done for the good of others does not necessarily amount to karma-yoga if it is done with the purpose gaining fame or even for, say, booking a luxury suite in the heaven for oneself. The work should not only be selfless and done without arrogating to oneself its agency or doer-ship, but also be sincere, efficient, duly regardful of consequences, and not indifferent or sloppy or harmful to anyone. When one works leaving the outcome to God's will, and with single-minded devotion, it frees one from anxiety and tension and can thus promote efficiency too. These riders or qualifications to karma-yoga are not all mentioned together in one place, but need to be noted. Feeling non-doer-ship in spite of being actively engaged and renouncing doer-ship of all actions to God is stressed in II.19, III.30 and again in V.8. Renunciation of the fruit of action is commended in II.47, detachment (*sangam tyaktva*) and dedication (*yogasthah*) in II.48, and dexterity or efficiency in work (*karmasu kaushalam*) in II.50. The fact that the work is not to be done mindlessly or disregarding harmful consequences is emphasised by calling work done with such indifference as *t<u>a</u>masika* (XVIII.25). Also *tamasika* is absent-minded (*ayukta*) lazy work (*alasah*) taking unduly long time (*dirghasutri*), reluctant (*vishadi*), pedestrian (*prakritah*) or malicious (*naishkritika*) work (XVIII.28). On the other hand, work done with fortitude and enthusiasm is praised as *sattvika* (XVIII.26). The only incentive permitted in karma-yoga is that it purifies one's mind, avoids tension and brings peace and fulfilment. It is thus purely a labour of love, to be enjoyed for its own sake. It may not be everybody's cup of tea, and that is why everyone is not a karma-yogi though everyone may be working on something or the other.

But is the recommendation practical at all? The bulk of modern economic activity is motivated by desire for personal gain or profit. Adam Smith, called the father of economics, thought that self-interest is not bad for the world. According to him, when each person acts according to self-interest, there is a mutual balance and natural order in a market system, and the common good is promoted. In an oft-quoted passage which has made him famous even among non-economists, he said: 'It is not from the benevolence of the butcher, the brewer, or the baker, that we expect our dinner, but from their regard to their own interest. We address ourselves, not to their humanity but to their self-love, and never talk to them of our own necessities but of their advantages' (Smith 1776; as quoted by Sen 1990: 23). Yet, Smith himself in another book, *The Theory of Moral Sentiments* (1790), chastised philosophers who saw virtue entirely in terms of prudence or self-interest, and he doubted whether prudence was enough for a good society (Sen 1990: 23–24). It has been realised since long that a 'natural order' produced exclusively by narrow self-interest can be very unfair with a lot of exploitation of the weak by the strong and can also be environmentally unsustainable. The Gita calls for reining in selfishness and narrow desires, if not preventing them altogether, so that it is within socially or morally acceptable bounds. Moreover, human nature is not entirely selfish. For example, without the selfless love of the mother for her child, humanity would not have even survived. As the society has developed over the millennia, human beings have learnt to broaden their self-interest to go beyond their own narrow self and cover larger and larger circles around them, family to society and ultimately all the world. Economic rationality seen narrowly in terms of selfishness alone would be a case of what Amartya Sen called as 'rational fools', and not sensible and wise human behaviour (Sen 1982). There is a plurality of motivations governing human behaviour, not self-interest alone (Sen 1990: 19). With the progress of human civilisation, the role of motivations other than narrow self-interest can be said to have been expanding more and more significantly, though it may certainly not have obliterated it. The Gita encourages this trend only in the interest of both the spiritual advance of the individuals themselves and the overall advance of the society. The Gita accepts all the *purusharthas* including *artha* and *kama*, but with due qualifications. In fact an implication of karma-yoga is that thereby worldly activity including work for livelihood is reconciled with *sadhana*.[7] The Gita does not prohibit even the accumulation of wealth; it prohibits only doing it through dishonest or unjust means (*anyayena artha-sanchaya*) (XVI.12). To do good to others selflessly, which the Gita recommends, one cannot himself be a destitute after all!

Nevertheless, the Gita recommends work as worship. This idea comes out clearly when it discusses varieties of *yajna* in Chapter 4 in eleven verses from 23 to 33. There are references to *yajna* elsewhere too. The Gita transforms the Vedic concept of yajna as a ritual offering in sacred fire with elaborate mantras into a metaphor for offering in any form to either God or humanity. Not only the fruit of work but also the pride of doer-ship is sacrificed or offered. In the yajna described in the Gita, everything and everyone is taken as Brahman – the act of offering, the offering itself, the person offering and the object of offering; it is also offered into the fire of Brahman. The Gita assures that one who performs the yajna in any form in such a spirit reaches Brahman surely (IV.24). The varieties of yajna mentioned in the Gita are work, wealth (by way of donation), austerity, knowledge, prayer, devotional worship, *japa*, meditation and even *pranayama*. Yajna is usually translated as sacrifice; it is sacrificing oneself, fruits of one's actions, one's possessions for the sake of world welfare, seeing God in everything and acknowledging everything including oneself as His. All yogas are fused into yajna. All actions performed by a karma-yogi are yajnas, says Swami Bhoomananda (2014, Vol. II: 12). As Parthasarathy explains, 'Yajna denotes conversion of any activity into worship. Each and every activity becomes a prayer' (2011: 306).

An important qualification of karma-yoga is that both the doer-ship of work and its fruit are surrendered to God, but this cannot be done without bhakti or devotion to Him. It means that according to the Gita at least, there cannot be a 'secular karma-yogi'. This qualification is spelt out in several verses. Verse III.30 calls for renunciation of all works in favour of the Lord with the mind centred on one's spiritual self. Verse V.10 says that karma does not bind one who has dedicated his works to the Brahman with no attachment to them. Verse IX.27 asks a devotee to make an offering to the Lord of whatever one does, eats, sacrifices or gives. The requirement of bhakti dominates even over karma in some of the verses. There are two almost repetitious verses, which are considered as crucially significant for *sadhana* by almost all the interpreters:

> *Manmana bhava madbhakto madyaji mam namaskuru /*
> *Mamevaishyasi yuktaivam atmanam matparayanah //*
> (IX.34)
>
> ('Fill thy mind with Me, be My devotee, sacrifice unto Me, bow down to Me; thus having made my heart steadfast in Me, taking Me as the Supreme Goal, thou shalt come to Me.'
> – Tr. by Swarupananda 1982: 217–18)
>
> *Manmana bhava madbhakto madyaji mam namaskuru /*
> *Mamevaishyasi satyam te pratijane priyosi me //*
> (XVIII.65)
>
> ('Occupy thy mind with Me, be devoted to Me, sacrifice to Me, bow down to Me. Thou shalt reach Myself; truly do I promise unto thee, (for) thou art dear to Me.'
> – Tr. by Swarupananda 1982: 397).
> The repetition involved is for emphasis.

Interpreters who have emphasised bhakti above everything have been particularly fond of quoting verse IX.26, which makes God accessible to the poorest of the poor if only he or she has devotion for Him. It says: 'Whatever one offers with devotion and a pure heart, whether it is a leaf, flower, fruit or a bit of water, I accept that as a loving gift' (Tr. by the author). Roopa Pai writes about this verse: 'In one stroke, through this single, deceptively simple verse, the Gita makes it clear God does not belong to the privileged. He does not need gold and fine silks and sumptuous food. All He needs is love' (Pai 2015: 135).

There is a separate chapter also on bhakti-yoga (the twelfth), which commends devotion to God in a personal form, as it is easier. What is more, actions can be dedicated to a personal God one loves, who is amenable to meditation too (XII.6). It is noteworthy here that karma-yoga and bhakti-yoga are not offered as substitutes; they go together closely. There is no question of which of them is better or more important, as both are equally necessary and complement each other. Yet, the Lord leaves the relative emphasis between the two entirely to the personal inclination of the devotee. If the person finds it difficult to fix the mind on the Supreme firmly, he or she can get themselves in actions dedicating them with devotion to God, without desiring personal benefit from these actions (XII.9–11). It is clarified that a true devotee has also to be compassionate and friendly to all beings, free from egoism, forgiving and always have a happy or pleasant disposition (*santushtah satatam*) (XII.13–14). By implication, it applies to karma-yogi as well, for the Gita makes no difference between the two. A devotee, moreover, is equitable both to friend and to foe, and even minded between honour and dishonour, between praise and censure; nothing deters him or her from steadfast devotion to the Lord (XII.18–19).

In spite of commending both karma-yoga and bhakti-yoga together almost throughout the dialogue of the Gita, there is a verse at the end of the advice which appears almost as a concluding summary of Krishna's teaching, but which is intriguing and needs some discussion. The verse is

> *Sarva-dharman parityajya mamekam sharanam vraja /*
> *Aham tvam sarva-papebhyo mokshayishyami ma shuchah //*
> (XVIII.66)

> ('Relinquishing all Dharmas take refuge in Me alone; I will liberate thee from all sins; grieve not.'
> – Tr. Swarupananda 1982: 398)

What is meant by 'dharmas' here? Shankara in his commentary on the verse says that dharmas mean karmas, that is, all works, and renouncing dharma includes renouncing *adharma* (unrighteousness) also. He explains further that renouncing karma means giving up not only fruits of action but also any sense of doer-ship or agency in oneself. The intention of the Gita according to Shankara is to show that works by themselves cannot be the means for *moksha* ultimately; only the knowledge of the self leads one to it (Warrier 1983: 616–18). Dayananda Saraswati, interpreting Shankara, clarifies that it does not mean karma-yoga is irrelevant in *sadhana*, since it is through karma-yoga that the mind is purified and prepared to awaken to self-knowledge and thus to *moksha* (Dayananda 2011, Vol. 9: 329). In asking Arjuna to give up his dharma/karma, the Lord expects him to give up only his doer-ship by surrendering everything and himself too to the Lord. That is how Ramanuja also interprets. Complete surrender asked for is giving up any sense of agency or doer-ship, and all sense of possessiveness.

It is only such a surrender that purifies and cleanses one of all sins and guilt. Ramanuja explains that several expiatory rites were in vogue at the time of the Gita, which meant spending a lot of time and money on them with no assured effect. According to the Gita, none of these are necessary; in fact, such rites have to be given up. It is only surrender with complete devotion to God which ensures expiation of all sins, and purifies one, according to this verse in the Gita (Adidevananda 2014: 598–99). Madhva also agrees with such an interpretation and says that the call to abandon all duties (dharmas) is not to give them up physically, but only to give up the fruits thereof. Otherwise, Madhva asks, how can one explain the Lord's injunction to Arjuna to fight the war to the finish? (Sharma 1989: 314). The Lord's intention is to emphasise bhakti, and not necessarily to undermine karma-yoga.

The ultimate goal of a passionate devotee is to be united with God. The Gita assures that one who leaves his or her body and departs remembering only Him attains Him without doubt (VIII.5). But it may not always happen that one meditates on God or remembers Him at the time of death. To ensure that this happens, the Gita suggests cultivating the habit of remembering Him all the time (VIII.7). It means that even if engaged in some work or the other, there has always to be awareness or consciousness of God's presence and benevolence at the back of one's mind. Even normal day-to-day activities like eating and giving are done in the spirit of an offering to God (IX.27). Then there is no question of being lost to God or failing to remember Him at the crucial times including death.

We have thus far discussed only karma-yoga and bhakti-yoga, and found that they go together in the Gita. Where does jnana-yoga come then? Jnana-yoga is referred also as *buddhi-yoga* in the Gita. It appears that *sadhana* can be pursued in different ways, depending on one's concept of the ultimate goal, and different goals may suggest different ways. If one's goal is personal fulfilment through unselfish service to humanity, seeing God in every being and serving Him through serving humanity, the chosen path obviously would be karma-yoga. When the goal is seen as personal fulfilment through union with a personal God, one follows bhakti-yoga, the path of love and worship. If, on the other hand, self-realisation is perceived as the ultimate goal of *sadhana*, the path followed is one of *jnana-yoga* combined with *raja-yoga*, as the two go together. The emphasis of karma-yoga is on using the will power, or conation, the capacity to detach oneself from desiring the fruits of one's actions, while the emphasis of *bhakti-yoga* is on using and developing one's inclination to love and feel, to sympathise and where necessary commiserate with others and consoling them assuring them of the love of God and His protection. The emphasis of jnana-yoga is on using buddhi, the capacity to discriminate between the real and unreal, momentary and everlasting. It needs a certain ability for abstraction, to go beyond multiplicity and detail to unity and synthesis. It is not the analytical ability which is demanded, but an ability for holistic conceptualisation. Though all the three paths seem to be individual affairs where the striving is by individuals, and not group affairs of collective effort, the striving even by individuals is not in complete isolation from others. This is because all the three paths require seeing God not only in one's self but also in the selves of every being. This is most obvious in karma-yoga, where selfless service for the welfare of all is commended (*sarva-bhuta-hita*). Bhakti towards a personal God cannot be complete unless this God is seen in all. And jnana cannot similarly be complete unless one sees the Self in all and all in the Self. There is no problem if the Self is substituted by one's concept of God, personal or impersonal.

There is no conflict at all between these three paths, and the Gita seems to prefer their integration or combination. In combination, they would have a synergetic effect, since they mutually help each other. A sadhaka does not at all have to make a neat distinction between karma, bhakti and jnana, following only one exclusively. The Gita itself makes no clear separation of the three paths, as is clear from three verses which are among the concluding ones in the last chapter (XVIII.55–57). They say: 'By loving [*bhaktya*] Me, he shares in my glory and enters into my boundless being [Verse 55]. All his acts are performed in my service, and through my grace he wins eternal life [Verse 56]. Make every act an offering to Me; regard Me as your only protector. [Resorting to Buddhi-yoga], make every thought an offering to Me; meditate on Me always [Verse 57] (Tr. Easwaran 1997, Vol. 3: 446 for verses 55 and 56, and 448 for verse 57). Karma-yoga, jnana [buddhi]-yoga and bhakti are all explicitly united here. If *sadhana* is done in an integrated way, the whole personality and mind of the seeker is raised to a great moral and spiritual height, finding fulfilment, confidence and lasting happiness even when faced with numerous vicissitudes of the mundane world. This indeed is the clear promise of the Gita. This indeed is *moksha*, that is, freedom from bondage to desires, from anxieties and tensions, from petty narrowness, problems and foibles, in spite of being engaged in the world. This freedom has no meaning if it comes only after death. It is something which one can expect even while living in the world. This is clear from verses 50 to

57 in the last chapter of the Gita. *Moksha* while living is not escapism, but is depicted as a life of perfection here. Freedom from karmic cycle of rebirth is a matter of belief, and not every seeker may bother about it, if the verse from the *Srimad-Bhagavatam* quoted earlier is an indication. What matters is fulfilment while living the present life itself and making it meaningful.

Most interpreters, particularly Swami Dayananda Saraswati, regard *jnana* or realisation of the ultimate truth as the final stage of *sadhana*, karma-yoga and bhakti-yoga being the means of preparing and purifying the mind for it (Dayananda 2011, Vol. 9: 329). Shankara himself composed many hymns of fervent bhakti addressed to personal deities. A very interesting example of such a hymn, addressed to Shiva, which is at the same time an earnest prayer to purify the mind, is as follows:

> *Ma gatchcha tvam itasthatah Girish bho mayyeva vasam kuru*
> *Swaminnadikirata mamaka-manah-kantara-simantare* /
>
> *Vartante bahusha mriga-mada-jusho matsarya-mohadayah*
> *Tan hatva mrigaya vinoda-ruchita labham cha samprapyasi* //
> (From *Shivananda-lahari* by Shri Shankaracharya,
> as quoted in Herur 2001: 356)
>
> ('My Lord, the Lord of Mountains, the Primeval hunter! Do not go here and there, but reside in Me! Within the wilderness of my mind, there are many animals – arrogance, jealousy, infatuation, and the like! Have the pleasure of a hunt by hunting them down!'
> – Tr. by author)

There is no conflict between bhakti and jnana. But bhakti is expected to lead to jnana, as otherwise it remains at the level of raw sentimentalism or emotion. Similarly, bhakti has to be combined with karma, because bhakti without karma (when one is physically capable of working) would be pure idleness and a burden on the society. Karma-yoga is designed to achieve jnana, because karma-yoga has no meaning if the ego is not dropped and all fruits of work and even doer-ship are not surrendered to God in the service of humanity. Thus it would appear that jnana-yoga is not a separate *sadhana*, but simply a culmination of *sadhana* through karma-yoga and bhakti.

The purpose of jnana-yoga is realisation of the Ultimate Truth. In Advaita philosophy, the ultimate truth is seen as the identity of one's individual spiritual self, the Atman, with the Parabrahman or

Paramatman. In Vishishta-advaita, it is seen as the Atman being a part of the body of Paramatman, but dependent on Him. In Dvaita, it is seen as total dependence of the Atman on the Paramatman, the relationship being one of a servant to the master. The realisation is aided by meditation on the Self/Parabrahman in Advaita, and on the personal deity in the two schools. The Gita does not make a distinction between the three schools, and the object of meditation is left to the choice of the seeker. It can be on a personal deity in a form of one's choice, or it can be on the Self in an impersonal and pure form of consciousness or simply awareness of what goes on in the mind, tracking the mind consciously and bringing it back to focus on the chosen object. In Advaita, the paradox is one of the subjects, the Self, itself being the object of meditation. The method of meditation recommended by the Gita is briefly 'Fix the mind on the Self and think of nothing else'. The full verse is as follows:

> *Shanaih shanairuparamet buddhya dhriti-grihitaya /*
> *Atmasamstham manah kritva na kinchid api chintayet //*
> (VI.25)

> ('With the intellect endowed with perseverance, may one slowly resolve [quieten] the mind (in *atma*). Making the mind abide in the self, may one not think of anything else.'
> – Tr. by Dayananda 2011, Vol. 5: 147;
> square brackets added)

Dayananda says that it is not difficult as one might fear. 'The pursuit of [spiritual] knowledge is not like climbing Mount Everest; it is more like dropping that you are holding in your hand. Because it is more dropping than climbing, it is not as difficult as you might think. It is simply a question of dissociating yourself from your own identity of being only so much' (Dayananda 2011: 148). What it means that one has to simply drop the things that the mind is burdened with including not only anxieties and fears but also the notion of one's limited self. Dayananda explains that according to Krishna, yoga can be pursued without despair (*anirvinna chetasa*) (Dayananda 2011: 147).

The science of yoga particularly as codified by Patanjali developed after the Gita. But one can see the seeds of it in the Gita. The Gita even explains breath control (*pranayama*) as a practice, which can precede meditation, as it helps in focusing the mind (IV.29). Swami Vivekananda has presented a lucid and detailed exposition of Patanjali's *Yogasutras* (CWSV 2000, Vol. 1: 110–313), along with the eight steps of raja-yoga. All of them are mentioned in the Gita, though not necessarily in one place one after another, and though not in exactly the same words – *yama* (practising virtues like non-violence, non-possessiveness), *niyama* (cleanliness – both internal and external, contentment, austerity, etc.), *asana* (right but comfortable posture),[8] *pranayama* (breath control), *pratyahara* (withdrawing sense organs from their objects and shutting down external 'noises'), *dharana* (fixing the mind on an object – may be on a part of one's body such as the tip of one's nose or the middle of the brows, or on a mantra, or a favourite form of God), *dhyana* (meditation proper) and, finally, *samadhi* (a state of being fully absorbed).

Meditation consists first of observing the mind itself, being aware of all that goes in the mind, as a *sakshi* or witness. The *sadhaka* becomes her or his own psychoanalyst here. It is a deep state of introspection. This is where the Gita's advice to fix the mind on the self and think of nothing else becomes relevant. Once this state is reached, the mind becomes objectless, unburdened, with nothing (*shunya*) left in the mind except super-consciousness. This is the stage when the Self is realised, leaving the sadhaka in peace with ineffable joy. When this state is maintained effortlessly and a little longer, it can be said to be *samadhi*, where a unity with the Ultimate is experienced. This is not a state of deep sleep. Deep sleep is when one is 'beneath consciousness'. In deep meditation, on the other hand, one is all the while not only awake but also fully aware and conscious. Initially, such a state may be experienced for only a fraction of a minute, but the duration can significantly improve with practice, provided that the person has *shraddha* (perseverance and commitment) and has also been following the mental and moral discipline of keeping the mind and conduct pure.

For those who find it difficult to focus on the self or one's own consciousness as a method of meditation, the Gita recommends *japa* – repeated recitation of God's name or a *mantra* in one's mind with awareness, not allowing the mind to stray. Even if it strays, one has to, with practice, try to bring it back on track (VI.35). Krishna regards *japa* so highly that he identifies himself with it, saying that among the yajnas, He is yajna in the form of japa (X.25). There are a few longish mantras like the Gayatri and Mrityunjaya, which have their own rich benefits. However, for holding the mind fixed for meditation, shorter mantras, preferably those which can be uttered mentally along with breathing, are advisable. For example, while inhaling, utter *Om* (stretching it longer to synchronise with deep inhaling), and *Namah*

Shivaya while releasing the breath or exhaling. Similarly, *Shree Hari* can be recited repeatedly. The Gita itself does not prescribe any particular mantra, leaving it to the *sadhaka*, though it does mention *Om tat sat* as the triple designation or expression (*nirdesha*) of Brahman (XVII.23), to be uttered with *shraddha* while performing all rituals or worship (XVII.24–28). *Om* is Brahman, and together the three words mean Brahman, that (is) the truth. The Gita explains that *sat* means both truth and goodness or benignity (XVII.26). In spite of the great popularity of *japa* in *sadhana*, it is not considered as meditation proper, the latter being focusing on the abstract, formless Self, that is, *sat chit ananda* (Tejomayananda 1997: 5). However, japa is an invaluable aid in preparing the mind for meditation proper.

Whatever be the object and form of meditation, its great benefits – hinted at in the Gita itself – are widely acknowledged all over the world, and its popularity is soaring. The benefits of meditation are not just momentary, but also lasting and go well beyond the duration of time when it is practised. The enduring benefits claimed are increased ability to concentrate, reduction in stress and anxiety, prevention of depression, control over blood pressure, sound sleep, a healthy check on anger and other emotions, increased clarity of mind with consequent improvement in decision making and a better physical as well as mental health, on the whole resulting in a state of always feeling happy, cheerful, compassionate and friendly to all. I know of cases where through the practice of meditation, people have been able to give up addictions like smoking and drinking. Incidentally, these benefits are at the mundane level, not necessarily spiritual benefits, though in this case they go together.

Is there a conflict between self-realisation and continuing to work in the world for the welfare of all? Does not a self-realised yogi become indifferent to the world, immersed in his newfound bliss? Not so, if we understand the Gita correctly. Self-realisation does not require sitting in meditation all day and night. On the contrary, as Sri Aurobindo warns, such excesses may be self-defeating and un-harmonious (Aurobindo 2010: 145). A self-realised person sees God in everyone and that his or her own self-realisation is further enriched and fulfilled when he or she serves others selflessly. Such a person has no desire for oneself, and all his or her actions become spiritual.

Arjuna puts a question which is relevant to all *sadhakas*. What if someone, even if endowed with faith, falls short of expectations of *sadhana*, by wandering off the right path? Does he or she not lose both the worlds – the pleasures of this world and also the promise in the other world, and get destroyed? (VI.37–38). Krishna dispels this anxiety and fear by assuring that there is no destruction whatsoever for such persons and that anyone who has done some good will never perish (*na hi kalyanakrit kaschit durgatim tata gatchchati* – VI.40). On the contrary, there is ample hope for them of redemption and spiritual success eventually (VI.41–45). One need not be afraid of committing honest mistakes, of faltering on the path to God, for there is always an assurance of help and support.

A significant feature of the different paths of *sadhana* is its accessibility to all irrespective of social or economic differences and also irrespective of 'karmic luggage' as Malinar puts it (2009: 7). There is no emphasis on rituals, and any offering which a seeker can afford is accepted and appreciated (IX.26). Even a manual worker working on a wage can be a spiritual seeker. He or she does not have to sit in meditation for hours and forgo remunerative work. Even if busy all the day with work for livelihood, a few minutes for remembering God with devotion assures grace from Him.[9] *Sadhana* is not meant only for the luxury class. Moreover, even a sinner has hope as per the Gita.

Notes

1 The discussion here about *trigunas* and Table 6.1 is mainly based on Nadkarni (2013: 58–61).
2 Jayant Kalawar thinks that *shraddha* is much more than 'faith' as usually translated; according to him, it means 'a disposition to keep acting regardless of obstacles' or 'passionate focused commitment', with which I agree (Kalawar 2012: 97, 150).
3 The discussion here about the *sattvika* economy is mainly based on Nadkarni (2013: 77, n-9).
4 See the last row under Shankara in the table given as Appendix to Chapter 2 for examples of such verses.
5 This para and the preceding one are a summary of Chopra (2001: 39–174), but at the same time relating the account with the Gita's language and philosophy.
6 This section uses to some extent Chapter 4 on 'Sadhana in Hinduism' in Nadkarni (2013: 78–101), but it is much more than a mere summary of that chapter having several new things to say.
7 About taming desire and selfishness as commended by the Gita, see also the discussion on karma-yoga under the first section of this chapter.
8 The *Yoga-shastra* mentions different postures for exercise, but in the context of meditation, *asana* means sitting in an erect posture with the back, neck and the head in one straight line, comfortably (so that one is not distracted by discomfort), but not so comfortably as to go to sleep (as when slouching). The Gita commends sitting cross-legged in a clean and lonely

place free from distractions, on a dry and firm floor on a grass mat covered by soft cloth. For elderly people, sitting cross-legged on the floor is not mandatory; they can as well sit on a straight-backed chair with legs drawn in. The trick is in sitting relaxed but being alert and mindful at the same time.

9 There is a *pauranik* story about Lord Vishnu telling the celestial saint Narada why He values a farmer's devotion as of higher spiritual quality than that of Narada himself because the concerned farmer devotes a few minutes of his busy day for remembering Him, while Narada has no such constraints (Nadkarni 2013: 91–92).

7

CRITICISMS OF THE GITA AND RESPONSES

Contradictions

Like the Bible, the Gita also has attracted a lot of critical scrutiny both in the West and in India. Hinduism has so far at least been quite tolerant of criticism, as it should be, but sometimes so 'tolerant' that even major points of criticism have not been responded to by many. Interpreters of the Gita such as Gandhi and Aurobindo did respond to some of them, but by and large, the criticisms have been ignored. Such an attitude, however, may not be quite helpful for a proper understanding of the texts criticised. However, it is wiser to attend to criticism and respond through logic and politeness than to launch abusive attacks or to threaten the critics physically. Surely, that kind of response is not in the spirit of Hinduism and even the Gita itself. The whole dialogue between Arjuna and Krishna is in the spirit of friendly and calm logical discussion. This chapter attempts a fairly comprehensive response to major criticisms made about the Gita, taking also into account responses made by others too. Though the Gita attracted a good deal of criticism mainly in the West before India's independence, almost all the criticism made after independence has come from Indians, that too Hindus themselves. This is a healthy sign, indicating the scope for scepticism and openness in Hindu society. Faith should not be forcibly imposed; it should be heartfelt. In any case, criticisms merit response.

German philosopher, Karl Jaspers, is said to have remarked to an Indian friend that he thought the Gita to be full of contradictions. After a pause, he also added: 'That is why it is a great book' (Lash 2000: 1). Arjuna himself was baffled, and charged his mentor, Krishna, as confusing him and asked him to be clear and definite, as recorded in the Gita itself (III.2). Take, for example the eighteenth verse in the fourth chapter of the Gita, which says: 'One who sees inaction in action, and action in inaction, even while being engaged (*yukta*) in all action, is a wise human being.' Apparently, it is a very confusing and self-contradictory verse. Yet going by what is said earlier in the Gita, the verse only means that the Gita expects a yogi to be engaged all the while in action but with selflessness, humility without any sense of doer-ship, and without worrying about the final outcome. To understand the Gita, one needs to understand its intent and perspective. That is also why it is a challenging text for interpreters. The task of deriving a coherent philosophy from it has therefore been exciting and, I should add, fruitful too. It has been fruitful because the Gita has been a marvellous attempt at reconciling the seeming opposites and arriving at a synthesis. That is why M. R. Yardi calls his book on the Gita 'As a Synthesis' (1991). There is a lot of conflict and confusion in life, and yet we need to face it and seek enough balance and peace of mind to pursue our chosen goals. Along with conflicts and confusion, there comes complexity too. Many conflicts and contradictions appear so because of complexity. Life is quite complex, the universe no less so. At a superficial level, things may look very simple. But when you begin to probe into them, understand them in depth, complexities emerge at once. Sri Sri Ravi Shankar says, 'life is simple and complex at the same time' (Shankar 2013: 47). He takes the instance of eating a banana. It is so simple. But its digestion is quite a complex process, and a lot of 'work' is involved. The origin of the Gita itself owes to conflict and confusion in the mind of Arjuna. In a way, using Sri Sri Ravishankar's words, the Gita is also simple and complex at the same time. We can, while trying to comprehend its complexity, savour its simplicity too. As Hirst observes, 'contradictory statements need not indicate inconsistency or textual additions, but can be seen as part of a process of understanding which drives Arjuna and the reader beyond initial preconceptions' (Hirst 2000: 50).

Historicity

The criticism about the historicity of the Gita, and by implication its authenticity, was raised first by Western scholars. However, as noted in Chapter 3 of this book earlier, Western scholarship also helped the Gita to go global. It also stimulated a lot of critical scholarly writing on the Gita and its translation both in the West and in India, and both in English and in Indian regional languages. Western scholarship included Christian theologians and missionaries who also played an important role in disseminating the Gita in the West.[1] Though missionaries studied it mainly to show how it falls much short of the Holy Bible, there were also large-hearted Christian scholars who thought highly of it and considered it as a sacred text of Hinduism on par with the significance that the Bible has for Christianity. The study of the Gita also occasioned a search for common ground between Hinduism and Christianity. For example, Robinson mentions R. D. Griffith, who in 1849 likened the incarnation of Krishna to that of Christ, and the concepts of Trimurty and the syllable AUM (Om) in Hinduism to Trinity in Christianity. Griffith also found several points of similarity between the Bible and the Gita, though he insisted on the primacy of the former and inadequacy of the latter, and claimed that Hinduism could not meet the challenge of Christianity. Griffith felt that proselytisation of Hindus would be expedited more by appealing to features common to the two religions than by arrogant assertion of Christian truth which could cause resentment (Robinson 2006: 73–74). But contrary to expectations of Griffith, the common features only boosted the confidence in Hinduism among its followers and justified their faith in the Gita. Christian missionaries could not in any case obliterate Hinduism though they won many converts. Hinduism has still remained the religion of the bulk of the people of India and has emerged as a global religion in its own right, criticisms notwithstanding.

There have been quite a few points of Christian critique that were taken up even more forcefully by Hindu scholars themselves, which will be taken up subsequently. A major point of Christian critique of the Gita, however, is its lack of historicity, expressed, for example by J. N. Farquhar (1861–1929) notwithstanding his full praise for it on other counts like its theism and emphasis on personal morality. According to him, Jesus Christ is a historical personality, while Krishna is not; incarnation stories of Krishna are myths, and 'the Gita did not come from Krishna' (quoted in Robinson 2006: 78). So, the Bible has a historical authenticity, which the Gita does not have. Farquhar felt that human nature was such that 'man needs an incarnate saviour', and where there was no such saviour, this saviour would be imagined and a mythological substitute capable of inspiring faith and devotion would be created (Robinson 2006: 79). He saw in Christianity and in the historic real person of Jesus Christ the fulfilment of Hinduism's hopes and dreams (Robinson 2006: 80). As a religion, Hinduism lacks a historical founder which other religions have; its major sacred text also does not have a historicity, which the texts of other religions have. Thus, this critique does not stop with the Gita, but covers Hinduism itself as a whole.

A major problem about establishing historicity of Hinduism and its texts is their very hoary unparalleled past. One has to appreciate that their history starts some two millennia BCE. Dating systems comparable with the present were not developed for a long time. But it does not mean that there is no evidence of historical reality of the Ramayana and the Mahabharata events. The criticism about lack of historicity was made before archaeological work was done on the Mahabharata sites and can therefore be considered as outdated now.

B. B. Lal, an eminent archaeologist, whose excavation work in Kalibangan in Rajasthan brought to light a prosperous city of Harappan civilisation, points out that 'all the sites associated with the Mahabharata story continue to bear the same name even to this day', and there is not more than one place having the same name. 'For example, there is only one Hastinapura, one Mathura, one Kurukshetra and so on' (Lal 2013: 60). Hastinapura was the capital of the Kuru (Kaurava) kingdom of the Mahabharata and is located at right bank of Ganga in Meerut district of Uttar Pradesh. Excavations at Hastinapura were carried out by Lal during 1950–52, which showed several layers of the old city indicating at least five historical periods with breaks in between. The first period is characterised by finds of pottery known as Ochre Colour Ware dating back to pre-1200 BCE, and the remains of the period were found on natural soil showing them to be the oldest. Period II is characterised by Painted Grey Ware, belonging to *ca.* 1100–800 BCE, period III by Northern Black Polished Ware dated between early sixth and early third century BCE, period IV by Shunga terracotta of early second century BCE to the end of third century CE and period V by Early Medieval Ware of late eleventh to the early fifteenth century CE (Lal 2013: 64). Several things like bowls, a 'dining set' (consisting of a *tha̠li* or dish, *katoris* or small bowls and *lota̠* or tumbler), iron-and-copper objects, a stone mould for casting jewellery, gamesmen pieces and dice used in the game of *chaupar* have been retrieved belonging to period II (Painted Grey Ware). Many of these things had artistic designs painted in black including swastikas, sigmas and spirals. Even a large house consisting of thirteen rooms and courtyard (with roof and much of the walls destroyed) of the same period was unearthed. Photographs of these things have been presented in the book by Lal (Lal 2013: 66–75). An enormous flood of the Ganga eroded or washed away many things associated with this period. There is evidence of a huge fire ending the third occupation as well (Lal 2013: 73, 77). After giving considerable thought and cross-checking with evidence obtained from other Ochre Colour Ware and

Painted Grey Ware sites, Lal concludes that only Painted Grey Ware Culture was associated with the Mahabharata period (1100–800 BCE) (Lal 2013: 83). Lal estimates the most probable date of the Mahabharata war as between 860 and 900 BCE (Lal 2013: 86). Lal rejects the earlier dates estimated on the basis of astronomical data, since at the dates so arrived (viz. 3102–3067 BCE), none of the Mahabharata sites such as Hastinapura, Mathura and Kurukshetra had existed (Lal 2013: 87). Thus, there is some concrete archaeological evidence of the Mahabharata period. There are, however, no contemporary inscriptions proving the historicity of either Mahabharata or of Krishna. But Lal observes that there are also no such inscriptions to prove the historicity of either the Buddha or Mahavira, and the historical reality of Krishna cannot be rejected on this ground (Lal 2013: 89). Lal points out at several references to Vasudeva (Krishna) and some of the other characters in the Mahabharata in ancient literary tradition right from the *Atharva Veda* to Kautilya's *Arthashastra* – texts which are independent of the Mahabharata (Lal 2013: 90). Lal concludes that 'the epic has a basis in history' (Lal 2013: 91) to prove, which was the purpose of his whole book (*Historicity of the Mahabharata – Evidence of Literature, Art & Archaeology*). The book also discusses the extensive impact of the epic on art and literature, coins and inscriptions in India and abroad (Laos, Cambodia, Java and Bali) in the ancient as well as the medieval periods, along with many interesting photographs of paintings and sculpture which include those relating to the Gita.

An eminent Marxist scholar, Damodar D. Kosambi, doubted – if not the historicity of the Mahabharata events – at least the scale of the Kurukshetra war as described in the epic. According to the epic, some four to five million men killed each other with only a few survivors left, in the eighteen-day war. Unrealistically large number of chariots, horses and elephants were reportedly deployed (see Note 3 of Chapter 1). Kosambi felt that there would certainly have been as many camp followers and attendants as fighters. He says: 'A host of this size could not be applied without a total population of 200 million which India did not attain till the British period' (Kosambi 1962: 12–13; as quoted in Desai 2014: 28). Desai adds that exaggeration was a norm in the epics, and with each successive rendition, it would have only increased further (Desai 2014: 28). Kosambi criticised the Gita on other grounds too (taken up later), but as for this criticism about the exaggeration of the scale of war, it does not affect either the historicity or the authenticity of the Gita as such.

But is historicity that important as to make religion history-centric? There have been responses to the Christian critique on the ground of historicity, not by proving the historicity of Hinduism or of the Ramayana and the Mahabharata, but by challenging the relevance or the necessity of historicity itself as the basis of religion (or its sacred books) or as the criterion of judging them. Balagangadhara questioned the propriety of applying the characteristics of Semitic religions (like having a single historical founder and having a common and historically dated sacred text) to all religions as the necessary criteria of defining religion. He remarked that 'what makes Christianity into religion is not what makes Hinduism into a religion' (1994: 22). Rajiv Malhotra also took up this issue assertively in two books – *Being Different* (2011) and *Indra's Net* (2014). He rejects insistence on history centrism, that is 'the mandated belief that God has revealed himself in history only in unique events and only to specific peoples or prophets, and in a way that is forever unavailable to others directly. This dogma demands that the exclusive path can be found only in the literal words of god as heard by specific projects and mentioned in some particular text that comprises literal history' (Malhotra 2014: 283). By contrast, *avatars* and gurus play the role of 'fresh entrepreneurial start-ups' (Malhotra 2011: 100)[2] from time to time according to Hinduism to establish dharma and fight *adharma*, responding to changing circumstances and providing continuity. Even while recognising the authority of sacred texts, as Radhakrishnan says, Hinduism always tempered this respect by 'the recognition of the truth that God has never finished the revelation of His wisdom and love' (1971: 16). Radhakrishnan adds: 'Hinduism is a movement, not a position; a process, not a result; a growing tradition, not a fixed revelation' (1971: 91). Realisation of the Ultimate Truth or the Divine is not claimed to be anybody's monopoly and is accessible to all. There is scope for debate, not for fundamentalism. There is 'built-in pluralism and context sensitivity' (Malhotra 2011: 100).

As for the Gita's status and authority as a sacred text, we have already explained the factors contributing to it in the first section of the first chapter of this book. This status does not have to depend upon its dating according to some calendar or the other. Moreover, the sayings or teachings of even the Buddha and Jesus Christ were not as written down by themselves, but were recorded by others. This has not reduced the authenticity of their teaching. The same thing happened in the case of Krishna and the Gita too.

However, the development of Hinduism independent of historical dating involved a price to pay. Though the ancient sages did have a concept of time, no concerted effort was made towards evolving a long-term calendar acceptable widely and with a commonly accepted benchmark until after the Buddha's time. The ancient Hindus had a cyclical – not a linear – concept of time. Not only seasons, but also the names given to years were based on a cycle of sixty *samvatsaras*. It is not that their time horizon did not extend beyond sixty years, for they had the concept of four *yugas* each extending over many millennia, with the yugas also moving cyclically. This is a paradox because the ancient Indians had a fascination for astronomy and enumeration, for which there is evidence in the Vedas. Though it is claimed that the Kali-yuga calendar is the oldest having a zero point in the year 3102 BCE, it is not clear when the calendar was actually adopted. As Amartya Sen says, there is always a difference in point of time between the bench-mark zero year and the adoption of a calendar, just as the Christian calendar was not adopted right when Christ was born. Sen points out that there is reference to dating according to the Kaliyuga era neither in any of the Vedas, nor even in the Ramayana and the Mahabharata. Sen cites the opinion of the Calendar Reform Committee that it was probably started during the time of A̱ryabhaṯa in 499 CE. There were other calendars also in ancient India, namely the Buddha Nirvana Era with a zero point of 544 BCE, Mahavira Nirvana Era with a zero point of 527 BCE, Vikrama Samvat with a zero point of 57 BCE, and Shaka calendar with a zero point of 78 CE.[3] These calendars came into vogue after the Gita was composed. Even otherwise, there was no established practice of dating according to any of these calendars in much of the literary work in ancient and even medieval India. While the Christian criticism about the lack of historicity may not reduce the authenticity of Hinduism and its texts, it does point to a genuine lack of adequate awareness to properly date the texts, whatever the calendar.

Is the Gita other-worldly? amoral? deterministic?

One of the major criticisms of Hinduism and other eastern religions by some Christian and even secular Western scholars is that they are world-denying or life-negating. They have not charged the Gita specifically as such, but being a major sacred text of Hinduism, we need to consider whether this is applicable to it. This criticism about the eastern religions has been made mainly by Max Weber, Albert Schweitzer and K. W. Kapp, and has been dealt with elsewhere in necessary detail (Nadkarni 2014: 157–67). Concerning the Gita, we have already noted earlier that it has nowhere mentioned or hinted that the world is unreal or a mere illusion. On the other hand, it has a rich ethical content (presented in the preceding chapter), which would have had no purpose or meaning if the world was unreal, since ethics has application only in this world and not beyond. The Gita's ethical teaching is intended to make our lives more meaningful and purposive. There is also no conflict between working for a living or even earning wealth and spiritual striving in the Gita, though unjust or dishonest means of earning a living or wealth are not allowed.

R. D. Griffith, however, felt that the Gita, as a general principle, prioritised metaphysical truth over moral truth. He was uncomfortable particularly with what he thought was a reliance on the Divine that detracted from moral responsibility (as quoted in Robinson 2006: 73). Even some of the Hindu interpreters of the Gita, like Aurobindo and later Dayananda Saraswati (of south India), have interpreted the Gita as having prioritised the Divine, not as a criticism of the Gita but as an exposition. Both felt that the ultimate purpose of life is to realise the Divine, and ethics prepare the mind for it by purifying and raising its potential to realise the goal (Dayananda 2011, Vol. 9: 329). Ethics are part of *s̲adhan̲a*, spiritual striving, and as a means, it is subordinated to the goal. This does not mean that the significance or role of ethics is negated or even undermined, or considered dispensable. There is no question of detracting from moral responsibility, because there cannot be a conflict between the Divine and moral responsibility. The confusion is caused probably by misinterpreting the verse, *Sarva dharman̲ parityajya* . . . (XVIII.66), taking *dharma* to be moral responsibility (which admittedly is the literal meaning of the word), but as explained in the last section of the preceding chapter, it is not the purport of the verse to abandon all morality! If the intention of the verse was to advise relinquishing all moral responsibilities as a general principle, Krishna would not have taken the trouble to emphasise ethics and ethical behaviour so much (see the second section of the preceding chapter). The Gita is not amoral. What the verse expects from a devotee is ultimately a total surrender to the Divine and its will, without any sense of 'I' and doer-ship, and forgetting all mundane problems. This is not an advice for inaction either, but only an advice to give up the ego and even the sense of oneself being the cause of any action. No devout Hindu would interpret the verse as a license to be amoral; he or she will take it in the right spirit of a call for total submission to the Divine forgetting one's separate individuality completely, submerging into the one and the only one ultimate reality in the final and decisive stage of *s̲adhan̲a*. Even after realising this state, the Gita expects the seeker to remain active, and such a person by the very nature of the state would also remain moral carrying out duties automatically if not self-consciously.

Griffith does not seem to give up his criticism, however. If everything is left to God, it amounts to determinism or even fatalism! (Robinson 2006: 73). A few other critics also have charged the Gita of being deterministic. This criticism seems to be based on Krishna's declaring after assuming his cosmic form (*Vishwarupa*) that Drona, Bhishma and other warriors are already killed (or destined to be killed) and that Arjuna would be a mere *nimitta*, an instrument (XI.33–34). In the last chapter of the Gita again, Krishna tells people behave according to their inborn nature, and even if one wishes to act otherwise, they would be bound by their nature. Further, the indwelling Ishwara (Lord) causes all beings to move as if they are mounted on a machine (XVIII.60–61).

There is apparently a huge self-contradiction in the Gita on this point, which was briefly discussed at the end of the first section of the preceding chapter. It bears some reiteration given the importance of the point. If the Gita is deterministic as implied by the two verses referred earlier, why indeed in the next-but-one verse (sixty-third) of the same chapter (eighteenth) does Krishna ask Arjuna to ponder critically over the teaching and act as per his choice? Obviously, Arjuna is not regarded as a mere instrument without any decision-making power. What is the meaning of preaching ethics to a mere instrument? Why did Arjuna need so much persuasion if he was a mere cog in the machine? The self-contradiction arises because the problem is not a simple one. There is a huge debate in philosophy after all about free will vs. determinism. We seem to have free will, but that is within severe limits imposed not only by the laws of nature including our own nature but also by the similar freedom given to others. That is why the Gita takes the stand that our right or freedom is only in acting; the outcome depends on so many factors, some of which cannot be foreseen that we cannot presume ourselves to be the cause of the outcome. Ramakrishna Paramahamsa compared our freedom with the freedom of a tethered animal. But the length of the rope by which we are tied appears to be long enough to give us the freedom of moral choice and perform our moral responsibilities. Such being the case, self-contradiction in the Gita on this point is understandable. To call it as deterministic would, however, be misleading and incorrect.

These difficulties of reconciling *sadhana* with making a living in the world, aspiring for spiritual liberation with dharma in the world, and free will and surrender to God, do no doubt indicate tensions, but the Gita itself shows the way of reconciling and resolving them. As Malinar observes, 'the impact of the *BhG* [Gita] lies in its attempt to mediate between two opposing referential frameworks of human aspirations on the one hand, the realm of socio-cosmic relationships encompassed by *dharma* and based on ritual performances as transmitted in Vedic texts; and on the other, the quest for liberation from this very realm through ascetic practices and the employment of new forms of knowledge' (Malinar 2009: 5). She explains further that this mediation is achieved on two levels: (a) through working in the world in the spirit or attitude of karma-yoga, and (b) through the concept of a single highest God, Krishna, who is both the lord of the world and its dharmic order as well as the ever-liberated yogi. He mediates between 'ascetic detachment and royal engagement' (Malinar 2009: 6). God is not at all seen as a hindrance in an active engagement in the world but a help, a supporter and a guide, provided that the engagement is according to dharma or moral principles, with this help, support and guidance leading ultimately to spiritual liberation. For a believer, all difficulties and tensions are resolved in Krishna ultimately. An important message of the Gita, especially as hinted in its last verse (*Yatra Yogeshwarah Krishno* . . . – XVIII.78), as Roopa Pai points out, is: 'man's actions are incomplete and eventually "unsuccessful" – both in terms of being right and in terms of bringing him lasting joy – if he does not work hand in hand with God, or if he does not have God's blessings (this is a religious text we are talking about, after all!)' (Pai 2015: 259; parentheses in original).

Is the Gita reactionary?

Dr Ambedkar, Kosambi and a few other rationalists and Marxists consider the Gita as a reactionary text, its main purpose being to reverse the social reform initiated by the Buddha and to uphold the dominance of Brahminism, if not of only Brahmins. It may be recalled (from the first chapter) that Dr Ambedkar takes the Gita as post-Buddhist. The gist of the contention of the critics[4] who charge the Gita of being reactionary is as follows. The Buddha had preached against the *chaturvarnya* system and also violence involved in animal sacrifices. Even Shudras and women could be admitted as monks in the Buddhist *sangha*. Around the same time when the Gita was being composed, Charvaka's *Lokayata* philosophy of atheism was gaining ground. This philosophy had rejected religion and rituals. Jainism also was spreading which too rejected violence and theism. All the three influences together broke the hegemony of Brahmins and even threatened their livelihood and their very survival. Brahmins desperately wanted a text which could help reviving Brahminism or the Vedic religion of rituals priest-craft, and the Gita was the result. The real meaning of karma as commended in the Gita is not work in general but rituals of *karma-kanda*, so that the priests are assured of their livelihood. The Brahmins cleverly chose Krishna, a Kshatriya, instead of a Brahmin to be its formal spokesman of the preaching in the Gita to make it more convincing. The Buddha and Mahavira were also Kshatriyas who were in the forefront of a revolution against the Vedic religion, and Krishna was projected to counter them. Thus the Gita in its very essence is counter-revolutionary. It is casteist as is indicated by the emphasis on *swadharma* which is nothing but caste duty. It seeks to consolidate the caste division in the society by threatening that there would be no salvation for those who transgress their caste duties. Its attitude of contempt towards the two lower castes – Vaishyas and Shudras – as well as to women is evident from the verse which puts them together as those with sinful breeds (*papa-yonayah*) (IX.32) (though, of course, they are all assured of reaching the Supreme Goal if they take refuge in Krishna). The real intention behind karma-yoga is to exploit the working class by indoctrinating them to believe that they should work wholeheartedly without expecting a due reward for work but be content with whatever they get as God-given. This is to avoid any class struggle and ensure submission to the established order under the hegemony of Brahmins.

The criticism is based on a thorough misunderstanding and needs a detailed response. First of all, the Gita's stand on the birth-based caste system is presented. A few verses in it do refer to the existing *varnas* which by then had become birth based. In Chapter 1, Arjuna refers to the threat of mixing of *varnas* (*varna-sankara*) as a result of the catastrophic war leading to a breakdown of countless families (verses 41–43), but these verses are a part of his misgivings which Krishna removes later. A key quotation in this context is the first line of verse IV.13, where Krishna tells Arjuna that the four *varnas* were created by him on the basis of *guna* (aptitude, nature) and *karma* (work or occupation) (*Chaturvarnyam maya srishtam guna-karma vibhagashah*). Krishna does not say here that the *varna* is based on birth, which is deliberate. Kane observes that if Krishna wanted to make birth as the basis of his division of labour, he could have easily said *jati-karma vibhagashah* or *janma-karma vibhagashah* instead of *guna-karma vibhagashah* as actually stated (Kane 1990, Vol. II: 1635–36). Sardar K. M.

Panikkar considers the verse as constituting a devastating attack on caste based on birth, far from supporting it. He says: 'It is the most unequivocal repudiation of divine origin of caste based on birth, the most categorical denial of Brahmin claim to inherent superiority' (Panikkar 1961: 40–41). The second line in the same verse (IV.13) has also some significance. Krishna says in it: 'I am the author (*kartara*) of this (*varna* system), I am also its non-doer (*a-kartara*)'. It implies that though the system of division of labour based on aptitude and work is natural (made by Him), its later transformation into a birth-based system is man-made and He does not support it. *Uttara-Gita* which is also a dialogue between Krishna and Arjuna makes the same point explicitly. When Arjuna specifically asks Krishna how *varna* is determined, he replies:

> *Na jatih karanam tata gunah kalyanakaranam/*
> *Vratastham api chandalam tam devah brahmanam viduh//*
>
> ('Birth is not the cause, my friend; it is virtues which are the cause of welfare. Even a *chandala* observing the vow is considered as a Brahmana by the gods.')[5]

It follows that when Krishna advising Arjuna (in II.31) to do his duty as a Kshatriya, he was asking him to follow his chosen duty as a soldier, not his caste or *jati*. Not all those fighting in the Kurukshetra war were born as Kshatriyas. Arjuna's guru himself was a Brahmin who took a leading part in the war on Kaurava side by being the chief of the army after Bhishma fell. There were also others like Ashwatthama and Kripa who fought in the same war.

There is again an explanation in XVIII.41–44 about how the division of labour into the four *varnas* is based on their nature. Thus, only those having a pure mind and righteousness can be called as Brahmins. It just cannot be the case that only those born in Brahmin families would be considered as having a pure mind; Krishna could not surely have meant such perversion. Some responsibility and common sense would have to be exercised in interpreting the texts after all. The Gita nowhere says that one's nature or *svabhava* is based on *jati* or the community of birth. The verses concerned only classify human nature into four types, which in turn influences their work. Radhakrishnan says: 'The four-fold order is not peculiar to Hindu society. It is of universal application. The classification depends on types human nature' (1998: 364). He further quotes Gerard Heard from his book, *Man the*

Master (1942): 'It would seem that there have always been present in human community four types or strata of consciousness. . . . the Aryan-Sanskrit sociological thought, which first defined and named this four-fold structure of society, is as much ours as India's' (quoted in Radhakrishnan 1998: 367, fn-1).

Radhakrishnan also observes in this regard: 'All men are not equal in their capacities but all men are equally necessary for society, and their contributions from their different stations are of equal value' (Radhakrishnan 1998: 366–67). The Gita also teaches this equality clearly, for example in Chapter 6, where Krishna says in as many as four verses (29–32) that yogi treats all beings with evenness, sees Krishna in all beings, and considers pleasure and pain everywhere as his own. Such an attitude cannot allow any unequal and exploitative caste system. Krishna reiterates this philosophy of equality again when he declares, *samoham sarva-bhuteshu* (I am the same to all beings) (IX.29). Much is made of the Gita bracketing together persons of 'sinful breed' (*papa-yonayah*), women, Vaishyas and Shudras in IX.32, as mentioned earlier under criticisms summarised. Having declared that He is the same to all beings, it could not just have been Krishna's intention to view women and the two lower castes as of 'sinful breeds' as translated by Kosambi (quoted by Desai 2014: 38). What Krishna says in the verse is only that all those who take refuge in Him, *be they sinners, women, vaishyas and shudras* (*or anyone*), they all attain the highest spiritual goal. Kosambi translates the phrase as 'sinful breeds such as women, vaishyas and shudras'. Instead of 'such as', it is more logical and consistent with the intention of Krishna to read it with a coma after 'sinful breeds' as done here, others being separate categories. *Papa-yonayah* only means those born with a 'karmic luggage', and they could be anyone, not necessarily women and the low castes. What Krishna meant is that salvation is open to all, sinners as well as those having a low social status. There is absolutely no hint of any support to such a low status given by the society to women and lower castes. On the contrary, the accessibility of all to the Divine and salvation or liberation is assured regardless of gender and social status.

Now about the alleged attempt by the Gita to revive ritualism and restore the hegemony of Brahmins in religion. According to Dr Ambedkar, the Gita defends the dogmas of counter-revolution by Jaimini's *Purva Mimamsa*, and '[b]y Karma yoga or action, the Gita means the dogmas contained in Jaimini's Karma kanda' (as quoted in Rodriguese ed. 2004: 195). On another page of the same article, Dr Ambedkar says: 'Jaimini preaches pure and simple Karma yoga [rituals]. The *Bhagavad Gita* on the other hand preaches *anasakti karma*. Thus the Gita preaches a doctrine which is fundamentally modified' (2004: 200). He is right in observing that the concept of karma-yoga fundamentally modifies the ritualism of not only the ritualism of Jaimini's *Purva Mimamsa* but also the earlier *Yajurveda*.[6] While ritualism of the two texts was meant for achieving certain selfish ends like getting a son or wealth or for ensuring that one goes to heaven after death, the Gita's karma-yoga meant undertaking selfless action in general for the benefit of people and even of all beings (*loka-sangraha* or *sarva-bhuta-hita*). But Dr Ambedkar is wrong in contending that karma in the Gita simply means ritualism or it simply intends to revive ritualism and support Jaimini's counter-revolution.

There is no doubt a reference to yajna in several places in the Gita, particularly in Chapter 3, verses 9–15, which Dr Ambedkar cites in support of his argument about the Gita being ritualist. However, the Gita changes the very meaning of yajna as selfless offering, not necessarily ritual sacrifices. Verse 9 itself clearly asks Arjuna to do his work or duty (karma) unattached, since any work other than for the sake of *yajna* is binding (not liberating). It is only if *yajna* is interpreted as a selfless offering, the word fits in properly in the verse. *Yajnas* were normally performed to earn merit (*puṉya*) for oneself and family, for protection against evil spirits, for expiating sins, to seek the birth of a son and also for the welfare of the world. These goals were not exclusive, but often combined. Yajnas always had a purpose and could not have been done without attachment as advised in the Gita. The Gita did not of course prohibit Vedic *yajnas*, but did not encourage them either, and emphasised selfless action instead as spiritually more fulfilling. It is clear from the previous verse (III.8) that what Krishna had in mind while referring to karma was not ritual sacrifices but action in general. He says here that one cannot even 'travel in body' (do *shar̲ira-ya̲tra*) or maintain oneself through inaction and asks Arjuna to do his obligatory work (without being tempted by renunciation of work since that is not possible). The meaning of 'karma' in the Gita is very clear from this verse, which is so elsewhere too. Even in verse III.10, where again there is a reference to yajna, the Gita treats the act of creation itself as a yajna, which makes sense only if taken as a selfless service or action. Easwaran translates this verse as follows: 'At the time of creation the Lord gave humanity the path of selfless service and said: "Through selfless service you will always be fruitful and find the fulfilment of your desires."'[7] (Easwaran 1997, Vol. I: 160). In verses 12–15 also, *yajna* makes much better sense when interpreted as selfless service or action than as a Vedic ritual. The gist of these verses is that one who enjoys without making a selfless offering or service is as good as a thief; he is a sinner (III.12, 13). Even rain which makes it possible for us to have our daily food is the result of a selfless service (III.14). Brahman, as the creative and blissful energy, is present in every selfless act (III.15). The next verse (sixteenth) calls upon us to participate in this virtuous cycle of selfless service, instead of thinking always in terms of indulging in sensual pleasures. These verses together (in fact, the whole of the third chapter, which is on karma-yoga) are a powerful plea for selfless service. It makes little sense here if karma is interpreted narrowly as Vedic rituals.

Rationalists, particularly if they are Marxists, do not give up easily in argument. Well, they say, if karma-yoga is selfless work, it is only a ploy of the elite to exploit the working class to get free labour! This is the contention of Veerabhadrappa, who has devoted a full chapter on 'Work without reward' for it (2004: 154–65). He rightly asks, 'Is it ever thinkable that one can do one's work without having one's eye on the return of one's labour? After the Gita propounded this idea, in any part of the world, including India or any society, has this principle been practised? Is translating this principle into action beneficial to any individual or human society?' (2004: 154). He contends that such a teaching was brought up only as an instrument of the two uppermost castes to indoctrinate the lower but producing and working castes into unprotesting submission. The aim was only to consolidate feudalism.

First of all, karma-yoga is not meant for preaching to others but for following it oneself. It is not as if one can free oneself from its obligations and expect only others to follow it. Before an employer expects selfless work from his workers, he too should render selfless service to his workers and society.[8] Second, was the Gita addressed to the lower castes as such? Formally at least, the Gita's teaching is addressed to Arjuna, asking him to fight without attachment to outcome but as a duty. Even if Arjuna was only a pretext and the teaching was meant for others too, it is accepted by all the interpreters of the Gita that the teaching has a general and universal application. It is not meant for the working class alone in a capitalist economy, but also to capitalists earning interest and making profits. Gandhi addressed his proposal of the trusteeship ideal to treat wealth as a trust for the benefit of the society mainly to the capitalists, but the idea is essentially the same. Even before Gandhi, the Communist ideal of 'From each according to his ability; and to each according his needs' was proposed for the working class itself. Is this also not based on the same idea as the

Gita's? Is preaching some altruism in a world dominated by unbridled selfishness as unrealistic as Veerabhadrappa and his likes think? There was an occasion to indirectly take up the questions posed by him, in the preceding chapter itself. It was argued that the Gita cannot be interpreted as expecting workers to work, or doctors to treat patients, or capitalists to invest without any due return. The Gita teaches moderation. What it teaches us is to balance our selfishness with some altruism, some regard for the welfare of the society. What would you tell a doctor in a government or municipal hospital who expects a bribe from patients even though on a regular salary? What moral principle would you apply to a minister who wants a cut in every deal or project that is sanctioned by him, or to a prosecution lawyer who is willing to moderate his attack on a criminal against a secret consideration, or to a cricketer who is willing to drop a catch or two against payment? The Gita's teaching of karma-yoga is particularly addressed to such people, who expect an unduly high and morally unacceptable reward for what little they do and tend to hold the society to ransom. To the extent that even the poor have been capable of and inclined to altruism (why not?), they too can be taken as believing in karma-yoga of the Gita.

The Gita is not a reactionary text; on the contrary, it is a revolutionary text no less than Buddhism. It rejected the claim of upper castes for superiority based on birth by taking instead the criteria of quality and aptitude. It brought religion to the masses, making it inclusive. This was by undermining the role of rituals and emphasising the role of simple bhakti as an important path of reaching God. Whatever little one offers, be it a humble leaf, flower or even a little water, is accepted by God if only offered with devotion (IX.26). No expensive or elaborate rituals are necessary. Bhakti-yoga preached by the Gita opened the doors of religion to the lower castes and women. The Gita stressed the equality of all on the ground that the self resides in all (VI.29). It declared that one who sees God in all and all in God is never lost to God, nor is God lost to such a person (VI.30). Even if the Gita is taken as post-Buddhist, it can be accused of trying to take the wind out of the sails of Buddhism, or of borrowing its reformist zeal, but not of thwarting its progressive elements. Buddhism had left a gap by its agnosticism, but the Gita gave a personal God to the masses whom they could pray to, love and aspire to be united with. The Gita fulfilled a mass need and helped to improve their sense of well-being, even if Marxists may say that it provided opium to the masses. By emphasising karma-yoga and altruism, it also opened a way to help the masses. The Gita did not want to make it appear as condescending charity, because whatever you give has to be with no contempt to receivers, and what is more, it has also to be without any feeling of pride or egoism, as it stressed (XVII.21). If I give to anyone with contempt, it only means I have no humility. The Gita played an important role in democratising Hinduism and paved the way for the bhakti movements later.[9]

The Gita and its deontology

The Gita has been criticised by several on several counts as we have reviewed earlier. An important point of criticism is that the Gita is not against violence and war if duty required them. This owes mainly to the immediate context of the Gita – Arjuna's reluctance to fight his relatives and particularly his teacher, and Krishna's persuasion that Arjuna should do his duty as a soldier. In his book, *The Idea of Justice* (2009), Amartya Sen questions the wisdom of focusing on duty irrespective of the consequences and makes his criticism in the context of his assessment of deontology – priority for doing one's duty as a candidate principle for the basis of justice.[10] Sen does not of course charge the Gita with inciting violence, but is only critical of its rigid deontology even where it results in the massive violence of war, which certainly was not unexpected. Sen brings out Arjuna's predicament clearly. Arjuna has no doubt that he would be fighting for a just cause and also has no doubt about his victory. His fear is not the fear of defeat (Sen 2009: 209). He is doubtful only whether he would be doing the right thing if it ends up killing all those whom he had loved and respected, causing also large-scale death and carnage. Sen feels that 'Krishna got away with an incomplete and unconvincing argument against Arjuna' (Sen 2009: 212-fn). Doing one's duty regardless of consequences is not acceptable to Sen as a principle. He is aware that several other important issues too are raised in the Gita and that the Gita is not about deontology only. He also concedes that 'there is nothing to prevent a general deontological approach from taking considerable note of consequences' (Sen 2009: 216). What bothers him, however, is that the general principle of doing one's duty is raised in the Gita to a purist or absolute status. Sen takes care to distance his emphasis on consequences from the old debate in the West between deontological and consequential approaches to justice. In this debate, consequential ethic was considered as relativist, with end justifying any means adopted. For Sen, 'processes' too are important (which Gandhi calls as the means).

Much before Sen's critique of the Gita, Gandhi too faced the problem of interpreting Krishna's urging Arjuna to fight the war. Gandhi took the firm view that the Gita preaches non-violence, because not only does it mention ahimsa as a virtue to be practised but also advocates several other virtues which are not consistent with violence. He saw the war background of the Gita only as a metaphor for life's struggle that cannot be avoided but should be faced with equanimity. Gandhi certainly bases his argument on the evidence in the Gita itself. For example, the Gita explicitly advocates ahimsa along with other virtues like truthfulness, compassion, absence of anger, peacefulness, gentleness and humility as the divine qualities to be cultivated (XVI.2). On the other hand, demonical (*asuree*) qualities emerging from lust and anger are deplored (XVI.12, 13). There is a special denunciation of an *asuree* attitude of: 'I have eliminated this enemy today and I will eliminate others too. I am the lord, I am powerful, I will succeed and will enjoy' (XVI.14). This is precisely an attitude of violence and warmongering, and precisely what the Gita denounces. We have noted earlier that many other modern and contemporary interpreters also consider the war background of the Gita as a metaphor for the struggle between the forces of good represented by Pandavas and forces of evil represented by Kauravas.

However, even if the war was real and not just a metaphor, we need to appreciate that it was thrust on the Pandavas; it was not their choice. Krishna had himself tried his best to avoid the war and went to the court of Kauravas as an emissary to negotiate for an honourable settlement. He said that the Pandavas want peace and would be willing to settle for a village each for the five brothers, so that they could live outside the vicious rule of the Kauravas. Duryodhana arrogantly retorted that he would not part with even a tiny bit of land equal to a needle-top – forget five villages. The elders watched helplessly though sympathetic to the Pandavas. The war became inevitable, as it was a point of self-respect for Pandavas to fight for their right. The elders including the common teacher of Pandavas and Kauravas, who were under the patronage of the latter, had to be on their side. Paradoxically, they wished victory for the Pandavas and their cause, though fighting sincerely on the side of the Kauravas. There was no doubt in their minds that the Pandavas were virtuous persons and theirs was a just cause, and the Kauravas were vicious and greedy, but they felt duty-bound to be on the Kaurava side. For them also, duty prevailed over other considerations of ethics like virtue. They failed to exercise their weight and influence over the Kauravas to accept a peaceful settlement. What is puzzling, there were several kings around who were common relatives and friends of both Pandavas and Kauravas, and they too could not avoid the war, but instead took one side or the other to support and participated in the war with their huge armies. The war was hardly Krishna's decision or choice. It was as if everyone around was itching for a good fight and willed the war. It was beyond anyone to withdraw from it at the final point when the dialogue of the Gita took place. It may seem that Krishna being an *avatar* of God could have prevented it. But we have to remember that humans have been granted freedom of will by God, and the war was entirely within the free will of everyone and it would have been against the principle of free will if Krishna were to interfere at the late stage and prevented it as a miracle. The freedom of will had to simply work itself out.[11] It is another matter that free will was abused by the Kauravas. A moral lesson that the Mahabharata teaches is that free will has to be exercised with responsibility and at the right time.

Moreover, a pertinent question is if it is ethically alright for a soldier on the battlefront to withdraw from war unilaterally, particularly one so responsible a leader as Arjuna. How should it be interpreted? Krishna warns Arjuna that he would be regarded as a coward if he withdraws at this stage. Is absolute non-violence practicable or even ethical, particularly if there is a risk of its being one sided? As we noted earlier, Gandhi thought that if Arjuna and with him the Pandavas were to withdraw from war at that stage, they would have been pursued and massacred. Were Russia and France wrong in resisting Hitler when he invaded them?

Further, Sen is not quite correct in thinking that the Gita's deontology is indifferent to consequences. The Gita condemns action taken without regard to consequences as *tamasika* (XVIII.25). Sen misinterprets the Gita's advice to act without aspiring for fruits as an exhortation to disregard consequences. The exhortation is to only act unselfishly. Moreover, the Gita's concept of duty is not limited to a soldier's fighting in a battle, but goes beyond and covers other concerns too like serving people and promoting their welfare (*loka-sangraha*) as observed in the preceding chapter. The Gita's emphasis on duty is quite understandable since the bulk of human activity in any civilisation is governed by a sense of duty, as Gandhi observed. Otherwise, no human society can run smoothly. Different kinds of duties evolved in a society precisely because of their expected beneficial consequences. Affection and sentiments alone are not enough. It is the duty of parents to take care of their children, get them educated and cultured, and keep them healthy.

It is the duty of a married couple to respect each other, be loyal and help each other. If someone is hit by a vehicle and is lying on the road, it is the duty of passers-by to help that person. It is the duty of government servants to serve people without seeking gratification. The whole system of law and order can be said to be based on duty-ethics. The consequences of ignoring duty will be far more disastrous than those of doing one's duty regardless of consequences. Action guided only by consequences, disregarding one's moral duty, could mean sliding down into a relativist or opportunistic ethic of the end justifying the means.

The Gita is not alone in emphasising duty. The Holy Bible asks us to love our neighbour and be a Good Samaritan in an hour of need. The Ten Commandments are duty centred. Kant, the most respected leader of the Enlightenment Age, formulated his ethical doctrines in terms of 'categorical imperatives' as he called. It is said that Kant's ethical theory is one of the best ever devised (Richter 2008: 139). For him, ethics requires responsibility, not just sentiment. We fulfil this responsibility through 'orders that we give ourselves' or 'imperatives'. He distinguishes between 'hypothetical imperatives' from 'categorical imperatives'. 'If you want a pie, then go to a bakery' is an example of the former; it does not come under the ethical domain. Some things must be simply done, regardless of what you want, and these acts come under categorical imperatives or duties, and come under ethics. Kant distinguishes between imperfect duties and perfect duties. Imperfect duties are the ones which one may not do all the time, but as much as possible, like helping people. Perfect duties are the ones which one must do all the time. Kant gives an example of a perfect duty – never make a false promise, that is, we must never pretend to be promising to do something which in fact we have no intention of doing (Richter 2008: 127). Some duties may be pleasant and some unpleasant, but the Gita says that we must not attach ourselves to doing only the former and avoiding the latter. We may not know the consequences of doing some duties, but moral duties remain categorical imperatives. Krishna and Kant seem to have a lot of common ground! Sen's call to prevent manifest instances of injustice such as poverty itself can be considered as an instance of deontological ethic, though of course he is explicit and insistent on taking into account the consequences of one's action, with which the Gita also agrees.

Miscellaneous criticisms

A point of criticism which has been made by most of the critics of the Gita is that its arguments are not logically ordered; they are jerky, unconvincing and often lack consistency. It is, for example unrealistic to argue about the irrelevance of human agency. A conspicuous instance, as pointed out by Dr Ambedkar, is Krishna's argument that Arjuna could fight and kill because the Atman is immortal and he would not be killing the real self of anyone, and even the bodies are after all mortal and he would not be able to prevent them from dying. Dr Ambedkar writes: 'If Krishna were to appear as a lawyer acting for a client who is being tried for murder and pleaded the defence set out by him in the *Bhagavad Gita* there is not the slightest doubt that he would be sent to the lunatic asylum' (2004: 197). Dr Ambedkar's point is that it was alright to argue that Arjuna could not back out of the war at that stage, but to use such a logic would be hardly convincing. If Krishna's logic and his theory of irrelevance of human agency were to prevail, what is the meaning left to ahimsa and crime? Desai asks, is death so trivial? He terms such a logic as sheer escapism. Under this, 'the responsibility of human action is completely evaded', and if I take a bribe, 'I can convince myself that it is not I who take a bribe nor you who give it to me' (2004: 65). He adds: 'Since certain though my death may be, should I not insist that you the murderer who threatens me, have no right to kill me? . . . Just because death is inevitable, its timing cannot be of no consequence' (2004: 66–67).

This criticism also is based on a serious misunderstanding of the Gita and misapplication of its theory. The reality is quite complex, and statements made with a particular meaning and motive in a particular situation cannot be literally applied in all contexts and situations. In such a kind of distorted universalism, the Gita's arguments may sometimes do look conflicting and inconsistent. For example, the Gita not only accepts freedom of will in some situations but also denies it in others as discussed in the preceding chapter. Similarly, human agency or responsibility is certainly accepted in asking man to be ethical and do his duty, but is to be taken as irrelevant in situations such as a soldier fighting in a legally declared war involving killing. A soldier who participated in such a war would always be tortured by a heavy conscience all his life, if he accepts moral responsibility for the deaths he caused in a war. Arjuna would have had the same problem, but for Krishna's arguments. He wanted to have a clean conscience before going to war, and Krishna enabled him to have it. It does not mean that anyone can indulge in murder with a clean conscience. War is certainly bad, and as pointed out earlier, Krishna tried his best to avoid it and negotiate a solution. Kauravas forced the war on the Pandavas, but Arjuna could not just forget that those with whom he would be fighting were not his enemies but his near and dear ones and wanted to escape from the war when it was too late. Krishna deplored such escapism and inspired him to have the will to fight. Krishna said that you cannot solve problems by escaping from them, but by facing them with a sense of duty. Thus Krishna's logic was not one of escapism as alleged but was a remedy for escapism in a particular situation. This cannot be interpreted as Krishna having given a free run for all sins, crimes and murders. That would amount to complete twisting and distortion, and cannot certainly be accepted as the message of the Gita. It does not mean that the Gita's teachings are all purely contextual and relativist. They do have general significance and relevance, but this has to be interpreted without giving up common sense. If the Gita's philosophy was only a pep talk to Arjuna and had no significance to other situations and other people, it would not have been accepted as a popular sacred text. Even then, it cannot be interpreted mechanically in all circumstances. The theory that Atman is immortal and does not die with the body has been a source of immense solace to many Hindus who are grieved by the death of their dear ones. Man in search of immortality finds it in this theory; they believe that there is something immortal in man in spite of the body being perishable which gives solace. It may sound irrational to rationalists, but it is a matter of faith. It looks that very common people at large have shown more common sense and logic in interpreting the Gita than rationalist intellectuals!

Kosambi points out at the variety of interpretations of the Gita, each opposed to the other, and says: 'No question remains of its basic validity if the meaning is so flexible' (quoted approvingly in Desai 2014: 27). It is indeed true that apparently very different interpretations in terms of *Advaita, Vishishta-advaita* and *Dvaita* have been made by Indian philosophers, but we have also observed while discussing them that they express different aspects of the Ultimate. Differences are bound to arise while explaining philosophy, particularly when a text like the Gita is not intended to be partisan but aims at achieving a synthesis. The Gita, after all, is not a do-it-yourself manual for assembling a TV set or a car!

Veerabhadrappa takes the Gita to task for being strongly critical of atheists and has devoted a full chapter of his book to explain why the Gita is anti-rational and wants to promote blind belief in whatever is said in the Gita and in Krishna (2004: 115–23). Far from being anti-rational, Charles Wilkins, who first translated the Gita into English, and Warren Hastings, who patronised the translation, saw in the Gita a potential to raise the level of 'vernacular religion' from 'venality and corruption' it had fallen into and making it comparable with Christianity (Robinson 2013: 39). They appreciated its being capable of lifting popular religion from superstition to a higher form of religion, more amenable to reason (if only it reaches the masses). The Gita accepts several paths to one goal and even freedom to conceptualise several forms of God. It is not fanatical and, at least for this reason, should be accepted as more rational than other faiths which are fanatical about both the issues. Robinson observes, 'the *Bhagavad-gita* can be read as proving that the Hindu tradition is more experiential and less dogmatic than Western faiths' (2006: 152). If you read the Gita with an open mind, you will not find it anti-rational. The fact that Krishna did not want Arjuna to simply and blindly follow him is evident from his almost final advice to Arjuna to critically think over what all was said and then do as per his choice (XVIII.63). The general spirit of the Gita should also be appreciated. It points out different paths of *sadhana*; it gives the choice of the form of deity to the devotee and says in whatever form you worship or to whomsoever you worship, it reaches the same God, Krishna. The Gita is liberal in its religion, not fanatical. It does not, after all, call upon believers to kill all non-believers or harass them until they become believers! Moreover, the attack is more on the incorrigibly arrogant, those tending to greedily amass wealth through foul means and those given to indulging in sensual pleasures without compunctions, than on atheists (XVI.10–18). The reference to atheists is only in one verse, viz., XVI.8, which may well have been an insertion in the final version of the Gita by someone hating them. How could Krishna having taught non-hatred elsewhere permit hatred only for atheists? In the last chapter, Krishna of course says that the Gita is not for those who are devoid of devotion, who do not render any service [to others in the society or to God] and those 'who cavil at Me' (XVIII.67). This hardly amounts to a strong attack on the atheists. Krishna does not want anyone to be forced to believe in the Gita, and that is all.

Staunch rationalists are poor psychologists. They do not comprehend the vast scope of human aspirations and confine these aspirations only to the mundane. Anyone who does not fit it into rationalists' narrow conception of human mind is taken as irrational. To assume that believers are necessarily irrational and only the non-believers are rational is itself very unreasonable and irrational.

In any case, too much emphasis on rationality in matters of religion is itself not rational. Religion is not science, and their spheres are different, though they need not conflict. Gandhi thought that religion has no business in matters to be resolved by science, and science and rigid logic have in turn no business to be judgemental about religion. He felt that 'attribution of omnipotence to reason' is as bad as idolatry. He said: 'I do not know a single rationalist who has never done anything in simple faith. . . . But we all know millions of human beings living their more or less orderly lives because of their child-like faith in the maker of us all. . . . I plead not for the suppression of reason, but for due recognition of that in us which sanctions reason itself' (quoted in Fischer 1998: 308). The Gita also pleads for the same.

Let us savour a sample of Veerabhadrappa's own rationality. According to him, the Mahabharata war was a conflict between interests of Brahmins represented by Pandavas and Kshatriyas represented by Kauravas (2004: 42–43). He forgets that Pandavas and Kauravas were cousins and that both were Kshatriyas. The war hardly had any caste basis. In fact, Brahmin leaders like Drona, Ashwatthama and Kripa fought on the side of Kauravas. There were no such Brahmin leaders on the Pandava side. Krishna himself was a Kshatriya.

Desai calls the Gita 'toxic' because he thinks that it is casteist, misogynist and even racist, and therefore irrelevant for the modern times (Desai 2014: 138). The misunderstanding about its being casteist and misogynist has been cleared earlier already. The charge about its being racist rests on the basis of deliberate misinterpretation of Chapter 16, where Krishna distinguishes between divine and demonical qualities (Desai 2014: 150). Desai thinks that the reference to *daivee* and *asuree* is to *devas* and *asuras*, whom he considers as races. He interprets that Krishna praises devas and condemns non-aryan asuras as respective races. It is beyond Desai's 'rationalist' and 'secular' mind to think that Krishna was referring only to ethical differences between the good (divine) and the bad (demonical or devilish). As a matter of fact, there is absolutely no hint of racism either in the chapter or in the entire Gita.

It is a healthy sign of the Hindu society that it has permitted a critical scrutiny of its sacred texts. The sacred texts of all religions should be open to such criticism and reinterpretations to make them relevant to the times as the Gita. However, the teachings of sacred texts, be it the Gita, the Bible or the Koran, have to be interpreted with some responsibility, objectivity, reasonable positiveness of attitude and balance. They should not be distorted merely for the thrill of attacking a text respected as sacred by millions and be happy in the thought that it is being progressive. Calling the Gita as 'terrorist tract' or 'toxic' betrays a complete lack of balance, responsibility, sensitivity and even rationality. Criticism of sacred texts, however, should be responded to with logic, not intolerance. The texts should neither be fanatically defended to the point of not permitting any criticism and even threatening the critics, nor be ridiculed by critics to the point of twisting the logic and the context of the teachings unduly hurting the sentiments of believers. While tolerance to criticism and freedom of thought is necessary for a healthy, humane and a progressive society, such freedom should be expressed with responsibility, and not recklessly.

Notes

1 The account of Christian critiques of the Gita here is based mainly on Chapter 3, 'Christian Theological and Missionary Critiques' in Robinson (2006: 71–85).

2 There is obviously a major typing error in the table on page 100 of Malhotra's book (2011). To be consistent, the sub-column titled 'Open Architecture Spiritual Eco-system' should be shifted to the left column under 'Human bottom-up potential independent of history', and the sub-column titled 'Non-negotiable Grand Narrative of History' should be shifted to the right column under 'God makes top-down history'.

3 For a critical discussion of India's own calendars, see Chapter 15 on 'India through its Calendars' in Sen (2005: 317–33).

4 The gist of arguments of three critics is given here: Kosambi (1968) as quoted in Desai (2014: 37–38), Ambedkar (2004: 193–2000) and Veerabhadrappa (2004).

5 As quoted by Sharma (2000: 165). His source is S. V. Oka (1957) *The Uttaragita with a Translation into English and Appendices*, Poona: Bhandarkar Oriental Research Institute.

6 Dr Ambedkar contends that since the Gita's aim was to defend the ritualism of Jaimini's *P<u>u</u>rva M<u>i</u>m<u>a</u>ms<u>a</u>*, the Gita must have been composed thereafter. However, Jaimini is not the founder of ritualism, since the *Yajurveda*, which was composed much earlier than both the Gita and *P<u>u</u>rva M<u>i</u>m<u>a</u>ms<u>a</u>*, had its main contents in ritualism. Dr Ambedkar also contends that Jaimini does not refer to the Gita and must therefore have been prior to it. But the Gita also does not refer to Jaimini or his work, though it refers to the Veda(s).

7 The verse, at least as translated by Easwaran, may sound self-contradictory. How can a selfless work be expected to fulfil one's desires? This point has been addressed in the first section of the preceding chapter while discussing desirelessness in the context of the Gita's teaching, and is taken up again in the next two paras here while responding to the criticism by Veerabhadrappa.

8 This point has been taken up for further elaboration with examples in the next chapter.

9 For a fairly detailed account of the bhakti movements and their role, see Nadkarni (2013: 203–50).

10 The account of Amartya Sen's criticism and my response to here are developed further from Nadkarni (2014: 136–41).

11 There is an apparent self-contradiction on this point in the Gita. Freedom of will is clear from the pains that Krishna has taken to persuade Arjuna to do his duty and his advice that he can do what he wants after critically thinking over what all was said to him and then do what he liked. If Arjuna was a mere puppet in the hands of God, the Gita was not needed. On the other hand, in Chapter 11 of the Gita, Krishna also says after showing His universal form (*Vishwarupa*) that all the people with whom Arjuna would be fighting are already destined to be killed and that Arjuna was only an instrument (*nimitta*). The contradiction can be resolved by distinguishing between two planes of reality. In the practical plane of what Shankara called as *vyavaharika satya*, there is freedom of will. But in the ultimate plane of *paramarthika satya*, everything is Brahman, and the question of separate individual freewill does not arise.

8

NOVEL APPLICATIONS

The Gita as a guide to leadership, enterprise and management[1]

The Gita was traditionally seen only as a source of spiritual guidance and also as a means of earning *punya* or merit through daily recitation. In applying the Gita to novel situations, which were not visualised at the time of its composition, it is important to appreciate that one should transcend the literal meaning of the verses and grasp the general spirit or purport (*tatparya*) behind them. The application of this requirement begins with the very first verse of the Gita, which includes a reference to the battlefield. A few novel applications of the Gita have already been presented in earlier chapters, such as the efficacy of a business executive and the nature of a national economy in Chapter 6 while discussing Table 6.1. The verses of the Gita have a remarkable profundity to enable this, which is what makes it a timeless and living sacred text which continues to inspire millions even after two and a half millennia of its composition.

After the first English translation of the Gita by Charles Wilkins appeared in 1785 in London, many Western thinkers saw it as a source of deliverance from excessive materialism. The value of the Gita as a source of inspiration and guidance in mundane problems, at both the national and individual levels, was realised only recently since the eighteenth century, compared with its long recognition as a sacred book. This use had to do with the Gita's practical approach to ethics. Practical approach does not mean sacrificing ethics for the sake of convenience. That would be hypocrisy, and the Gita abhors hypocrisy as *mithyachara* (III.6) or *dambha* (XVI.10). Practical approach to ethics means having the potential to guide through ethical problems one faces in day-to-day life. These problems arise at various levels – in the private lives of individuals, in community or national problems, and of course in business enterprises. The very background of the Gita is set in a battlefield. Gandhi and many others took it as a metaphor. The triumph of the good over the evil, or of justice over injustice, does not take place automatically, but only through a relentless struggle. During the days of India's freedom struggle, the Gita was taken as a direct source of inspiration for the national movement by such luminaries as Bankim Chandra and Bal Gangadhar Tilak. Raja Rammohan Roy used the Gita as a source of support for reforming the Hindu society and for eradicating such social evils. He used the Gita even to oppose idolatry and superstition.[2] Mahatma Gandhi treated the Gita as his mother, as a source of solace and as a guide in all practical problems he faced in the freedom struggle he led and in social reforms he launched. He wrote in 1925:

> I find a solace in the *Bhagavadgita* that I miss even in the Sermon on the Mount. When disappointment stares me in the face and all alone I see not a ray of light, I go back to the *Bhagavadgita*. I find a verse here and a verse there and I immediately begin to smile in the midst of overwhelming tragedies – and my life has been full of external tragedies – and if they have left no visible, no credible scar on me, I owe it to the teachings of the *Bhagavadgita*.
>
> – Mahatma Gandhi in *Young India* 1925 (pp. 1078–79); *CWMG* Vol. 32: 195

Shriranga, an eminent modern writer in Kannada, also known as Adya Rangacharya, takes the Gita as a guide to leadership, as it transformed a confused, indecisive and forlorn Arjuna into a clear-headed, determined and self-confident leader prepared to fight his battle finally. At the critical moment, Arjuna forgot that he was an important leader of his army which was vitally dependent on him and allowed his mind to wander to irrelevant things as a common individual without thinking the implications of his temptation to give up the battle for his army and for his own honour. Krishna brought him back to an awareness of his duty and gave him a philosophy of selfless duty and dedication suited to a leader (Shriranga 1972: 63, 143–44, 147, 249–50). Shriranga makes another point also. Justice requires that a wrongdoer is duly punished; to desist from so punishing because the punishment hurts and it amounts to violence would plunge the society into deep trouble. As a leader, Arjuna should have been aware of this, but lapses into sentimentalism. Krishna removes his confusion by asking him, among other things, to make his thinking focused on the most relevant, instead of allowing it get diffused into multiple directions (II.41) (Shriranga 1941: 32, 35). A very important requirement of a leader is to be focused on the relevant. The final decision has to be by the leader, but, as said by Krishna, it has to be based on critical thinking (XVIII.63). Since decisions by leaders affect a large number of people, it is people's responsibility to see that only persons of *sattvika* qualities as described in the Gita are selected as leaders in a democracy (Shriranga 1972: 250). Leaders themselves, if they care for a good reputation, should take the initiative to be virtuous and be persons with enormous self-control who will refuse to yield to temptations of abusing their power. The Gita has a lot to teach about self-control, as explained under 'Ethics in the Gita' in Chapter 6.

It is no wonder that the Gita has now come to be seen as a source of inspiration for business enterprise and business leaders, and guide to management. In a sense, the modern business environment under competitive capitalism also looks like a ruthless battlefield. Starting a new business needs courage, an enterprising spirit and pride in doing it. A timid person neither can start business enterprises nor can satisfactorily run them as they may buckle down under pressure of competition. What verse can be more inspiring and invigorating than the third one in Chapter 2? It says:

> *Klaibyam masma gamah Partha naitat tvaiyyupapadyate /*
> *Kshudram hridaya daurbalyam tyaktvotthishta Parantapa //*

It means: 'Yield not to unmanliness, O Son of Pritha! Ill doth it become thee. Cast off this mean faint-heartedness and arise, O Scorcher of thine enemies!' (Tr. Swarupananda 1982: 28).

Swami Vivekananda considered this verse as containing the whole message of the Gita (CWSV 1998, Vol. IV: 110). He thought it to be particularly relevant to the then mass of Indians immersed in ignorance and superstition who needed to struggle for a respectable place in the comity of nations. They had to fight numerous social evils like untouchability and mass illiteracy. But the verse can be considered to be equally relevant to talented young men inspiring them to start their own enterprises and create new employment instead of tamely being content with being employed by others. An unenterprising or inert nature (*apravritti*) is condemned by the Gita as *tamasika* (of the quality of dullness or passivity) (XIV.13).

However, the enterprising will always find ups and downs, which they have to face with equanimity and patience. 'Have patience' (*titikshasva*), says the Gita emphatically (II.14). An important message of the Gita is: Treat joy and sorrow, profit and loss, success and failure with equipoise and be ready to struggle (II.38). How is it possible? The Gita says, through detachment (*sangam tyaktvaa*). A certain amount of detachment even while actively engaged in work helps one to gain an evenness of mind (*samatvam*) against ups and downs, success and failure (II.48). Apart from avoiding stress and depression, detachment equips one to deal with all vicissitudes calmly and efficiently. Detachment does not mean non-seriousness with work or lack of commitment. The Gita is very emphatic about working with dexterity (*yogah karmasu kaushalam*) (II.50). It considers working with fortitude (*dhriti*) and enthusiasm (*utsaha*) as *sattvika,* the most desired of the three *gunas* or mental qualities (XVIII.26). There is no question of the Gita accepting indifference to quality of work as detachment. But the detachment as taught by the Gita is a key to both success and survival. An entrepreneur, whether an industrialist or farmer, has to accept risks and uncertainties as unavoidable facts of life and be ready to face them with boldness and confidence. The tragic suicides of numerous farmers or even of small businessmen are a consequence of not imbibing this teaching of the Gita. Even if a business goes into liquidation, a business person should not loose cool and equipoise, and be ready to reincarnate himself or herself within this God-given life. There is a famous verse in the Gita (II.22) which has served as a source of solace in the context of passing away of a dear one. It says: 'Even as a man casts off worn-out clothes, and puts on new ones, so the embodied casts off worn-out bodies, and enters into others which are new' (Tr. Swarupananda 1982: 42). This verse could as well be applied to situations of failure or liquidation of a business enterprise. An entrepreneur should not lose his or her cool in such situations, but be ready to learn from experience and start a new enterprise. Professor B. Mahadevan interprets this verse as teaching the need to discard obsolete ideas and experiment with new ones in business; it is a mantra for innovation.[3] Old models which do not any longer work may have to be given up and new ones tried. Chatterjee observes that 'a core capability that all leaders of all times must possess is the ability to lead change' (2012: 215). He thinks that the Gita teaches business leaders to remain relevant and be useful to the world. 'To do that, they need to deal with discontinuities and question their own mental models' and 'go beyond wishful leadership to wilful leadership' that leads to action. They triumph when they merge their individual will with the life's larger purpose, which is what was taught by Krishna (2012: 216–17).

Hindu scriptures have accepted the goal of earning wealth as a valid *purushartha* (human goal). Earning wealth per se is not regarded as a sin, but is encouraged on the contrary. It is considered as the duty of a householder to earn, take care of family, be hospitable and help others. The principles of morality are applicable to all including householders. They have no concessions or exemptions from them just because they need to earn, though sannyasis are subject to even more rigorous moral and spiritual discipline. Similarly, business enterprises enjoy no exemptions from the principles of morality, just because they are in business. They have in fact special responsibilities because they are in a position to affect the lives of others. The Rigveda gave a general advice which is relevant even today, both for individuals and for business enterprises. It is pertinent in the context of what the Gita also has to say further on the issue. The *Rigveda* (X.31.2) says:

> *Parichin marto dravinam mamanyad ritasya patha namasa vivaset /*
> *Uta svena kratuna samvadeta shreyamsam daksham manasa jagribhyat*

> ('Let a man/woman ponder well on wealth, earn it through the path of moral law and with humility, consulting one's own conscience, and then heartily gain upright prosperity.'
> Tr. by the author)

Wealth does not come on its own. One has to consciously ponder (*parichin*) over how it has to be earned through the path of moral law or truth (*ritasya patha*), and not by dishonest means. It has to be earned with humility (*namasa*), since success depends on the grace of God and one owes it to the society at large for making it possible. Ethical dilemmas are bound to arise, which have to be resolved through consulting one's conscience (*kratuna samvadeta*) or inner voice as Gandhi called it. Once these qualifications or conditions are respected and followed, one can heartily (*manasa*) earn wealth and gain well-deserved (*daksham*) prosperity (*shreyamsam*).[4]

The Gita not only implicitly accepts this, but also adds that the wealth earned must also be shared and be used for the welfare of humanity (*loka-hita*). Earning wealth has to be done in the spirit of a *yajna*, an offering, and one should enjoy its fruit only after meeting the dues of all; that is one has a right to eat only the remnants of *yajna*. The Gita further explains this by saying that those who cook only for themselves eat sin (III.13). Even food that one prepares has to be shared, what then of earning wealth through business? A further extension of the idea that one has a right only to the remnants after meeting the dues of all is that the moral responsibility of a corporate enterprise is not confined only to its shareholders, but extends to other stakeholders as well like employees, customers, suppliers, state and society.[5] Shareholders come last; they are entitled only to what remains after all dues and liabilities are met. The business enterprises have no right also to unsustainable and/or illegal exploitation of nature. If the business operations cause some negative externalities like depriving some people of their land or livelihoods, they need to be first compensated and rehabilitated. If any pollution is involved, the business enterprise has to honestly take steps to avoid or at least minimise pollution within permissible or acceptable limits, and duly compensate the victims of pollution. All these are implied when the Gita says that one has a right only to the remnants of *yajna*.

The great thing about the Gita is that it does not stop at teaching ethics, though it is important. It goes beyond and teaches how to be effective and efficient too. As a matter of fact, being ethical in business also contributes to efficiency and effectiveness. There is no conflict between ethics and business efficiency. The management should not be guided by only short-term gains and sacrifice its long-term credibility. Micro-economic theory is developed on the premise that a firm has the goal of profit maximisation. A healthy firm, however, aims at maximising profits over a long run and not tempted by short-run gains, which harm long-run profitability. We often talk about the brand value of an enterprise, which is essentially a long-term concept. Brand value does not so much depend on the profitability of business, as profitability depends on brand value. Brand value depends in the main on the moral integrity with which business is conducted, the confidence the customers have in the product and services of business, the reputation of the enterprise on the treatment of its employees and suppliers, its social welfare projects and also the extent of eco-friendliness of the enterprise. A good management has to ensure all these for success. The secret of success in business management lies in following the Gita's advice: *Parasparam bhavayantah shreyah paramavapsyatha* (III.11). It means: 'Cherish each other, support each other, you gain the highest good'. A little further, in verse 16 of the same chapter, the Gita refers to a cycle (*chakra*) of good works, involving helping each other and gaining mutual benefit, and warns that one who does not participate in this virtuous cycle lives in vain (*mogham jeevati*). But if this cycle is followed, it contributes to the longevity and brand value of the enterprise. Yes, as explained earlier, ups and downs, and even mortality, of business enterprises have to be faced with equanimity. But it does not mean that management cannot do anything about it. Brand value helps a business greatly to tide over ups and downs and promotes its longevity. However, brand value is not dropped to an enterprise from the high heavens as a gift; it has to be created and assiduously patiently built. The secret of boosting brand value lies in following the Gita's twin principles of eating only the remainder after sharing and cherishing each other. It cannot be ignored that cherishing each other covers our natural environment also. When the environment is protected, it nourishes us too!

Another advice which the Gita gives is to have humility, and not only to avoid arrogance but also to be cautious about not giving any such impression to others. Arrogance, even an impression of being arrogant, is highly counterproductive. In the old days, many used to think that throwing one's weight around and creating an aura of fear works best in getting work done. But it also creates unconsciously or consciously resistance and an attitude of withdrawing from wholehearted cooperation. A mature way is to prefer being loved rather than being feared. Amiability and exuding warmth in relationships with all are not so much as a way of getting willing obedience from those below, but essentially because it is the person's very nature. Such a person is quick to give credit to others for both small and big things, and not appropriate all credit for oneself. A good manager, even a CEO, is open to suggestions and advice from others, and attends to complaints on time and sincerely, and even when a complaint has to be rejected, it has to be done after due consideration and respect to the complainant. A good and healthy organisation does not depend on the competence of just one or a few persons, but of most. A competent manager creates an environment where all contribute wholeheartedly and is quick to recognise the role of others. The Gita says that it is the deluded arrogant who thinks that he or she is the only doer (*Ahamkara-vimudhatma kartaram aham manyate*) (III.27).

The Gita insists that (even in private enterprises) due procedures and codes of conduct (*shastra-vidhi*) have to be followed wherever applicable. They should not be flouted under temptation or selfish impulse (*kamakaraka*), since any such irresponsible behaviour on the part of management does not lead to success (*na sa siddhim avapnoti*) (XVI.23) and could instead land it in disaster. Legal procedures and codes of conduct tell us what should be done and what should not be, and need to be taken into account (XVI.24). Decisions and their implementation have to be transparent, and in a spirit free from undue personal selfishness, anger and greed (XVI.21).

The Gita hints (in XVIII.20–22) that in taking important decisions or solving problems, it is best to have a total view of things involved, rather than be content with analysing a thing in isolation even if in depth. Taking a holistic view is expected to give the most satisfactory outcome, since it recognises that there are several dimensions to an issue all of which may be relevant directly or indirectly. It takes the larger picture into account, which may produce new insights that a purely analytical approach may miss. It will be very harmful for an enterprise to take decisions on the basis of what the Gita calls as *tamasika* knowledge. We have more to discuss about this in the next section. We may note, here, however, that taking a total view includes negative externalities imposed on the environment and other people, which the management cannot ignore. These negative externalities are side effects the cost of which is imposed on others of both the present and future generations, but not borne by the enterprise causing them. They are in the form of air and water pollution, and depletion of the stock of natural resources beyond sustainable limits. A *sattvika* management should take responsibility for all these damages and prevent them or duly compensate for them. For example, a factory which has come up on a farmland may have paid some price for land purchased and occupied, but it should also rehabilitate the displaced farmer who has lost his source of livelihood by employing him or his family members in suitable jobs. There is emphasis on *shaucham* (cleanliness) and *adroha* (non-treacherousness) in the Gita (XVI.3), which also mean avoiding or minimising air and water pollution and adverse side effects on other people. The implications of the Gita's teaching for environmental management and ethics have been brought out by Swami Ranganathananda in his work on the Gita and have been narrated in the section on him in Chapter 5.

There is a principle of work in the Gita, karma-yoga, which in simple English means selfless service. But if you try to spell it out particularly for general application, it can be seen as intriguing in spite of all the attention and publicity it has received. The essence of karma-yoga is considered to be as spelt out in Chapter 2, verse 47. It says: 'you have a right only to doing work (*Karmanye eva adhikaraste*); but never to its outcome or fruit (*ma phaleshu kadachana*); don't think of yourself as the cause of work (*ma karma-phala-heturbhu*); but don't abstain from work (*ma te sangostvakarmani*)'. If you take this verse in isolation, it may sound highly unacceptable, even revolting. If a manager goes before his workers with such a harsh injunction, he will be considered as a slave-driver. How can anyone be expected to work without anticipating a reward, be they workers or professionals? Let alone workers, how can a manager, who is supposed to be result oriented and has certain targets to achieve, be indifferent to the outcome of what he or she does? How can you expect an entrepreneur to be indifferent to profits or success of his enterprise, when his or her very motive is to make a surplus at least in the long run and make a success of his enterprise? Even a spiritual seeker is motivated by the desire for *moksha* or *nirvana*, and cannot be entirely desireless.

Actually, however, the Gita does not intend it. Krishna himself motivates Arjuna by saying: 'If you die in the battle, you will attain heaven; if you win, you will enjoy this earth. Stand up, therefore, and resolve to fight' (II.37). How can he, then, in just ten verses later in the same chapter ask the same Arjuna not to desire any fruit of his action? Nor does Krishna advise indifference to expected outcome. He denounces work done without heeding to the consequences as *tamasika* (XVIII.25). The Lord does not expect any work to be done in an 'unengaged' way (*ayukta*), that is mindlessly or thoughtlessly, nor lazily taking one's own sweet time (*dirghasutri*) (XVII.28). He insists on commitment (*shraddha*) and treats the lack of it as *tamasika* (XVII.13). He emphasises dexterity in work (*karmasu kaushalam*) (II.50) after recommending work without seeking a gain. Work has also to be done with fortitude and enthusiasm (XVIII.26). It means that one has to enjoy the work. The question is whether anyone can fulfil all these expectations without anticipating anything at all in return. What then does karma-yoga exactly mean? It is easier to do so through illustrations.

Basically, karma-yoga is meant for one's own self to practice and not for asking others to follow it freeing oneself from the obligation of it. That would amount to hypocrisy and an attempt at slave-driving. Karma-yoga is a mental discipline with practical applications for both efficiency and spiritual advancement. We can think of following karma-yoga at two levels, primary and advanced. We may illustrate it with the example of a doctor or a surgeon, who may charge a higher normal fee to well-to-do patients, but a much lower fee to the poor. The doctor has to meet expenses involved in giving a good service and also make a living, and cannot therefore afford to give free medical service for all. But having charged a fee, the doctor will not discriminate between a rich and a poor patient, giving a better and careful service to the former and indifferent service to the poor. In giving the medical service, a good doctor is guided by the motive of professional excellence and pride in work, and compassion for all patients, irrespective of what they pay. A more-paying rich indoor patient may be accommodated in a special AC room, and a common patient in a general ward. But as far as the medical service itself is concerned, there will be no discrimination between the two, and even the general ward will be kept as clean and hygienic as the special room. This is karma-yoga at a primary level, doing work with professionalism, pride in the quality of work, with complete care and mindfulness, and also of course with compassion to beneficiaries of work and to all. The doctor may charge fees, but is not guided only by the pecuniary considerations which in fact are pushed to background. A more enterprising doctor may intensify his or her social service by charging nothing or only a nominal fee, and meeting the expenses involved through donations from the admiring public, without compromising on the quality of service and professionalism. What really distinguishes a more mature or higher-level karma-yogi from the one at the primary level is that the sense of 'I am doing' totally vanishes in the mature who considers himself or herself as a mere instrument or puppet in the hands of the Divine, carrying out the Divine Will, not one's own will. The selflessness here is on two counts: the person does not work for a personal reward and, second, drops all the feeling of 'I' or 'mine'.

Similarly, a teacher may accept a salary to make a living, but as a karma-yogi, she will be totally lost in teaching, constantly improving herself in the profession, giving her best, enjoying teaching for its own sake and not working just for a salary. The teacher as a real karma-yogi would feel that she is just an instrument of the Divine, carrying out the Divine Will. Such a teacher cannot be unmindful of the outcome of the teaching, for it has to be ensured that the students absorb the knowledge and skills taught. But a karma-yogi does not judge the outcome in terms of the income gained. To that extent, the teacher is selfless or desireless (*anahamvadi, nispraha*), a requirement for a karma-yogi.

Can we apply the principle of selfless work to business enterprises in general? The bulk of economic activity in the world is assumed to be motivated by the desire for a personal gain or profit. According to Adam Smith, considered the father of economics, self-interest is not necessarily bad for the world. When each person acts according to self-interest, according to him, there is a mutual balance and natural order as in a market, and the common good is protected. Smith's view has not gone unchallenged. A natural order produced exclusively by narrow self-interest can be very unfair with a lot exploitation of the weak by the strong and can also be environmentally unsustainable. What is needed is to rein selfishness. This can be done either by the government through regulation and control, or by self-restraint, or through both. What the Gita does is to emphasise voluntary self-restraint. This aspect of the Gita was later developed by Mahatma Gandhi, who asked for treating the surplus wealth as a trust for the benefit of the society. Economic rationality seen narrowly in terms of selfishness would be a case of 'rational fools', and not a sensible or wise behaviour (Sen 1977). One is free to earn enough to prove one's self-worth, but it is not necessary that all the earning be spent on oneself and family only. Just as individuals can, and many do, devote part of their wealth for philanthropy, corporate enterprises can also, and do, devote some of their earnings for the benefit of the larger society. This is a part of their social responsibility.[6]

Social responsibility of business enterprises has several dimensions and is in addition to their responsibility to their stakeholders. Only some of the social responsibility has direct monetary implications, like contributing to social projects of the country to enhance the welfare and environmental improvement, and promoting education and culture. The company can even persuade their highly paid employees to make similar contributions. It creates an environment of social awareness in the company. The other dimensions of social responsibility are avoiding any discrimination against women in employment including in top positions, deliberately diversifying the social background of employees so that SCs and STs and religious minorities are adequately represented including the middle and top positions, and giving some preference and proper facilities to the physically challenged persons in employment. Doing all these would amount to following the Gita's advice of caring for *loka-hita* or *loka-sangraha* (promoting people's welfare). It is no longer left to the sweet will of the companies to do this. The Companies Act 2013 stipulates in Section 135 that every company having a net worth of 5,000 million rupees or more, or having a net profit of 50 million rupees or more, shall spend at least 2 per cent of its net profit before distribution (averaged over the preceding three years) on social welfare projects as its corporate social responsibility.[7] Do I hear a voice from somewhere that such a provision discourages enterprise and investment? Those having such a feeling should reread the third verse in the second chapter of the Gita quoted earlier (*Klaibyam ma̲sma gamah . . .*).

In the foregoing part of this section, we have seen the Gita only from the point of what guidance it gives to business leaders, enterprises and management. What about ordinary employees or workers? The criticism of the Gita that its advice to do work regardless of reward is only to deprive the workers of their due and to ideologically indoctrinate them to work like slaves has been duly refuted in the previous chapter, and it is not necessary to revisit it here. An important aspect of management is managing the human resources. A *tamasika* approach to personnel management is viewing employees narrowly as instruments hired for certain tasks and nothing more. A holistic and *sattvika* way would be to treat them as whole human beings with aspirations and families, and caring for all their concerns. Workers would then get a feeling that they are a vital part of an extended family in the form of the employing organisation, in which they count, resulting in a significant improvement in their loyalty and commitment. The workers have their responsibilities too.

The distinction made in the Gita between *sattvika, rajasika and tamasika* is a useful source of guidance for workers. Nobody can either expect any worker to work without a due and reasonable remuneration, or expect any worker to meekly put up with a remuneration which is not just and fair. But any enterprise or organisation would not expect a worker to be *tamasika*, which means being lazy, slow, irregular, deceitful, quarrelsome and clumsy in work and uncivilised towards other workers particularly women. In other words, such a worker is without any work ethic. The Gita deplores being *tamasika*. If there is enough proof of a worker having such a record, the employing enterprise is within its right to terminate his or her services provided that a due legal procedure is followed. Dismissing workers on false charges would amount to cruelty or *himsa*, and the Gita is definitely against *himsa*. A *rajasika* worker works only for salary, obsessively attached to personal reward, working with just enough efficiency to retain his or her job, but without a sincere commitment to the interests of the enterprise employing him or her. Such a worker may survive, but this kind of attitude is not conducive either to the moral and material progress of the worker or to the success and prosperity of the enterprise. Workers indulging in such behaviour believe in the philosophy of free ride. The crux of free-riding philosophy is the attitude of 'What if I don't work enough? In the totality of work, my being uncommitted does not matter'. But this philosophy militates against both the individual and collective interest. It will corrode the integrity and the very personality of the person believing in it. A *sattvika* worker by contrast, even if working for a due remuneration for work, believes that his or her long-run interest lies in working honestly and efficiently, maintains good interpersonal relationship with all workers as well as with those to whom he or she has to report, and does not subscribe to the philosophy of free ride. A *sattvika* worker does not have such a calculating mind as to expect an immediate reward for every little extra thing done. A *sattvika* attitude will contribute to the welfare of not only the enterprise but also of the worker.

It is not claimed here that the Gita contains within its 700 verses all the issues of the ethics, art and science of management.[8] But the Gita can be quite inspiring and invigorating to business leaders and managers, when properly understood. The attempt of this chapter has been to promote such an understanding.

Pursuit of truth in scientific research[9]

A contribution of the Gita, which so far had largely gone unnoticed, relates to approach to pursuing true knowledge and scientific research including methodology of social science research. The Gita has an astoundingly direct relevance to scientific research and has the potential to make it more insightful and productive. An important problem in research is objectivity. Objectivity does not mean value-neutrality. A research may be oriented to help in promoting health and human welfare in general, and also social justice. But there is often a risk of having pet biases and prejudices including pet theories which one tries to prove somehow, especially in social sciences. There is sometimes a risk of the research being doctored to promote certain interests. Technocrats interested in carrying out say, a power generation project, who are asked to do a social cost–benefit analysis, may somehow underestimate costs, especially social costs, and exaggerate benefits, just to get the project approved. The Gita's advice to be emotionally detached from the outcome of work and also do it with honesty and efficiency is useful in ensuring some objectivity.

There is another problem in research, one of adopting a right approach. An approach which compartmentalises a problem, splitting it into several parts and studying each in isolation, is quite common with academics. This goes under the name of rigorous analysis. This is in contrast with the holistic approach which looks at the problem as a whole, with all its aspects and parts and their cross connections. Both these find their place in the Gita. A common mistake is that we tend to miss the whole, while being obsessed too much with the parts, as in the famous fable of the elephant and the nine blind men. It is usually referred to also as 'missing the forest for the trees'. It is not that there is any essential conflict between the approaches, and both may be necessary in full and proper research. Even while a holistic approach takes note of the whole, it cannot also ignore the parts, just as a car mechanic cannot afford to ignore the working of individual parts while test-driving the car.

In the Gita, there is a direct and explicit discussion of both these approaches. When contemplating or probing into the nature of reality, the approach adopted in the Upanishads was holistic, irrespective of whether the perceived ultimate reality allowed for diversity or not. But their discussion in the Gita has relevance in the context of not only philosophical or metaphysical questions, but also mundane issues raised in sciences including social sciences and in governance and management.

The Gita acknowledges that there could be genuine differences in perception and conclusions in the pursuit of knowledge. According to it, there is a unity or consistency between knowledge (*jnanam*), object of knowledge (*jneyam*) and the knower (*parijnata*), just as there is coherence between the means of action (*karanam*), action (*karma*) and the actor or agent of action (*karta*) (XVIII.18). They influence each other and differences in the nature of the knower (particularly innate biases or prejudices), and the means or approach to knowledge may produce differences in the outcome of the process – perceptions and knowledge produced. The Gita makes an assessment of perceptions and approaches adopted in terms of the theory of *Gunas*, which has already been discussed at length in earlier chapters.

Three verses in Chapter 18 (20–22) of the Gita present this assessment in brief directly. In addition to them, there are other statements in the Gita which are of indirect help, which are also taken into account here. The first of these three key verses is as follows:

> *Sarva-bhuteshu yenaikyam bhavam avyayam ikshate /*
> *Avibhaktam vibhakteshu tat jnanam viddhi sattvikam //*
> (XVIII.20)

> ('Understand this to be *sattvika* or the highest knowledge which sees the enduring unity in different things or the universal in differences.'
> – Tr. by the author)

Any understanding or knowledge which views the object of knowledge holistically, finds what is unifying, universal or common from the diversity of particulars, and sees how different parts relate to each other, thus constituting the whole, such knowledge is the highest, according to the Gita. A knowledge of only the discrete particulars can be descriptive; it does not explain the particulars. Real knowledge is what leads us beyond the particulars and explains the totality of particulars. In other words, *s<u>a</u>ttvik* is totalising, synthesising or philosophical knowledge, which finds the meaning that lies behind everything observed. Seeing the universal from the particulars is a part of the holistic approach, but it is also much more. The approach looks at the whole, as more than a sum of its parts. It is not necessary that the whole should exist or should be seen as an organic unity in an undifferentiated way. It does not deny diversity. It does not have to declare the diversity as false. In fact, the Gita declares elsewhere that truth can be approached both as one and as of separate or manifold parts (*ekatvena prathaktvena bahudh<u>a</u> vishwato mukham*, IX.15). There are also several other verses in the Gita which emphasise the diverse and pluralistic nature of truth (XI.5, 13; XIII.3, 27 and 30). But truth is fully perceived and knowledge emerges only when the unity in diversity is grasped, which is what the *s<u>a</u>ttvika* approach is about. The approach can even look at parts as wholes within a whole, each part having its own diversity and yet bound together either conceptually or ontologically in a unity. The essence of holism does not depend on the level of aggregation, but on whether to the maximum extent possible, all facets, all components, all connections and all the factors bearing on the object of the study are taken into account.

Swami Vivekananda asserts that only when a particular is related to the universal, it leads to knowledge. There can of course be several universals, since more than one generalisation can be drawn from a particular group of the observed material. He asks, 'What is knowledge?' and answers, 'Destruction of peculiarity. Suppose a boy goes into a street or a menagerie and sees a peculiarly shaped animal. He does not know what it is. Then he goes to a country where there are hundreds like that one, and he is satisfied; he knows what the species is. Our knowledge is knowing the principle. Our non-knowledge is finding the particular without reference to the principle' (quoted in Vidyatmananda 2006: 12).

Most research is holistic in the sense that it seeks to get a larger picture or the meaning that lies behind the particulars. It is totalising. Explaining what real research is and how it is different from mere data or information gathering, Kurien gives the example of a crime investigation. A police constable may record all particulars of the crime scene, which is the first step in investigation. Research starts when a senior police officer has a close look at the overall scene, studies all the particulars, forms hypotheses and tests them, seeing the larger picture and taking a holistic view of the crime (Kurien 1973). This is not the end of the process and needs validation in a court of law by a detached judge, who also has to take a holistic view. In such a view, particulars are not ignored, but are related and totalised.

We can thus speak of two ways to holistic research: One is conceptualising the whole comprising parts, viewing the parts in relation to the whole and to each other, and seeing how the whole characterises the parts taken together, as in studying a forest or an economy. The other is deriving the general from diverse particulars, finding what is common or universal among them, as in the case of studying a set of individuals making up a distinct community or society. Both are valid ways to holistic knowledge, in fact to any meaningful knowledge. In the first, you start from the whole, and in the second, you start from the parts. But both take due note of the whole as well as parts and the interrelation between the two.

An approach which stops at the particulars without transcending to the whole is considered by the Gita as a lower level of knowledge, which it calls *rajasika*. The next verse in the Gita (XVIII.21) deals with it. But in this context, *rajasika* does not mean emotional or selfish, but simply a stage lower than the highest. If the highest knowledge is totalising or holistic or synthesising, the lower is disaggregating and analytical. While *satvika* transcends the particulars even while grasping them, the *rajasika* is focused on the particulars and their diversity without seeking the connectivity between them. The concerned verse is:

> *Prathaktvena tu yat jnanam nana bhavan prathak-vidhan //*
> *Vetti sarveshu bhuteshu tat jnanam viddhi rajasam //*
> (XVIII.21)

> ('Understand that knowledge to be *rajasik* which view different entities separately, treating each as different and separate.'
> – Tr. by author)

The *rajasika* approach is not condemned here. A concern for the particulars may be necessary both in any plan of action and also in ascending to the higher approach to knowledge (*sattvika*). The method, however, has limitations, a major one being it stops short of full or holistic knowledge, which alone can provide full insights. What makes a *rajasika* approach inferior or inadequate is not that it includes analytical techniques, but that it excludes a holistic vision or misses the larger picture. Once it includes the larger picture, it becomes *sattvika*. A *sattvika* approach may not only include but may also need analytical techniques. Intuition plays an important role in *sattvika* approach, but intuition unsupported by analytical corroboration may not carry conviction. In this sense, the *sattvika* need not necessarily exclude *rajasika*, and the two can be complementary.

The Gita cautions against grave mistakes in the pursuit of knowledge and research. The next verse (XVIII.22) describes what can lead to false or misleading knowledge, and in turn to ignorance. The verse is:

> *Yat tu kritsnavad ekasmin karye saktam ahaitukam /*
> *Atatvarthavat alpam cha tat tamasam udahritam //*
> (XVIII.22)

> ('The *tamasika* is said to be that which treats a small unit or thing as if it is the whole, in a purposeless way or without understanding the objective and without grasping the essence.'
> – Tr. by author)

Tamasik means dark, which sheds no light. It cannot be said to be contributing to knowledge; on the contrary, it may be misleading. Taking a small sample and examining it as representing the whole is not *tamasika* by itself. What makes it *tamasika* is if it is done without a proper awareness of the objectives of or reasons for investigation (*ahaitukam*) and without any theoretical framework to guide (*atatvarthavat*), and if the sample is too small (*alpam*) to be the representative of the whole. Under such conditions, the investigation would be misleading and hence *tamasika*. This one verse captures thus the essence of sampling theory and cautions against the pitfalls of sample surveys. What makes an approach to knowledge or scientific research *tamasika* is narrow-mindedness due to conscious or unconscious prejudice, which can lead to ignoring some parts or aspects of the whole, and even the objectives of our search. The outcome is not just ignorance but misleading or wrong understanding.

It is common knowledge in scientific research that there can be two types of errors in testing hypotheses: Type I error consists in the rejection of a hypothesis which is true; and Type II error is acceptance of a hypothesis which is false. The Gita comes astoundingly close to stating this in the following verse:

> *Nasato vidyate bhavo nabhavo vidyate satah /*
> *Ubhayorapi drishtontahstvanayoh tatva-darshibhih //*
> (II.16)
>
> ('The unreal never is. The Real never is not. Men possessed of the knowledge of the Truth fully know both these.'
> Tr. by Swarupananda 1982: 37)

The crux of knowledge is to know what is real or true, and what is false. According to this verse, truth alone exists. It is the essence of falsehood (*asat*) that it cannot exist. We may, however, commit the mistake of thinking something to be false what really is true and exists (Type I error), and of taking something to be real and existing what really is false and does not exist (Type II error). The Gita wants a seeker of truth to be wary of both these errors. Gandhi captured the original purport of the verse pithily as: 'Truth is God. . . . God alone is real and all else is unreal' (Gandhi 1927: xi). But the verse is as relevant even to the seekers of mundane knowledge. And the Gita's criterion of distinguishing the real from the unreal, presented with clarity and precision, is simply that the former alone exists.

It is important to appreciate that no backdoor entry to monism is proposed by advancing the case for the holistic method. Monism tends to disregard diversities and disjunctions as either unreal or secondary. By contrast, a holistic method takes full note of them as important parts or aspects of the whole and probes into the interconnectedness and functioning of the system as a whole. When Gandhi said that 'he endeavoured always to look at all the sides of a question' (CWMG 1972, Vol. 53: 441), he was describing a basic requirement of the holistic approach. Holism does not deny that reality is complex and multifaceted, evolving over time, with parts interacting with each other and having such a synergetic outcome that it is more than a mere sum of its parts. In the case of social issues, a holistic approach may be even more important than in the case of machine like a car. Social reality is evolutionary, and a society or community is more than a collection of individuals.

The type of questions asked may qualitatively and quantitatively differ between a holistic and a purely analytical approach. For instance, when it comes to agriculture and increasing the crop yields, the analyst may focus on increasing the dose of inputs like fertilisers, pesticides, weedicides and irrigation. A holist, on the other hand, will think over how to improve the capability or knowledge of the farmer and ensure the sustainability of the ecosystem, with the question of increasing crop yields being a part of the probe. However, a holistic method can be said to have gone astray if it is divorced from parts or particulars. A doctor is welcome to treat a human being as whole instead of doing a symptomatic treatment, but in the name of holistic treatment, the diseased part or limb can hardly be ignored. A focus only on the whole, ignoring the parts, may not be enlightening. In India, for example poverty was viewed mainly in general or on the whole for the country in terms of its economic backwardness for a long time. It was when V. M. Dandekar and Nilakanth Rath came out with their study on *Poverty in India* in 1971 that poverty began to be viewed in its particularities, identifying who and how many were poor. This was a more meaningful approach and helped in formulating policies for poverty alleviation. It is quite possible that even if a country is not economically backward or its national income and infrastructure is improving, such prosperity on the whole may bypass a significant number who constitute the poor. That is why a seeker of knowledge has to be clear about what he or she wants to know or do and ask right type of questions.

The Gita does not propose mere logical rigour or formal correctness of the method employed to seek knowledge. Its insistence on the coherence among the object of knowledge, the knower and knowledge may be recalled here. A cold-blooded murder may be planned by seeking to know the whereabouts and movements of the person selected for killing. Seeking knowledge may not always be innocent or guided by noble motives. The Gita insists on the purity of intention of the knower, her or his selflessness, honesty and moral status in general. *Sattvika* knowledge implies all these; it is not enough whether it is just holistic.

Employing a *sattvika* approach, however, need not necessarily lead to unanimity, because perceptions and situational contexts of knowledge seekers may differ and their conclusions may not be the same. It may be misleading to adopt the criterion of unanimity for objectivity. A more helpful criterion of objectivity is to see whether the knowledge seeker has his own axe to grind or is, on the contrary, unselfish, detached and open in the pursuit of knowledge. Even if *sattvika* holism need not lead to unanimity, it may promote greater understanding. And what is more, tolerance and respect for differences in views. It is possible that all views may not stand the scrutiny of critical inquiry, but the inquiry should be honest and detached. That is why the Gita insists on moral purity of motive or purpose of the knowledge seeker.

Knowledge may well be sought by a team together. Different members of the team may be assigned different tasks, but the team leader at least should necessarily have a holistic grasp of the purpose and approach of the research project as a whole. It is more desirable, however, that all the members of the team share this holistic perspective or vision. Otherwise, the different members doing segregated tasks may develop a sense of alienation, making their work joyless and mechanical, which may in turn supress their creativity. Holism promotes creativity, and if creativity is expected from all members of the team – as it should be – the holistic vision of the project should also be shared by all.

A few examples from social sciences are given here to see how a holistic perspective makes a difference. A classic case is that of the Great Depression in the world economy, which started in 1929. As employment and prices started crashing, wage cuts were advised with the hope that enterprises will not then cut back on jobs, even if they do not increase them. The wage-cut policy was based on the confused reasoning that what applies at the individual or micro-level would hold at the aggregate or macro level too – which what the Gita called as a *tāmasik* approach. As a result of widespread wage cuts, the Depression only deepened and widened. John Maynard Keynes argued that wage cuts made the aggregate demand decline and increased *un*employment. He recommended deficit budgets and increased public spending to boost aggregate demand and fight the Depression. Thanks to this lesson learnt, the recession during 2008–09 though widespread did not reach the same magnitude as the Great Depression of the 1930s. Another example of the use of the holistic method is Karl Marx's analysis of the working of the capitalist system as a whole, showing how the system produced frequent crises and generated poverty and inequality. Both the governments and the working class learnt a good deal from this analysis and took steps in their own respective ways, which moderated the worst evils of capitalism and helped it to improve.

Identifying the well-being of a country mainly in terms of its per capita income and its development mainly in terms of growth of GNP is an instance of what the Gita calls a *tāmasik* approach. A holistic and *sāttvika* view of development, on the other hand, would take into account not only the growth of GNP, but also indicators like reduction in poverty, inequality, illiteracy, gender disparity, environmental pollution and crime rate.

The holistic method has the advantage of enabling the emergence of new paradigms, which may be needed to solve newly emerging problems. This can lead to better informed, better perceived policies which will be more effective and welfare-promoting, since as the Gita says, it is the *sattvika* which leads to knowledge (*sattvat sanjayate jnanam*, XIV.17) and binds with happiness (*sattvam . . . sukhasangena badhnati*, XIV.6). More than formal training in a fixed set of techniques, one awakens to such an approach by an open mind and wide reading, very necessary for researchers. Even others may benefit by making a habit of it, as it enables wiser decisions in day-to-day life or career.

Success in career and life

This leads us to the enormous guidance which the Gita provides in making our lives and careers more successful and meaningful, quite apart from spiritual striving or *sadhana*. Our life is a *loka-yatra* (travel of the soul in this world) as the Mahabharata terms it. It is in this 'travel' or pilgrimage, as Amur explains the metaphor used in the great epic, that we seek to achieve the four goals of *purusharthas* (Amur 2013). Amur's scholarly and perceptive book in Kannada, *Loka-yatre*, covers major dialogues in the entire Mahabharata, but we are focused here only on the Gita. The Gita calls it as *sharira-yatra* ('travel in body') (III.8). All of us like to have an enjoyable and also successful ride of life by our body. It is clear from the metaphor that what travels is our *jiva* or soul, and its vehicle is the body.

First of all, what constitutes success in life? We begin as a starting point from the narrow context of mundane careers in pursuit of *artha* (wealth, power, status) and then go on to wider goals. It is certainly good to be ambitious and realise one's highest potential, but everyone cannot ultimately become the president of the United States of America, or a Rabindranath Tagore, or an Albert Einstein or a Bill Gates. There is bound to be inequality in power, wealth, creativity and talent. Success in life cannot be measured only in terms of becoming any of these. Vacancies at the top are bound to be limited in any sphere, and all those who fail to make it to the very top cannot be termed as failures in life or even in career however ambitious, merited and self-confident one may be. Often public recognition eludes many, even if highly merited and deserving. For example, for every Nobel Prize winner, there may be several others who may have missed it but are no less deserving. But they cannot be considered as failures in life.

The Gita's approach to success in life is that even when one is working in a given career (*sve sve karmani abhiratah*), one can attain the highest perfection (*samsiddhim labhate*) (XVIII.45). This is facilitated when one chooses a career best suited to the person's nature and quality or ability (XVIII.47), because that is when the highest potential is reached. All undertakings and careers have shortcomings or hazards, just as fire is accompanied with smoke (XVIII.48), and wisdom lies in choosing work or career where one's potential is the highest. One need not mechanically interpret what constitutes the career where one's potential is the highest. It need not be seen in absolute terms, but in terms of where one's comparative advantage lies, including the aspect of what the society or economy values most amongst various alternative potentials that one has. The statement in the first line of the verse XVIII.47 (viz., 'better to do one's own duty even if it has shortcomings, than doing others' work well') does not at all have to be interpreted as an advice to stick to the hereditary work of one's caste, because the Gita speaks about the division of labour according to one's quality and aptitude and chosen work and not about *jati* or castes. This point has already been discussed fully in the preceding chapters.[10] One's potential need not be seen in static or rigid terms. If, as a result of training and acquiring new skills, one's potential changes, there is no bar on changing one's work or career. There is, for example no bar on a nurse getting herself trained as a doctor, but as long as she is a nurse, she cannot take up the duty of a doctor even if she is good at it. According to the Gita, even if one's job is less paying or less prestigious, one should strive to do it perfectly with utmost sincerity and selflessly, because that is the way one contributes to the welfare of the society and also to one's own moral, spiritual and even material (why not?) development.

There is more to success in life than success in career and earning, though the latter is certainly a very important ingredient of the former. We need also to be happy and successful with our relationships within and outside the family, making them harmonious, enjoyable and constructive. A happy, mutually loving, supportive, trusting and encouraging family contributes very positively to success in career too. In fact, such a family is an end in itself. The theory of *purusharthas* insists on a balanced development of moral, material, emotional and spiritual goals or aspects of life. *Moksha* is not necessarily liberation from the world physically; it is freedom from bondage to narrowness of mind, self-imposed limitations and complexes. It is when such freedom is achieved that one reaches one's highest potential, and this requires consistency and coherence in the way of achieving the *purusharthas*.

An interesting thing about the Gita is that it shows a way in which there is no conflict between its key to success in work and success in life, and similarly between success in life and spiritual progress. There has to be a large degree of coherence in this regard. A yogi need not necessarily be a sannyasi; a family man and a housewife are also yogis in their own rights. Success in life inclusive of career can be defined almost in the same terms as success in yoga. The Gita gives this definition, which is also the criterion of success for each individual. It is that one should feel happy, peaceful, content and blissful within, relaxed within, find his or her light within and experience freedom (V.24; VI.27). It is not that there are no sorrows or pains for such a person, but they would be overcome with dignity and without self-destruction (II.65).

The Gita is full of verses which can guide towards *success on all the three fronts together* – career, life and spiritual striving. We may go through some of these verses and draw out their guidance in this respect. Perhaps the most important advice is to make sure that your self is your friend and not an enemy and uplift yourself by your own self (VI.5). This is obviously by pushing away thoughts that depress you, overcoming guilt complex and avoiding brooding over your past mistakes as well as mistakes of others that have hurt you. The Gita focuses on the present and what can be done here and now. This is implied by the famous verse, *Vasamsi jirnani yatha vihaya* (just as old worn out clothes are cast off) (II.22), which was used in the context of management also earlier. One should have self-respect and self-confidence, without being conceited, and should acknowledge the self-respect of all others as well, since the same Lord dwells in us all. A person who respects himself or herself as well as others is respected by all. Humility does not require anyone to demean oneself. The first requirement of self-confidence and getting rid of any guilty feelings is to live a moral life and making it a matter of habit. Verses 13 and 14 in Chapter 12 and again verses 1–4 in Chapter 16 stress the moral qualities one has to try to cultivate, like truthfulness, *ahimsa*, freedom from hatred and egoism, a compassionate and generous disposition, forgiveness, not losing mental balance and calm over pains and sorrows, self-control, dedication to a worthy cause like welfare of all beings, developing contentment and avoiding hypocrisy and treacherousness absolutely. The Gita says that neither sentimental attachment nor hatred, but self-control and evenness of mind, take you to a life of peace and happiness (II.64). It teaches tolerance and ability to stand up to vicissitudes in life (II.14, VI.7). Obsessive anxieties over loss and other fears often disturb this evenness, and it is wise to learn to cope with them (II.56). The Gita's recipe for this is to develop detachment over the outcome of all endeavours, leaving them to God. It stresses the importance of cultivating a calm, cool and composed mind (VI.19), as a great asset. The Gita assures that those who inculcate such *s̱attvik* qualities always tend to rise to great heights; those confined only to selfish pursuits (*ṟajasiks*) stagnate; and those *ṯamasiks* who are visionless, ignorant and lazy fall down in life (XIV.18).[11]

A valuable teaching of the Gita is to care for and nurture mutuality in relationships – crucial for success in career as well as in personal life. It is by caring for each other (*parasparam bhavayantah*) that one can gain success (III.11). We should trust others, avoid being habitually cynical and doubtful, for that can be counterproductive and self-destructive (*samshayatma vinashyati* – IV.40). There is a natural virtuous cycle at work in the world contributing to the welfare of all (III.14), and we should be a part of this contributing to it. A physical evidence of the virtuous circle at work is a wound healing even without medication. Even when there is medication, we have to depend on the natural healing process. This is the evidence of God at work promoting the welfare of all. The Gita expects us to participate in this process as active partners of God. According to the Gita, one who does not do so lives in vain (*mogham jivati*, III.16). The good begets good, which further begets it; a good deed produces more such deeds, moving in an exponentially virtuous cycle. An important way of participating in this cycle, as suggested by the Gita, is to selflessly promote the protection or welfare of people (*loka-sangraha*) to the best of one's ability (III.20, 25) and being generous. The Gita's idea of *yajna* is sharing one's wealth, both material and mental, with others. Genuine generosity is selfless and non-egoistic. It should not, however, be reckless. Help should be given only to the deserving who need and value it, at the right time, with *shraddha*, and without a trace of disrespect to the recipients (XVII.22, 23). When done so, the giver is blessed more than the recipient, and the giver's living becomes meaningful and successful.

The Gita advises us also about how we ought to work. In fact, this advice constitutes the most important part of it, accounting for more verses than any other issue. Karma-yoga has been discussed earlier in several chapters, especially in the sixth on the philosophy of the Gita. But we are not referring to it here as a path of *sadhana*. Several interpreters such as Tilak, Aurobindo and Gandhi discussed it as a philosophy of life, not necessarily as part of *sadhana*. Though the original purpose of advising karma-yoga is to escape from the karmic binding and the cycle of births and deaths, interpreters of the Gita found it valuable in making our work effective and our life purposeful. We are not concerned here with karma-yoga for *sadhana* only. Our interest is in seeing what guidance the Gita gives in making our work more effective yet stress free at the same time. The key to this lies in giving up our obsessive attachment to the fruit of work, though taking care to do it skilfully and with dedication and also with due regard to consequence on others. In other words, there should be no desire to selfishly appropriate the fruit of work or even the credit for work done.[12] Share even the credit with others, acknowledging it explicitly from the beginning. This is what a good leader also does. There is no question here of disowning either legal or moral responsibility for the work done. The advice is with reference to mental or psychological responsibility only. It is a matter of cultivating this mental attitude which helps in avoiding stress. It does not also mean that one should not enjoy one's work. One can certainly learn to enjoy one's work and even take pride in doing it well, in spite of not being interested in appropriating either the fruit or the exclusive credit for doing it. However, interpreters like Swami Dayananda have pointed out that it is nearly impossible for anyone to do karma-yoga with all these qualifications, particularly giving up any feeling of doer-ship or agency, unless one believes deeply in God, surrendering the agency and also the fruit or outcome completely to Him. Only a dedicated devotee of God is able to do so, they feel. The Gita, for example expects work to be done in the spirit of a *yajna*, as an offering to God, with detachment but with a sense of freedom (*muktah*) (IV.23, 33). However, an agnostic can certainly be as unselfish as a fervent devotee of God and even be broad-minded enough to share the credit for work and success with others, though he or she may not be willing to surrender the doer-ship and outcome to God.

Detachment from outcome by itself may not make our work effective and enjoyable. The Gita has some more things to teach in this regard too. There are two teachings which may *seem* mutually contradictory, but can be reconciled by the wise. One is, be focused and single minded in tackling any problem setting aside considerations irrelevant to the problem at hand (*Vyavasayatmika buddhirekeha kuru*, II.41). The second teaching is what we discussed in the previous section – to treat a problem at hand holistically taking all its sides, implications or aspects into account including the ethical. While evaluating a PhD thesis, for example, the referee has to evaluate all its aspects – the perspective, literature cited, clarity of objectives, methodology adopted, rigour of analysis and the logic of conclusions and policy implications. This is being holistic. But considerations like gender, race, religion, caste, place of origin, mother tongue and wealth of the candidate are all absolutely irrelevant. If there is any 'conflict of interest', such as the candidate being the son or daughter of a close relative, the evaluator should not accept the concerned work, so that any irrelevant matter prejudicing evaluation is avoided. This is being single-minded. One can be both holistic and single minded.

The Gita's teaching about being focused, concentrating on the process instead of outcome, and taking success and failure with equanimity – not allowing them to make one either complacent or depressed – is of highest relevance in a competitive world. Not only in business, but also in careers like sports, it can make a significant difference. Tenacity and dogged pursuit of one's goal will be difficult otherwise. One cannot afford to lose cool amidst adversity. Not allowing any feeling of frustration even in dismal failure is the key to bounce back to success. The Gita preaches optimism, hope and active engagement, telling you emphatically to avoid despair and escapism.

In my view, the ultimate message of the Gita is summarised in just four verses in Chapter 6, verses 29–32, especially the last one among these. It conveys a golden rule for ethics in all walks of both private and public lives. It is to see oneself in others and others in oneself, and to place oneself in others' problems and situations and think how one would have reacted to them. It is a message of not merely sympathy but also empathy and harmony. It is to establish harmony with other beings, harmony with environment and harmony with oneself. That really is Advaita – non-separateness. The opposite of Advaita is egocentric separateness, which is the source of all trouble and all violence in the world.

Important teachings of the Gita relevant in making for success in life may be briefly listed (some of them already discussed earlier):

- Believe in yourself. You are not just a perishable and insignificant piece of matter, but Atman the immortal (II.23, 24). You are not a sinner, you are pure. Be good and true to yourself as well as to others, and thus be your true self.
- Make yourself your friend, not your enemy. Raise yourself by your own self, by your efforts. You can also destroy your life, career and yourself by yourself, but never do it (*na a̱tma̱nam avasa̱dayet*, VI.5). Obsessive attachment (*ra̱ga*) and hatred (*dvesha*) are your worst enemies; subjugate them (II.64).

- Respect all beings as equals, as there is divinity in all (VI.30, 31). Respect their life, feelings and right to dignified treatment. Treat others' pain and pleasures as yours (VI.32). God is impartial to all (*samoham sarva bhuteshu*, IX.29), cares equally for all (IX.29; XIII.27). The Gita does not teach fanaticism and parochialism; on the contrary, it explicitly teaches respect for differences in faiths and forms of worship (IV.11; VII.21).
- Respect the code of conduct. Be *sattvik*, even while being active. *Sattva* is the single-most dependable source of lasting happiness (*Sattvam sukhe sanjayati*, XIV.9) and also of knowledge (XIV.11). Make a good name for yourself, as an example for others to follow (III.21). Even individuals have 'brand' values or reputations like companies; if reputation is gone, it is worse than death (II.34).
- Be assured that a doer of good never perishes; a good deed never goes in vain (VI.40). Participate in the cosmic virtuous cycle (III.11–16).
- Make a distinction between *karma* (action to be performed), *vikarma* (forbidden action) and *akarma* (inaction). Avoid the latter two. Even inaction is karmically binding (sinful), if what is necessary to be done is avoided (IV.15).
- Do your chosen work with dedication and commitment (*shraddha*). Perseverance with *shraddha* helps you to get what you aim at (VII.22).
- Do your duty with humility. Don't worry about the outcome of your struggle (II.47, 48). Work has to be performed with detachment (*asakta*, III.19; XVIII.49), with no desire to appropriate its fruit (II.47). Instead enjoy the work, doing it with skill (*kaushalam*) (II.50), with enthusiasm and fortitude (*dhrityutsaha-samanvita*) (XVIII.26) and with due regard to consequences.[13]
- Don't be attached only to pleasant work, avoiding the unpleasant, but do your duty (XVIII.10). There is nothing superior, nothing inferior in work; all works and their fruits are offered to God (XII.6).
- When faced with a choice between what is perishable or momentary and what is enduring or lasting, choose the lasting. Fight for the lasting (II.18).
- Have a higher purpose in life. Enjoy your life, but don't get bogged down to momentary sensual pleasures. Don't aim only at quick success though tempting (II.44; IV.12). Through your work, contribute to the protection or welfare of people (*loka-sangraha*), for that makes your life meaningful (III.20, 25).

- Consciously aim at moderation and make it a habit. Neither extreme abstinence nor indulgence is good for success; they can instead be self-destructive (VI.16–17).
- Mind is fickle, tempted too easily, and can divert you from your higher aims. Proper management of mind is a key teaching of the Gita as it leads to success and happiness in life. Manage your anger, as it can cloud your reasoning, lead to confusion and divert you from your path. Try to keep it calm, cool and composed. Sometimes anger is justified where it plays a corrective role, but keep it well under control and apologise later for losing your temper. Steady and focused mind is a great asset. Cultivating a sense of detachment, meditation and conscious practice can help in this (VI.25–27, 35). Detachment is neither being absent minded nor indifferent. Be mindful or aware of what you do. That is what the Lord means when he advises *vyavasayatmika buddhi* (engaged mind) and to avoid wandering in many directions at the same time (II.41).
- Be focused on your goal (II.41), but take all aspects of the problem at hand (II.20–22).
- Don't lose opportunities of fighting for a good cause if you have the aptitude of a fighter. Cowardice is worse than defeat (II.35, 36).
- Have equanimity of mind even while fighting (II.38). Transcend the pair of opposites like a mature person (II.45; XII.18, 19).
- Learn to adjust to change in circumstances even if adverse and try to innovate by adopting novel ideas, just as you discard old worn out clothes and wear new ones (*vasamsi jirnani yatha vihaya navani grihnati naroparani*, II.22). Be enterprising.
- Depend upon what is wise without being narrowly selfish (II.49). Be cautious that even knowledge or information may be at times masked by ignorance or misinformation, resulting in confusion and misleading you (V.15). Prejudices – either your own or of others – caused by selfish interests create this confusion (III.39). Beware of them.

We have thus eighteen main teachings of the Gita in this list, which incidentally tally with the number of chapters in the Gita. Significantly, the relevance of the Gita as our guide to even daily life and to career, not to mention *sadhana* has remained the same ever or more probably increased. That is why its popularity is accelerating, with more and more people reading, and also more and more saints, philosophers and scholars writing about it discovering new meanings and new applications. Over the time, it has proved itself to be a timeless and living sacred text.

Notes

1 A smaller earlier version of the first section of this chapter was published in *Nitte Management Review*, IX(1), July 2015, pp. 1–13, as an invited article, under the title 'The Bhagavad-gita as an Inspiration to Enterprise and Guide to Management'. The author is grateful to NMR for permission to use the article here.

2 For details, see Agarwal (1993: 19, 48) and Nadkarni (2013: 257).

3 See B. Mahadevan, 'Bhagavad Gita: Ideas for Modern Management', talk delivered in a Seminar on 'Towards a new paradigm of business management: Alternative perspectives from ancient Indian wisdom', at IIM, Bangalore, 12 December 2009, http://www.samskritibookfair.org.archives/882, p. 2.

4 The translation of the verse and its explanation are taken from Nadkarni (2013: 62).

5 For details, see Chapter 10 on 'Ethics in Business', in Nadkarni (2014: 243–70).

6 The explanation of karma-yoga here is based on Nadkarni (2013: 89–94).

7 For details, see Nadkarni (2014: 264–68).

8 For a more detailed discussion in a broader context, see Chapter 10 on 'Ethics in Business' in Nadkarni (2014: 243–70).

9 This section not only draws some points from Chapter 7 in Nadkarni (2014: 169–95), but also has additional inputs. See this chapter for detailed applications in several social and ethical problems of today. Only a few of them are dealt with in the present book that too in brief.

10 See the sections on 'Ethics in the Gita' in Chapter 6, and 'Is the Gita reactionary?' in Chapter 7 of the present book.

11 However, not all those who have failed in life or are poor and deprived are visionless, ignorant and lazy. Similarly not all those who have succeeded in their career and have hoarded a lot of wealth are necessarily *sattvik*. Life is too complex for easy generalisations. We can only speak about tendencies, given other things.

12 See especially verses II.47–51.

13 Work done without heed to expected consequences (including any harm to others) is considered as *tamasik* (XVIII.25).

GLOSSARY

Advaita – A school of Vedanta/philosophy which regards the Ultimate Truth as One, where the Supreme/Brahman and the Atman are one and the same; monism.

Ahamkara – Ego-consciousness; 'I'-maker; arrogance.

Ahimsa – Non-violence.

Ananda – Bliss, blissful joy; everlasting happiness/ecstasy; an attribute of Brahman/the Divine and Atman.

Anasakti – Detachment.

Artha – see *Purusharthas*.

Atman – The self, identified with one's consciousness (*chit*).

Avatar/Avatara – Descent of God in the world to solve its problems/to restore dharma.

Bhakta – A spiritual/religious devotee.

Bhakti – Spiritual/religious devotion.

Bhashya – Commentary, gloss.

Bhedabheda/Dvaitadvaita – A school of philosophy which takes the Ultimate Truth vis-à-vis the world as one of difference-cum-non-difference or dualism-cum-monism, as in the case of waves in the sea, both being real.

Bhoga – Sensual enjoyment.

Bhuta-hita – Welfare of (all) beings.

Brahman/Parabrahma – The Ultimate Truth/Reality; the Absolute (not to be confused either with Brahma, the Creator, first of the Trinity of Deities; or with Brahmana, a caste).

Brahma-vidya – Science of knowing Brahman.

Brahma-nirvana Brahmi-sthiti – Ultimate and lasting happiness/positioning in the Brahman.

Buddhi – Sense of discrimination, wisdom.

Chaitanya – Pure consciousness, pure energy.

Chit – Pure consciousness; an attribute of the Divine and the Atman.

Dharma – Code of moral conduct, system of rules of ethics/justice; duty (See *Purusharthas*).

Dharma-shastras – Texts like the *Manu Smriti* which prescribe codes of conduct.

Dharma-yuddha – Fighting for defending a lofty value/s; war justified by the need to protect one's life, property or honour; war fought on the basis of a code of conduct.

Duhkha – Sorrow (opposite of *sukha*).

Dvaita – A philosophy which takes God, the insentient world and the *jivas* to be basically different from each other, all being real, but the latter two being dependent on God.

Harsha – Cheer, rejoice.

Hita – Welfare, well-being.

Ishwara – The Supreme with attributes; saguna Brahman; God.

Japa – Repeatedly reciting in mind a holy mantra or a name of God.

Jiva – Embodied Atman.

Jivan-mukti – Liberation while living.

Jnana – Spiritual knowledge; knowledge of the Brahman and the Atman; a path of *sadhana*.

Kama – Desire; sensual pleasure (See *Purusharthas*).

Karma – (1) Action or work as in karma-yoga. (2) Accumulated effects of past deeds with potential to affect the present and the future until they are exhausted by their 'enjoyment'.

Karma-marga Karma-yoga – The path of works in which work is done selflessly without desiring the fruit of work, or as God's work.

Karta – Agent/doer of action.

Lila – Sport.

Loka-hita – Welfare or well-being of the world; benefiting the people at large.

Loka-sangraha – Promoting the welfare or maintenance of people.

Matha – Monastery, usually headed by a monk.

Maya – Appearance, projection as on a screen; creative power of God.

Mayavada – A doctrine which takes the world as illusory or unreal.

Mithya – Unreal.

Moha – Infatuation, sentimental attachment.

Moksha/Mukti – Liberation from the cycle of births and deaths (See *Purusharthas*).

Nimitta – Instrument.

Nirguna – Attributeless, formless (opposite of *saguna*).

Nirvaira – Absence of enmity.

Nirvana – Ultimate and lasting happiness.

Nivritti – Spiritual pursuit (as opposed to pravritti); renunciation; release.

Papa – Sin (opposite of *punya*).

Paramarthika satya – Spiritual or transcendental truth (opposite of *vyavaharika-satya*).

Paramatman – The Supreme.

Prapatti – Total surrender to God.

Prasada – (1) Grace; (2) Tranquillity, coolness (Gita II.64, 65).
Prasthana-triyi – The three sacred texts (literally, points of departure in acquiring *jnana*): the Upanishads, the *Bhagavad-Gita* and the *Brahmasutras*.
Pravritti – (1) Material advancement (as opposed to *nivritti*). (2) Tendency.
Priti – Pleasure (Gita I.36).
Punya – Merit, credit (opposite of *papa*).
Puranas – Popular religious texts in Sanskrit like the *Bhagavata Purana*, which narrate stories and glories of the Divine, convey moral lessons and philosophy in easy-to-understand way and promote bhakti.
Purna – Perfect, complete, full, not lacking in anything; an attribute of the Supreme.
Purusharthas – The four human goals/pursuits: *dharma* (good/just conduct, dutifulness), *artha* (wealth, power), *kama* (sensual pleasure, desire) and *moksha* (liberation).
Rajasika – See *Trigunas*.
Sadhaka – Person engaged in *sadhana*.
Sadhana – Spiritual striving.
Saguna – With attributes, with form (opposite of *nirguna*).
Samsara/Sansara – Cycle of births and deaths; day-to-day life in the mundane world.
Sanatana Dharma – Ancient and eternal dharma; traditional name for Hinduism.
Sannyasa – Renunciation.
Sat – Pure existence, truth, an attribute of Atman and the Divine.
Sattvika – see *Trigunas*.
Satya – Truth.
Sharira-yatra – Embodied passage/travel through the world (synonym of *loka-yatra*).
Shastra/s – Science, system of knowledge as in *yoga-shastra*; texts like *Manu Smriti* which prescribe codes of conduct as in *Dharma-shastras*.
Shraddha – Dedication, commitment, faith.
Shreya – What is morally/spiritually most desirable; good/beneficial in the long run.
Shruti – Texts which are taken as authoritative, foundational and sacred (like the Vedas) (as distinct from *Smritis*, which are secondary or supplementary).
Smritis – see under *Shruti*.
Sthitaprajna – Person of equipoise; mentally steady, cool and balanced; person of perfection.
Suhrida – Friend.
Sukha – Happiness, pleasure.
Swadeshi – Self-reliance.
Swadharma – Following one's aptitude and skills, and thus realising full human potential for good (not to be confused with caste duty).
Tamasika – See *Trigunas*.

Tatparya – Purport.

Trigunas – Three characteristics or qualities: *sattvika (sattva)* (good, upright), *rajasika (rajas)* (pleasure loving, emotional) and *tamasika (tamas)* (dull, lethargic).

Tripti – Satisfaction.

Varnas – The four classes based on traditional division of labour: *Brahmanas* (those learned in Vedic texts, priests), *Kshatriyas* (soldiers), *Vaishyas* (traders and agriculturists) and *Shudras* (labourers). (Not to be confused with birth-based *jatis* or castes.)

Vedanta – Spiritual knowledge as contained in the Upanishads, the *Brahmasutras* and the Gita.

Vishishta-advaita – Qualified monism; a philosophy which believes in 'Pan-organistic system' in which the Supreme, the world and the *jivas*, though different, form a unity in the body of the Supreme, the latter two being dependent on the former.

Vyavaharika satya – Practical/empirical truth, mundane truth.

Yajna – Offering, sacrifice.

Yoga – (1) Yoking, joining, striving, a path of *sadhana* as in bhakti-yoga. (2) A suffix to the title of each chapter in the Gita.

Yoga-kshema – Meeting the needs and providing security or well-being.

Yoga-shastra – Science of spiritual striving.

Yogi – Person engaged in yoga.

Yuga – Era.

BIBLIOGRAPHY

Adidevananda, Svami (Tr.) (2014; first published in 1992). *Shri Ramanuja Gita Bhashya (with Text and English Translation)*. (With an Introduction by Svami Tapasyananda). Madras (Chennai): Sri Ramakrishna Math.

Agarwal, Satya P. (1993). *The Social Role of the Gita – How and Why*. Delhi: Motilal Banarasidass.

Agrawal, Purushottam (2004). *Nija Brahma Vichar – Dharma, Samaj, aur Dharmetar Adhyatm* (Hindi). New Delhi: Rajakamal Prakashan.

Agrawal, Purushottam (2006). 'Decoding the Ethics of *Srimadbhagavadgita*', *The Book Review*, 30(1 and 2), January–February, p. 29.

Ambedkar, B. R. (2004). 'Krishna and His Gita', in Valerian Rodrigues (Ed.), *The Essential Writings of B. R. Ambedkar*. New Delhi: Oxford University Press, pp. 193–204.

Amur, G. S. (2013). *Lokayatre* (Kannada). Bengaluru: Priyadarshini Prakashana.

Anandashram, Swami (2014). 'Advaita Vedanta ani Bhaktiyogu' (from a lecture in Konkani), *The Chitrapur Sunbeam*, 21, July 7, pp. 5–8.

Anon (2011). *Nagarasa Kaviya Karnataka Bhagavadgite* (Kannada). Bengaluru: Bharatiya Vidya Bhavan.

Arendt, Hannah (1970). *On Violence*. San Diego: Harcourt Brace.

Aurobindo, Sri (1996; ninth edition). *Essays on the Gita*. Pondicherry: Sri Aurobindo Ashram.

Aurobindo, Sri (1999). *The Synthesis of Yoga*. Pondicherry: Sri Aurobindo Ashram.

Aurobindo, Sri (2010; first published in 1993). *Integral Yoga: Sri Aurobindo's Teachings and Method of Practice* (Selected Letters of –) . Pondicherry: Sri Aurobindo Ashram.

Badrinath, Chaturvedi (2007; first published in 2006). *The Mahabharata: An Inquiry in the Human Condition*. Hyderabad: Orient Longman.

Balagangadhara, S. N. (1994). *'The Heathen in His Blindness . . .' Asia, the West and the Dynamic of Religion*. Leiden: E. J. Brill (published in India by Manohar, New Delhi, in 2005).

Banavathy, Vinayachandra K. and Anuradha Choudry (2014). 'Understanding Happiness: A Vedantic Perspective', *Psychological Studies*, 59(2), June, pp. 141–52.

Besant, Annie (1907). *The Bhagavad Gita or the Lord's Song*. Madras (Chennai): G. A. Natesan & Co.

Basham, A. L. (1967; third edition). *The Wonder That Was India: A Survey of the History and Culture of the Indian Sub-Continent before the Coming of the Muslims*. London: Sidgwick & Jackson.

Bhaumik, Mani (2005). *Code Name God*. New Delhi: Penguin.

Bhave, Vinoba (1964; first edition in English in 1958). *Talks on the Gita*. Varanasi: Sarva-Seva-Sangh Prakashan.

Bhoomananda Tirtha, Swami (2014; first published in 1999). *Essential Concepts in Bhagavadgita* (6 Volumes). Thrissur: Narayanashrama Tapovanam.

Brockington, John (2002). 'Translating the Sanskrit Epics', *Indologica*, 27, pp. 97–126.

Chatterjee, Debashis (2012). *Timeless Leadership – 18 Leadership Sutras from the Bhagavad Gita*. Singapore: John Wiley; New Delhi: Wiley India.

Chatterji, Mohini M. (1960). *The Bhagavad Gita or the Lord's Lay*. New York: Julian Press.

Chinmayananda, Swami (1978). *The Art of Man-making – 114 Short Talks on the Bhagavad Geeta*. Mumbai: Central Chinmaya Mission Trust.

Chinmayananda, Swami (Tr. and Commentary) (1996; new edition). *The Holy Geeta*. Mumbai: Central Chinmaya Mission Trust.

Chopra, Deepak (2001). *How to Know God – The Soul's Journey into the Mystery of Mysteries*. London: Rider, Random House.

CWMG (*Collected Works of Mahatma Gandhi*) (98 Volumes, Electronic Book, 1999). New Delhi: Government of India, Publications Division.

CWSV (*Complete Works of Swami Vivekananda*) (9 Volumes, 1997–2001). Calcutta: Advaita Ashrama.

Dalal, Neil Akshay (2009). *Texts beyond Words: Contemplation and Practise in Shankara's Advaita Vedanta*. Austin: University of Texas.

Das, Arvind N. (1982). 'Peasants and Peasant Organisations: The Kisan Sabha in Bihar', in Arvind N. Das (Ed.), *Agrarian Movements in India: Studies in 20th Century Bihar*. London: Frank Cass, pp. 48–87.

Das, Arvind N. (2008). 'Swami and His Friends: Sahajananda Saraswati and Those Who Refused to Let the Past of Bihar's Peasant Movements to Become History', in William R. Pinch (Ed.), *Speaking of Peasants in Indian History and Politics – Essays in Honour of Walter Hauser*. New Delhi: Manohar, pp. 193–232.

Das, Gurcharan (2009). *The Difficulty of Being Good – On the Subtle Art of Dharma*. New Delhi: Allen Lane (Penguin).

Dasgupta, Surendra Nath (1975; first edition in 1922). *A History of Indian Philosophy* (5 Volumes). Delhi: Motilal Banarasidass.

Davis, Richard H. (2015). *The Bhagavad Gita: A Biography*. Princeton: Princeton University Press.

Dayananda Saraswati, Swami (1989). *The Teaching of the Bhagavad Gita*. New Delhi: Vision Books.

Dayananda Saraswati, Swami (2007-a). *Value of Values*. Chennai: Arsha Vidya Research & Publication Trust.

Dayananda Saraswati, Swami (2007-b). *Srimad Bhagavad Gita*. Chennai: Arsha Vidya Research & Publication Trust.

Dayananda Saraswati, Swami (2011). *Bhagavad Gita: Home Study Course* (9 Volumes). Chennai: Arsha Vidya Research and Publication Trust.

Desai, Mahadev (Tr. with additional Introduction by) (1946). *The Gospel of Selfless Action or the Gita according to Mahatma Gandhi*. Ahmedabad: Navjivan Publishing House.

Desai, Meghnad (2014). *Who Wrote the Bhagavadgita? A Secular Inquiry into a Sacred Text*. Noida: Element (Harper Collins).

Disciples, His Eastern and Western (1989). *The Life of Swami Vivekananda* (2 Volumes). Calcutta: Advaita Ashrama.

Disciples, His Eastern and Western (2001; Seventh Edition.). *The Life of Swami Vivekananda* (Two Volumes). Kolkata: Advaita Ashrama.

Diwakar, R. R. (1999; first published in 1953). *Mahayogi – Life, Sadhana & Teachings of Sri Aurobindo*. Mumbai: Bharatiya Vidya Bhavan.

Easwaran, Eknath (1997). *The Bhagavad Gita for Daily Living – Volume I: The End of Sorrow; Volume II: Like a Thousand Sons; Volume III: To Love Is to Know Me*. Mumbai: Jaico, in association with Nilgiri Press, Tomales, CA.

Easwaran, Eknath (2012). *Essence of the Bhagavad Gita – A Contemporary Guide to Yoga, Meditation and Indian Philosophy*. Mumbai: Jaico, in association with Nilgiri Press, Tomales, CA.

Edgerton, Franklin (Ed. and Tr.) (1944). *The Bhagavad Gita* (2 Volumes). Cambridge, MA: Harvard Oriental Series – 38.

Farquhar, J. N. (1925). 'The Organisation of Sannyasis of Vedanta', *The Journal of the Bombay Branch of the Royal Asiatic Society*, 1 (new series), July, pp. 479–86.

Fischer, Louis (1998; first published in 1953). *The Life of Mahatma Gandhi*. Mumbai: Bharatiya Vidya Bhavan.

French, Harold W. (1991). 'Swami Vivekananda's Use of the Bhagavadgita', in Minor (Ed.), pp. 131–46.

Gambhirananda, Swami (Tr. and Ed.) (1984). *Bhagavadgita with the Commentary of Sankaracharya*. Kolkata: Advaita Ashrama.

Gambhirananda, Swami (Tr.) (1998). *Bhagavad-Gita with an Annotation, Gudhartha-Dipika by Madhsudana Saraswati*. Kolkata: Advaita Ashrama.

Gandhi, M. K. (1927). *An Autobiography or the Story of My Experiments with Truth*. Ahmedabad: Navjivan Trust.

Gandhi, M. K. (1972). *Collected Works of Mahatma Gandhi*. New Delhi: Government of India, Publications Division.

Gandhi, M. K. (1980). *The Bhagavadgita*. Delhi: Orient Paperback.

Gowda, Nagappa K. (2011). *The Bhagavadgita in the Nationalist Discourse*. New Delhi: Oxford University Press.

Griffith, R. D. (1849). 'An Essay on the Bhagavat-Geeta', in J. Garret (Ed.), *The Bhagavat-Geeta or Dialogues of Krishna and Arjoon in Eighteen Lectures*. Bangalore: Wesleyan Missionary Press, pp. xxxvii–lvii.

Gundappa, D. V. (2001). *Shrimad-Bhagavad-Gita Tatparya Athava Jeevana Dharma Yoga* (Kannada). Mysuru (Mysore): Kavyalaya.

Harder, Hans (2001). *Bankimchandra Chattopadhyay's Srimadbhabadgita – Translation and Analysis*. Delhi: Manohar.

Harshananda, Swami (2008). *A Concise Encyclopaedia of Hinduism* (3 Volumes). Bangalore: Ramakrishna Math.

Hauser, Walter (1995). *Swami Sahajananda and the Peasants of Jharkhand*. New Delhi: Manohar.

Heehs, Peter (1989). *Sri Aurobindo: A Brief Biography*. New Delhi: Oxford University Press.

Heehs, Peter (Ed.) (1999). *The Essential Writings of Sri Aurobindo*. New Delhi: Oxford University Press.

Herur, Suresh (2001). *Subhashita-Manjari* (Script and Tr. in Kannada). Bengaluru: Kannada Sahitya Parishattu.

Hiltebeitel, Alf (2011). *Dharma – Its Early History in Law, Religion, and Narrative*. New Delhi: Oxford University Press.

Hirst, Jaqueline (2000). 'Upholding the World: Dharma in the Bhagavadgita', in Lipner (Ed.), pp. 48–66.

Iyer, Raghavan (Ed.) (1993). *The Essential Writings of Mahatma Gandhi*. New Delhi: Oxford University Press.

Jinarajadasa, C. (1996). *A Short Biography of Annie Besant*. Adyar: TPH (Theosophical Publishing House).

Jordens, J.T.F. (1991). 'Gandhi and the Bhagavadgita', in Minor (Ed.), pp. 88–109.

Judge, William Quan (1969). *Bhagavad Gita, Recension Combined with Essays on the Gita*. Pasadena: Theosophical University Press.

Kalawar, Jayant (2012). *The Advaita Life Practice: Balancing Relationships, Work & Money in the Twenty-first Century*. West Windsor, NJ: First Windsor Group LLC.

Kane, P. V. (1990; first published in 1932–62). *History of Dharma-shastras (Ancient and Medieval Religious and Civil Law in India)*. Poona (Pune): Bhandarkar Oriental Research Institute.

Kapoor, J. C. (1983). *Bhagavadgita: An International Bibliography of 1785–1979 Imprints*. New York: Garland Publishers.

Karve, Irawati (1991). *Yuganta – The End of an Epoch*. Hyderabad: Disha Books (Orient Longman) (first published in Marathi in 1967, and first English Tr. in 1969).

Khair, Gajanan Shripat (1997; first edition in 1969). *Quest for the Original Gita*. Mumbai: Somaiya.

Kosambi, D. D. (1962). 'Social and Economic Aspects of the Bhagavad-Gita', in his *Myth and Reality: Studies in the Formation of Indian Culture*. Bombay: Popular Prakashan, pp. 12–41.

Kumarappa, Bharatan (1979; first published in 1933). *The Hindu Conception of the Deity*. Delhi: Inter-India.

Kurien, C. T. (1973). *Guide to Research in Economics*. Madras (Chennai): Sangam Publishers.

Lal, B. B. (2013). *Historicity of the Mahabharata: Evidence of Literature, Art & Archaeology*. New Delhi: Aryan Books International.

Lash, Nicholas (2000). 'The Purification of Desire', in Lipner (Ed.), pp. 1–10.

Malhotra, Rajiv (2011). *Being Different – An Indian Challenge to Western Universalism*. Noida: Harper Collins.

Malhotra, Rajiv (2014). *Indra's Net – Defending Hinduism's Philosophical Unity*. Noida: Harper Collins.

Malinar, Angelika (2009; first published in 2007). *The Bhagavadgita – Doctrines and Contexts*. Cambridge: Cambridge University Press.

Minor, Robert N. (Ed.) (1991; first edition in New York in 1986). *Modern Indian Interpreters of the Bhagavadgita*. Delhi: Sri Satguru Publications (A Division of Indian Books Centre).

Minor, Robert N. (1991-a). 'Sri Aurobindo as a Gita-yogin', in Minor (Ed.), pp. 61–87.

Minor, Robert N. (1991-b). 'Sarvepalli Radhakrishnan and "Hinduism" Defined and Defended', in Robet D. Baird (Ed.), *Religion in Modern India*. New Delhi: Manohar, pp. 421–54.

Monier-Williams, Monier (2001; first published in 1875). *Indian Wisdom*. New Delhi: Rupa.

Munshi, K. M. (1988; first published in 1947). *Bhagavad Gita & Modern Life*. Mumbai: Bharatiya Vidya Bhavan.

Nadkarni, M. V. (2013). *Handbook of Hinduism – Ancient to Contemporary*. New Delhi: Ane Books Pvt Ltd.

Nadkarni, M. V. (2014; second edition). *Ethics for Our Times: Essays in Gandhian Perspective*. New Delhi: Oxford University Press.

Nehru, Jawaharlal (1981; first published in 1946). *The Discovery of India*. New Delhi: Oxford University Press.

Neufeldt, Ronald N. (1991). 'A Lesson in Allegory: Theosophical Interpretations of the Bhagavadgita', in Minor (Ed.), pp. 11–33.

Nirodbaran (1990). *Sri Aurobindo for All Ages*. Pondicherry: Sri Aurobindo Ashram.

Oka, S. V. (1957). *The Uttara Gita with a Translation into English with Appendices*. Poona (Pune): Bhandarakar Oriental Research Institute.

Osho (2006; first edition in 1980). *Krishna – The Man and His Philosophy*. Mumbai: Jaico.

Otto, Rudolf (1939; first published in German in 1933). *The Original Gita: The Song of the Supreme Exalted One* (English Tr. by J. E. Turner). London: George Allen & Unwin.

Pai, Roopa (2015). *The Gita for Children*. Gurgaon: Hachette India.

Palshikar, Sanjay (2014). *Evil and the Philosophy of Retribution – Modern Commentaries on the Bhagavad-gita*. New Delhi: Routledge.

Pande, Govind Chandra (1994). *Life and Thought of Shankaracharya*. Delhi: Motilal Banarasidass.

Pandit, M. P. (1998). *Sri Aurobindo*. New Delhi: Munshiram Manoharlal.

Panikkar, K. M. (1961). *Hindu Society at Cross Roads*. Delhi: Asia Publishing House.

Parekh, Bhikhu (2001). *Gandhi – A Very Short Introduction*. Oxford: Oxford University Press.

Parel, Anthony J. (Ed.) (2009). *M. K. Gandhi – Hind Swaraj and Other Writings*. New Delhi: Cambridge University Press.

Parthasarathy, A. (2011; first edition in 2008). *Bhagavad Gita*. Mumbai: A. Parthasarathy.

Patchen, Nancy (2003 Reprint). *The Journey of a Master – Swami Chinmayananda – The Man, the Path, the Teaching*. Mumbai: Central Chinmaya Mission Trust.

Prabhavananda, Swami and Christopher Isherwood (Trs.) (1944). *The Song of God: Bhagavadgita* (with an Introduction by Aldous Huxley). Hollywood: M. Rodd Co.

Prabhupada, A. C. Bhakti Vedanta Swami (1983; first published in 1968). *The Bhagavad Gita as It Is*. Los Angeles: The Bhaktivedanta Book Trust.

Purani, A. B. (1978). *The Life of Sri Aurobindo*. Pondicherry: Sri Aurobindo Ashram.

Purohit Swami (Tr.) (1935). *The Geeta: The Gospel of the Lord Shri Krishna*. London: Faber.

Pusalker, A. D. (1955). *Studies in the Epics and Puranas*. Bombay (Mumbai): Bharatiya Vidya Bhavan.

Radhakrishnan, S. (1939). *Eastern Religions and Western Thought*. Oxford: Clarendon Press.

Radhakrishnan, S. (1971; first published in 1927). *The Hindu View of Life*. London: Unwin.

Radhakrishnan, S. (1996; first published in 1923). *Indian Philosophy* (2 Volumes). New Delhi: Oxford University Press.

Radhakrishnan, S. (1998; first published in 1948). *The Bhagavadgita (with an Introductory Essay, Sanskrit Text, English Translation, and Notes)*. New Delhi: Harper Collins.

Rajagopalachari, C. (2006; first published in 1951). *Mahabharata*. Mumbai: Bharatiya Vidya Bhavan.

Ramakrishnananda, Swami (1959). *Life of Sri Ramanuja*. Madras (Chennai): Sri Ramakrishna Math.

Ramdas, Swami (1976; first published in 1966). *Gita Sandesh (Message of the Gita)*. Bombay (Mumbai): Bharatiya Vidya Bhavan.

Ranganathananda, Swami (2000). *Universal Message of the Bhagavad Gita – An Exposition of the Gita in the Light of Modern Thought and Modern Needs* (3 Volumes). Kolkata: Advaita Ashrama.

Rangaswami, Sudhakshina (Ed.) (2012). *The Roots of Vedanta: Selections from Shankara's Writings*. New Delhi: Penguin.

Richter, Duncan (2008). *Why Be Good? A Historical Introduction to Ethics.* New York and Oxford: Oxford University Press.

Robinson, Catherine A. (2013; first published in 2006). *Interpretations of the* Bhagavad-gita *and Images of the Hindu Tradition – The Song of the Lord.* London and New York: Routledge.

Row, Subba (1921). *The Philosophy of the Bhagavad Gita.* Madras (Chennai): Theosophical Publishing House.

Row, Subba (1934). *Notes on the Bhagavad Gita.* Point Loma, CA: Theosophical University Press.

Sampatkumaran, M. R. (1985). *The Gitabhashya of Ramanuja.* Mumbai: Ananthacharya Indological Research Institute.

Saraswati, Swami Sahajananda (2000; first published in 1952). *Mera Jeevan Sangharsh (My Life Struggle)* (Hindi) (Edited by Awadesh Pradhan). Delhi: Granth Shilpi.

Saraswati, Swami Sahajananda (2003). *Gita Hridaya.* Volume 3 under *Swami Sahajananda Saraswati Rachanavali* (Hindi) (Edited by Raghav Sharan Sharma, 6 Volumes). New Delhi: Prakashan Samsthan.

Sastri, Alladi Mahadeva (1977). *The Bhagavadgita with the Commentary of Sri Sankaracharya.* Madras (Chennai): Samata Books.

Sen, Amartya (1982). 'Rational Fools', in his *Choice, Measurement and Growth.* Oxford: Oxford University Press, pp. 84–106 (First published in 1977 as 'Rational Fools: A Critique of the Behavioural Foundation of Economic Theory', *Philosophy and Public Affairs*, Vol. 6(4), pp. 317–44.)

Sen, Amartya (1990; first published in 1987). *On Ethics and Economics.* New Delhi: Oxford University Press.

Sen, Amartya (2005). *The Argumentative Indian – Writings on Indian History, Culture and Identity.* London and New Delhi: Allen Lane (Penguin).

Sen, Amartya (2009). *The Idea of Justice.* London and New Delhi: Allen Lane (Penguin).

Seshadri, Kandadai (1996). 'Ramanuja: Social Influence of His Life and Teaching', *Economic and Political Weekly*, 31(5), February 3, pp. 292–98.

Shankar, Pandit Bhavani (1966).*The Docrine of the Bhagavad Gita – The Path of Initiation.* Bombay (Mumbai): Popular Prakashan.

Shankar, Sri Sri Ravi (2013). *Bhagavad Gita – Commentary* (Chapters 1 to 6). Bangalore: Sri Sri Publications Trust.

Sharma, Arvind (1985). *The Hindu Gita: Ancient and Classical Interpretations of the Bhagavadgita.* La Salle, IL: Open Court.

Sharma, Arvind (2000). *Classical Hindu Thought – An Introduction.* New Delhi: Oxford University Press.

Sharma, B.N.K. (1986; first edition in 1962). *Philosophy of Shri Madhvacharya.* Delhi: Motilal Banarasidass.

Sharma, B.N.K. (1989). *The Bhagavadgita Bhashya of Shri Madhvacharya* (Tr. with an Introduction). Bangalore: Anandatirtha Pratishthana.

Sharma, B.N.K. (1997; first edition in1961). *Madhva's Teachings in His Own Words.* Mumbai: Bharatiya Vidya Bhavan.

Sharma, R. S. (2011). *Economic History of Early India*. New Delhi: Viva Books.

Shriranga (Adya Rangacharya) (1941). *Gita-gambhirya Athava Shrikrishnana Samaja-shastra* (Kannada) (The Profundity of the Gita, or Sociology of Shrikrishna). Dharwad: Rangamanga Prakashana.

Shriranga (Adya Rangacharya) (1972). *Gita-darpana* (Kannada) (A Mirror to the Gita). Sagar: Akshara Prakashana.

Sinha, Mishka (2010). 'Corrigibility, Allegory, Universality – A History of the Gita's Transnational Reception, 1785–1945', *Modern Intellectual History*, 7(2), pp. 297–317.

Sivananda, Swami (2009). *Ethics of the Bhagavad Gita*. Shivanandanagar: The Divine Life Society.

Sivananda, Swami (2013). *The Bhagavad Gita*. Shivanandanagar: The Divine Life Society.

Smith, Adam (1776). *An Inquiry into the Nature and Causes of the Wealth of Nations*. Reprinted R. H. Campbell and A. S. Skinner (Eds) (1976). Oxford: Clarendon Press.

Smith, Adam (1790, first published 1759). *The Theory of Moral Sentiments*. London: T. Cadell. (Republished by Clarendon Press, Oxford, in 1976).

Srinivasachari, P. N. (2009 reprint of the third edition in 1996; first edition in 1943). *The Ethical Philosophy of the Gita*. Madras (Chennai): Sri Ramakrishna Math.

Stevenson, Robert N. (1991). 'Tilak and the Bhagavadgita's Doctrine of Karmayoga', in Minor (Ed.), pp. 44–60.

Swarupananda, Swami (1982; thirteenth edition). *Srimad Bhagavad-gita (with Text, Word-for-word Translation, English Rendering, Comments, & Index)*. Calcutta (Kolkata): Advaita Ashrama.

Tapasyananda, Swami (year na). *Shri Ramanuja – His Life, Religion & Philosophy*. Madras (Chennai): Sri Ramakrishna Math.

Tejomayananda, Swami (1997). *Dhyanasvarupam – The Principles and Practice of Meditation*. Mumbai: Central Chinmaya Mission Trust.

Telang, K. T. (1970; first published in 1882). *The Bhagavadgita with the Sanatsujatiya and the Anugita* (Under the Series – *Sacred Books of the East* (Tr. with an Introduction and Edited by Max Muller, Volume VIII). Delhi: Motilal Banarasidass.

Thapan, Anita Raina (Ed.) (2005). *Swami Chinmayananda Reader*. New Delhi: Penguin.

Tilak, Bal Gangadhar (1936). *Shrimad-Bhagavad-gita-rahasya or Karmayoga-shastra* (English Tr. by B. S. Sukthankar, 2 Volumes). Poona (Pune): Tilak Bros. [http://sanskritebooks.org].

Upadhyaya, Kashi Nath (1971). *Early Buddhism and the Bhagavadgita*. Delhi: Motilal Banarasidass.

Veerabhadrappa, B. V. (2004). *The Bhagavadgita – A Rational Enquiry*. Bangalore: Navakarnataka (Tr. from Kannada original published in 1997 by D. K. Seetharama Sastry).

Vidyatmananda, Swami (Ed.) (2006; first published in 1972). *What Religion Is: In the Words of Swami Vivekananda*. Kolkata: Advaita Ashram.

Vivekananda, Swami (1997–2001). *The Complete Works of Swami Vivekananda* (CWSV). Kolkata: Advaita Ashram.

Warrier, A. G. Krishna (Tr.) (1983). *Srimad Bhagavad Gita Bhashya of Sri Shankaracharya*. Madras (Chennai): Sri Ramakrishna Math.

Wilkins, Charles (1785). *The Bhagavadgeeta, or Dialogues of Kreeshna and Arjoon; in Eighteen Lectures; with Notes, Translated from the Original in Sanskreet*. London: C Nourse.

Yamunacharya, M. (1988; first edition in 1963). *Ramanuja's Teachings in His Own Words*. Mumbai: Bharatiya Vidya Bhavan.

Yardi, M. R. (1991). *The Bhagavadgita as a Synthesis*. Poona (Pune): Bhandarkar Oriental Research Institute.

Yardi, M. R. (2011; first edition in 1991). *Shri Jnaneshwar's* Bhavartha-Dipika *Popularly Known as Jnaneshwari* (Translated from Marathi). Mumbai: Bharatiya Vidya Bhavan.

Yogananda, Sri Sri Paramahansa (Indian Edition 2002; first edition from Los Angeles in 1995). *God Talks with Arjuna: The Bhagavad Gita – Royal Science of God Realisation – The Immortal Dialogue between Soul and Spirit – A New Translation and Commentary* (2 Volumes). Kolkata: Yogoda Satsang Society of India.

Zaehner, R. (Ed. and Tr.) (1969). *The Bhagavad-Gita*. Oxford: Clarendon.

NAME INDEX

SUBJECT INDEX

Note: Page numbers in italics indicate tables.